Transformation of Resource Towns and Peripheries

Most developed economies, including single-industry and resource-dependent rural or small town regions, are transforming rapidly as a result of social, political, and economic change. Collectively, they face a number of challenges as well as new opportunities. This international collaboration describes a critical political economy framework that will be useful for understanding these transitions.

Transformation of Resource Towns and Peripheries describes the multifaceted process of transition and change in resource-dependent rural and small town regions since the end of World War Two. The book incorporates international case studies from Australia, Canada, Finland, and New Zealand, with the express purpose of highlighting similarities and differences in patterns and practices in each country. Chapters explore three main themes: how corporate ties and trade linkages are changing and impacting rural communities and regions; how resource industry employment is changing in these small communities; and how local community capacity and leadership are working to mitigate challenges and take advantage of new opportunities.

This book will be of interest to students of regional studies, geography, and rural and industrial sociology. It will also have a strong appeal to policy-makers and local regional development practitioners.

Greg Halseth is a Professor in the Geography Program at the University of Northern British Columbia, where he is also the Canada Research Chair in Rural and Small Town Studies and Co-Director of UNBC's Community Development Institute, Canada.

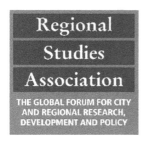

Regions and Cities

Series Editor in Chief
Susan M. Christopherson, *Cornell University, USA*

Editors
Maryann Feldman, *University of Georgia, USA*
Gernot Grabher, *HafenCity University Hamburg, Germany*
Ron Martin, *University of Cambridge, UK*
Martin Perry, *Massey University, New Zealand*
Kieran P. Donaghy, *Cornell University, USA*

In today's globalised, knowledge-driven and networked world, regions and cities have assumed heightened significance as the interconnected nodes of economic, social and cultural production, and as sites of new modes of economic and territorial governance and policy experimentation. This book series brings together incisive and critically engaged international and interdisciplinary research on this resurgence of regions and cities, and should be of interest to geographers, economists, sociologists, political scientists and cultural scholars, as well as to policy-makers involved in regional and urban development.

For more information on the Regional Studies Association visit www.regionalstudies.org

There is a **30% discount** available to RSA members on books in the *Regions and Cities* series, and other subject related Taylor and Francis books and e-books including Routledge titles. To order just e-mail alex.robinson@tandf.co.uk, or phone on +44 (0) 20 7017 6924 and declare your RSA membership. You can also visit www.routledge.com and use the discount code: **RSA0901**

Transformation of Resource Towns and Peripheries

Political economy perspectives

Edited by Greg Halseth

Routledge
Taylor & Francis Group

LONDON AND NEW YORK

First published 2017 by Routledge

2 Park Square, Milton Park, Abingdon, Oxfordshire OX14 4RN
52 Vanderbilt Avenue, New York, NY 10017

Routledge is an imprint of the Taylor & Francis Group, an informa business

First issued in paperback 2019

British Library Cataloguing in Publication Data
A catalogue record for this book is available from the British Library

Library of Congress Cataloging in Publication Data
Names: Halseth, Greg, editor.Title: Transformation of resource towns and peripheries : political economy perspectives / edited by Greg Halseth.
Description: Abingdon, Oxon ; New York, NY : Routledge, 2016. | Includes index.Identifiers: LCCN 2016004974 | ISBN 9781138960893 (hardback) | ISBN 9781315660110 (ebook)
Subjects: LCSH: Regional planning. | Rural development. | Urban economics.
Classification: LCC HT391 .T6956 2016 | DDC 307.1/2--dc23
LC record available at http://lccn.loc.gov/2016004974

ISBN: 978-1-138-96089-3 (hbk)
ISBN: 978-0-367-87519-0 (pbk)

Typeset in Times New Roman
by Saxon Graphics Ltd, Derby

Contents

Figures

Tables

Contributors

Neil Argent is Professor of Human Geography in the Division of Geography and Planning at the University of New England, Australia. His research focuses on critical and applied approaches to local and regional economic development and analyzing demographic and social change in rural settings.

Sean Connelly is a lecturer in the Department of Geography at the University of Otago in Dunedin, New Zealand. His research interests are in sustainable community development, alternative food networks, and rural and regional development.

Maija Halonen (MSSc) is a doctoral student in Social Sciences affiliated with the Karelian Institute in the University of Eastern Finland. Her research interests include structural development of peripheries, rural migration, and everyday life experience in marginal localities.

Greg Halseth is a Professor in the Geography Program at the University of Northern British Columbia, Canada, where he is also the Canada Research Chair in Rural and Small Town Studies and Co-Director of UNBC's Community Development Institute. His research examines rural and small town community development, and local and regional strategies for coping with social and economic change.

Roger Hayter is a Professor in the Department of Geography, Simon Fraser University, Canada. He is an economic geographer with research interests in industrial location dynamics, evolutionary geographies of firms, development issues facing resource peripheries, and the forest sector.

Juha Kotilainen is a Professor in the University of Eastern Finland, Department of Geographical and Historical Studies, Environmental Policy section. His research focuses on transformations, development, and resilience of communities and towns with a connection to the extraction of natural resources, as well as debates over the environmental and social impacts of mining and forestry.

Sean Markey is an Associate Professor with the Resource and Environmental Management Department in the Faculty of Environment at Simon Fraser

University, Canada. His research concerns issues of local and regional economic development, community sustainability, rural development, and sustainable infrastructure.

Etienne Nel is a Professor in the Geography Department at the University of Otago in Dunedin, New Zealand. His research interests are in regional, local, and community economic development, and small town development. His research focuses on Southern Africa and Australasia.

Laura Ryser is the Research Manager of the Rural and Small Town Studies Program at the University of Northern British Columbia, Canada. Her research interests include small town community change, institutional barriers to change, building resiliency to respond to restructuring trends, labor restructuring, and rural poverty.

Anthony Sorensen is Adjunct Professor in Geography and Planning at the University of New England at Armidale in Northern NSW, Australia. Much of his research has focused on the development of small town economies in Australia's rural regions and on the adjustment of agricultural systems to changes in technology and competition in global markets. He is also on the steering committee of the IGU Commission on Local and Regional Development.

Markku Tykkyläinen is a Professor at the Department of Geographical and Historical Studies in the University of Eastern Finland. His research interests include local and regional development, health and welfare geography, socioeconomic transformation of societies, regions, and localities, use of natural resources, and the environment. He has applied regional and geospatial analysis, modeling, and simulations in several research projects.

Eero Vatanen is a freelance economist and input–output analyst who is specialized in issues of tourism, reindeer herding, economies of wood for construction, and food in resource-based economies. His clients and employers include University of Eastern Finland, the Finnish Forest Research Institute, the University of Lapland, and Natural Resources Institute Finland.

Acknowledgments

When I first began thinking about this book and the goal of sharing the experiences of rural regions in developed nations around the world, I knew it would need a strong group of respected scholars to join the undertaking. I was so very fortunate that each of the national groups asked to participate agreed enthusiastically to be part of the undertaking. My first important thanks, therefore, go to Neil Argent and Tony Sorenson from Australia, Markku Tykkyläinen, Maija Halonen, Juha Kotilainen, and Eero Vatanen from Finland, Sean Connelly and Etienne Nel from New Zealand, and of course my co-authors on the British Columbia chapters my longtime friends and colleagues Laura Ryser and Sean Markey.

I would like to make note of a special thank you to Roger Hayter. In some of the most interesting edited volumes that I have read, the critical contribution was made through the introductions to each of the book sections. These introductory essays helped tie together the larger themes and always resonated with me. When asked, Roger agreed without hesitation to contribute three introductory essays and the book is much stronger for it.

I would also like to thank the publishing team at Routledge. Robert Langham was the commissioning editor and has been a generous and patient supporter of the project. Emily Kindleysides took over from Robert and helped see the project through to completion. Lisa Thomson was our first editorial assistant and was a pleasure to work with. Her tasks were picked up expertly by Elanor Best. Thank you as well to Kelly Cracknell, my production editor at Routledge. I would also like to especially thank Sue Littleford of Apt Words for her expert assistance in copyediting the manuscript and Dave Wright and the team at Saxon Graphics for their typesetting work.

I am sure that readers will appreciate the fine and comprehensive index which allows the book to be a ready reference tool. I would like to recognize and thank Kathy Plett for contributing an expertly crafted index for the book.

I would also like to thank Tashi Sherpa and Danielle Patterson for their careful work in harmonizing the text and bibliographies across the various chapters as well as for their help with numerous other production tasks. Kyle Kusch helped, as he always does, with many technical, mapping, and graphics matters and it made my work easier.

My time in pulling together this edited volume was generously supported through the Canada Research Chair program (award numbers 950-200244, 950-203491, and 950-222604).

The British Columbia chapters in this book focus on the forest industry of BC's central interior region. A good deal of that focus is in the community of Mackenzie—a place where my research team has worked for many years. I would like to recognize the three mayors of Mackenzie with whom we have worked. Tom Briggs, longtime mayor of Mackenzie, was always very generous with his time, deeply interested in his community and in the forest industry, and willing to help us out whenever we called. Tom passed away after a courageous battle with cancer in 2013 and he is missed. Stephanie Killam, also a long-serving mayor of Mackenzie, has been a close friend and colleague now for many years as she shepherded the town through trying times and into a more optimistic future. Finally, Pat Crook is the current mayor and someone we have known for years through our many projects.

In closing, I would like to thank my family for their ongoing support of my research.

Greg Halseth

1 Introduction

Political Economy Perspectives on the Transformation of Resource Towns and Peripheries

Greg Halseth

Introduction

Across most developed economies, single-industry and resource-dependent rural and small town regions are changing rapidly as a result of social, political, and economic restructuring. Collectively, they face numbers of challenges as well as new opportunities. This international collaborative book takes a critical political economy approach to understanding the transitions being experienced in these rural and small town regions. The book builds upon an international comparative perspective and includes university-based research teams contributing original work from Australia, Canada, Finland, and New Zealand. The focus is upon the processes and implications of economic restructuring within each case study region's historic resource base.

The book makes several contributions. At a general level, it describes the multifaceted process of transition and change in resource-dependent rural and small town regions since the end of World War Two. The book incorporates international cases with the express purpose of highlighting similarities and differences in patterns and practices in each country. Each research team provides state-of-the-art summaries of their national research literature to bring concise summaries to an international audience. As well, the individual chapters contribute original research gathered through field investigations in rural and small town regions experiencing transition. The goal is to support a better understanding of the key external and internal processes contributing to change in rural and small town regions.

Book Structure

The overall structure of the book is relatively straightforward. Following this introductory chapter, there are three substantive parts. The first part is entitled "Global-Local Perspectives on Restructuring." This part includes a specific interest in industrial development and corporate restructuring over time. It includes coverage of the strategies used by firms, the organization of the economy within a global context, changes in products, markets, and trading relationships, and the pace of change over time driven by economic restructuring.

The second part is entitled "Labor and Employment Perspectives on Restructuring." This part includes reviews and discussions of labor force transitions in the highlighted rural regions and their resource industries. This includes transitions in the amount and type of employment, implications for the labor force, and the structures or organizations that support labor and labor force transition.

The third part is entitled "Community Implications." This part covers the types of approaches that rural communities and regions have used to cope with, or adapt to, the wider restructuring of the economy. General trends include the evolution from local economic development approaches to community economic development approaches, and now to place-based community development approaches.

The book wraps up with a concluding chapter, together with an index. The concluding chapter not only provides summary comments and observations linked to the major themes of the book, but it also provides forward looking comments with respect to the trajectories of change in rural and small town regions as well as the critical issues that need attention from research, policy, economic development, and community development interests.

National Contributions

This edited collection includes contributions from four countries. These are Australia, Canada, Finland, and New Zealand. The notes below describe the contributions from each of the national research teams.

Australia—Neil Argent and Anthony Sorensen

Following each part's introduction, the various sections of this book begin with a chapter drawn from the Northern Tablelands region of New South Wales, Australia. The region has a historic economic dependence upon agriculture, especially export-oriented pastoral production in lamb and beef, and fine wools, together with field crops such as wheat, barley, oilseeds, and cotton. Much of this agricultural production developed in response to local climatic and topographic conditions, and within the preferential trade environment of the British Empire.

The first of the Australia chapters about global-local connections is written by Neil Argent. The chapter's theoretical framework is drawn from Innis' Staples Theory and the elements of geography, institutions, and technology. Geography and technology are closely intertwined over time through the development of transportation infrastructure managed by various state agencies. To this foundation, Argent incorporates Evolutionary Economic Geography and its interest in how changes in geographic, institutional, and technological circumstances can support economic shifts over time.

Argent also notes that, as a settler landscape, change has been a dominant theme in the Northern Tablelands. Path- and place-dependent agricultural development characterized the nineteenth and early twentieth centuries for this region as early settler homesteads were replaced with state-sponsored settlement and the expansion of agriculture. This productivist economy was jarred into transition beginning in the 1970s by the deregulation of the Australian economy that opened up protected industries to international competition, and by the removal of state-sponsored supportive policies and programs that had buoyed agricultural sectors.

The second Australian chapter is also by Neil Argent. With a focus upon labor issues, Argent traces the early growth of labor needs within a number of expanding agricultural sectors, through later processes of transition, contraction, and rationalization that actively reduced demand for farm labor, through to current challenges within a number of agricultural sectors for access to temporary and low-cost sources of farm labor. In doing so, Argent also traces the shifts from regional population growth via local labor pools to the current expansion of various immigrant labor programs.

Through the late nineteenth and early twentieth centuries, a great deal of attention was given in Australia to the quality of working conditions, the expansion of wages and benefits, and more generally to the quality of working people's lives. A strong labor movement protected workers—although as Argent points out it was focused primarily on white, Anglo-Saxon men. A strong set of both institutions and institutional practices pervaded Australian labor relations generally, and the agricultural sector was no exception. While always an economic challenge for agricultural producers, the protected nature of the pre-1970s agricultural industry helped somewhat to mitigate these challenges.

But economic restructuring was especially hard on agriculture. With reductions in employment came sets of migration trends, including youth out-migration from rural regions. The seasonal nature of labor demand by agriculture, together with the loss of the regional reserve army of labor via these national migration trends, has led to increasing attention being given to international migration as a tool for meeting seasonal agricultural labor needs. Argent describes numbers of these migrant labor programs, and how increasingly large agricultural producers are able to use such worker schemes to address the structural crisis in seasonal rural labor.

The third Australian chapter is by Anthony Sorensen. Drawing upon the same region of New South Wales, Australia, the chapter focuses specifically upon the regional service center of Armidale. Building from the earlier chapters, this contribution specifically explores community responses and strategies as a regional agricultural service center adjusts to change over time. The chapter includes a review of some of the typical approaches to economic transition, as well as some of the opportunities and challenges posed to such approaches via concomitant changes in state policy, program focus, and capacity.

The theoretical focus of the chapter is on processes of technological change. As Armidale is also home to the University of New England, the chapter spends time considering the processes central to developing creative communities and economies. The discussion includes various types of indices that have been used to support creative economies, including such topics as funding, talent, support, mindset, and capacity to set trends. The chapter also evaluates a suite of regional performance indicators that are helpful to decision-makers in focusing upon potential areas of opportunity.

The case study work in the chapter focuses upon a suite of tactics and strategies being employed in Armidale. These include a Digital Economy Taskforce and the connected Digital Economy Implementation Group. The chapter also touches upon some of the international activities of these two initiatives. The success of such work, as Sorensen suggests, is not via the application of 'cookie-cutter' approaches, but rather ones that rely upon local assets such as the human, social, physical, financial, and built capitals available for supporting regional development.

British Columbia—Greg Halseth, Laura Ryser, and Sean Markey

The book also includes three chapters drawn from the experience of resource industry restructuring in British Columbia, Canada. The chapters, written by Greg Halseth, Laura Ryser, and Sean Markey, draw on the case of the forest industry and focus on the experiences of the central interior region of the province. Specific case study detail is drawn from the forest-industry dependent town of Mackenzie.

The first of the British Colombia chapters explores industrial, specifically corporate, restructuring. Building from a historical overview of the development trajectories within British Columbia's forest industry, the chapter details the changing corporate structure of the industry over time. In recent years, this story has been one of decreasing international investment together with increasing corporate consolidation. A most recent change has been that the now large British Columbia-based firms are investing aggressively in forest product companies in the United States. This investment is especially focused in the southeastern United States, with an interest in plantations of the fast-growing Southern Yellow Pine.

The second part of the industry-focused chapter concentrates on the dramatic shifts that have occurred in the market, and the impacts of these shifts on industry behavior. Especially important in recent years have been various trade and tariff debates with British Columbia's largest forest product market—the United States. Also important have been efforts to reorient the industry to new markets, especially the Asian markets of China and India. While there has been growth in these markets, that growth has largely been in terms of traditional forest products and the challenge for the future is getting more value, rather than volume, out of British Columbia's increasingly limited forest resource base.

The second of the British Colombia chapters examines the implications of industrial and corporate restructuring on the labor force. The first part of this chapter looks specifically at patterns of job losses over time. While production efficiencies and the adoption of new equipment or new processes that could reduce the number of workers needed is an old story in the forest industry, changes after the global economic recession of the early 1980s greatly accelerated job losses. The second part of the labor chapter then explores the implications of job losses and corporate consolidation on the structure of union representation for workers.

The final part of the labor chapter focuses on a particular labor dispute at one company's operations in Mackenzie. Taken at face value, the story is one of a contract negotiation dispute over company plans to implement greater job flexibility through the collective agreement. The story covers the events before, during, and after a significant strike that occurred in the community. Beneath the surface, however, the story is more complex and is linked to the increasingly mobile nature of capital versus the relative rootedness of labor.

The third British Columbia chapter looks at local responses to industrial restructuring and the pressures that come from declining local employment. The focus is on how small forest-dependent communities have responded to the sweep of changes occurring in their key local economic sector. At the conceptual core of the chapter is the changing set of expectations for how local governments work, namely they are set within the transformation and reorientation of local government operations from 'managerialism' to 'entrepreneurialism.'

Following a review of local initiatives designed to help broaden the economic foundations of the community, attention is also turned to the transformation of approaches from economic development to a broader-based community development approach. Among the challenges for continuing with an economic-only focused approach is that numbers of critical supports for local transformation have been successively removed or downsized by senior governments. As a result, local government not only has to be entrepreneurial in seeking out new economic options, but it also has to build those vital community supports necessary for not only attracting businesses and labor, but also retaining the existing businesses and labor.

In looking at the options for economic renewal, as with other chapters in this book, a place-based approach is seen as a fruitful option for moving forward. The chapter highlights that some of the challenges or influencing factors around the place-based approach include levels of local capacity, experience with collaboration, the need for leadership, use of available social capital, the availability of public policy supports, the geographic variables of location and accessibility, and the need for local innovation.

Taken together, the British Columbia chapters highlight that while corporate interests have quite deliberately recognized the changing competitive environment of the global economy, and have made decisive moves to reposition themselves to be more competitive in that environment, public policy and local community efforts have not been as transformative. While senior government has instructed communities to be more entrepreneurial in searching for economic opportunities and attracting new business ventures, it has at the same time removed many of the critical supports necessary to help communities secure those new economic activities or businesses. At the same time, local government has, at times, struggled with the transformation from managerialism to entrepreneurialism. For some, there is a desire to return to the halcyon days of the 1970s when big industry brought large numbers of jobs and significant local tax revenue such that local government really had little to do beyond managing basic infrastructure maintenance. Today the circumstances are more dynamic and complex.

Finland—Maija Halonen, Juha Kotilainen, Markku Tykkyläinen, and Eero Vatanen

The three chapters drawing on the example of Finland take a long-term perspective to questions of rural development. Markku Tykkyläinen, Maija Halonen, Juha Kotilainen, and Eero Vatanen deploy this long-term perspective through their case study of the resource town of Lieksa. Located in the Finnish borderlands region of Karelia, the town has experienced the booms and busts of a resource-dependent economy since the late 1800s. Through their chapters, the authors discuss not only contemporary issues around rural restructuring, but also the impacts of the region's developmental and political history. These past trajectories, it is clear, play an important role in directing change over time.

In their first chapter exploring global-local linkages and industrial restructuring, the authors adopt the theoretical framework of long wave economic development. Using this industrial life-cycle approach, they proceed to sketch the evolution of the case study region. The first long wave is described as involving the development of a local iron ore industry. The second wave involved the extensive rural 'colonization' that came about increasing small farming and forestry due to increasing demand, population growth, land reforms, and postwar settlement policy. The third wave involved the development of a regional forestry sector, while the fourth wave involve the extension of that forestry sector through a Fordist model of industrial production which also served to mark a late mature stage of development. The fifth wave involved the extension of the Nordic model of the welfare state and the associated growth of the services economy.

The first chapter also provides a detailed sketch of the historical development of the forestry sector in Finland generally, and in the town of Lieksa specifically. Topics that resonate with discussions in other chapters around forest-based economies include the importance of the opening of new opportunities to 'access' raw natural resources at a relatively low cost as the signal for new investment. Also included are the development of new technologies that created a competitive advantage in the transformation of raw materials into marketable products, and the concomitant changing opportunities found within regional and global markets.

The critical elements discussed within each long wave cycle involve the techno-economic paradigms that, for a time, dominated and set the conditions for each economic wave. Associated with these techno-economic paradigms are national development policies and geopolitical relationships. The breakdown of each techno-economic paradigm, shifts in geopolitical relationships, and the failure of national policies to adapt in a timely fashion, are interwoven and mark the transition points between economic long waves.

The second Finnish chapter explores the implications of economic restructuring on industrial labor. Following from the long wave economic cycle framework established in their first chapter, the authors describe how labor demand fluctuated across the different waves. Over time, issues of productivity relative to profitability pressures on resource industries are important in determining changes in the demand for labor and the quality of the work environment. While wages in the forestry sector in Lieksa remain high, for example, the substitution of capital for labor now means that there are markedly fewer workers in that sector. The chapter also employs the concepts of labor market corporatism, specifically how the changing relations between economic policies, social policies, the reproduction of labor, and the global market opportunities for natural resource industries all play key roles.

In the case study town of Lieksa, the general Finnish pattern of rural job losses is repeated. These appear in all economic sectors, with the most dramatic being in the historically labor-intensive sectors of agriculture and forestry but also in paper, paper board, and solid wood product manufacturing. Due to the rationalization of the service sector and depopulation, the sector has also faced job losses. In reviewing these changes over time, the authors again draw upon the economic long wave model.

Taken together, the chapter describes the interconnectivity between the restructuring of companies, changes in state policy, and the associated linkages to shifts in the global economy. These come together in the discussion of the restructuring of the Finnish public sector during the 1990s. With changes in the global economy, and losses of state revenue, the Finnish government reorganized the welfare state model and dramatically cut public sector spending (and public sector jobs). In small communities and rural regions, these cuts to the public sector had disproportionately large impacts.

The third Finnish chapter looks at local impacts and policy responses to resource town transitions in the case study town of Lieksa. While the earlier Finnish chapters focused on industrial life cycles and long wave economic development theory, the final chapter draws upon the concepts of resilience and adaptive capacity.

As economic restructuring and associated changes in the labor force have played out, demographic aging has also been one noticeable outcome. By 2014, the majority of the area's population was over age 50 and many are over 60 years of age. In opening their study of responses, the authors start with a review of changes in regional policies as the state responded to the long-run pressures of decreasing rural employment and increasing rural out-migration. In Finland, regional development policies are guided by a recognized connectivity between the issues of employment, education, and well-being. These policies are generally enshrined in legislation and have recently been supported by EU initiatives such as those within the LEADER program. In the study area of Lieksa, however, these new regional development policies appear to have had a limited impact.

The authors then highlight the importance of local development strategies, which have also been connected to the nationally driven regional development policies. In the 1970s, these followed one of the predictable global 'fads' through the creation of an industrial park to attract new businesses. While new businesses were attracted, they relied upon imported raw materials, abundant labor, and available subsidies to the point where over the long term the strategy and the new businesses were unsuccessful.

Other local strategies focused on diversifying the economy have focused on a 're-exploitation' of already developed economic sectors. In the case of local natural resources, with the continuing dominance of the regional forest industry for jobs as a cornerstone, there have been efforts to broaden the forestry 'cluster' through new opportunities in bioenergy. However, long-term job reductions in various industries may be difficult to make up via bioenergy, or related, opportunities.

In the case of the service sector, the all-time promising option is in the tourism sector and leveraging the area's lakes and the nearby Koli and Patvinsuo national parks. A new minor strategy is with the emerging seniors population and the second-home population. Both may increase demand for services but are dependent on population development.

The three Finnish chapters together describe long-term processes of change. Looking forward they suggest that place-based approaches that build upon local assets which are then reorganized and realigned in new ways may create the potential for resilience and renewal. They conclude, however, that future pathways are immensely complex, and that chance, surprises, and contingencies "play such major roles in their trajectories, that predicting the future of a resource periphery is, after all, a complicated task."

New Zealand—Sean Connelly and Etienne Nel

The New Zealand chapters document a particularly interesting case of transformation. This is because of the dramatic shifts that occurred as the country went from a Keynesian-style interventionist economy and social democratic welfare state to a much more open neoliberal economy and state. Sean Connelly and Etienne Nel provide three chapters that explore this transition and its implications for peripheral rural regions and places.

To start, their opening chapter describes in some detail the critical policy shifts that began with significant austerity measures, sweeping deregulation, and the removal of specific industrial supports. There was considerable geographic unevenness and differential impacts from this neoliberal policy shift. Aspatial impacts include economic shifts in production (i.e. from sheep to cattle in the agricultural sector) while spatial impacts include growth in service sector employment in urban areas. The authors outline not only the broad sweep of these changes, but also their short- and long-term impacts. These changes are also set against external forces such as changes in the price of energy and the generally increasing trend of globalization within the international economy. Among the many issues raised is the increasing direct foreign investment, especially in agricultural and forest lands. Using case study examples from the West Coast of Southland regions, they highlight the geographic unevenness of adaptation and economic development in neoliberal New Zealand.

Their second chapter looks at the transformation of New Zealand's welfare state into a neoliberal state through the lens of labor practices. In this case, two stories are interwoven throughout the chapter.

The first of the stories involves the dramatic shifts experienced in employment numbers. As fits with their earlier chapter, this includes discussion of employment declines in the primary and secondary manufacturing sectors, accompanied by employment increases in tertiary and service sector employment. The spatial expression of these employment number changes is twofold. The first is the creation of what has become known as the 'two economies' of New Zealand—one urban based (especially Auckland centered) and one rural based. The second is the clear expression of geographic unevenness as experienced in resource-producing regions such as the West Coast and Southland case study areas.

The second labor story has to do with the purposeful dismantling of the strong labor movement and of labor unions themselves. The story also involves labor's replacement in political power via the ascendancy of corporate and business interests. Changes to collective-bargaining rules, national bargaining practices, and rules governing worker organization, and an enhanced focus in both legislation and practice on job flexibility are all part of this second labor story.

Their third chapter looks at the community-level responses to the challenges described for peripheral rural regions in New Zealand. Building on the dramatic employment impacts of the neoliberal policy transformation, they identify a range of 'transition supports' put in place by the central government as well as by some other agencies.

With that background, they explore the West Coast and Southland case regions by describing two key initiatives. In the Southland's region, it was the Venture Southland partnership, while in the West Coast region it was the formation of the Development West Coast trust fund created when much of the forest landscape was redesignated from forestry to national park land. For Development West Coast, the approach is based on the region's traditional strengths. In contrast, Venture Southland has adopted the approach of a regional developer and is focused on facilitating a breadth of economic and community development opportunities. Through it all, the challenging impacts of the neoliberal policy turn persist in these rural regions of New Zealand.

Closing

Taken together, the three sets of chapters from each of the four countries included in this edited book provide fascinating explorations of the changing political economy of resource-dependent towns and rural peripheries. The cases from Australia, Canada, Finland, and New Zealand explore, in turn, the implications of changing global-local economic relationships, the impacts of dramatic change on labor and employment in various resource sectors, and the broader implications for communities in the profiled rural and small town places and regions. That they highlight differences in experience is certainly no surprise, for there are some very different development histories, different political histories, and different economic sectors between the cases.

However, they also highlight considerable similarity. Such similarities include a long-boom of resource-dependent economic development after World War Two; the growth of those resource sectors within a relatively protected trading network; and the significant investment made by the state in developing the infrastructure needed to complement the employment and productivity gains of the long-boom. The similarities also include the disruption of those protected trading networks by globalization and political change; the disruption of state investment by the adoption of neoliberal policy approaches; the dramatic restructuring of employment that came from industry adjustment, downsizing, or closure beginning in the 1970s and accelerating after the 1980s. The implications have been considerable for the rural and small town places where these industries had once thrived.

Another part of the similarities in the cases has being the challenges faced by public policy and its seeming inability to adjust to the post-1970s/1980s restructuring of the political economy of resource-dependent regions. Part of the public policy shift has involve the removal of many protective or supportive programs, leaving struggling resource sectors even more exposed to global market fluctuations. Another has been the overt encouragement of greater local and regional responsibility for economic development and diversification, something that has resulted in a proliferation of economic plans (and economic planning processes) as well as local and regional development agencies. However, without some of the significant public policy levers available to the state, such localist initiatives have seen limited success.

In this collection, the authors have sought to provide a political economy perspective on the restructuring of resource-dependent regions within developed economies. Given that a political economy perspective does not legitimize purely political, purely social, or purely economic explanations, the collection contributes to a much broader sense and understanding of the driving forces behind, and of the implications that derive from, resource sector restructuring. As also fits with a political economy perspective, the collection highlights the critical role of historical development trajectories in shaping both responses to change and the possibilities for the future. The rural and small town regions profiled in the various cases have shown tremendous resilience, adaptability, and flexibility, something that bodes well for their own futures. Making better decisions about those futures can be informed by the stories in this collection.

Part I
Global-Local Perspectives on Restructuring

Introduction

Geography and History Matter

Roger Hayter

Economic geography has given priority to understanding the relentless centripetal cause and effect implications of economic development. Such a focus makes sense; after all rich nations are already urbanized, urbanization is rapid in other countries, and 'megacity' regions are emerging around the world. Yet, the centrifugal effects of economic development are simultaneously powerful, evident at multiple scales and relentlessly reaching out to increasingly remote resource peripheries and communities. Indeed, resource communities and peripheries are essential cogs in the global economic system and their variegated evolution is shaped by global-local interactions of institutional forces that are unappreciated in urban core-based theorizing. Moreover, in recent decades resource communities around the globe have experienced structural transition (restructuring) in their global role and as places. Part I of this book provides the theoretical and empirical context for understanding the nature of this transition for selected resource towns and peripheries located in selected rich economies of the global north, specifically the New World 'settler' economies of Australia, Canada, and New Zealand, along with Finland as an old world economy, albeit a late-industrializer on the European periphery.

The overarching theme of this book, firmly established in Part I, is to reveal how resource communities are shaped by distinctive, interdependent evolutionary and global-local dynamics, that is, that history and geography matter. This focus closely complements a literature on the remapping or reterritorialization of resource peripheries that has also embraced Australia, New Zealand, and Canada. While this latter literature emphasizes resource-cycle dynamics, conflicts, and changing resource values and governance, the present text addresses the changing lives, opportunities, and routines of rural residents that are transitioning or restructuring from established patterns of resource dependency. The book's particular focus is on contemporary processes of transition or restructuring of established or mature communities and settlements of varying sizes, but none big.

In conceptualizing transition, the four chapters in Part I draw upon related, albeit different evolutionary-institutional concepts in economics and economic geography. From an old world perspective, Tykkyläinen *et al.* explicitly draw upon long wave theory and in particular the techno-economic paradigm (TEP) model as the theoretical framework for their analysis of industry life cycles in and around Lieksa, Finland over the last 250 years. Within Australia's settler economy, Argent similarly adopts a long view by connecting the staple thesis of development (originally conceived in a Canadian context), particularly as expressed by the geography, territory, institutional triad, with the concept of path dependency to situate the economic evolution of the Northern Tablelands in New South Wales since the 1830s. For their study of Mackenzie, British Columbia (BC), a new, planned resource town of the late 1960s/early 1970s, Halseth *et al.* draw implicitly from the TEP model to focus on the shift from Fordism to the Information and Communication Techno-economic Paradigm (ICT) and its emphasis on flexibility principles. With respect to the transitions of the West Coast and Southlands' communities of South Island, New Zealand, Connelly and Nel highlight the political economy perspective of post-Keynesian and the rise of neoliberalism in the transition from Fordism, and its implications for growing inequality.

These related historical/evolutionary platforms readily appreciate the path-dependent, cumulative, and crisis-ridden nature of resource periphery development. There is also recognition of the importance of those busts that are not just cyclical but are 'turning point' crises that provide an immediate stimulus to community transitions and restructurings. Indeed, the severe crisis of the late 1970s/early 1980s that signaled profound changes in the global economy, including the deindustrialization of established core regions, effectively provides the starting point for understanding the restructuring of Lieksa, Mackenzie, and the West Coast and Southlands' communities, especially in relation to forestry and mineral activities. In the agricultural, once primarily sheep-rearing region of the Northern Tablelands, if the winds of change were strongly evident a decade or so earlier, driven by changing technologies, substitute products, and consumer preferences, they were reinforced by this same global crisis. Since then, all the case study communities have been on a roller coaster ride of volatility, with further recessions, the Asian crisis of 1997, the dot-com bust of 2001, and the financial meltdown beginning in 2008 posing ongoing challenges in their bids for rejuvenation and stability.

But the local implications of crisis for resource communities cannot be divorced from their geography, in the first instance as defined by their relative isolation. The case study communities and peripheries introduced in Part I are all in remote regions where resource exploitation is fundamentally export-dependent and vulnerable to the changing prices and demands of urban cores. To be sure, both the enormous fixed and sunk costs of capital-intensive resource exploitation, as evident in Mackenzie's pulp and paper operations, and the personal place-attachments of entrepreneurial resource exploitation, as evident among the farmers of the Northern Tablelands or in New Zealand's Southlands, has helped maintain production to some extent in the face of low prices. Nevertheless, the contemporary restructuring of the case study communities has featured secular changes in their economies that have featured major adjustments in resource-based activities, and the rise of the service sector as a job generator. Resource-cycle dynamics, competition, technological innovation, natural hazards, and policy regime changes have combined to stimulate resource activity adjustments in the case study peripheries that have variously involved rationalization and job loss, product and geographic market diversification, and shifts in product-mix, the latter perhaps most vicariously (and unexpectedly) revealed by the Northern Tableland's decline as a sheep-rearing region and its emergence as a cotton producer. Indeed, the case studies collectively emphasize that renewable resources, as well as nonrenewable resources, and the places they support, are vulnerable to long-term decline. Thus farming, fishing, and forestry-related activities comprise the principal resource-base of the case study communities while the mining of nonrenewables also feature in New Zealand's West Coast evolution.

If remoteness is a shared, albeit relative characteristic, the four chapters of Part I allow comparative insights into how the trajectories of the case study communities are distinguished by the particularities of global-local dynamics as they evolve over time. In practice, geography matters to understanding the case study community transitions because of variations in: resource endowments, the starting points for resource exploitation, the nature and organization of resources, national (and regional) contexts and policies, geopolitics, relative location and connectivities, and local cultures and institutions. These themes are interrelated and differences in resource endowment, for example, have implications for industrial organization, labor inputs, markets, and technology. Thus the agricultural staples that dominate the Northern Tablelands, and which occur in Lieksa and the New Zealand regions, are entrepreneurial and dispersed. In contrast, Mackenzie's pulp and paper is corporately owned and capital intensive, as are mining operations. The chapters in Part I further underline the significance of relative location or situation, including with respect to local, national, and international institutional contexts, for the trajectories of their case study communities.

As Connolly and Nel report, while New Zealand's West Coast and Southland communities were jolted by the 'enforced' loss of Commonwealth preference in 1973, their coastal locations and geographic proximity to Asia provided alternative markets potentials, albeit ones that required overcoming cultural and political distance. The subsequent onset of neoliberalism, or 'Rogernomics' after 1980 posed a more brutal challenge, based on privatization and deregulation, that removed long-established subsidies, forms of protection, and social supports from these communities and in turn stimulated restructuring toward a more specialized resource-base, the flexibilization of labor and more uneven returns to community populations. Whether for better or worse, Rogernomics also demonstrated that path-dependent behavior can be changed as a matter of policy choice.

In contrast to New Zealand, in federal Canada resource exploitation is largely controlled by provincial governments, with forests under public ownership. As Halseth *et al.* indicate, in BC since the 1980s some, but not all, provincial governments have been sympathetic to neoliberalism, but not with New Zealand's zeal. Thus following an interventionist left-wing government during the 1990s with the return of a right-wing government in 2001, neoliberalism is reflected in the removal of the 'appurtenancy' requirement for forests to be used locally, and a degree of deregulation. Yet, unlike New Zealand, privatizing BC's forests is not an issue, and if environmental regulations have been relaxed since 2001 they are now much stronger than they were in 1991. Indeed, conservation has become an important trend in BC, as in New Zealand and Australia, while Aboriginal rights have become highly contested and widespread throughout the province. For the most part treaties were not signed in BC and a major policy concern of recent decades has sought to redress this situation, including by facilitating control over resources, notably forest resources, by Indigenous peoples. Yet in Mackenzie itself the flexibility mantra of neoliberalism captures the challenge of restructuring a highly specialized, forest-product mass production model that is capital intensive and facing a high cost, dwindling natural resource-base. Here a highly structured workforce is threatened by capital substitution, and flexible changes to work practices. Forestry industry adjustments are further complicated by US protectionism, and if Asian markets beckon they must overcome the distance to ports, about 1,000 or 1,500 kilometers respectively to Vancouver and Prince Rupert. Indeed, the ideal of Mackenzie as a planned new town in the wilderness, once part of a Canada-wide initiative that began in the 1950s, is now obsolete, replaced by more flexible fly-in-fly out thinking.

Meanwhile back across the Pacific, Argent emphasizes that the commercial opening up of the isolated inland region of the Northern Tablelands of New South Wales depended on various state-led initiatives, initially by the national government especially with the provision of key infrastructure, by technological changes, and by an influx of settlers, initially especially from the UK as part of the Pax Britannica that dominated the nineteenth century (trends equally evident in New Zealand and BC). The zenith of this evolution occurred—in tandem with the resource industries of the other case study communities—in the 1950s and 1960s, during which time government support in the form of tax breaks, R&D investment, and price stabilization schemes were introduced. If this farming-wool economy was showing signs of strain by 1970, with technological changes reducing labor requirements and substitute products replacing wool garments, as with New Zealand's Southlands and West Coast, the loss of Commonwealth preference when the UK entered the EU posed a major threat, and helped stimulate restructuring. In the 1980s and 1990s this restructuring was then reinforced by the national government's replacement of its historically protectionist policies that raised costs with an across-the-board commitment to free trade that included withdrawal from wool price stabilization.

Finally, as part of the old world of Europe, Tykkyläinen *et al.* situate Lieksa's industrial evolution within the context of all five TEPs that first embraced iron-ore exploitation in the nineteenth century, and then agriculture and forest-product activities. Moreover, its distinctive evolution is rooted in Finland's (and Scandinavia's) unique blending of welfare and development state thinking. Regarding the latter, for example, the Finnish state long recognized the potential of resource exports to generate backward, forward, and fiscal linkages throughout the economy; in forestry this has meant stronger national resolve (than in Canada, BC, or New Zealand) to promote local R&D, value-added activities, domestic ownership, and equipment and producer service suppliers. It has also meant a longer contemplation, admittedly not always successful, of seeking to diversify remote places like Lieksa. Further, Finland (and Lieksa) has become increasingly integrated into the EU with its diverse, rich markets, and less marked power asymmetries than those facing Canada's or New Zealand's resource communities.

The following chapters in Part I articulate the broad contours of why geography and history matter to the case study resource communities and peripheries, and the springboard for discussion in Parts II and III.

2 Trap or Opportunity?

Natural Resource Dependence, Scale, and the Evolution of New Economies in the Space/Time of New South Wales' Northern Tablelands

Neil Argent

Introduction

The fortunes of rural economies, alongside the housing, labor, financial, and industrial subsystems of which they are at least partly comprised, seem to depend increasingly on the extent and nature of their incorporation into national, international, and/or global trading networks. Unfortunately, not all regions—or nations—have equal capability to choose the nature of their insertion into such networks. A core message of the geographical political economy literature (Sheppard, 2011), and the "variegated capitalism" research (Peck and Theodore, 2007), is that, due to a mixture of differing histories, initial resource endowments and institutional frameworks, the global economic landscape strongly resembles a mosaic, a patchwork of strongly and subtly contrasting hues, even where capitalism is the dominant paradigm for organizing an economic system. History and place matter! The case study regions considered in this edited collection have, by and large, a shared history of being inserted into national and international economies based on their capacities to provide abundant cheap and good quality (and largely untransformed) natural resource commodities to the metropolitan cores of their imperial masters. Not surprisingly, such long-established patterns of development have produced—or at least substantially shaped—the industrial structure of these regions and their constituent local economies and labor markets. Such structural formations, once established, tend to have an enduring influence over the future social, demographic, and economic trajectories of the region.

The empirical focus of this chapter, and the other two chapters on Australia included in the broader project, is the Northern Tablelands of New South Wales, Australia (Figure 2.1). With a long historical dependence on, and comparative advantage in, export-oriented pastoral production (i.e. fine wool growing, fat lambs, and beef cattle grazing) and broadacre cropping (e.g. wheat, barley, oilseeds, cotton), the Tablelands provide an illuminating case study of rural demographic, economic, and social development in a so-called 'settler state.' From early in its post-colonization history, the Tablelands had a dual local/colonial and international orientation, responsible to and dependent on the colonial (after 1901, State) society and political authority but also the export markets of the British Empire which provided much of the region's income. However, as the nation's agricultural sector

Figure 2.1 Map Showing Northern Statistical Division of New South Wales and Regional
        Development Australia—Northern Inland Australia.
Source: Author.

underwent a troubled and protracted transition from the era of productivism to
multifunctionality during the 1980s and 1990s (Wilson, 2001; Argent, 2002;
Holmes, 2006), the Northern Tablelands' relationships with other scales changed
both quantitatively and qualitatively, inducing a period of substantial change and
restructuring within region. The chief purpose of this chapter is to outline the
Northern Tablelands' evolving interrelationships, over time and space, with
broader regional, national, international, and global scales, and to document their
economic, demographic, and social ramifications for the region.

While the succeeding chapter focuses on the impacts of these changes on the
Northern Tablelands' labor force, this chapter concentrates its attention on the
region's major industries and the particular economic geography that their
interrelationships created. This analysis draws conceptually on some recent
applications of Innis' staples theory and evolutionary economic geography (EEG)

to rural economic analysis, and an outline of these bodies of thought follows next. The remainder of the chapter involves an exploration of the historical and geographical development of the Northern Tablelands and its key industries, with a particular focus on the ways in which these—and leading entrepreneurs within each—have both adapted to globalizing tendencies and forces within their own sectors but also played a role in molding the ways in which those globalizing tendencies anchor down in place. We are particularly interested in the fluctuating fortunes of four subregions within the Tablelands: the local government areas (LGAs) of Armidale-Dumaresq, Guyra, Inverell, and Narrabri. Together these represent the (limited) variety of land uses on the Tablelands, together with the past and current challenges and opportunities the region faces from a range of scales.

Conceptualizing Change in Natural-Resource-Dependent, Settler Nation Regions: Staples Theory and Evolutionary Economic Geography

Despite the widespread awareness of the peculiarities of the 'resource' or remote rural region among economic geographers and regional scientists, discussion of these regional types has up until recently been largely confined to the margins of regional development research and teaching. Cities, urban agglomerations, and industrial districts seemed to hold much more fascination for most academic theorists, policy-makers, and practitioners. More recently, however, perhaps in response to recent mineral and energy resource 'booms' around the globe, interest has shifted to better understand the peculiarities of natural resource-producing economies (Tonts *et al.*, 2012, 2014; Argent and Measham, 2014). One, admittedly dated, body of thought developed especially for just this regional type is the staples theory of Harold Innis (1929).

Innis' staples theory is best regarded as a broad approach to understanding the causes of uneven development over space and time (Hayter and Barnes, 1990). More particularly, staples theory emanated from Innis' antipathy toward conventional economic development theories, concepts, and modes of thought, developed in the 'imperial core' and then foisted on colonial nations and their constituent regions, often with long-term negative consequences for the latter. In contradistinction to mainstream, neoclassical economic thought, *geography*, *institutions*, and *technology* form central elements of staples theory.

For Innis, *geography* plays a central role in shaping the developmental fortunes of staples-dependent regions. A number of separate but related dimensions of space and spatiality are relevant here. First, Innis explicitly recognized the crucial role of the physical resource-base (e.g. underlying geology) in dictating the location of the primary stages of resource extraction. Second, and relatedly, staples theory incorporates an understanding of the multifarious roles of the broader physical environment (e.g. climate, topography) in both enabling and constraining access to resources, labor, and higher order goods and services. A powerful illustration of this element can be seen in the starkly zonated population distributions of Canada and Australia (i.e. the ecumene). The extended socio-spatial relationships that develop between primary extraction and processing firms and their corporate headquarters, financiers, regulators, supporting education and training institutions, and labor form a third component of staples theory: spatiality. A centrally important aspect here is the distanciation of strategic decision-making and economic power across the geographical landscape and corporate hierarchy, such that the peripheral position of the hinterlands is reinforced vis-à-vis metropolitan centers (see Massey, 1984). The broad 'heartland/hinterland' structure of the Canadian space economy (see McCann, 1982; McCann and Gunn, 1998) is a reflection of these factors.

Institutions and institutional networks constitute the second major element of staples theory. Not surprisingly, the predominant institution in this context is the state. In federated polities such as those of Canada and Australia, the 'state' is neither a solitary nor unitary entity. Rather, political power and regulatory oversight is spread in a multiscalar fashion across numerous jurisdictions. Responsibilities are often shared between different tiers of the political system though not always in a well-coordinated manner. In Australia, it is the federal government (also known as the Commonwealth) that holds constitutional responsibility for managing the nation's diplomatic, economic, social, and environmental relations with the rest of the globe, incorporating such matters as the issuing of licenses for mineral and energy exports. Yet it is the state governments that possess the key responsibilities for the management of, including access to, the country's natural resources (Emy and Hughes, 1991; Aplin, 1998). At least in the initial stages of development, staples production involves investment in large and costly infrastructure (e.g. efficient roads, railroads, telecommunications), machinery, and equipment. In the Australian context, in the earliest colonial stages of economic development it was government that acted as lead entrepreneur and financier (Butlin *et al.*, 1982). Over time, though, the state's role—both federal and state—shifted to a more facilitatory, comprador role, establishing and maintaining the conditions for initial and ongoing foreign investment in staples production (Armstrong and Bradbury, 1983).

Finally, *technology* greatly influences the relative demand for, and supply of, different types of staples, facilitating the flow of commodities, capital, and information between site of extraction, corporate headquarters, processing center, financiers, end markets, and the like. Transport and communications technology changes are seen as particularly important, with their capacity to destroy obsolete modes together with the businesses and the settlements that relied on these. Technological changes are, therefore, in a Schumpeterian sense, a force for creative destruction (Innis, 1930).

From Innis' perspective, each staple embodies a particular set of geographical, institutional, and technological relationships: the staple commodity's space/time bias (see Barnes, 2005). Along the spatial axis, each staple by necessity implies a location in which the resource is extracted and, frequently, another to which it is transported for further processing and final shipping/freighting. More broadly, a staple's spatiality can be measured by the extent to which it becomes emblematic of the locality and/or region in which it is produced (e.g. steel and steel products and Sheffield in the UK; computing technology and California's Silicon Valley) (Barnes, 2005). However, it is important to remember that each staple is a product of its time, with the extraction and consumption of natural resources heavily dependent on: the prevailing state of technology; the changing condition of the natural environment from which the resource is extracted; changing institutional frameworks and approaches; and the varying profitability of staples production (Barnes, 2005). The fortunes of the staples-producing region, then, are often prone to great volatility.

A fundamental mechanism within staples theory is the 'staples trap.' This refers to the structural vulnerability to which every staples-dependent economy and society is potentially susceptible. The staples trap reflects national-level weaknesses in industrial structure, macroeconomic management, and external orientation—themselves a legacy of structurally biased trading conditions between the Imperial core and the dominions. However, the staples trap impacts most immediately on the single industry resource towns (SIRTs) and regions that are the "fulcrum point(s) between the resources themselves and the global metropoles that require them" (Barnes *et al.*, 2001 p. 2130). For Innis, SIRTs are "'storm centres to the modern international economy'" (cited in Barnes, 2005 p. 111); subject to the cyclonic winds of rapid and intensive investment and disinvestment in response to sudden shifts in demand, resource availability, and corporate restructuring (also see Hayter, 2000). At least in the initial stages of a settler colony's economic development much of the rest of the economy is, to a greater or lesser degree, dependent on multiplier effects from the export sector (Hayter and Barnes, 1990; Barnes *et al.*, 2001). This 'export mentality,' in the context of the highly uneven economic and demographic structures and systems that have accreted over time and space within the nation, is something of a double-edged sword for hinterland regions.

During buoyant times when, for instance, international markets require continuous supplies of natural resources at rising prices, local workforces, families, and entire communities partake in the rising tide of prosperity (Barnes *et al.*, 2001). For example, in Australia social welfare provisions and fundamental democratic reforms (e.g. women's suffrage) were established in the late ninteenth century on the back of flourishing demand for the nation's staples from the imperial center. These social and political advances made Australia the envy of much of the remainder of the industrialized world at the time (Emy and Hughes, 1991). When the staples economy turns bad, though, it can turn horrid (Barnes, 2005). Widespread redundancies and lay-offs and/or plant closure or 'mothballing' in the face of sudden commodity price declines, resource-base exhaustion, or corporate restructuring (or a combination of all three) can turn once vibrant regional economies into ghost towns, laying bare the potentially dire consequences of this structural dependence (also see Barnes *et al.*, 2001).

As already noted, natural resource-dependent regional economies (and communities) rarely enjoy sustained periods of prosperity. Rather, they are subject to innumerable forces and one-off factors that can just as easily trigger crises or periods of buoyant growth. Crises can impact severely on the narrowly based economies of hinterland regions: workers and their families usually have few alternative employment opportunities locally and so begins the race to liquidate housing and other 'sunk' assets and move out before housing markets collapse. After Markusen (1996), Hayter (2003) regards the so-called resource peripheries of the hinterland as 'slippery spaces' in which physical commodities and resource rents are efficiently extracted and transported to the 'sticky places' of the core/heartland. So, just as labor and capital can—and do—flow easily into the site of staples commodity exploitation/extraction they can just as easily flow out.

The tendency for staples production to be dominated by a few large firms introduces a further dimension to the staples trap. In the contemporary era, with governments adopting a more laissez-faire approach to industry support than that used in the Fordist era, the usually capital-intensive nature of staples exploration and extraction (e.g. transport and storage infrastructure; plant and machinery; workers' accommodation and services) is increasingly being footed by private capital, often involving foreign direct investment. In former settler societies, such as Canada and Australia, such developments have often reinforced or exacerbated oligopolistic private market structures in, for instance, the Canadian lumber, pulp, and paper processing industries and the Australian food processing and grain handling sectors (Hayter and Barnes, 1997; Pritchard, 1999; Hayter, 2003; Botterill, 2012).

Although the potentially negative consequences of staples dependence can be overstated it is important to appreciate the powerful structural and behavioral processes that help produce, and reproduce, the staples trap. During 'boom' times, national, regional, and local governments, and private capital (including local chambers of commerce, etc.), unions, and local workforces are often temporarily unified (albeit uncomfortably at times) in defense of the 'propulsive' sector (Barnes *et al.*, 2001). Thus, staples dependence is reproduced throughout the community, permeating local cultural practice (e.g. company sponsorship of local sporting teams; industry displays at the local annual show) and political affairs. In this way, the path dependence at the core of the staples trap is buttressed by local 'cognitive lock-in' (Hudson. 2005).

To better account for this inevitable spatial and temporal dynamism, we combine staples theory with insights from evolutionary economic geography (EEG) in this analysis of the (partial) integration of the New South Wales Northern Tablelands with the national, international, and global economies. EEG is concerned with explaining the transformation of economic landscapes over various temporal and spatial scales and, in particular, explicitly recognizing and accounting for the causal roles of time and space in economic change and continuity (see Boschma and Martin. 2010). From our perspective EEG provides a broad theoretical platform—and one thoroughly compatible with staples theory—upon which to explore the particular structural features, strengths, and weaknesses of the NSW Northern Tablelands and to investigate the causal and contingent factors and processes that drive industrial, economic, and demographic change over time in this setting.

EEG stands in contradistinction to neoclassical economics for a number of reasons. First, in contrast to the latter's treatment of space and time as passive dimensions within the economic development process, EEG's ontology regards these two fundamental dimensions as intertwining and interrelated active forces shaping societies and economies. Whereas orthodox equilibrium economic models downplay the significance of historical events and processes of spatial competition in molding the economic landscape, EEG research accentuates the roles of technological innovation, bounded rationality among economic agents (e.g. entrepreneurs), and the role of institutions in driving economic change. True to the label, EEG research is strongly influenced by a number of fundamental Darwinian concepts, such as 'selection,' 'variety,' and 'self-replication' (Essletzbichler and Rigby, 2007). Second, against the atomistic ontology of neoclassical economics (e.g. the centrality of *homo economicus* to the rational allocation of resources), EEG explicitly recognizes the role of behavioral factors, such as routines and norms, in explaining how individuals, firms, and institutions shape economic systems. One of the most significant ideas to emerge out of this work is the notion of 'path dependence.'

In earlier usages, path dependence was typically associated with particular technologies that had, via processes of ongoing innovation, improvement, and promotion, become adopted as the industry standard (e.g. the QWERTY keyboard (David, 2001)). While path dependence helps to explain how a branch of industry becomes 'locked-in' to the use of a specific innovation, for economic geographers *path* dependence is often equated with *place* dependence in which local or regional economic processes can be said to be, in one way or another, substantially dependent on or correlated with past events and trajectories (Plummer and Tonts, 2013a). In analytical terms, this means understanding the ways in which past applications of specific technologies, previous rounds of investment, sunk costs, dynamic increasing returns, historical institutional structures, and social routines contribute to cumulative and self-reinforcing spatial development (Plummer and Tonts, 2013a, 2013b; Tonts *et al.*, 2014). One of the concerns of economic geographers has been with how these cumulative and self-reinforcing processes eventually 'lock' regions in to a particular developmental trajectory (Hudson, 2005). Once this lock-in occurs, it often takes a sizable external shock to destabilize (or unlock) the system and set it on an entirely new developmental pathway.

Recently, attempts have been made to deepen EEG's explanatory power through the incorporation of the seemingly ubiquitous notion of resilience (Hudson, 2010; Martin and Sunley, 2014; Tonts *et al.*, 2014). Though subject to some criticism (see Martin and Sunley, 2014, for a summary), resilience appears to have some relevance to regional economic analysis, especially when included within an EEG and staples theory framework. First, given EEG's concern to explain how and why regional economies evolve, resilience provides a ready focus on how shocks or perturbations—regardless of whether they are generated by endogenous or exogenous factors or processes, or a combination of the two—affect the competitive selection processes central to regional economic evolution. Contemporary staples-dependent regional economies tend to be especially susceptible to such crises, and often lack the critical tools, including institutional frameworks and settings, to be able to avoid the worst effects of a downturn or to be able to independently forge a new sustainable pathway out of recession.

Second, adopting a resilience perspective to the analysis of shocks and their regional impacts (and causes) directs attention to the strategic initiatives and 'fixes' adopted by a region's collective business sector, labor, and public institutions, before, during, and after a crisis. In itself, this provides a means for clarifying the meaning and operation of other crucial (but equally occasionally imprecise) ideas such as lock-in and path and place dependence.

However, as emphasized by others (McManus *et al.*, 2012; Martin and Sunley, 2014; Tonts *et al.*, 2014), resilience is suggestive of a number of different dynamics, post disturbance or shock, depending on the philosophical and disciplinary standpoint of the researcher. Unlike the ecological and engineering senses of the term, resilience in the context of more-or-less isolated, natural resource-dependent rural economies and communities does not (necessarily) refer to these entities' capacities to either absorb stress or 'bounce back' to a prior steady-state (Wolfe, 2013; Martin and Sunley, 2014). Rather, it seeks to encompass the frequently complex and complicated process of adaptation and adjustment that occurs in empirically real rural settings when social, demographic, cultural, and economic systems are challenged or threatened. The concept enables the exploration of the multiple trajectories that 'the community' may embark upon, or be forced into, taking into consideration the influential role of past experiences and multiscalar forces. From an EEG perspective, recovery frequently suggests a transition to a new set of functional arrangements that aim to underpin economic and social wellbeing (Christopherson *et al.*, 2010). For Martin and Sunley (2014 p. 11), "The study of regional resilience is very much about the dynamics of systems that are internally heterogeneous, highly open, relationally connected externally and the subject to decisions and influences arising at a multitude of scales."

Concepts embedded within the resilience literature, such as 'adaptive capacity,' 'self-organization,' 'complexity,' and 'learning' have become increasingly influential in recent theoretical work in evolutionary economic geography (Hudson, 2010; Wilson, 2012; Franklin *et al.*, 2011). Of relevance to this research for its focus on *social* resilience in Australian agriculturally dependent regions is McManus *et al.*'s (2012) and Pritchard *et al.*'s (2012) findings that farmers' attachment and loyalty to their home community formed an important plank in their case study communities' search for viability and vitality in spite of the depredations of drought, a tightening cost–price squeeze, and population mobility. Acknowledging contentions made in the regional development literature regarding the presumed poorer adaptive capacity of narrowly based rural economies in the face of crisis conditions, Martin and Sunley (2014 p. 27) note that,

> The implication is that a region with a narrow economic base, that is one specialized in a limited range of activities, will not only be more susceptible to idiosyncratic sector-specific shocks, but will have fewer opportunities to re-orientate its economy, and hence fewer alternative routes to recovery.

For them, whether or not such a regional economy actually does fall into a downward spiral of decline from which recovery is prolonged or unachievable remains an essentially empirical question.

Becoming Britain's Farm: Path- (and Place-) Dependent Pastoralism on the Northern Tablelands of New South Wales?

As already noted, the empirical focus of this set of chapters is the Northern Tablelands of New South Wales, Australia (see Figure 2.1). This broad region, covering approximately 99,100 square kilometers (ABARES, 2015), is encompassed by the official administrative spatial unit of the Northern Statistical Division (SD), and lies in the northern section of the state, inland of the popular coastal strip of the Far North and Mid-North Coasts. The region's centroid sits approximately six hours' drive north of the State's capital, Sydney, and five hours' drive south from the Queensland capital, Brisbane. As discussed elsewhere (Argent *et al.*, 2010), a critical account of the region's historical geography—including its shifting interlinkages with international and global markets and trading networks—must pay due recognition to the process of colonization (or invasion, as the Indigenous inhabitants would see it) and the particular position that non-metropolitan regions such as the NSW Northern Tablelands fulfilled in the colony's (later the State's) and the nation's development as suppliers of vital food and fiber and export income. A staples theory perspective is, therefore, potentially relevant and instructive for this task.

As observed above, an Innisian approach to understanding the most significant factors underlying settlement and the ensuing economic, demographic, and social development of the Northern Tablelands involves explicitly understanding the three key factors—geography, institutions, and technology—and their separate but highly interrelated roles.

Although European settlement in New South Wales officially began on January 26, 1788, the New England plateau (also known as the New England Tablelands)—the easternmost half of the Northern Tablelands—was virtually unknown to the new settlers until 1818 when explorer John Oxley navigated his way onto the region's open, savannah-like landscape (Premier's Department, 1951). Of course, the Indigenous tribes of the area—principally the Anaiwan and the Kamilaroi—knew the Tablelands well and it is they who felt the full force of the extension of pastoralism into the region from the 1830s. With Australian wool experiencing growing demand from British markets from the 1820s, pressure mounted for access to grazing lands outside of the geographical confines of the 19 counties on the Cumberland Plain that marked the "limits of location" (Atchison, 1977). The New England Tablelands, bounded on three sides by steep, rugged ranges, was largely inaccessible to bulk transport (even the bullock dray) from the major entrepôts and population centers to the south and east. Once a way was found through the Moonbi Ranges in 1832, though, squatters and their pastoral 'runs' (or stations) expanded quickly, numerically and spatially, on the plateau, seeking to find out for themselves whether or not the area's potential for fine wool production was deserved. Official registers of the time record 21 'runs' on the New England Tablelands by 1836 and observed that a decade later two-thirds of the area was occupied by squatters and their 300,000 sheep (Premier's Department, 1951).

The pastoral "mode of occupance" (Holmes, 2006) practiced in colonial Australia was necessarily a spatially extensive, low-intensity form of economic exploitation, involving relatively few resources, including labor. The New England Tablelands was tied to the seat of official administration and port facilities located in Sydney and, later, also Newcastle (see Figure 2.1). However, during the early decades of European settlement in the region these links were tenuous and oftentimes ruptured due to the very basic standard of transport and communications networks in the new colony. In a scenario strongly reminiscent of Vance's mercantile model of settlement (1970), the squatters, the producers of the prized fleece, relied for their supplies and access to end markets on towns and cities located at some distance from the Tablelands. A sparse road network meandered its way up the ranges and onto the plateau, draining agricultural and pastoral commodities from the Tablelands into the Hunter Valley port of Morpeth (later Newcastle) and Sydney and carrying back necessary inputs (Smailes and Molyneux, 1965). A lack of telecommunications infrastructure further exacerbated commercial and social isolation (Premier's Department, 1951).

Given the prevailing environmental, locational, and technological limits on settlement on the Tablelands, the squatting occupance mode ensured that population densities and overall population levels remained low through the 1800s and early 1900s (Premier's Department, 1951). From the 1840s onward, an incipient local urban system emerged as villages and towns sprang up at the major crossing points of creeks and rivers (Atchison, 1977). The railway arrived on the Tablelands in the 1880s (Premier's Department, 1951), reaching Armidale in 1883, and a second wave of settlements developed at the junctions of roads and railway lines (Smailes and Molyneux, 1965). The location of homesteads on the major runs also formed important nodes and, although not all survived as functional service centers, some did:

> Of the fifty homesteads (identified in 1848) forty remained as functioning pastoral stations in 1862, while three of the remaining ten (Bendemeer, Bundarra and Walcha) had acted as the original focal points for towns. The old station names have become firmly established in local usage, usually as parish and district as well as property names.
>
> (Smailes and Molyneux, 1965 p. 35)

Although many of these centers effectively disappeared as functioning urban centers with subsequent improvements in transport infrastructure and technology, still others had their original advantage reinforced by the "impress of colonial administration" (Jeans, 1975). Colonial authorities in Sydney established police forces, courts of law, and land administration powers and facilities in several towns—including Armidale—thereby conferring on them a central importance that they would retain for generations (Atchison, 1977). While spontaneous and spasmodic mining ventures (chiefly gold, antimony, tin, and sapphires) did trigger the emergence of small towns such as Emmaville, Tingha, and Hillgrove, most were short-lived ventures. Nonetheless, the influx of miners and their families did lend some demographic and economic support to the more established towns. Legislative attempts to break up the pastoral runs and 'unlock the lands' in favor of small-scale 'selectors,'[1] as in the NSW Robertson Land Acts of 1861, served to establish a nascent yeomanry and to lift local population levels in some areas of the Northern Tablelands but success was patchy.

Demographic, urban, and economic development on the Northern Tablelands remained highly fluid well into the twentieth century. The 'closer settlement' policies of the late 1800s and early 1900s facilitated both the amalgamation of small properties and the subdivision of large runs. Together with the progressive improvement of housing conditions and the progressive tendency for houses to be located (or relocated) alongside road frontages instead of watercourses, these structural shifts (Smailes and Molyneux, 1965) caused much flux in the regional settlement pattern. Change was most dramatic on the poorer granitic soils to the west of the New England plateau where homestead abandonment was relatively high. Amid this flux, though, the settlement hierarchy that originally formed along the favored central spine of the New England Tablelands, and which the current major highway and railway still follow to this day, was consolidated. That process of consolidation came at the cost of many smaller settlements toward the bottom of the urban hierarchy, such as mining camps, agglomerations of dwellings on pastoral stations, and small, isolated villages, which either disappeared quickly or progressively lost functions and population as the more favorably located towns gained dominance in the regional urban hierarchy. In many respects, this is a process that continues to the present day.

Industry, Population, and Interscalar Relationships on the Northern Tablelands During the Productivist Era, 1945–1980s

Irrespective of quibbles over terminology and conceptual definitions (see Roche and Argent, 2015), the international literature on the 'post-productivist transition' (PPT) highlighted the structural similarities between national-scale agricultural development regimes that developed post-World War Two in order to meet international concerns over food shortages. Nations, such as Australia, New Zealand, Canada, United States, and Britain, introduced a raft of legislative programs in order to expand *and* intensify farming and agricultural output (Wilson, 2001; Argent, 2002), installing agriculture as an industry of national strategic significance. In Australia, the policies and programs of the 'productivist era' could be seen as a continuation of a long-standing public worship of farming and rural settlement (Powell, 1988; Williams, 1975) but were also designed to lift the productivity of a farm sector still recovering from the long-term effects of wartime capital rationing, as well as tackling recurrent balance of payments and terms of trade problems at the scale of the national economy (Hefford, 1985). Simple, stark arithmetic gave a sense of the potential crisis that Australia alone was facing in the post-World War Two era. Agricultural production during the late 1940s and early 1950s had increased by approximately 1 percent per annum; over the same period the national population was growing at an average annual rate of 3 percent (Hooke, 1970).

In his policy speech of February 1952, the Minister for Commerce and Agriculture, John McEwen, placed agriculture upon the mantle it would hold for the next two decades:

> The Commonwealth Government has, therefore, decided to adopt as its policy objective, a Commonwealth-wide programme of agricultural expansion, not only to meet direct defence requirements, but also to provide food for the growing population, to maintain our capacity to import, and to make our proper contribution to relieving the dollar problem. Out of consideration of all these circumstances, the Commonwealth Government has decided that activities directly concerned with the production of essential items of food and agricultural products in this country shall be classified in importance with defence and coal production.
>
> (Hooke, 1970 p. 205)

This announcement was accompanied by five-year production plans for a wide range of farm commodities, a depreciation rate of 20 percent per annum on all farm plant, equipment, and structures, the introduction of a home consumption price scheme for wheat, and the advent of concessionary lending by major trading banks to farmers (Hooke, 1970; Lawrence, 1987). These programs had a direct effect on farm production, facilitating output increases of 35 percent through the 1950s and again in the 1960s (Gruen, 1990).

In wool-dominant regions, such as the New England Tablelands, investment in agricultural expansion and intensification was also greatly facilitated by buoyant market conditions, themselves strongly influenced by international events. Allied involvement, including US and Australian troops, in the Korean War (1950–1953) saw demand for wool increase significantly, driving the wool price index up from 592 in July 1950 to 1,437 in March 1951 (base 1936–1939 = 100) (Hefford, 1985). Supported by a reinvigorated public agriculture research, development, and extension effort (e.g. via the Commonwealth Scientific and Industrial Research Organisation (CSIRO) and state government departments of agriculture), graziers were able to increase animal performance via improved pasture species, including clovers, application of superphosphate fertilizers, and biological rabbit control (Hefford, 1985).

In the Northern SD, high national and international demand for wool and meat, together with a concerted research, development, and extension effort to lift pasture productivity, led to a 75 percent increase in the area sown to 'improved' (exotic) clovers and grasses between 1961 and 1971 (ABS, 1983). The post-World War Two agricultural expansion is evident in Table 2.1. Farm numbers increased and average farm sizes declined during the 1950s in response to the combined effects of soldier settlement schemes and the broader stimulatory policy settings. Farming families, often spanning two or three generations, comprised the

Table 2.1 Selected Agricultural Statistics: Northern Tablelands of New South Wales, 1951–2007

	1951	1961	1971	1981[1]	1996[2]	2001[2]	2011[2]
Farm numbers	9,678	10,037	9,909	8,061	6,706	6,098	7,041
Average farm size (ha)	920.34	840.9	842.8	946.3	1,091.3	1,078.7	1,015.2
Sheep ('000s)	11,833	13,713	8,204	7,486	6,480	6,025	3,770
Beef cattle ('000s)	827	817	1,691	1,222	1,663	1,629	1,628
Wool ('000 kg)	41,544	49,853	27,670	28,012	21,386	23,082	11,223
Cereal crops ('000 tonnes)	196.5	450.2	699	1,919	–	1,929	3,008
Cotton (tonnes)	–	–	53,401	209,591	–	703,307	919,565

Source: Carver, 1955; Bureau of Census and Statistics various years, ABS various years, Australian Wool Testing Authority various years.

Notes
1 Farms needed to have an estimated value of operations (EVAO) of $2,500 or greater to be included in statistical returns.
2 EVAO ≥ $5,000 or greater.

overwhelming majority of operating units. Not surprisingly, sheep numbers and the wool clip also increased substantially, as did cereal crop production; the latter concentrated primarily in the western portions of the Northern SD.

As highlighted above, a combination of environment, terrain, relative location, and history saw the Northern Tablelands develop a solid reputation as a region with a distinct comparative advantage in mixed livestock and broadacre farming (see Argent *et al.*, 2010). Consistent with the notion of the staples trap, though, local farmers—and the broader regional economy—had few alternative industries that they could turn to when an inevitable downturn affected a particular sector. Table 2.1 shows that a collapse in the international wool market in 1970 caused a sudden, dramatic decline in sheep numbers and wool production. Apart from cutting sheep numbers and wool production in response to the 1970 downturn, local farmers diversified into beef cattle production (Table 2.1). For those broadacre farmers located in the western portion of the Northern SD, and able to access irrigation water from the inland-flowing rivers (e.g. the Namoi and the Gwydir), cotton has proved to be a generally very lucrative crop, and plantings have increased substantially since its introduction (Table 2.1).

An indication of farming's importance to the broader regional economy during this phase can be gauged from its contribution to employment. In 1947, agriculture comprised 39.2 percent of total employment on the New England Tablelands; manufacturing accounted for just 7 percent (Premier's Department, 1951). Industry other than agriculture and pastoralism on the broader Northern SD remained poorly developed well into the twentieth century. Manufacturing was virtually nonexistent. The vast bulk of the primary commodities left the region for export markets with "a minimum of processing and do not undergo in it any stages of what would normally be regarded as manufacturing" (Premier's Department, 1951 p. 56). This said, one category of manufacturing that maintained a presence within the region up until late in the twentieth century was first-stage processing of local products (or by-products) for local or extra-regional markets: timber mills, brick kilns, tanneries, and shoe makers (Premier's Department, 1951). What other more elaborately transformed manufactured goods the small local population required were simply 'shipped' in—often from the 'Mother Country'—via Sydney or Newcastle by bullock dray, horse and cart, then train, truck, or by air.

Table 2.2 shows the relative shares of employment by industry for the Northern SD and New South Wales for 1961, 1971, and 1981. In spite of the breaks in continuity for some industry categories due to changes in national industrial classificatory systems, it is clear that agriculture remained the dominant mainstay of employment for this vast region into the 1980s. Although its share of regional employment declined over the two decades from 1961, farming still provided close to one-quarter of all Northern SD jobs at the 1981 census. This said, the capital intensification of farming—a central plank of federal government policy for agriculture—could be seen to be having its impact on the Tablelands, with farming employment declining in numerical terms by quarter between 1961 and 1971. At the scale of the broader state of New South Wales, agriculture saw its share of employment almost halve over the same period, dwindling to the status of a minor employment category. By contrast, whereas manufacturing employment expanded dramatically in the early post-World War Two years in New South Wales as part of a national industrialization and import-replacement strategy, in the Northern SD the sector remained relatively small. Tertiary services (e.g. retail and wholesale trade) made up another important, if subsidiary, sector, as did the quaternary services as the regional economy matured. Over this two-decade period—the putative halcyon years of the productivist era—employment in the Northern SD grew by 22 percent. The corresponding statistic for New South Wales was 39 percent.

Table 2.2 Employment by Industry: Northern Tablelands and New South Wales, 1961, 1971, and 1981

Industry	Northern Tablelands	NSW	Northern Tablelands	NSW	Northern Tablelands	NSW
	1961 (%)	1961 (%)	1971 (%)	1971 (%)	1981 (%)	1981 (%)
Agriculture	36.13	8.87	26.01	5.84	23.48	4.93
Mining	0.72	1.45	1.57	1.40	1.34	1.39
Manufacturing	7.92	28.87	7.90	24.74	6.44	18.45
Electricity, gas, water	1.17	2.16	1.40	1.90	1.61	2.08
Construction	8.21	8.55	8.97	7.39	5.85	6.24
Wholesale/retail trade	–	–	17.35	18.46	16.20	17.30
Transport and storage	5.24	6.62	5.01	5.37	5.03	5.55
Communication	2.56	2.12	2.53	2.03	2.02	2.04
Finance and property	2.01	3.54	4.82	8.17	5.34	9.61
Commerce	14.86	16.23	–	–	–	–
Public administration, defense	1.68	3.72	3.22	5.12	4.09	5.11
Community and business services	10.34	9.63	11.67	10.04	–	–
Health and community services	–	–	–	–	7.03	8.38
Amusements, hotels, etc.	6.48	6.07	5.76	5.47	–	–
Education	–	–	–	–	7.89	5.51
Recreation and cultural services	–	–	–	–	5.37	5.55
Other	2.69	2.17	3.78	4.08	8.30	7.85
Total employment (nos.)	59,345	1,602,716	61,866	1,937,666	72,399	2,233,111

Source: ABS various censuses.

Figure 2.2 shows the changing population levels of the Northern SD—incorporating the official spatial units of the New England Tablelands, the North Central Plain, and the North West Slopes—from 1961 to 2011. As is clear from this graph, the Northern SD experienced sustained population growth (20 percent, or 1 percent per annum) over the two decades from 1961 to 1981.

This growth was driven mainly by expansion in the mixed livestock farming belt of the North West Slopes. However, population increase in this subregion was only partially related to agriculture. In fact, during the 1950s and 1960s farming in this region—as in the rest of the nation—underwent an unprecedented process of capital intensification, a dynamic that caused considerable retrenchment in farm employment. Tamworth, the then and, to this day, dominant commercial, industrial, and administrative center in the entire Northern SD, grew by over 38 percent over the corresponding period. The New England Tablelands' population growth also exceeded that of the aggregate SD (21.1 percent) while the drier, broadacre farming-dependent North Central Plain, incorporating Moree and Narrabri, grew more slowly (14.5 percent). Over the same period, each major region's population share shifted little: an approximate two percentage point decline for the North Central Plain was absorbed by its neighbor, the North West Slopes. Somewhat surprisingly, levels of urbanization remained largely unchanged. On the Northern Tablelands, the historical experiment with 'closer settlement' combined with the newer raft of farming-specific concessions and subsidies to expand regional settlement and agriculture (e.g. wheat farming), especially in the western sector of the Northern Tablelands (Atchison, 1977). Smaller but significant post-World War Two soldier settlement schemes were also opened up around Kentucky and Enmore on the New England Tablelands (Smailes

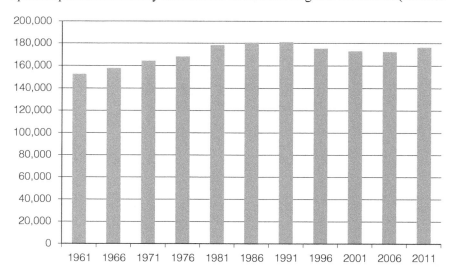

Figure 2.2 Total Population, Northern Statistical Division, New South Wales, 1961–2011.
Source: ABS various censuses.

and Molyneux, 1965). In other words, due to the dramatic reshaping of the region's settlement structures, itself influenced by the eventual working-out of the effects of 'closer settlement' policies, evolving transport technologies and networks and ongoing adaptation to the landscape and environment, the balance between dispersed—or farm/station—and town population remained relatively stable in spite of ongoing dramatic changes to the economic base.

Changing Places, Shifting Scales: The Northern Tablelands and the Multifunctional Transition, 1980s–Present

As has been described and discussed elsewhere (e.g. Pritchard and McManus, 2000; Gray and Lawrence, 2002), the 1980s and 1990s have been troubled decades for Australian agriculture and rural Australia more generally. In many respects, the early 1970s were a harbinger of the troubled times ahead. The election of the reformist Whitlam Labor government to federal power in 1972 saw heavy cuts to tariffs, quotas, and other forms of protection for virtually all industries (Hefford, 1985; Lawrence, 1987). Among the reforms was a 25 percent 'across-the-board' reduction in tariffs for all manufacturing industries. With the considerable benefit of hindsight, this wholesale repeal of industry assistance could not have been more poorly timed, coming as it did just ahead of the 1973 OPEC-inspired oil price hike which helped tip most of the industrialized world into a protracted recession. Additional pain for some farm industries (chiefly dairy and fresh fruit) came with the news of Britain's accession to the European Common Market in 1973, effectively ending protected Commonwealth trade (Hefford, 1985).

The 1980s ushered in more changes and mixed circumstances for Australian farmers. Although the subject of some debate, a peculiarly Australian strain of neoliberal thought and statecraft infused a range of Commonwealth and state government policies, from social welfare, to education, to trade (O'Neill and Argent, 2005; O'Neill and Moore, 2005; Weller and O'Neill, 2014). As a pioneering member of the so-called Cairns Group of free-trading nations, Australia has long championed the virtues of open and free markets to domestic and global audiences. Consistent with this stance, during the 1980s, 1990s, and 2000s Australia undertook to remove as many institutions, mechanisms, and programs that could be deemed as distorting of the so-called natural operation of free markets. Via a series of reports over this time (e.g. the 1974 Green Paper on Rural Policy (Harris *et al.*, 1974); the 1982 Balderstone Report (Balderstone *et al.*, 1982); the 1986 Economic and Rural Policy (Australian Government, 1986)), successive federal governments conveyed the message to farmers and rural communities that the generous support provided during the productivist era needed to come to an end to ensure that both groups responded appropriately to market signals. Concessions to farm production (e.g. fertilizer bounties, subsidies for farm fencing, free agricultural research and development advice) and in support of rural settlement (e.g. subsidized water and electricity, maintenance of rural roads and railway lines) were wound back. Targeted financial support continued to be provided to farmers hard-hit by sudden commodity price collapses and/or seasonal calamities (e.g. drought, flood) but increasingly such funds were subject to strict eligibility criteria, including financial viability into the medium and long term. In other words, contrary to the political rhetoric of 'agricultural exceptionalism' that pervaded much of the productivist era, from the early 1980s farmers found that their status had been reduced to that of just another industry.

Following this logic, the major macroeconomic and microeconomic reforms of the 1980s and 1990s were undertaken with the viability of the national economy at the forefront of policy-makers' minds, rather than the more-or-less unique circumstances of particular industry sectors. The floating of the Australia dollar and the deregulation of the Australian banking and financial services sector—both undertaken in the early 1980s—were seen as fundamental to incorporating Australia into the global economy, thereby minimizing the role of government in key resource allocation decision-making and introducing the rigors of global competition into the national economy. The deregulatory zeal spread to key institutions assembled prior to or during the post-World War Two period, including farm sector-specific major statutory marketing authorities that managed trade for each major commodity (e.g. Egg Marketing Board, Australian Wool Corporation). Under 'National Competition' legislation introduced in the mid-1990s, such cooperative and managed trade mechanisms were deemed anticompetitive and, as such, disbanded or corporatized and then privatized (Pritchard, 1999, 2005).

For economic geographers it is a truism that the effects of macroeconomic policies necessarily play out in different ways across what is always a variegated social, economic, and physical landscape. Deregulation of the dairy sector commencing at the start of the new millennium, for example, caused tumultuous change in the major dairying regions concentrated in the major cities' peri-urban fringes and the eastern and southwestern coastal belts, for example. Sudden exposure to global markets—with all of their own perversions, biases, and inbuilt volatility—caught many farmers in their own staples trap. In the early years after financial deregulation, aggregate farm debt ballooned through a combination of lax lending policies (e.g. poorly managed foreign currency loans), a wildly fluctuating Australian dollar, and volatile commodity prices. As Pritchard *et al.* (2007 p. 80) observed, "The net effect of these neo-liberal policies has been to radically destabilize family farming as a social and economic formation." Farmer militancy, previously rarely observed among a traditionally conservative group, erupted in the late 1980s and early 1990s, with farmers mounting protests in the major capital cities against what they saw as a plague of government-induced problems (Lawrence, 1987; Gray and Lawrence, 2002).

Arguably, the abolition of the wool price reserve scheme in 1991 was the deregulatory reform that had the most dramatic impact on rural economies and communities. Merino wool had become a staple of most rural regions following the conclusion of World War Two in spite of occasional severe market fluctuations (as in 1970, noted above). Alongside beef cattle grazing, raising sheep for wool was a key plank in the Australian mixed farming model. In areas well-suited to fine wool Merino production, such as the New England Tablelands, it became the dominant agricultural industry. For most regions, though, Merino sheep grazing formed a vital element in farmers' and the rural economy's diversification strategy. It was highly unusual for grain, beef, sheepmeat, and wool sectors to be in crisis conditions simultaneously, and while there were occasions in a given production season in which routine tasks for each sector could clash, generally these were manageable. For farmers—many of whom worked as shearers or shed hands for extra income or in exchange for work performed on their own farm—and the broader rural economy and society, the Merino wool industry provided a vital source of at least part-time income through the various seasonal tasks associated with wool growing (e.g. lamb marking (applying ear tags, tail docking, vaccinating), crutching (shearing of soiled wool from the breech area), shearing). Thus, the wool industry was responsible for an important component of regional employment as well as farm-level income.

The dismantling of the wool reserve price scheme and its supporting infrastructure and institutional framework could be seen to be a product of the (neoliberalizing) times but it was also substantially attributable to the failure of the floor price mechanism itself, at least as administered during the 1980s and 1990s (Argent, 1999). Regardless, the sudden introduction of free market conditions for Australian Merino wool in 1991 had an almost immediate and traumatic impact on most of rural Australia (see Tonts *et al.*, 2014). On the Northern Tablelands, a region with an international reputation for fine wool growing, the end of the wool reserve price scheme ushered in a period of profound restructuring. As Table 2.1 shows, the region's flock contracted by over 2.5 million head while the annual wool clip also declined. By 2011, the Northern SD wool clip was about the half that of the 1996 clip and less than a quarter the weight of that in 1961 (Table 2.1). On the New England Tablelands, the epicenter of fine wool Merino production, the rate of decline was not as dramatic as that for the entire SD (−37.5 percent). Nonetheless, given the Tableland's environment and climate, not to mention the expertise and experience of local graziers and farmers, local landholders struggled to find reliable income sources except via pluriactivity (e.g. finding off-farm work or establishing new on-farm businesses) or to find alternative grazing enterprises. Fat lamb production and/or grazing of dual wool/ meat sheep breeds such as the SAMM, or meat-only breeds such as the Dorper, became increasingly popular. In the context of dramatically lowered returns, some more entrepreneurial wool producers sought to take greater control of the entire wool commodity chain so as to reduce transactional costs and capture more of the value-added of woolen wear. New England graziers, the Frasers, provide an example of this approach. They established 'Frasers of Arran,' an upmarket woolen garment label soon after the abolition of the wool reserve price scheme and associated industry decline, using the services of domestic woolen mills and designers to create and market garments from their own wool to sell direct to Australian consumers. The 'Frasers of Arran' label was closed in 2013 though the Frasers remain involved in farming in the New England region (see Frasers of Arran—New England, 2016).

Over the decade from 1991 to 2001, farm numbers on the Tablelands decreased, as did farm employment (see Table 2.3). In the local government areas (LGAs) of the New England Tablelands—the part of the Northern SD most dependent on wool production—populations declined by an average of 6 percent. The biggest decreases occurred in the fine wool 'heartlands' of Guyra and Walcha (−11 percent and −12.2 percent respectively) though the closure of the Guyra abattoir in 1996 (Stayner, 2003), and ongoing restructuring of the timber sawmilling sector in Walcha throughout the decade were important contributing factors. Notably, all but Walcha and Armidale-Dumaresq LGAs recorded population growth over the succeeding decade (2001–2011).

As is obvious from Table 2.3, the industry structure of the Northern SD since the turn of the millennium has converged with the broader New South Wales economy, with the notable exceptions of agriculture, fishing, and other primary industries (overrepresented relative to NSW) and, to a lesser extent, professional, scientific, and technical services (underrepresented relative to NSW). The long-

Table 2.3 Employment by Industry: Northern Tablelands and New South Wales, 1991, 2001, and 2011

Industry	Northern Tablelands	NSW	Northern Tablelands	NSW	Northern Tablelands	NSW
	1991 (%)	1991 (%)	2001 (%)	2001 (%)	2011 (%)	2011 (%)
Agriculture	19.86	3.92	19.36	3.36	14.63	2.20
Mining	0.93	0.98	0.41	0.54	1.49	0.98
Manufacturing	7.00	13.11	6.70	10.97	6.71	8.45
Electricity, gas, water	1.37	1.42	0.73	0.95	1.09	1.09
Construction	5.04	6.17	5.14	6.71	6.54	7.31
Wholesale/retail trade	17.79	18.93	15.51	16.10	13.98	14.78
Accommodation and food services	–	–	6.65	6.68	6.62	6.71
Transport, postal, warehousing	4.07	4.96	4.33	4.95	4.47	4.93
Information media and telecommunications	–	–	1.23	3.00	0.84	2.31
Communications	1.48	1.73	–	–	–	–
Finance and insurance	–	–	1.23	4.80	1.91	5.05
Rental, hire and real estate	–	–	1.05	1.79	1.19	1.65
Finance, property and business services	6.26	12.72	–	–	–	–
Professional, scientific and technical services	–	–	3.90	7.40	3.82	7.87
Administration and support services	–	–	3.90	3.37	2.22	3.26
Public administration and safety	4.12	5.03	5.02	5.23	5.71	6.15
Community services	18.43	16.96	–	–	–	–
Education and training	–	–	8.97	7.15	9.79	7.94
Healthcare and social assistance	–	–	9.48	9.26	11.87	11.61
Arts and recreation serv.	–	–	0.75	1.29	0.83	1.48
Recreation, personal and other services	6.39	7.26	–	–	–	–
Other services	7.27	6.82	3.92	4.07	4.03	3.75
Total employment (nos.)	72,118	2,406,931	71,104	2,748,396	75,598	3,130,219

Source: ABS various censuses.

term impact of the manufacturing sector tariff cuts implemented from the early 1970s can be seen in the relatively narrow gap in the proportion of employment attributable to manufacturing between the Northern SD and NSW.

A better analytical tool for assessing the relative differences in employment performance and economic structure over time between two (or more) regions is shift/share analysis. Not without its critics, shift/share analysis is a relatively simple and straightforward technique that allows the performance of regional economies and labor markets to be disentangled from the influence of national and/or state industry trends, and from factors specific to each region. Shift/share analysis divides a region's employment growth into three main components:

1   the contribution that the region's particular industry mix makes to regional employment growth (the national effect);
2   that portion of regional employment growth attributable to the region's share of national or state growth (the *share* or structural component); and
3   that made by 'other factors' within the region (the regional *shift* or differential component) (Stimson *et al.*, 2006).

A shift/share analysis of the Northern SD and New South Wales was conducted for the decade spanning 2001 to 2011.[2] Not surprisingly, perhaps, the employment capacities of the Northern SD are far below those of the New South Wales: employment in the former grew by 6.32 percent over the decade compared to nearly 14 percent for New South Wales. Explanations for this discrepancy can be found in the employment structure of both entities. In spite of the apparent increasing structural convergence of the two economies and labor markets noted above, the regional share (or structural) component was −5.03. The chief contributors to this negative result were, again not surprisingly, the Northern SD's relatively high concentration of employment in agriculture and, perversely, manufacturing. Both industries offset the positive structural component effects of elements of the quaternary services sector (e.g. healthcare, education, public administration). The Northern SD also exhibited a differential component of −2.54 percent. Inter alia, the differential component can be seen as something of a proxy for a region's competitiveness and capacity for innovation. The major culprits in this case were wholesale trade (a notional loss of over 900 jobs), education, and healthcare (notional losses of over 600 jobs each), public administration and professional, scientific, and technical services (notional losses of over 450 jobs each). By and large, major decision-making affecting employment in these sectors lies outside of the region. For example, the healthcare, education, and public administration, and professional, scientific, and technical services sectors, although growing substantially at the scale of the state and nation, are overwhelmingly controlled by governments. In the wake of chronic budgetary crises at both tiers of government, regional services have been forced to prune nonessential employment and to produce 'efficiency dividends' to the responsible administration, especially in health and education (both state-level government responsibilities). Similarly, the professional, scientific, and technical services sector is predominantly publicly owned and managed, incorporating scientists employed by the nation's chief scientific organization, CSIRO, state government departments of agriculture and the sole university within the region, the University of New England. In all cases, restructuring and downsizing have been the mantra of the decade in order to meet dictates originating from Sydney—and/or Canberra—to save costs and departmental/agency budgets. In the case of wholesale trade, the dramatic declines in regional employment can, at least in part, attributed to decisions by major retailers, such as Woolworths, consolidating their freight forwarding services in ever-larger regional centers such as Wyong on the NSW Central Coast (Wilkinson, 2014).

Beyond Narrow and Remote: Changing Scale Relations and Avoiding Staples Traps

Of course, patterns detected at the scale of a region the size of the Northern SD can often camouflage or subsume highly distinctive or even divergent trends occurring within the region. In this penultimate section, we explore the varied and dynamic economic structures of a number of Northern SD local government areas (LGAs), concentrating on the role of interscalar economic, political, and strategic relationships in shaping change in these areas. The influence of international and global companies in the Northern SD has become more important and pervasive since the 1980s and directly linked to the region's comparative and competitive advantages in agricultural production. Our exploration begins with a shift/share analysis of the five Northern SD LGAs for the decade 2001 to 2011 (Table 2.4), followed by an analysis of major economic development issues in each LGA, focusing on the extent to which these have been influenced by events, processes and/or actions at national, international, and/or global scales. The selection of LGAs was not fortuitous but meant to represent the varied land uses and economic bases of what is an internally heterogeneous region.

Table 2.4 reveals a number of insights about the regional economy and labor markets of the Northern SD. First, the LGAs in the eastern half of the SD experienced overall growth in employment over the decade, though none came close to the overall state average growth rate. Narrabri, in spite of the relatively recent development of new coal mines and the creation of a substantial number of new jobs, saw its labor force shrink over the same period. Not surprisingly, perhaps, given the fundamental role that farming still plays in local labor markets, all LGAs—with the exception of Armidale-Dumaresq—had negative structural components—or industry mix effects. Given secular decreases in manufacturing employment since the mid-1970s, the sector automatically attracts a negative weighting in the shift/share analysis (Narrabri and Inverell). On the other hand, the healthcare and education sectors provided the strongest positive contribution to the structural component for those Northern LGAs with sizable shares of employment in these industries (all but Guyra). Armidale's mildly positive structural component is due overwhelmingly to its role as a university town and major regional administrative and service center.

Table 2.4 Shift/Share Analysis of Select New South Wales Northern Statistical Division Local Government Areas (or Parts Thereof), 2001–2011

	Employment Change, 2001–11	State Component	Regional Shift (Structural Component)	Key Industries (+ & −)	Regional Share (Differential Component)	Key Industries (+ & −)
Narrabri	−1.60	13.89	−9.09	Agriculture, manufacturing (−) Healthcare (+)	−6.40	Wholesale and retail, accommodation, food services (−) Mining (+)
Guyra	8.19	13.89	−12.79	Agriculture (−)	7.10	Agriculture (+)
Inverell	9.15	13.89	−5.25	Agriculture, manufacturing (−) Healthcare (+)	0.51	Manufacturing (+) Wholesale (−)
Armidale-Dumaresq	9.74	13.89	3.16	Agriculture (−) Healthcare, Education (+)	−7.31	Education, mining, healthcare, accommodation, food services, public administration (−) Retail (+)

Source: ABS 2012.

The differential component—or regional share—displays some other key facts about the character of the various subregional economies of the Northern SD. First, despite their relatively small population size, subsidiary position in the regional urban hierarchy, and dependence on farming, Guyra and Inverell had positive differential components. Interestingly, the otherwise declining (in employment terms) sectors of agriculture and manufacturing were the major sources of these results in Guyra and Inverell, meaning that both industries were causes of structural weakness *and* competitive strength in each local economy. These results point to the successful adaptation of key local businesses to the challenging economic, demographic, and political environment that has enveloped land-based production over the past three decades. On the other hand, though, the strong negative differential component effect results for both Narrabri and Armidale highlight important performance issues in each LGA.

Narrabri is situated in the western portion of the SD (see Figure 2.1) and is a typically broadacre farming LGA. At the 2011 Census, agriculture—the LGA's dominant industry sector—provided nearly 21 percent of all Narrabri's jobs. Over recent decades, it has become—with Moree LGA to the immediate north—the epicenter of cotton production in the region. This is a sector that is increasingly internationally and globally integrated. Although it has experienced considerable fluctuations in price over recent years, in 2010–2011 the crop was the most valuable farm commodity in the entire SD, returning approximately $800 million to the region (Wilkinson, 2014). Cotton cropping in the region began in the 1960s with substantial US investment, expertise, and practical involvement: 27 of the 60 cotton growers in the Narrabri area in 1967 were Americans (Wilkinson, 2014). Leading the US participation in the development of cotton in NSW's northwest was Californian company, J. G. Boswell, which established the Auscott business to manage the growing and processing of cotton in the region, including substantial irrigation developments (see Auscott Ltd., 2015; Wilkinson, 2014). As at 2013, Auscott operations covered 35,220 hectares, with ginning facilities at Moree and Narrabri (Wilkinson, 2014). The international dimensions of NSW northwest cotton farming extends beyond US direct investment and knowledge transfer with nearly a third of the crop exported to Indonesia and a further 20 percent exported to Japan (Wilkinson, 2014).

Growing international demand for cheap, quality energy resources is also playing an increasingly influential role in shaping land use and economic development in and around Narrabri. Black coal exports from Australia have grown rapidly over the past decade, consistent with China's and India's industrialization, making the nation the world's largest exporter of the commodity (Minerals Council of Australia, 2015). Although the Bowen Basin in Queensland and the Hunter Valley in NSW are the dominant coal provinces in Australia currently, the Gunnedah Basin, located in the western portion of the Northern SD, is emerging as an important province in its own right (Franks *et al.*, 2010). In 2006, Narrabri also become host to a significant coal-mining venture near the town of Boggabri. The mine is owned and controlled by Japanese resource company, Idemitsu, but significant shareholdings are also held by Japanese steelmakers such as Nippon Steel and Sumitomo (Wilkinson, 2014; Tasker, 2015). This was followed by the opening of a further coal mine to the south of the town in 2010—operated by Australian mining interest Whitehaven—and more recently, the controversial Maules Creek coal mine east of Narrabri.

As important as these new coal-mining developments may be to the NSW state government's revenue and to local and regional employment, they have come at a time of intensive public scrutiny of and activism against coal mining and related fossil fuel-based development. As international concern mounts over global warming and its consequences, a growing body of scientific, philosophical, and investor opinion (including Nobel Prize-winning medical scientist, Prof. Peter Doherty and British economist Lord Nicholas Stern) (Gittens, 2015) has aligned itself against one of the chief culprits of carbon dioxide emissions, coal mining, including all new mining projects. In the context of a mounting groundswell of farmer and broader public antipathy toward coal seam gas (CSG) and mining exploration and extraction; a tide that has coalesced into the 'Lock the Gate' protest movement (see Lock the Gate Alliance, 2015) the Maules Creek mine proposal has attracted sustained community activism against Whitehaven's activities. While global-scale concerns about the mine's contribution to future climate warming have been an important strand of the protestors' focus, so has the impact of the mining development on local ecosystems and water tables, given the mine's location on former State Forest land. In Narrabri, and in spite of the expansion of mining in the LGA, the population has continued to decline (−6.5 percent 2001 to 2011), undercutting demand in the wholesale, retail, accommodation, and food service sectors. The widespread use of fly-in-fly-out (FIFO) and drive-in-drive-out (DIDO) worker travel arrangements in the construction phase (at least) of the Narrabri coal mines can be seen as something of a missed local opportunity in this regard.

Guyra is a small LGA located in the center of the New England Tablelands and positioned almost equidistant between the major service and administrative center of Armidale and the medium-sized regional service town of Glen Innes. Long an agriculturally dependent area, with comparative advantages in fine wool growing, fat lamb, beef cattle, and some vegetable production (e.g. potatoes, tomatoes) (see Argent *et al.*, 2010), at the 2011 Census farming and closely related activities comprised over a third (34.1 percent) of local jobs. As noted by Argent *et al.* (2010) the town of Guyra is host to the largest glasshouse tomato-growing facility in the southern hemisphere, owned and operated by national horticultural producer and processor Costa Group, based in Geelong, Victoria. With 20 hectares under glass and in full production, the company has recently completed a further 10 hectares extension to the north of Guyra. Australia's largest single fruit and vegetable producer, Costa is a contracted supplier to the country's major retailers, including Coles, Woolworths, IGA, and Aldi (Sykes, 2015). Costa's transformation from a Victorian family-owned and -managed fruit and vegetable growing and wholesaling business to a powerful national-scale corporation has been facilitated by recent substantial injections of foreign direct investment (via US private equity company Paine and Partners) and a stock market float, estimated to raise approximately $A600 million (Neales, 2015). These recent injections of funds have been crucial to the successful extension of the company's tomato glasshouse facilities at Guyra but, as will be discussed in Chapter 6, the extra labor required to manage and harvest tomatoes has been a major boon for the town.

Inverell LGA borders Guyra to the west and is a mixed farming area, involving livestock grazing and broadacre cropping. The town of Inverell is home to the Bindaree Beef abattoir which employs over 600 people. At the 2011 Census, farming provided nearly 13 percent of the LGA's jobs, while manufacturing—dominated by Bindaree Beef—accounted for another 10.5 percent. A family company founded by John McDonald in 1981, Bindaree Beef has recently sought to take greater control of its position in the beef commodity chain, merging with Australian meat exporter, Sanger, to form Bindaree Beef Group. The new company then purchased nearby beef feedlot, Myola, near Moree (Hough, 2015). The merger was in part triggered by the opportunities provided by the recently concluded Free Trade Agreement between Australia and China and the need to develop sufficient economies of scale to participate in the Chinese market. This strategy appears to have paid dividends, with Chinese pork processor, Shandong Delisi Food Co., paying $A140 million to take a 45 percent stake in Bindaree Beef Group in October 2015. Beef processed at Bindaree's Inverell plant and destined for Chinese markets will be sold and distributed via Shandong Delisi's networks (Hough, 2015).

Armidale-Dumaresq's case is a little more puzzling, given its superior position in the regional hierarchy and the location of the only university campus in the region. Its strong research and development, service, and administrative functions should provide it with the basis for a much stronger employment (and demographic) performance. Armidale's population has been remarkably stable over the past 30 years in spite or perhaps even because of the university presence. The town and the broader shire has long experienced among the highest in-migration and out-migration volumes and rates of all non-metropolitan LGAs (Argent *et al.*, 2011). This is likely attributable, at least in part, to the fact that university-level education and research is now very much a national and, increasingly, an international labor market. Nonetheless, there are promising signs that Armidale and its hinterlands are beginning to capitalize on their very substantial and rich stocks of human capital, some of which relate directly to the farming and pastoral background of the area, others of which do not.

Livestock grazing, including beef and wool production, in the New England Tablelands has long been supported by a weak agglomeration economy—centered on Armidale—of the University of New England (UNE), the CSIRO, and an assortment of breed societies. Over recent years, UNE has greatly expanded its technical and technological capacities in virtually all facets of livestock and farm management, including the development of state-of-the-art monitoring and measurement of beef and sheep rumen activity (for the measurement of grazing's greenhouse gas contributions), plants' dynamic responses to environmental stress, including water shortage, the use of broadband Internet in everyday farm management, and the like. Complementing UNE's SMART Farm are locally based firms such as ICT International. Formed by UNE postgraduate Dr. Peter Cull, ICT International has developed into a highly credentialed business serving national and international markets with its soil, plant, and environmental monitoring equipment and programs. Based around the husband and wife team of Peter and Susan Cull, ICT International manufactures their monitoring tools locally but exports to 45 countries. Applications for their equipment include long-term environmental (including climate) monitoring in the northern Canadian permafrost, sap flow of tree species in the Brazilian Atlantic rainforest, and mine site rehabilitation. A key aim of their work is to contribute to the development of new scientific knowledge in environmental management in vulnerable areas around the globe (interview with Susan Cull).

A final example of ICT-led business innovation and entrepreneurship perhaps serves to indicate the extent to which the Armidale region's path dependence on the agricultural and pastoral economy is being complemented if not completely reshaped. WhiteHack, an ethical hacking business serving a global marketplace, is based in Armidale and the brainchild of Adrian Wood. WhiteHack identifies and nullifies cyber-attacks on private business and public sector organizations by hostile hackers. WhiteHack's success is measured in the rapid growth in its national and global client base, and in its Armidale workforce, which has doubled from 7 to 14 in 12 months (interview with Adrian Wood). Although the company's location in a regional center may appear strange at first blush, it needs to borne in mind that Armidale was the first location for the 'roll-out' of the National Broadband Network: effectively the first town or suburb in the nation to be provided with fiber optic cable to the node. For businesses such as Wood's then, providing the technological infrastructure and access to labor is satisfactory, physical location is relatively unimportant. While labor recruitment to such a specialized field has proved difficult at times for Wood, his adjunct status at UNE allows him to provide targeted training in information systems security and mentor 'up-and-coming' ethical hackers (interview with Adrian Wood).

Conclusion

Consistent with the conceptual insights of staples theory and evolutionary economic geography this chapter has provided an interpretation of the New South Wales Northern Statistical Division's evolution since European settlement that deals explicitly with the region's physical geography and relative location (vis-à-vis colonial and later state capital and regional cities and international markets), changing institutional frameworks and settings, and dynamic technologically dependent constraints and opportunities. In weaving this tale, we have been concerned to understand and explain the separate though interrelated influences of space/time (Massey, 2005) in shaping the developmental trajectories of the region's industries, together with that of its towns and rural hinterlands and, particularly, the extent to which these pathways have been influenced by changing interscalar relations.

The Northern SD's demographic and economic development through the nineteenth and early twentieth centuries could be seen as a largely path- and place-dependent process, at least partly forced along by the impetus of the Australian colonial project of wealth creation and nation-building via primary commodity exports to the 'Mother Country.' This was not an endeavor that proceeded harmoniously: many local Aboriginal people lost their lives via warfare and introduced sickness (Reynolds, 1982), and the squatters who leapt over the legislative and cartographic boundaries of the 'Limits of Location' to establish their 'runs' on the Tablelands were in direct conflict with the colonial authorities. Later attempts to 'unlock the lands' via 'closer settlement' legislation and establish a yeomanry as the basis for agricultural and rural development were similarly resisted. These battles have left a more-or-less indelible palimpsest on the Tablelands in terms of a cadastral framework and cultural heritage (including place-names and significant built and natural environment). Additionally, though, the nature of settlement and economic development in the Northern SD over the century from the 1850s helped it to develop an "area reputation" (Amin, 2003), nationally and internationally, for wool, sheepmeat, and beef production. It was this reputation, together with the experience and expertise in pastoral production, often passed down through generations, and supporting infrastructure, that the Northern SD carried into the productivist era.

National and international market conditions, along with a battery of concessional schemes and subsidies and state-led scientific improvements in farm management, underpinned the relative prosperity of Northern SD farmers and their townships. In circumstances in which agriculture was still the mainstay of local labor markets well into the 1980s, what was good for the farmer was seen as good for the whole region. However, rapid technological change also saw the demand for farm labor decline rapidly over this period. Although recent research has demonstrated the active support of New England Tableland farmers for their local towns (Pritchard *et al.*, 2012), the success of individual farms during the 1950s–1970s did not necessarily always flow to the Northern SD's towns and villages. The region's general inability to develop more diverse and robust industry structures and, thus, more functionally complex urban hierarchies, could be seen as a weakness of this dependent trajectory.

The radical political and institutional changes wrought at international and national scales after the 1970s exposed the Northern SD's vulnerability to a staples trap. The twin jaws of this trap could be seen in the removal of a swathe of supportive policy mechanisms for farming, together with the de(re)regulation of previously sacrosanct national-scale regulations defending the national economy and financial system, on the one side, and farmers' consequent exposure to greater market volatility, on the other. The removal of the wool reserve price scheme had particularly catastrophic effects for many individual farmers and their communities, and this event alone triggered a traumatic restructuring of the inland farm sector and rural economic and settlement system. And yet, in spite of the real financial, demographic, and social disruption caused by the neoliberalization of farm and regional development in Australia, as this chapter has illustrated, there are many positive signs and instructive stories of individuals and communities that have broken long-established cognitive lock-in collective mindsets and selectively harnessed aspects of regional or local path/place dependence to forge new and actually rewarding developmental trajectories. As such, then, what this chapter has demonstrated is, inter alia, the capacity of a region and its constituent communities, to adaptively respond to adversity without complete reinvention of the established economic base and supporting infrastructure, but through intelligent selection and capitalization on emergent strengths. In doing so, though, the chapter has also demonstrated the increasingly important role of extra-local and multiscalar relations—financial, strategic, political—in this process of adaptive adjustment.

Notes

1 Selectors, unlike squatters, were the individuals permitted to purchase surveyed land following the various land reform acts of the 1860s.
2 Unfortunately, due to numerous changes to the national (and international) system of industrial classification used by Australia after 1945 and prior to the 1990s a shift/share analysis comparing the Northern SD and NSW was not feasible.

References

ABARES (Australian Bureau of Agricultural and Resource Economics and Sciences). 2015. *Agriculture and forestry in the New England and North West region of New South Wales, 2015, About my region 15.10*. Canberra, Australia: ABARES.

ABS (Australian Bureau of Statistics). 1983. *Handbook of local statistics—New South Wales 1983*. Sydney, Australia: Australian Bureau of Statistics.

ABS (Australian Bureau of Statistics). 1989. *1981 census on Supermap*. Canberra, Australia: Australian Bureau of Statistics.

ABS (Australian Bureau of Statistics). 1998. *Regional statistics—New South Wales 1998*. Sydney, Australia: Australian Bureau of Statistics.

ABS (Australian Bureau of Statistics). 2003. *2001 census on CData*. Canberra, Australia: Australian Bureau of Statistics.

ABS (Australian Bureau of Statistics). 2007. 2006 basic community profile series (Cat. No. 2001.0). Available online at: www.censusdata.abs.gov.au/census_services/getproduct/census/2006/communityprofile/130?opendocument&navpos=220. Accessed February 25, 2016.

ABS (Australian Bureau of Statistics). 2008. Agricultural commodities: Small area data, Australia, 2005/2006. Available online at: www.abs.gov.au/AUSSTATS/abs@.nsf/Lookup/7125.0Main+Features12005-06%20(Reissue)?OpenDocument. Accessed February 25, 2016.

ABS (Australian Bureau of Statistics). 2012. *2011 Census of population and housing time series profile* Cat. No. 2003.0. Canberra, Australia: Australian Bureau of Statistics.

Amin, A. 2003. Industrial districts. In E. Sheppard and T. Barnes (eds.), *A companion to economic geography* (pp. 149–168). Oxford: Blackwell.

Aplin, G. 1998. *Australians and their environment: An introduction to environmental studies*. Melbourne, Australia: Oxford University Press.

Argent, N. 1999. Inside the black box: Dimensions of gender, generation and scale in the Australian rural restructuring process, *Journal of Rural Studies* 15: 1–15.

Argent, N. 2002. From pillar to post? In search of the post-productivist countryside in Australia, *Australian Geographer* 33: 97–114.

Argent, N. and Measham, T. 2014. New rural economies: Introduction to the special themed issue, *Journal of Rural Studies* 36: 328–329.

Argent, N., Tonts, M., Jones, R., and Holmes, J. 2011. Amenity-led migration in rural Australia: A new driver of local demographic and environmental change? In G. Luck, R. Black, and D. Race (eds.), *Demographic change in rural landscapes: What does it mean for society and the environment?* (pp. 23–44). Dordrecht: Springer.

Argent, N., Walmsley, D., and Sorensen, A. 2010. Something old, something new, something borrowed, something …? Rediscovering the comparative advantage of the 'new' pastoral economies of northern New South Wales, Australia. In G. Halseth, S. Markey, and D. Bruce (eds.), *The next rural economies: Constructing rural place in global economies* (pp. 17–31). Wallingford: CABI Publishing.

Armstrong, W. and Bradbury, J. 1983. Industrialisation and class structure in Australia, Canada and Argentina: 1870 to 1980. In E. Wheelwright and F. Buckley (eds.), *Essays in the political economy of Australian capitalism, vol. 5* (pp. 43–74). Brookvale, Australia: Australia & New Zealand Book Company.

Atchison, J. 1977. The evolution of settlement. In D. Lea, J. Pigram, and L. Greenwood (eds.), *An atlas of New England, Vol. 2—The commentaries* (pp. 171–181). Armidale, Australia: Department of Geography, University of New England.

Auscott Ltd. 2015. About us. Available online at: www.auscott.com.au/AboutUs/default. aspx. Accessed November 20, 2015.

Australian Government. 1986. *Economic and rural policy.* Canberra, Australia: Australian Government Publishing Service.

Australian Wool Testing Authority. 2015. *New South Wales—Production by wool statistical area—net tonnes—Jul 14 to Jun 15*, Sydney, Australia: Australian Wool Testing Authority.

Balderstone, J., Duthie, L., Eckersley, D., Jarrett, F., and McColl, J. 1982. *Working group report to the Minister for Primary Industries.* Canberra, Australia: Australian Government Publishing Service.

Barnes, T. 2005. Borderline communities: Canadian single industry towns, staples and Harold Innis. In H. van Houtum, O. Kramsch, and W. Zierhofer (eds.), *B/ordering Space* (pp. 109–122). Aldershot: Ashgate.

Barnes, T., Hayter, R., and Hay, E. 2001. Stormy weather: Cyclones, Harold Innis, and Port Alberni, BC, *Environment and Planning A* 33: 2127–2147.

Boschma, R. and Martin, R. (eds.). 2010. *The handbook of evolutionary economic geography.* Cheltenham: Edward Elgar.

Botterill, L. 2012. *Wheat marketing in transition: The transformation of the Australian Wheat Board* (Vol. 53). Dordrecht: Springer Science & Business Media.

Bureau of Census and Statistics. 1970. *Statistical divisions and sub-divisions of New South Wales: Principal statistics, 1960 to 1969.* Sydney, Australia: Bureau of Census and Statistics.

Bureau of Census and Statistics. 1971. *New South Wales handbook of local statistics 1971.* Sydney, Australia: Bureau of Census and Statistics.

Butlin, N., Barnard, A., and Pincus, J. 1982. *Government and capitalism: Public and private choice in twentieth century Australia.* Sydney, Australia: Allen and Unwin.

Carver, S. 1955. *New South Wales statistical register for 1950–51.* Sydney, Australia: The Government of New South Wales.

Christopherson, S., Michie, J., and Tyler P. 2010. Regional resilience: theoretical and empirical perspectives, *Cambridge Journal of Regions, Economy and Society* 3: 3–10.

David, P. 2001. Path dependence, its critics and the quest for 'historical economics.' In P. Garrouste and S. Ioannides (eds.), *Evolution and path dependence in economic ideas* (pp. 15–40). Cheltenham: Edward Elgar.

Emy, H. and Hughes, O. 1991. *Australian politics: Realities in conflict,* 2nd edition. South Melbourne: Macmillan.

Essletzbichler, J. and Rigby, D. 2007. Exploring evolutionary economic geographies, *Journal of Economic Geography* 7: 549–571.

Franklin, A., Newton, J., and McEntee, J. 2011. Moving beyond the alternative: Sustainable communities, rural resilience and the mainstreaming of local food, *Local Environment* 16: 771–788.

Franks, D., Brereton, D., and Moran, C. 2010. Managing the cumulative impacts of coal mining on regional communities and environments in Australia, *Impact Assessment and Project Appraisal* 28: 299–312.

Frasers of Arran—New England. (2016) Available online at: www.frasersofarran.com.au/index.php?option=com_frontpage&Itemid=1. Accessed January 12, 2016.

Gittens, R. 2015. A move away from new coal mines adds up, *The Age.* Available online at: www.theage.com.au/comment/a-move-away-from-new-coal-mines-adds-up-20151013-gk7len.html. Accessed November 26, 2015.

Gray, I. and Lawrence, G. 2002. *A future of regional Australia: Escaping global misfortune.* Cambridge: Cambridge University Press.

Gruen, F. 1990. Economic development and agriculture since 1945. In D. Williams (ed.), *Agriculture in the Australian economy,* 3rd edition (pp. 19–26). South Melbourne, Australia: Sydney University Press in association with Oxford University Press.

Harris, S., Crawford, J., Gruen, F., and Honan, H. 1974. *The principles of rural policy in Australia: A discussion paper, Report to the Prime Minister by a Working Group.* Canberra, Australia: Australian Government Publishing Service.

Hayter, R. 2000. Single industry resource towns. In E. Sheppard and T. Barnes (eds.), *A companion to economic geography* (pp. 290–307). Oxford: Blackwell.

Hayter, R. 2003. 'The war in the woods': Post-Fordist restructuring, globalization, and the contested remapping of British Columbia's forest economy, *Annals of the Association of American Geographers* 93: 706–729.

Hayter, R. and Barnes, T. 1990. Innis' staple theory, exports and recession: British Columbia, 1981–86, *Economic Geography* 66: 156–173.

Hayter, R. and Barnes, T. 1997. Troubles in the Rainforest: British Columbia's Forest Economy in Transition. In T. Barnes and R. Hayter (eds.), *Troubles in the Rainforest: British Columbia's Forest Economy in Transition* (pp. 1–14). Victoria, Canada: Western Geographical Press.

Hefford, R. 1985. *Farm policy in Australia,* St. Lucia, Australia: University of Queensland Press.

Holmes, J. 2006. Impulses towards a multifunctional transition in rural Australia: Gaps in the research agenda, *Journal of Rural Studies* 22: 142–160.

Hooke, A. 1970. Farm investment. In D. Williams (ed.), *Agriculture in the Australian economy* (pp. 198–210). Sydney, Australia: Sydney University Press.

Hough, C. 2015. Bindaree Beef Group sells 45 per cent stake to Chinese processor. ABC Rural Online, Available online at: www.abc.net.au/news/2015-10-28/bindaree-sells-45-pc-stake-to-chinese-processor/6893886. Accessed November 26, 2015.

Hudson, R. 2005. Rethinking change in old industrial regions: Reflecting on the experiences of North East England, *Environment and Planning A* 37: 581–596.

Hudson, R. 2010. Resilient regions in an uncertain world: Wishful thinking or a practical reality? *Cambridge Journal of Regions, Economy and Society* 3: 11–25.

Innis, H. 1929. The teaching of economic history in Canada, *Contributions to Canadian Economics* 2: 52–68.

Innis, H. 1930. *The fur trade in Canada: An introduction to Canadian economic history.* New Haven: Yale University Press.

Jeans, D. 1975. The impress of central authority upon the landscape: South-Eastern Australia 1788–1850. In J. Powell and M. Williams (eds.), *Australian space, Australian time: Geographical perspectives* (pp. 7–12). Melbourne, Australia: Oxford University Press.

Lawrence, G. 1987. *Capitalism and the countryside: The rural crisis in Australia.* Leichhardt, Australia: Pluto Press.

Lock the Gate Alliance. 2015. Available online at: www.lockthegate.org.au. Accessed November 26, 2015.

McCann, L. (ed.). 1982. *Heartland and hinterland: A geography of Canada.* Scarborough, Canada: Prentice-Hall Canada Inc.

McCann, L. and Gunn, H. (eds.). 1998. *Heartland and hinterland: A geography of Canada.* Scarborough, Canada: Prentice-Hall Canada Inc.

McManus, P., Walmsley, D., Bourke, L., Argent, N., Pritchard, W., Sorensen, A., Martin J., and Baum, S. 2012. Rural resilience, network capital and belonging: How farmers keep country towns alive, *Journal of Rural Studies* 28: 20–29.

Markusen, A. 1996. Sticky places in slippery space: A typology of industrial districts, *Economic Geography* 72: 293–313.

Martin, R. and Sunley, P. 2014. On the notion of regional economic resilience: Conceptualization and explanation, *Journal of Economic Geography* 15: 1–42.

Massey, D. 1984. *Spatial divisions of labour: Social structures and the geography of production.* London: Macmillan.

Massey, D. 2005. *For space.* London: Sage.

Minerals Council of Australia. 2015. Characteristics of the Australian coal industry. Available online at: www.minerals.org.au/resources/coal/characteristics_of_the_australian_coal_industry. Accessed November 26, 2015.

Neales, S. 2015. Costa Group IPO likely to raise $600m, *The Australian Business Review.* Available online at: www.theaustralian.com.au/business/markets/costa-group-ipo-likely-to-raise-600m/story-e6frg916-1227408612186?sv=b2bbe73e9a6cdd700444573 7d64a5317. Accessed November 26, 2015.

O'Neill, P. and Argent, N. 2005. Neoliberalism in antipodean spaces and times: An introduction to the special theme issue, *Geographical Research* 43: 2–8.

O'Neill, P. and Moore, N. 2005. Real institutional responses to neoliberalism in Australia, *Geographical Research* 43: 19–28.

Peck, J. and Theodore, N. 2007. Variegated capitalism, *Progress in Human Geography* 31: 731–772.

Plummer, P. and Tonts, M. 2013a. Do history and geography matter? Regional unemployment dynamics in a resource dependent economy: Evidence from Western Australia, 1984–2010, *Environment and Planning A* 45: 2919–2938.

Plummer, P. and Tonts, M. 2013b. Income growth and unemployment in the Pilbara: An evolutionary analysis, *Australian Geographer* 44: 227–241.

Powell, J. 1988. *An historical geography of modern Australia: The restive fringe.* Cambridge: Cambridge University Press.

Premier's Department. 1951. *The New England region: A preliminary survey of resources.* Sydney, Australia: Government of New South Wales.

Pritchard, B. 1999. National competition policy in action: the politics of agricultural deregulation and the Murrumbidgee Irrigation Area Wine Grapes Marketing Board, *Rural Society* 9: 421–443.

Pritchard, B. 2005. Implementing and maintaining neo-liberal agriculture in Australia, *International Journal of Sociology of Agriculture and Food* 13: 1–12.

Pritchard, B. and McManus, P. (eds.). 2000. *Land of discontent: The dynamics of change in rural and regional Australia.* Sydney, Australia: University of New South Wales Press.

Pritchard, B., Burch, D., and Lawrence, G. 2007. Neither 'family' nor 'corporate' farming: Australian tomato growers as farm family entrepreneurs, *Journal of Rural Studies* 23: 75–87.

Pritchard, W., Argent, N., Baum, S., Bourke, L., Martin, J., McManus, P., Sorensen A., and Walmsley, D. 2012. Local-if-possible: How the spatial networking of economic relations amongst farm enterprises aids small town survival in rural Australia, *Regional Studies* 46: 539–557.

Reynolds, H. 1982. *The other side of the frontier: Aboriginal resistance to the European invasion of Australia.* Ringwood, New Jersey: Penguin Books.

Roche, M. and Argent, N. 2015. The fall and rise of agricultural productivism? An Antipodean viewpoint, *Progress in Human Geography* 39: 621–635.

Sheppard, E. 2011. Geographical political economy, *Journal of Economic Geography* 11: 319–331.

Smailes, P. and Molyneux, J. 1965. The evolution of an Australian rural settlement pattern: Southern New England, NSW, *Transactions of the Institute of British Geographers* 36: 31–54.

Stayner, R. 2003. Guyra, New South Wales. In C. Cocklin and M. Alston (eds.), *Community sustainability in rural Australia: A question of capital?* (pp. 38–64). Wagga Wagga, NSW: Centre for Rural Social Research.

Stimson, R., Stough, R., and Roberts, B. 2006. *Regional economic development: Analysis and planning strategy,* 2nd edition. Berlin: Springer.

Sykes, T. 2015. Will Costa's float bear fruit? Here's how to cost it. *Australian Financial Review.* Available online at: www.afr.com/business/agriculture/crops/will-costas-float-bear-fruit-heres-how-to-cost-it-20150714-gici0k. Accessed November 26, 2015.

Tasker, S. 2015. *Idemitsu sells coal mine stake to Nippon Steel,* The Australian Business Review March 25. Available online at: www.theaustralian.com.au/business/mining-energy/idemitsu-sells-coalmine-stake-to-nippon-steel/news-story/d15a15b0ad321a22d0a4f02d43317564. Accessed November 26, 2015.

Tonts, M., Argent, N., and Plummer, P. 2012. Evolutionary perspectives on rural Australia, *Geographical Research* 50: 291–303.

Tonts, M., Plummer, P., and Argent, N. 2014. Path dependence, resilience and the evolution of new rural economies: Perspectives from rural Western Australia, *Journal of Rural Studies* 36: 362–375.

Vance, J. 1970. *The merchant's world: The geography of wholesaling.* Englewood Cliffs, NJ: Prentice-Hall.

Weller, S. and O'Neill, P. 2014. An argument with neoliberalism: Australia's place in a global imaginary, *Dialogues in Human Geography* 4: 105–130.

Wilkinson, J. 2014. The New England-North West region: An economic profile, *e-brief*/2014, Sydney, Australia: NSW Parliamentary Research Service. Available at: www.parliament.nsw.gov.au/prod/parlment/publications.nsf/key/TheNewEngland-NorthWestRegion:AnEconomicProfile/$File/E-Brief+New+England+North+West. pdf. Accessed November 26, 2015.

Williams, M. 1975. More and smaller is better: Australian rural settlement 1788–1914. In J. Powell and M. Williams (eds.), *Australian Space/Australian Time: Geographical perspectives* (pp. 61–103). Melbourne, Australia: Oxford University Press.

Wilson, G. 2001. From productivism to post-productivism … and back again? Exploring the (un)changed natural and mental landscapes of European agriculture, *Transactions of the Institute British Geographers* 26: 77–102.

Wilson, G. 2012. Community resilience, policy corridors and the policy challenge, *Land Use Policy* 31: 298–310

Wolfe, D. 2013. Regional resilience, cross-sectoral knowledge platforms and the prospects for growth in Canadian city-regions. In P. Cooke (ed.), *Re-framing regional development: Evolution, innovation and transition* (pp. 54–72). Abingdon: Routledge.

3 Localization *and* Globalization

Industrial Reorganization in Mackenzie, British Columbia

Greg Halseth, Laura Ryser, and Sean Markey

Introduction

British Columbia (BC) is blessed with a rich and diverse landscape. That landscape is the product of a very complex geological structure and the opportunities that come from spanning many climatic zones. BC's forest industry takes advantage of this rich landscape and has grown into an internationally important forest product supplier. But changes in the global economy, especially since the economic recession of the 1980s and revisited after 2008, have been buffeting the industry. With the intention of exploring how the industry is changing 'on the ground' in BC's central interior as a result of these global pressures, this chapter examines corporate restructuring. In addition to looking at the pressures and changes, it also seeks to explore the resulting challenges and opportunities, both for industry and rural and small town communities associated with the forest sector.

Following this introduction, the chapter is organized into four sections. The first provides a background for understanding the historical trajectories of development and change in BC's forest industry. This is followed by a review of the changing corporate structure of industry ownership in BC's central interior over the past 30 years. The changing market conditions for BC's forest products, especially with recent changes affecting the industry in the central interior, are also reviewed. The final section provides a discussion of the impacts of global-local linkages and challenges on the organizational and market structure of the industry.

To explore the restructuring of the central interior forest industry, a small set of interviews were conducted with 14 key informants. These key informants had extensive experience in the region's forest industry that enabled them to share information about the critical changes that have occurred since the 1970s. Interviews were recorded and transcribed before transcripts were shared back with the participants for review. Latent and manifest content analysis was then used to compile themes from the data (Krippendorff and Bock, 2009; Andersen and Svensson, 2012).

Context

While 'restructuring' has emerged since the 1980s as a term to describe a new and particular set of changes and transformations in the industry, the process of change has been a constant companion of the BC forest industry. In this section, we provide a thumbnail sketch of the historical development of BC's forest sector. We then introduce the critical theoretical frameworks of institutional and evolutionary economic geography to understand more recent resource industry change.

Historical Thumbnail

As suggested above, BC's forest industry has experienced a long developmental process of change. In this section, we draw upon Marchak (1983), Hayter (2000), and Markey *et al.* (2012) to provide a thumbnail history of the industry.

BC's forest industry began on the southern coast over 130 years ago, and was centered close to the emerging city of Vancouver. This geography was shaped by the rich coastal ecosystem that supported dense stands of timber. It was also shaped by the fact that for the technology of the time it was much easier and cheaper to move logs by water to sawmills for processing. The focus on Vancouver took advantage of the city's emergent finance and trade center roles, and its port and railway connections to different markets. Across much of the rest of the province, the communication and transportation infrastructure was poorly developed.

Industrial scale development of natural resources requires access to three key elements: a natural resource base, transportation tools, and markets. The coming of the transcontinental rail line to Vancouver created the first coincidence of these key elements and a small nascent forest industry began developing around Vancouver and the southern part of Georgia Strait.

Following changes in these key elements, the forest industry set in place its first geographic structure. By 1914, two transcontinental rail lines (one with its terminus at Vancouver on the south coast and the other with its terminus at Prince Rupert on the north coast), as well as the rail lines serving the rich mining regions of Southeast BC, spurred an early dispersion of sawmilling activity. Hayter (2000) identified that in 1914, 56 percent of sawmilling in BC was in the Vancouver region, 27 percent was in southeastern BC, and 17 percent was along the northern transcontinental rail line.

With the evolution of transportation access, Farley (1979) mapped the dispersion of sawmilling across BC from its coastal and railroad line focal points. The number of sawmills, and the geographic dispersion of sawmills, reached its peak in the early 1960s. After that point, processes of corporate concentration of ownership and spatial consolidation of operations acted to contract the industry toward regional centers that met the needs of coincident access to transportation and resources, and where towns provided the amenities that would attract and retain workers and their families.

Forestry in the BC Central Interior

A number of authors have written histories of BC's central interior forest industry. Drushka (1998) explores how timing, and the evolution of both public policy and regional transportation systems, impacted the interior forest industry. As a result, its evolution has been quite different from the industry on the coast:

> Compared to the coast, the interior industry has been dominated less by large, integrated corporations than by local entrepreneurs and family-owned companies. Until recently, there had been few interior companies that operate in more than one part of the province, so a diverse cast of characters appears in this account. Thousands of people and hundreds of companies have played significant roles in the evolution of the industry.
>
> (Drushka, 1998 p. 7)

The result is that intense bonds formed between the industry and the communities. As the industry transformed after 1980, these bonds acted to the detriment of the small forestry-dependent communities. While the industry became dominated by fewer and larger firms, whose interests were increasingly focused on shareholder returns, the communities longed for a return to the 1970s and times of big employment and smaller companies, where the companies were partners in all aspects of community life.

Across BC's central interior, both Bernsohn (1981) and Drushka (1998) described the importance of the Grand Trunk Pacific Railway (later Canadian National after the Grand Trunk Pacific went bankrupt). The new transportation corridor going east to west connected markets in the rest of North America with a coastal port at Prince Rupert. Along the rail line through BC's central interior were rich coastal forests, the interior plateau with its easy access to stands of spruce and pine, and another rich interior wet belt closer to the Rocky Mountains.

This new transcontinental rail line provided new opportunities for the early pioneers of a nascent interior forest industry. The first was, of course, the need for railway ties and numbers of small operations received contracts. A second was the growing continental market for lumber. To address these opportunities, the early forest industry involved small mills located right beside the rail lines. Many of these were 'portable' mills in that they could be moved along the railway line when timber adjacent to the mill had been harvested.

The early years along the rail line were hard in a number of ways. As described by Drushka (1998 p. 83):

> Most of the new mills built during the postwar period were further north, along the new Grand Trunk Pacific line east of Prince George. The railway was completed in 1914. By 1919, it was broke and had been taken over by the federal government. Later, it was incorporated into Canadian National Railway. In the early years of the war, several of the small mills that had been established there attempted to stay in business at various points along the line,

which ran parallel to the Fraser River east to Tete Jaune Cache. Known as the East Line, this timber rich valley contained huge stands of spruce and was fed by several major tributaries. But during the economic downturn that occurred during the first half of the war, most of these mills disappeared.

Technology was limited. In the forests, felling was by hand, and transportation was by horses. The rivers and lakes of the area were also used to drive logs to mills. The swampy landscape necessitated the building of plank roads in the summer, and ice-covered skid trails in the winter. There was some railroad logging, but this was limited. Second, market fluctuations have always buffeted the central interior. Creativity in business was the order of the day in this start-up era:

- When World War One broke out, the boom ended. BC lumber production dropped by 40 percent from the 1910 level. Mills in the north that had been built to ship lumber via the new railroad went broke (Bernsohn, 1981 p. 24).
- Some mills lost money consistently on timber sales and made it back in other ways, such as by selling ties. During the early 1930s, Sinclair Mills lost money on lumber and made it back on the cookhouse and the horses (Drushka, 1998 p. 101).
- In its initial years, forest products included lumber, railway ties, and cedar shakes for roofing. Over time, the industry focused more and more attention on dimension lumber production as its core business.

Mechanization, which began in the 1930s, accelerated after World War Two. With mechanization also came larger mills and larger companies. The small portable mills of 30 years earlier were now replaced by large operations and large companies. Sawmills were active along the rail line, with a suite of planer mills being established in the regional center of Prince George (Bernsohn, 1981). This pattern settled in from the end of World War Two until the middle of the 1960s.

Changes beginning in the 1960s dramatically affected the central interior industry. While pulp and paper operations on the coast existed since the early days of the industry, changes in both technology and regulation through the 1960s led to a boom in pulp and paper mill construction in the early 1970s across the interior of the province. Among the key regulation changes were secure access to larger areas of Crown land for timber harvesting and 'close utilization.' As Bernsohn (1981 p. 86) describes:

> Every year from the late 30s until 1957, the number of firms in the north went up as more people entered the industry. Then the number began to drop until, in 1971, only 135 mills in the Prince George Forest District produced lumber, down from 704 in 1957. But during this period, the size of areas lumber firms had the right to cut in grew until some were larger than Scotland.

Close utilization demanded that more of the tree be 'converted' into products—a challenge well suited to increasing pulp production. To reduce risk for investors, the province introduced new forest tenures and new regulations to supply wood to new manufacturing facilities:

> The big problem that we were faced with was that nobody was going to put all the money into a pulp mill unless they knew where the wood was going to come from to get paid back, and everybody thought they were dreaming. Nobody's going to put hundreds of millions of dollars into pulp mills if they didn't have any assured wood supply.
>
> (Participant P4, 2000)

> By 1965, the pulp mills were under construction based on granting Pulp Harvesting Agreements that provided a guarantee of pulp timber to harvest if sufficient sawmill waste chips did not materialize. The lumber producers could see that there was much to be gained by moving to closer utilization and keeping all round logs from being used by the pulp mills. After much consultation, the new Close Utilization policy of the government was announced January 1, 1966.
>
> (Participant P2, 2013)

Change associated with the BC government's pulp and paper policies, as well as its close utilization regulations, attracted investment capital to the central interior. Two companies opened new pulp operations in Prince George in the latter half of the 1960s. Canfor, a major company in the coastal industry, together with its partner Reed Corporation from Britain opened the Prince George Pulp Mill. Noranda Mining Company, from Toronto, partnered with US-based Mead Paper to form the Northwood Pulp and Timber Company and open the Northwood Pulp Mill. Shortly thereafter, the Prince George Pulp Mill (Canfor and Reed) in partnership with Feldmühle of Germany built Prince George's third pulp mill—Intercontinental.

In the years that followed, Canfor and Northwood would buy up smaller sawmill operations to access their timber supplies. As explained by one participant:

> Well when we first started, Northwood and Canfor didn't own any sawmills, then they came in and started buying up sawmills. You know, little independents. I mean pretty near all the mills, they actually purchased them rather than building their own. The idea was that they wanted to secure fibre supply for their pulp mills. They did have a large pulp harvesting area. Northwood's was east of town, and Canfor's was north and west of town. When both mills started out, they had a wood room that went out and harvested chips. But that was until they could get the sawmills to put in chippers, and they slowly…within 10 years those wood rooms were shut down. They were surviving on 100 percent residual chips from their sawmills.
>
> (Participant P14, 2013)

Furthermore, as described by Bernsohn (1981 p.102):

The new pulp mills affected the lumber industry, of course. A firm could put in a barker and a chipper and get a higher quota and a new product from mill waste that had a guaranteed market, since a single pulp mill used at least fifty rail cars of chips per day. In addition, the pulp mills—with the exception of Prince George Pulp—were usually connected with existing lumber companies, and it was obvious that by increasing the size of the lumber side of the business, payment for chips would simply be taking money out of one pocket and putting it into another. So the firms building pulp mills tried to buy out other lumber firms and applied for any timber that hadn't been committed to a company.

The impacts of corporate concentration and spatial consolidation were clearly seen in BC's central interior. A retired forester notes that today:

> There is just a whole lot more attention to productivity, to making use of the productivity of the land. So in the last 40 years, that's a huge cultural change, huge policy change. In terms of forestry, in terms of the industry, I mean, it supported a need to continue to consolidate and consolidate… There was a time when there were something like 650 mills around Prince George. They consolidated down to 26. Now there's probably something like 5.
>
> (Participant P5, 2013)

Changes in technology, policy, and regulation were then combined with the increasing corporate concentration of ownership to provide economies of scale and opportunities for cost management through vertical integration of operations. A longtime observer described the value of vertical integration in the early years of the interior pulp and paper industry:

> When we started up, British Columbia Forest Products owned the pulp mill, they owned Sawmill A, they owned Sawmill B because B Mill started up just before the pulp mill did—that was a stud mill. When they built C Mill and started it up, we got all the hog fuel and we got all the chips for the pulp mill from that on conveyer systems. That kind of vertical integration is what made pulp and paper possible here in the interior because it meant you weren't paying for transporting your materials, your fibre.
>
> (Participant P1, 2013).

Product development was also changing. The first developments and investments were in plywood, but as sawmilling residuals became more valuable and firms began looking to capitalize on that value, there were later additions in terms of chipboard and particleboard products. Since the global economic recession of the 1980s, successive crises of profitability and an increasing opportunity cost within sawmilling residuals has meant new product development in terms of oriented strand boards and medium density fiberboard, as well as recent investments in various forms of fiber-based energy products. As argued by Canfor's Peter Bentley

(2012 p. 284), "We have come a long way in reducing our use of fossil fuels and replacing them with the industry's residuals. The greener we get by making positive contributions to the environment, the better it will be for our industry."

Fordism to Flexible Production

While not unique to industrial resource commodity production, the impacts of the shift from a Fordist to a more flexible regime of production are important in the transformation of BC's forest industry. Since the 1980s, resource commodity production has been undergoing a transformation, or restructuring, similar to that found in other production sectors. Sometimes cast as a response to a crisis of capitalism, or to the rise of competition from low-cost producer regions through increasingly globalized markets and international agreements that reduced protectionist barriers to trade, the general result was employment reductions, ownership concentration, production concentration in higher capacity mills, and ongoing agitation to lower the regulatory costs of production.

Most post-World War Two industrial resource commodity projects were seen as significant tools for both regional and national development (Mitchell, 1983; Hayter and Barnes, 1997; Gunton, 2003). The massive scale of production provided equally massive revenue flows to central governments through a host of tax, fee, and royalty schemes. They also provided for large numbers of jobs which stimulated and supported local and regional economies where the resources were being extracted.

Following the global economic recession of the early 1980s, the historic pattern of employment and benefits flows has changed radically. The older Fordist regime of production supported large workforces distributed across highly differentiated tasks in a repetitive, mass production approach to resource extraction. Since the early 1980s, these industries have followed the trend toward a more flexible regime of production (Barnes and Hayter, 1994, 1997; Hayter, 2000; Halseth and Sullivan, 2002). The reorganization of work toward multitasking, and the wholesale replacement of labor and tasks with increasingly advanced and computer-controlled machinery, has meant job losses in resource-producing regions that had previously experienced decades of employment growth and stability (Mackenzie and Norcliffe, 1997; Walter, 1997). Many in BC's interior industry agree with one longtime observer's comment that the introduction of technology had a "huge impact in terms of displacing labor" (Participant P5, 2013). In resource-producing regions such as BC's central interior, it is now common that less employment and fewer local benefits are derived from raw materials processing (Hutton, 2002; Halseth *et al.*, 2004; Markey *et al.*, 2012; Edenhoffer and Hayter, 2013b).

One area where the competition from low-cost producer regions and the challenge of flexibility have both been met is in pulp production. Northern BC's pulp is unique from many of its competitors. The climate creates slow growing conditions, and slow-growing trees produce long fibers. These long fibers add strength to products produced from such pulp. This product advantage has provided some resilience against market changes. As one person said:

> So our pulp is ... it's strength is what sells it. So it's used in areas that need lots of strength. Like in some of the writing papers and stuff like that, where you want the strength of the pulp. Our pulp has gone into products that need our strength, all over the world. Whereas before, pulp was pulp. Everybody used the same thing. Photocopy paper... a lot of them now are using eucalyptus, and hard and softwoods over in Indonesia and stuff like that. Again, it's an area where our pulp was getting pushed out of and into the more magazine strength, where you need good strength of paper.
>
> (Participant P14, 2013)

Reflecting on the competition from new low-cost pulp production facilities in the southern hemisphere, Canfor's Peter Bentley (2012 p. 282) confirms this view in that those southern products "cannot compete in quality with the strong long-fibered pulp that we produce in the Interior of British Columbia."

Crisis in the Resource Industry Life Cycle

Evolutionary economic geography provides a lens through which to view and characterize change within the resource sector. It understands that social-political-technological arrangements become established, and then embedded around temporally bounded regional economies. These include interfirm competition, support and supply chains, labor arrangements, knowledge and technical production, etc. Change over time is both expected, and expected to be circumscribed by past economies and dependencies.

For Boschma and Frenken (2006 p. 277), "Evolutionary Economic Geography applies core concepts and methodologies from evolutionary economics in the context of economic geography." Starting with the view that systems are sets of embedded routines—routines in firms, routines in policy, and routines in practice in institutions—evolutionary economic geography turns then to the issues of change and innovation. As befits its connections to geography, there is a concern with the spatial distribution of routines, and changes in these routines. As Martin (2012 p. 180) has argued, "any convincing theory of regional development needs to give explicit recognition to, and account for, the roles of history and path dependent dynamics and outcomes." But rather than viewing path dependence as inevitably supporting "locked-in" regional economies, he further argues that there must be room to admit other "more incremental and developmental patterns of evolution" (Martin, 2012 p. 183).

Edenhoffer and Hayter (2013b p. 139), drawing upon evolutionary economic geography, have recently described what they term to be the "broad contours of the restructuring of BC's forest industries between 1980 and 2010." Using a life cycle model approach, they describe the phases or stages for BC's forest industry development. As with similar models, their resource industry life cycle model understands change as an evolutionary process beginning with initiation, growth/ dispersion, plateau, and finally crisis stages. Within such a model, the potential development trajectories are more complex and "are interwoven with short-term business cycles *and* powerfully shaped by global shifts and technological, institutional and geographical conditions" (Edenhoffer and Hayter, 2013b p. 142, italics in original). These are mirrors of the resource community life cycle model from Halseth (1999). In both, the questions are how industries and communities respond to crises.

The challenges for firms come when expansion ends and a 'plateau' phase is reached. Such a plateau "signals the end of a region's competitive advantage based on low cost, high quality resources, and increasing competition from lower cost sources" (Edenhoffer and Hayter, 2013b p. 142). The plateau phase implies an end to increasing profit margins and challenges to returns on investment. Using their resource industry life cycle model, Edenhoffer and Hayter (2013b) consider BC's central interior forest industry to be at a mature stage of development within this plateau phase. They identify how

> maturity can be an extraordinarily long 'stage,' and take on many different forms in particular places, ranging from outright deindustrialization to various forms of survival and rejuvenation that can involve consolidation with job loss with or without output change, market and trade diversification, niche development, and greater emphasis on efficiency and product innovation.
> (Edenhoffer and Hayter, 2013b p. 140)

These response outcomes of consolidation, job loss, market diversification, and greater emphasis on efficiency are clearly seen in the interior's two dominant firms—Canfor and West Fraser.

A further challenge in the post-1980 period has been a rise in the number of debates regarding natural resource development in northern BC. Different 'voices' have sought to become engaged in debates over how land and resources are used and how the benefits and costs from any development should flow. Hayter (2000) refers to this as a 'contested re-mapping' of BC's forest landscape. These include groups concerned with environmental impacts and sustainability, First Nations concerned about Aboriginal rights and title on the land base, and the rise of trade disputes with BC's largest market—the United States.

Corporate Structure

Against the backdrop of technological and industrial change, this chapter is interested in how forest industry firms responded. In this section, we review four aspects of corporate structure. These include the de-internationalization of corporate ownership, the ownership structure of key firms, strategic partnerships, and the implications of such ownership changes in communities.

De-internationalization in Corporate Ownership

Edenhoffer and Hayter (2013a) provide a summary of the corporate ownership transition in the BC forest industry between 1975 and 2010 (Table 3.1). The most notable change has been the virtual abandonment of the BC forest sector by foreign-controlled firms. In 1975, six of the top ten forest companies in BC were foreign-owned. By 2010, only one of the top ten firms was foreign-owned. Interestingly, the top five BC companies in 2010 all began as family-owned firms and have long histories in the province and industry.

Prior to the recession of the early 1980s, BC's forest sector had significant participation by foreign-owned firms. Following that point, ownership transitioned dramatically to national firms. Hayter (2000) provides a summary of foreign firms exiting BC's forest sector from 1972 to 1999. He identifies a total of 13 firms that exited the industry. One of these companies exited through the closure of its BC operations, seven were acquired by other firms (several of these were intermediary international firms prior to later sale to Canadian firms), and the rest simply sold their interest in various joint ventures. It was during this period that Canfor acquired the operations of Balfour Forest Products and completed the buyout of its venture interests from Feldmühle and Reed. Also in this period, West Fraser acquired ownership of the Eurocan pulp mill in Kitimat.

Ownership Structure

In his treatment of BC's forest industry, Hayter (2000) devoted an entire chapter to the growth, evolution, and demise of MacMillan Bloedel Ltd. As the largest and preeminent company in BC's forest sector for many decades, Mac-Blo (as it was known) was often considered as the model for BC forest industry corporate operations. Mac-Blo began as a small timber-trading house and grew through

Table 3.1 Top Ten Forest Companies in British Columbia, 1975 and 2010: Rank by Share of Timber Tenure (Foreign-Controlled Firms in Bold)

Rank	1975	2010
1	MacMillan Bloedel	Canfor
2	**BC Forest Products**	Western Forest Products
3	BC Cellulose[1]	West Fraser
4	Canfor	Tolko
5	Northwood	Interfor
6	**Crown Zellerbach**	Tembec Industries
7	**Rayonier**	**Louisiana Pacific Canada**
8	**Weldwood**	RPP Holdings
9	**Eurocan**	Abitibi-Consolidated
10	**Tahsis**	N/A

Adapted from Edenhoffer and Hayter (2013a p. 379). Original sources cited by Edenhoffer and Hayter: Pearse (1976) and British Columbia. Ministry of Forests, Mines and Land (2011).

Note
1 BC Cellulose was a BC government-owned corporation that took over a bankrupt US-owned subsidiary.

and mergers with other firms. It integrated not only forest growth on the land base, but also integrated a multi-product suite of manufacturing facilities that could extract the best value possible from different sizes and types of timber, with international acquisitions supporting strategic access to products, markets, or technologies, and an international marketing operation that helped the company avoid the trap of single market dependency. The Mac-Blo story ended when it was acquired by US-based Weyerhaeuser in 1999.

West Fraser

In the interior of BC, we wish to highlight two key firms—West Fraser and Canfor. Their BC operations are shown in Figure 3.1.

West Fraser began in 1955 when the Ketchum family moved from Seattle and bought into a sawmill operation in Quesnel (Hodgins *et al.* 2006). From its initial founding until about 1980, West Fraser focused almost exclusively on adding new sawmills and increasing its lumber production capacity. In almost regular four- to five-year intervals, the company reinvested its earnings in new sawmills (Table 3.2). In most cases, this was via the purchase of existing operations in BC's central interior.

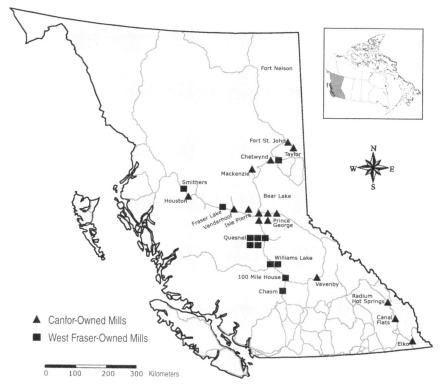

Figure 3.1 Canfor and West Fraser, British Columbia, Operations Locations.
Map by Kyle Kusch.

62   *G. Halseth* et al.

Table 3.2 West Fraser Timeline

1955	Ketchum Brothers buy Two Mile Planer in Quesnel
1957	Purchase Williams Lake sawmill. Company named West Fraser
1963	Purchase Brownmiller Bros. Lumber Co. in Quesnel
1967	Purchase A.L. Patchett & Sons sawmill in Quesnel along with Atlin sawmills
1967	Purchase Garner's Building Supply Store in Quesnel
1970	Builds Number One Sawmill in Quesnel
1976	Purchase Fraser Lake Sawmills (2 stud mills)
1978	Purchase Northern Wood Preservers in Dawson Creek
1979	Purchase Chetwynd Forest Industries (2 stud mills)
1979	Construction of Quesnel River Pulp Mill (partner with Daishowa Canada)
1979	Purchase 13% interest in Abitibi Paper Company
1981	Purchase 40% interest in Eurocan Pulp & Paper in Kitimat (liner-board mill, kraft paper mill, two sawmills, and partial interests in two joint venture sawmills)
1984	Increases interest in Eurocan to 50%
1986	West Fraser becomes a publicly traded company
1988	Acquires Revelstoke Building Supply Stores (Revy Home Centres)
1989	Partnership with Whitecourt Newsprint in new newsprint mill in Whitecourt, AB
1993	Acquires the remaining 50% interest in Eurocan
1995	Partnership Blue Ridge Lumber (medium density fiberboard) and Slave Lake Pulp Mill
1996	Construction of WestPine medium density fiberboard plant in Quesnel
1999	Purchase Zeidler Forest Industries (Alberta plywood plant, stud mill, veneer plant)
2000	Expands into the USA with sawmills in Huttig, AK and Joyce, LA
2000	Purchase Chasm Sawmill from Ainsworth Lumber Co.
2001	Revy Home Centres sold to RONA
2002	Interest in Quesnel River Pulp to 100%
2004	Purchase Weldwood Canada (7 sawmills, 2 plywood plants, 1 laminated veneer plant, and 2 pulp mills)
2006	Sells its interest in Burns Lake and Decker Lake sawmills to Hampton Lumber
2007	Purchase of 13 sawmills in southern USA from International Paper Company
2010	Permanent closure of Eurocan paper mill in Kitimat
2011	Sells Skeena Sawmills Division in Terrace
2012	Purchase Edson Forest Products in Edson, Alberta
2013	Exchanges timber rights with Canfor, closes Houston Mill
2014	Purchase Travis Lumber Co. in Mansfield, AK

Sources: www.westfraser.com/company/our-heritage/timeline; Hodgins *et al.* (2006).

From 1979 to 1993, the company moved aggressively into the emerging pulp and paper sector. In some cases, this was through joint ventures, in other cases it was by buying into existing operations and then securing greater control of some of those operations over time. In the late 1990s, the company extended the benefits that it saw by broadening its product base into pulp and paper. Through construction, joint partnerships, and the purchase of an existing plant, West Fraser added three new product areas—medium density fiberboard, plywood, and veneer production.

Beginning in 2000, the company began a new expansion strategy: "On the strength of a renewed commitment to their original goals, West Fraser boldly entered the new decade ... the company was determined to explore new opportunities for securing its industry-leading competitive position" (Hodgins *et al.*, 2006 p. 89). This strategy had three elements. The first involved a major expansion into the United States—specifically in the southeastern US where southern pine grew fast and supported a significant lumber industry. This strategy involved the purchase of some small firms, as well as the significant purchase of 13 sawmills from International Paper Company.

The second element of the strategy involved further securing their position as one of the preeminent forest products companies in BC. They did this through increasing their interest in Quesnel River Pulp, adding sawmill capacity in BC and Alberta through individual mill purchases, and purchasing the significant operations of Weldwood Canada. The Weldwood purchase was important as it not only eliminated a competitor, but added strength to existing West Fraser product sectors through the acquisition of seven sawmills, two plywood plants, one laminated veneer plant, and two pulp mills.

The third element of the strategy involved very careful consideration of, and action around, corporate vulnerability. They did this by closing some money-losing assets such as Skeena Sawmills in Terrace and the Eurocan pulp mill in Kitimat. They also sold off mills in the west central plateau of BC, an area of the province from which they further withdrew from via a trade of timber harvesting assets with Canfor and the closure of their Houston sawmill.

The West Fraser corporate strategy was fiscally conservative, focused on reinvesting income into expanding operations that solidified the firm's competitive position, the addition of new product lines to buffer the cycles of individual product demand, and moving quickly out of assets that did not have the desired revenue stream or long-term potential to grow that revenue stream.

Today, West Fraser is the largest lumber producer in North America (West Fraser, 2014). In 2014, it had about 7,000 employees and reported annual sales in the order of Cdn$3 billion. It operates 38 mills and facilities in Western Canada and the southern US. As an integrated wood products company, it has interests in lumber (mainly spruce, pine, and fir for dimension lumber), wood chips, laminated veneer lumber, medium density fiberboard, plywood, pulp, and newsprint. Table 3.3 shows the type and location of their operations.

West Fraser operates a total of 26 lumber production mills. Twelve of these are located in Western Canada (British Columbia and Alberta). An additional 14 are located in the southeastern United States. They have operations in North Carolina, South Carolina, Georgia, Tennessee, Alabama, Arkansas, Louisiana, Texas, and Florida. In addition to lumber production, they also operate five pulp and paper mills, three plywood plants, two medium density fiberboard plants, and two veneer board plants.

Table 3.3 West Fraser: Operations and Geography

Lumber	
Canada	*United States*
100 Mile House, BC	Armour, SD
Chasm, BC	Augusta, GA
Chetwynd, BC	Folkston, GA
Fraser Lake, BC	Henderson, TX
Quesnel, BC	Huttig, AR
Smithers, BC	Joyce, LA
Williams Lake, BC	Leola, AR
Blue Ridge, Ab	Maplesville. AL
Edson, Ab	Mansfield, AK
Hinton, Ab	McDavid, FL
Slave Lake, Ab	Newberry, SC
Sundre, Ab	New Boston, TX
	Opeika, AL
	Seaboard, NC
	Whitehouse, FL

Pulp and Paper
Hinton, Ab
Quesnel (2), BC
Slave Lake, Ab
Whitecourt, Ab

Plywood
Edmonton, Ab
Quesnel, BC
Williams Lake, BC

Medium Density Fiberboard
Blue Ridge, Ab
Quesnel, BC

Veneer and Laminated Veneer Lumber
Rocky Mountain House, Ab
Slave Lake, Ab

West Fraser, 2014.

Canfor

Canadian Forest Products, or Canfor as it is commonly known, has roots similar to, but somewhat older than, West Fraser. Canfor was created when brothers-in-law John Prentice and L.L.G. (Poldi) Bentley immigrated from Austria and in 1938 opened a small veneer plant along the Fraser River. This was soon followed by the purchase of the old sawmill complex at Eburne and its replacement with three new sawmills.

As shown in Table 3.4, corporate emphasis in the development of Canfor over time has followed four distinct eras. The first, prior to 1950, focused upon the acquisition of sawmill and cedar shingle mill capacity. At the start of the 1950s, the company was a significant Canadian producer of cedar shingles.

Table 3.4 Canfor Timeline

1938	Pacific Veneer panel company launched
1940	Purchase Eburne Sawmill (3 sawmills built on site)
1940–	Purchase timber operations at Vedder Crossing; Spring Creek Timber;
1943	Consolidated Timber
1943	Purchase Stave Lake Cedar shingle mill
1944	Purchase Englewood Logging Division and sawmill
1948	Purchase Hunting-Merritt shingle mill
1951	Purchase Port Mellon Pulp mill
1962	Joint venture with Reed Paper (UK) in Prince George Pulp and Paper mill
1963	Purchase Fort St. John Lumber Co. (planning mill, 2 sawmills)
1968	Joint venture in Intercontinental Pulp Prince George
1973	Purchase Westcoast Cellufibre
1981	Purchase Swanson Lumber Co. (sawmills AB and BC)
1985	Acquires full interest in Prince George Pulp and Paper, Intercontinental, and Takla Forest Products
1988	50% joint venture (Oji Paper Co.) in Howe Sound Pulp and Paper Mill
1989	Purchase Balfour Guthrie Forest Products
1999	Purchase Northwood Pulp and Timber (pulp mill, 6 sawmills, and research center)
2003	Purchase Daquaam Mill and Produit Forestiers Inc. Quebec
2004	Purchase Slocan Forest Products (4 sawmills, plywood plant, OSB mill, and pulp mill)
2006	Purchase New South in SC (3 sawmills, 1 remanufacturing plant, 2 lumber treatment plants, 1 trucking company, and an import business)
2006	Partnership with Pinnacle Pellet and Moricetown in Pellet Plant
2007	Purchase Chesterfield Sawmill in Darlington, SC
2011	Purchase Elko and Canal Flats Mills from Tembec Industries

Compiled from: Bentley (2012), Canfor (2012b).

Through the 1950s and 1960s, the company moved into a significant new product area—pulp and paper. In addition to its acquisitions and construction of new pulp and paper mills, the company also acquired additional holdings to increase its sawmill capacity and to provide the wood chip feed stock for its pulp mills.

Through the 1980s and 1990s, the company solidified its role as a major pulp and paper company. It also solidified its role as a major Canadian producer of lumber. It consolidated its industrial position in Canada with acquisitions in Alberta and Quebec. In BC, it took over two of its key rivals in the interior—Northwood Pulp and Timber, and Slocan. These latter acquisitions provided access to a much larger timber base as well as additional milling capacity.

From 2000 to the time of writing, Canfor has expanded its interests by purchasing a number of sawmills in the southeastern United States. It has also secured additional Canadian sawmill capacity by acquiring assets and mills from companies that had struggled to recover from the 2008 economic recession.

Today, Canfor is one of the world's largest integrated forest product manufacturers with more than 5,000 employees and sales in 2012 of more than Cdn$2.7 billion (Canfor, 2012a). In addition to its solid-wood operations, the company also maintains a 50.2 percent share of ownership in its former pulp and paper business now operated as Canfor Pulp Products Inc.

The geography of Canfor's operations are still dominated by its interests in BC. As shown in Table 3.5, Canfor has 19 operations in British Columbia and an additional operation in Alberta. Five of the BC operations are concentrated in Prince George. Canfor also operates a sawmill in southeastern Quebec. As with West Fraser, Canfor has also acquired sawmilling capacity in the United States, where they operate five facilities in North and South Carolina.

Edenhoffer and Hayter (2013a) examine the restructuring of Canfor and its operations from 1980 to 2010. Similar to our concern in this chapter, they focus upon the impacts flowing from the global economic recession of the early 1980s. Up until that time, BC's "forest industry experienced a spectacular expansion. The production of the main commodities, especially lumber, plywood, pulp and paper, was increasingly organized by relatively few vertically integrated

Table 3.5 Canfor: Operations and Geography

Sawmills	
Canada	*United States*
Grand Prairie, Ab	Graham, NC
Canal Flats, BC	Camden, SC
Chetwynd, BC	Conway, SC
Elko, BC	Darlington, SC
Fort St. John, BC	
Houston, BC	
Isle Pierre, BC	
Mackenzie, BC	
Plateau, BC	
Polar, BC	
Prince George, BC	
Radium, BC	
Vavenby, BC	
Daaquam, QC	
Pulp and Paper	
Intercontinental, [1] BC	(Prince George, BC)
Northwood,[1] BC	(Prince George, BC)
Prince George,[1] BC	
Taylor, BC	
Oriented Strand Board	
Peace Valley OSB[2]	(Fort St. John, BC)
Polar Board OSB	(Fort Nelson, BC)
Other	
J.D. Little Forest Centre	(Prince George, BC)
Marion, SC	

Canfor, 2014.

Notes
1 Canfor Pulp Limiter Partnership—50.2 percent ownership.
2 Limited Partnership—50 percent ownership.

widespread plant closures and job losses and marked a turning point in the corporations" (Edenhoffer and Hayter, 2013a p. 375). But the recession "stimulated fortunes of BC's forest industries, and corporate planning" (Edenhoffer and Hayter, 2013a p. 375). They then go on to explore the responses of Canfor to the new realities of BC's forest industry. They argue that Canfor's approach in the post-1980 period was illustrative of:

> the dominant corporate response to restructuring. It has survived by emphasizing cost minimization through rationalization, consolidation and acquisition, and even a degree of vertical disintegration. ... its strategies reflect a back to the future emphasis on a limited range of commodities.
>
> (Edenhoffer and Hayter, 2013a p. 376)

Explanation for this emphasis upon the historical core business activities of the firm around wood and pulp products includes the conservative nature of investment capital and the trajectory of past corporate experience and familiarity. However, the "implication of conservative, in-grained vertically integrated strategies become brutally exposed during deep-seated crises that signal the need for restructuring corporate and regional production systems" (Edenhoffer and Hayter, 2013a p. 377). In response to these pressures:

> Canfor's strategies remain emphatically focused on cost-minimizing and mass production. Computerization has permitted degrees of flexible mass production in lumber paper products, but internal economies of scale and size are key. ... Shifts in the geographical scope of this strategy are more profound. Apart from its control functions Canfor has divested its operations from its coastal roots and has shifted its focus to BC's interior (and Alberta) ... [as well as] diversification in North America outside of Western Canada.
>
> (Edenhoffer and Hayter, 2013a p. 382)

This strategy has been successful for Canfor, but it has not been successful for all of its pre-1980 rivals. Several of its largest earlier competitors, such as BC Forest Products and Mac-Blo, have disappeared from the industry.

The ownership timelines for both Canfor and West Fraser identify a wide range of corporate strategies and approaches to partnerships or controlling partnerships in various operations. At times, these strategies are helpful to reduce level of risk, acquire needed capital, acquire necessary expertise or markets, or to gain a foothold in a new product sector. Hayter (2000) tracks the participation of foreign firms in joint ventures during the establishment of the BC interior's pulp and paper industry from 1962 to 1973. He identifies eight pulp mills in the interior, and two on the north coast that were established under the new regulatory regime. In all of these cases, there was a partnership between a local firm and an international partner or set of partners. In all cases but two, the already-operating local firm was Canadian-based. Across these new pulp mills, international investment involved the participation of five Japanese firms, three US-based firms, two firms based in

Britain, two firms based in Finland, one in Sweden, and one in Germany. Strategic partnerships have always played an important role in the marketing and sales of BC forest products. Since 2000, however, new strategic partnerships have been created in key market locations. Canfor and West Fraser have been significant players in the opening of additional or new forest products markets.

Community Implications

How do such ownership changes appear 'on the ground.' Table 3.6 is a timeline of ownership changes at the major forest products facilities in Mackenzie, BC. As shown, during the 1960s there were several rapid ownership changes as the initial industrial infrastructure was established. Following that, there was a 20-year period where ownership was stable across the different companies and their operations.

Much of the early investment was by firms external to BC. It also included international partners from Germany, the US, and Japan and involved several joint partnership arrangements to secure enough capital financing and markets for products.

Table 3.6 Forest Firm Ownership Changes: Mackenzie, British Columbia

1964	Alexandra Forest Holdings (a division of the Wenner-Gren group), British Columbia Forest Products (BCFP), Argus Corporation, and Mead Corporation form Alexandra Forest Industries.
1964	First announcement for lumber, pulp, and paper complex at Mackenzie.
1967	Alexandra Forest Industries taken over by BCFP.
1968	Cattermole Timber (Finlay Forest Industries), Sumitomo Forestry Co. Ltd., and Jujo Paper Manufacturing Co. Ltd. announce new sawmill and pulp mill for Mackenzie.
1988	Fletcher Challenge Canada Limited buys BCFP.
1992	Royal Bank takes over Finlay Forest Industries.
1993	Slocan Forest Products and Donohue Inc. purchase Finlay Forest Industries.
1995	Fletcher Challenge sells its sawmills in Mackenzie to Timber West.
1997	Slocan Forest Products buys Timber West sawmills.
1999	Donohue Industries completes takeover of Finlay Forest Industries.
2000	Donohue Industries is taken over by Quebec-based Abitibi-Consolidated.
2000	Norske Skog ASA buys Fletcher Challenge.
2001	Pope and Talbot buys Norske Skog ASA's BC plants.
2004	Canfor and Slocan merge, Canfor take over.
2008	Conifex acquires Abitibi Bowater's Mackenzie sawmill.
2008	Edmonton-based Worthington Properties Inc. purchases Pope and Talbot pulp mill.
2009	Worthington Properties Inc. abandons Mackenzie mill, forcing provincial company Mackenzie Pulp Mill Environmental Management Inc. to pay for minimal maintenance.
2010	Netherlands-based Paper Excellence, a subsidiary of Asian-giant Sinarmas, purchases the shuttered Mackenzie pulp mill.

Developed from Mackenzie newspapers, local histories (Trade Union Research Bureau, 1974; Veemes, 1986; Williston and Keller, 1997), and fieldwork.

There then followed a 20-year period of ownership stability. This was broken in 1988 when New Zealand-based Fletcher Challenge purchased BC Forest Products. Economic uncertainty in the global economy through the early 1990s led to numbers of changes as well. Bankruptcy, takeovers, and the division and sale of corporate assets initiated a number of new rounds of ownership changes in Mackenzie and witnessed the coming, and going, of several international players.

The next significant set of changes was initiated with the 2008 recession. As one interviewee said:

> Well, a lot of the mills closed, some just downsized; a number have actually closed. A lot of the time, it's a combination of the implosion of the US market which we're very dependent on and the timber supply situation. Coming out of the recession, and also coming out of the pine beetle epidemic, we have a lot less timber.
>
> (Participant P5, 2013)

Sales after bankruptcies, and uncertainty over initial ownership changes, all led to a number of firms taking time to 'settle in' to Mackenzie's current industrial complex. The major players at present in Mackenzie are Canfor and Conifex, both of which are BC-based firms with operations concentrated in the central interior.

Historically, the major firms in a community were actively involved in the community. They provided not only jobs and local taxes, but they supported community groups and activities, they funded scholarships and recreation programs, and they hosted social events throughout the year. In other words, they had a close and almost paternalistic relationship with the host communities:

> FFI and BCFP [the two initial firms in Mackenzie] were both great for the community. If you look at the curling rink, they built that. They built this place here [community center].
>
> (Participant P3, 2013)

> The [housing and the community] were fairly good because the companies were not running down the houses. They were fixing them. Like I say, anything you wanted, anything you needed, you got it. You want to build a nice big fence, just ask for the lumber and you build it yourself. If you want to paint the outside of the house, there's how many gallons of paint you want, go right ahead.
>
> [QS](Participant P8, 2013)

The companies and their management staff were actively part of the community. As one interviewee described:

> When we started up here, BCFP said 'The only asset we have is our people. The rest of it is just stuff. We can change the stuff. What we've gotta do is train our people and stay in close touch with our people.' The first four mill

managers we had knew you, they knew your wife, they knew your kids' names; and when you met them downtown, they made a point of stopping to talk to you. You were people and everybody was equal because they knew that the people they were looking at there in the street might want to be the mill manager. They were always training, they were always recruiting.

(Participant P1, 2013)

Fiscal pressures have changed this relationship since the 1980s recession. The 'turnover' of firms in a locality, as well as the degree to which those firms may be involved in the community, was described by an interviewee:

Consolidation has changed the dynamic of the industry. That's the biggest change, in terms of how it affects communities, because it is a commodity business, it is global market, and it's hard to make commitments to a single community… No matter how much you want to stay there, if it doesn't work in that community then it doesn't work there.

(Participant P5, 2013)

A key concept to understanding how communities are affected by the changing corporate and market structures of the forest industry involves the notion of 'globalization.' Bowles (2013) explores several different processes at the heart of 'globalizing' northern BC. He argues for the importance of distinguishing between:

two distinct meanings of 'globalizing.' The first is 'globalizing' as an adjective, as a descriptor of increasing global economic integration and measured by trade and other flows. The second is as a verb, with agents 'globalizing' the region through a distinct set of actions and policies.

(Bowles, 2013 p. 262)

Bowles' analysis adopts a long-term perspective by examining the northern BC economy from approximately 1870 to present. He also focuses upon both economic development and policy. Using export data, Bowles looks at the degrees to which BC's economy was, over time, embedded within (or exposed to) of the global economy. The links to, and concerns about, dependence noted within staples theory resurface in the concerns here. Using this information, he shows how:

'globalizing' periods have differed in policy terms. For northern BC, the first period analyzed here combined globalizing with nation-building policies, the second combined globalizing with province-building policies, the third combined globalizing with neoliberal policies. Each has had different implications for the communities which populate the northern part of the province and illustrates how 'globalization' is experienced differently at different times depending on the policy environment.

(Bowles, 2013 p. 274)

One critical change of the neoliberal policy era was when:

> Forest firms were given greater operational control by the ending of appurtenancy in 2003 ... with this change, BC became the only province in Canada which has no kind of appurtenancy requirements. The umbilical cord between communities and the resources which surrounded them, a bedrock of the spatial contract with northern resource-based communities for decades, was cut and forest firms were now able to mill wood wherever in the province it was most profitable to so. This not only increased the economic insecurity of communities, but also made them more directly into competitors.
>
> (Bowles, 2013 p. 271)

The uncertainty and implications that is generated by this policy and structural change is described by our interviewees:

> There isn't hardly a place in the northern part of BC where wood from one community couldn't go to the next and still be in Canfor domain. I mean you look at central interior—the same exists with West Fraser. It could go in any direction, and from a market perspective, there are times when it should go different directions because there are certain mills and certain products, and certain timber, and if you don't match that up, somebody will beat you in the market.
>
> (Participant P5, 2013)

and

> The appurtenancy clauses affected the communities because when these communities were all built, it was on the premise that the wood cut in the valley was converted in the valley. So appurtenancy was a big issue for the community.
>
> (Participant P3, 2013)

Market Structure

Most treatments of BC's forest sector open with an acknowledgment that the industry has always been immersed in the global commodity marketplace. As a producer of minimally processed raw materials that form the inputs for higher order manufacturing in core industrial regions, BC's resource economy has been described as a staple producing economy. Canadian political economist Harold Innis developed staples theory to explain the circumstances of such a market orientation.

For Innis (1933, 1950), staples theory helps to describe the social, political, and economic implications for resource-producing regions occupying a peripheral place within the global economy. Innis argued that the institutional framework created through staples production posed long-term barriers to development (Drache, 1991). Two key problems that flow from a staples-based economy include dependency and truncated development (Markey *et al.* 2012). The dependency problem comes from functioning as a resource supply 'warehouse' for advanced economies. As price-takers, producing regions are dependent upon the demands of external markets. Edenhoffer and Hayter (2013b p. 140) note, "Resource industries and peripheries play vital roles in the global economy, their fortunes interdependent with cores even if the balance of decision-making power favours the latter." Over time, the fluctuations in global commodity demands and prices for raw materials have become more dramatic.

The dependence problem is exacerbated by the challenge of truncated development. World-scale resource exploitation projects require world-scale firms and access to requisite levels of financing. Once in place, large industrial capital manages a region's resource commodity production as one component of its needed service and supply chain. As Hayter (1982 p. 281) argued, the implication of such foreign ownership "relates to a loss of autonomy over strategic investments and technology decisions" (see also Haley, 2011). Halseth and Sullivan (2002 p. 258) expand upon this by arguing that, "foreign controlled firms are often content to continue exporting basic resource commodities that are needed in their home economies or for other components of their multi-national holdings."

This exposure has shifted along with the transformation of both markets and international trade. Beginning first with the topic of international trade regulation, the development of BC's forest industry was influenced in its early years by various forms of tariffs and protective trading relationships. This tended to focus trade internally to Canada or externally to British Empire markets. For some producers, internal markets focused on other local industries. For example, many sawmills in southwestern BC produced timber for the large underground mines of the region and the towns they supported. In northcentral BC, many of the sawmills along the northern transcontinental railroad line were owned and operated by prairie grain companies. This had a twofold advantage. First, timber harvesting on frozen ground in winter offered a way to employ seasonal labor when it was not needed in farming regions. Second, it supplied the lumber for the towns and the grain elevators of a rapidly expanding prairie settlement and agricultural region. The coastal industry was able to ship within the British Empire and build inroads into the US market, especially the booming economy of California immediately after the gold rush.

In the post-World War Two era, industrial forest development became a cornerstone of provincial policy. As noted earlier, purposeful public policy change created the conditions that were well suited to an expansion of the pulp and paper industry into the interior regions of the province. Policy also actively encouraged the types of investments needed from large international capital that were described earlier. But the increasing opportunities for growing the scale of forest product production needed to be matched with markets. Coincidentally, the growth of the US economy after World War Two, coupled with the baby boom of the 1950s and 1960s and the linked boom in suburban housing development, created just such a ready market for BC lumber. With easy rail and road access to US markets, the forest industry of the interior of BC expanded. This boom, and this market orientation on the US housing market, also acted to structure the industry, which placed an increasing focus on dimension lumber production.

These historical trends can be seen in Table 3.7, where data on the overseas shipment of wood products from 1955 to 1964 are shown. The table identifies significant shipments to the UK and the US—though it should be noted that most wood product exports to the US were via road or rail transportation. Also important are exports to Japan and Asia. Over this period, Japan shifted from a relatively small market to a significant market for BC wood products. It was on this market opportunity that the coastal BC forest industry focused its attention. The opposite holds true for Hong Kong, China, and Formosa. In this case, an already small market dwindles even further to the point of insignificance as a trading destination.

Hayter (2000) tracks the impacts of shifting markets on the BC forest industry. As the coastal industry turned more attention to the Japanese market, that market remained relatively stable until dropping off during the 2008 recession. As the interior industry was concentrating its activities on dimension lumber production, one of its main markets—the US housing market—boomed until 2008.

As shown in Table 3.8, coastal production remained relatively flat between 1971 and 1989. However, the target markets for its production shifted from being dominated by US exports to 'elsewhere.' In contrast, lumber shipments from interior mills nearly tripled over that same period. In addition, there was also some market diversification with growth in the Canadian market.

Table 3.9 shows the export value and volume of dimension lumber to the US market from 1988 to 2013. Three issues are important here. The first is that as the US housing market grew dramatically into the early 2000s, the interior BC forest industry capitalized on this growth opportunity in both value and volume of exports. One explanation for the greater rise in value over volume is that over part of this time period the Canadian dollar gained strength relative to the US dollar terms of currency exchange rates.

Table 3.7 Water-Borne[1] Exports of Wood Products, 1955–1964 ('000 Board Feet)

	Hong Kong, China, and Formosa	Japan	UK	US[2]	Totals
1955	1,909	1,623	607,240	345,694	1,412,059
1956	1,275	5,852	320,126	283,834	989,664
1957	1,256	2,301	384,754	275,452	1,078,918
1958	597	999	336,889	602,427	1,314,361
1959	509	1,201	267,293	595,170	1,197,653
1960	867	1,607	518,090	714,050	1,675,351
1961	360	155,550	422,939	838,080	1,789,115
1962	0	107,438	442,237	876,420	1,847,026
1963	172	278,168	465,428	963,783	2,149,132
1964	447	204,439	695,196	932,313	2,282,709

Source: BC Ministry of Forests (2014) and annual reports.

Notes
1 Rail and truck shipments are not included.
2 most wood exports to US are by rail or road.

Table 3.8 British Columbia Lumber Shipments From the Coast and Interior, 1971 and 1989

Coastal Shipments		1971	1989
	Total (MBF)	4,171.5	4,203.0
	% to Canada	17.1	21.7
	% to US	53.7	32.4
	% elsewhere	29.2	45.9
Interior Shipments			
	Total (MBF)	4,785.5	11,039.8
	% to Canada	19.9	30.1
	% to US	71.0	59.6
	% elsewhere	9.1	10.3

Original source: Hayter, 1992 p. 165. Adapted from Hayter, 2000 p. 242.

Note: MBF =million board feet.

Table 3.9 British Columbia Exports of Softwood Lumber to the United States

	Value (Cdn $)	Quantity (cubic meters)
1988	2,249,077,010	21,113,388
1989	2,223,401,760	20,550,325
1990	1,963,566,188	17,075,657
1991	1,935,382,343	16,805,277
1992	2,659,248,203	19,227,831
1993	3,883,071,469	20,588,106
1994	4,737,189,143	21,701,559
1995	4,160,691,701	21,867,228
1996	4,765,289,250	21,187,067
1997	5,076,848,465	20,522,303
1998	4,628,799,793	20,246,760
1999	5,250,432,263	20,031,801
2000	4,619,928,011	19,625,087
2001	4,786,346,852	21,444,420
2002	4,621,683,016	23,191,832
2003	3,672,858,089	23,989,883
2004	5,078,942,530	26,610,625
2005	4,805,107,483	28,660,182
2006	4,322,666,733	27,683,346
2007	3,376,875,570	22,981,112
2008	2,193,889,589	15,828,970
2009	1,542,556,548	11,861,087
2010	1,790,479,860	12,278,543
2011	1,598,253,101	11,192,506
2012	2,001,316,857	12,455,081
2013	2,557,693,498	13,603,532

Source: BC Stats, 2014a. From Statistics Canada, International Trade. Statistics custom extract, February 2014.

A second issue is the dramatic impact of the 2008 recession. A drop of nearly one-half of the volume and value of softwood lumber exports significantly affected BC's interior sawmills. In the town of Mackenzie, for example, all forest product facilities (three major sawmills, two pulp and paper mills, and a value-added mill) were shuttered for about one year. Some companies that had been operating in Mackenzie for many years, such as AbitibiBowater, went bankrupt. Prior to this, AbitibiBowater was the third largest pulp and paper company in North America, and the eighth largest in the world. The sawmill part of their operations in Mackenzie only reopened when a new firm (Conifex) took over under restructured labor and operating conditions. The pulp and paper mill component of their Mackenzie operations never reopened.

A third issue, and the reason the data were collected under the label of 'softwood' is that since 1980 there have been successive challenges by the US lumber industry claiming unfair trading, export, or business practices on the part of the Canadian industry. These challenges, and the seemingly endless rounds of appeals and negotiations, fall under the jurisdiction of the North American Free Trade Agreement (NAFTA) and its dispute resolution mechanisms.

Dependence upon the US market has been a key organizing feature of, and a key point of vulnerability for, BC's forest industry. As described by Hayter (2000 p. 219):

> BC's forest industries largely evolved within the implicit but powerful guidance of the principles of continentalism, which closely tied BC's fortunes to those of the US. In the early 1980s, these ties came under the unexpected threat (and reality) of protectionism.

Hayter (2000) then goes on to provide a detailed chronology of the various rounds of the softwood lumber trade dispute with the US. His research tracks a series of three disputes from 1981 through to 1996. In each of these cases, some form of countervail tariff is threatened by the US lumber lobby. Calls for a countervail tariff are generally made on the argument that Canadian producers may not be paying fair market value for the logs they harvest—and as such they are receiving an unfair trade subsidy. The financial return to the province for logs harvested from public lands is termed 'stumpage.' The calculation of stumpage has long been a complicated matter for governments and industries in Canada.

Further complicating each of these disputes is the number of groups and organizations involved. On the US side, there has been the US Coalition for Fair Canadian Lumber Imports and the Northwest Independent Forest Manufacturers. Organizations involved in various aspects of adjudicating these trade disputes have involved GATT (General Agreement on Trade and Tariffs), the International Trade Commission, the International Trade Administration, the Court of International Trade, the US Department of Commerce, the US Court of Appeal, the Canada–US Free Trade Agreement dispute resolution mechanism, and the World Trade Organization.

In each of these disputes, the Canadian industry and government has responded to the US claims. In the 1981 dispute, it invited an investigation of Canadian stumpage rates, and the result of that investigation was that the US Commerce Department rejected the call for a countervail tariff.

A new challenge in 1985 also claimed that stumpage rates provided an unfair subsidy to Canadian producers. In this case, the US Commerce Department accepted countervail tariff suggestions of up to 15 percent, to which Canada responded by self-imposing an export tax of 15 percent on softwood lumber.

The export tax remained in place until a new dispute was initiated in 1991. In this case, Canada terminated the 15 percent export tax and took the dispute to GATT. After many rounds of negotiations and challenges, a five-year Canada–US Softwood Lumber Agreement was put in place in 1996 that imposed quotas on Canadian exports beyond which tariffs would be automatically calculated. As one interviewee said: "The Softwood Lumber Agreement was like a suicide pill. When you start making money, you start paying higher tariffs on the wood to discourage the export" (Participant P3, 2013).

The outcomes of these three issues on the market orientations of BC's central interior forest industry since the 1980s have been fourfold. First, the industry has lost market share in the United States. This market share has been lost to US-based producers, but it has also been lost to new entrants from low-cost production regions taking advantage of increasingly liberalized global trading frameworks, decreasing relative transportation costs associated with containerized cargo, and the gap they saw in the US market as BC's producers adopted voluntary or imposed limits as part of the softwood lumber challenges.

Second, companies have adopted strategies that might allow them to 'leapfrog' the US border and continue to manage access into the US marketplace. This strategy is seen above for both West Fraser and Canfor, who since the early 2000s have bought into the southeast US sawmill industry. Canfor's acquisition of a number of sawmills under its Canfor Southern Pine division, for example, demonstrates how expansion and strategic partnerships in this region continues to be of corporate interest. In 2014 Canfor completed its purchase agreement with Scotch Gulf Lumber of Alabama to increase its marketable lumber capacity for the US (Canfor, 2013 p. 9). To further boost its US market capacity, in 2014, the company also announced that its Canfor Southern Pine operations would become "the exclusive sales and marketing agent for southern yellow pine products from the Southern Parallel Forest Products sawmill in Albertville, Alabama" (Canfor, 2014 p. 4). Canfor expects to market up to 125 million board feet annually from this arrangement.

Third, to compete with low-cost producers, BC's interior forest industry has aggressively adopted efficiency and cost-cutting measures to reduce the per-unit costs of their products. Such measures have included the substitution of capital and high technology equipment for labor, the closure of smaller and inefficient operations in favor of very large 'super mills,' and a short-lived focus on 'core business' activities. This last initiative involved the selling off of corporate assets in order to concentrate further on more high-efficiency dimension lumber production.

Fourth, in recognition of the significant loss of market share in the US, the industry has, in partnership with the provincial government, worked hard to open up access to new markets for dimension lumber products. The target markets have been the two most populous countries in the world—China and India. Recall from Table 3.7 that China was a small historical market for BC lumber, but that this market declined as the coastal industry shifted focus to the lucrative Japanese market and trade with Communist China declined during much of the Cold War era.

Table 3.10 shows the re-emergence of Asia in the last decade as a significant market for BC. As shown, total exports from BC have remained relatively stagnant from 2004 to 2013. Within this general trend, exports to the United States have dropped by nearly 25 percent. The continuing challenge for the US market to pull itself out of the 2008 recession highlights an ongoing market problem for BC's central interior forest industry. Also notable is that exports to Japan have remained relatively unchanged since 2004. The opportunity gap in export trade has been made up by focusing upon new opportunities in mainland China and India. While the Indian market remains small, it has grown by 250 percent since 2004. The significant change has been with exports to mainland China. In this case, there has been a nearly 450 percent increase over the past decade in total exports to mainland China.

Table 3.11 focuses only on wood products exports. Different from Table 3.10, is that total wood products exports have declined markedly since 2004. The impact of the 2008 global economic recession on the US housing market is shown dramatically by the significant dip in both total and wood products exports to the United States. This market simply has not recovered significantly to date. As with total exports, wood products exports to Japan have been affected by the 2008 recession, and have not recovered to their previous levels.

In terms of the new target markets, India has shown some initial growth and may be poised for significant potential future forest products growth. However, it is in mainland China that work to promote BC forest product exports has paid dividends. Growing from approximately Cdn$72 million worth of exports in 2004, wood products to mainland China in 2013 accounted for nearly Cdn$2 billion in value. In 2013, Canfor announced a strategic partnership arrangement with Chongqing Hongyun Trade Co. Ltd. to open a new store in the largest lumber-trading market in Chongqing City. The trading company will focus on

Table 3.10 British Columbia Exports to Selected Destinations (Cdn$'000,000)

	2004	2005	2006	2007	2008	2009	2010	2011	2012	2013
Mainland China	1,225	1,325	1,486	1,723	1,962	2,501	3,837	4,802	5,752	6,590
Japan	3,805	4,164	4,710	4,135	5,026	3,551	4,193	4,643	4,139	4,069
India	133	197	346	234	159	77	135	201	322	467
USA	20,137	22,101	20,517	19,077	17,582	12,920	13,252	14,005	14,031	15,750
Total International Exports										
	31,008	34,167	33,466	31,524	33,124	25,240	28,646	32,671	31,484	33,646

Source: BC Stats 2014b. Data contained in these tables are adapted from Statistics Canada, International Trade Statistics custom extract, February, 2014.

Table 3.11 British Columbia Wood Products Exports to Selected Destinations (Cdn$'000,000)

	2004	2005	2006	2007	2008	2009	2010	2011	2012	2013
Mainland China	72	78	88	134	206	362	798	1,403	1,358	1,837
Japan	1,693	1,368	1,347	1,037	982	753	892	935	946	1,165
India	1	1	1	1	1	1	3	11	9	11
USA	7,693	7,441	6,707	5,222	3,493	2,432	2,646	2,485	3,102	3,836
Total Wood Products Exports										
	10,062	9,485	8,776	7,164	5,408	4,127	5,106	5,706	6,175	7,749

Source: BC Stats 2014b. Data contained in these tables are adapted from Statistics Canada, International Trade Statistics custom extract, February, 2014.

dimension lumber for concrete forming and door frames (Canfor, 2013 p. 9). In addition, in 2014 Canfor announced a strategic partnership with Finnish based UPM Pulp. Under the agreement,

> UPM's Pulp sales network will represent and co-market Canfor Pulp products in Europe and China. In the initial phase, the cooperation agreement will consist of six grades of market pulp and approximately one million tonnes of pulp sales from eight mills on three continents.
>
> (Canfor, 2014 p. 4)

As Canfor's Peter Bentley (2012 p. 284) describes it, "China still has tremendous growth potential, and India offers significant new growth opportunities with the rapid expansion of its middle-class."

Discussion

This chapter has explored changes in BC's central interior forest industry using the lens of corporate restructuring in response to changes in the global economy. While some historical context is provided, our interest is especially with adjustments from the 1970s to present. The global economic recession of the early 1980s is considered a significant turning point in the organization and operation of the industry. The chapter focuses upon the corporate organization of industry ownership as well as changing markets for their wood products. The discussion covers four aspects of our chapter. The first is to provide a summary of significant trajectories in the industry. The second is to evaluate these trajectories against the impulses for change stemming from the global economy. The third is an evaluation of the processes of change and continuity within the industry, and their implications for its long-term vulnerability. Finally, we use evolutionary economic geography to explain both the processes of change and continuity.

There are a series of key trajectories that are identified in the BC central interior forest industry post-1980. On the corporate side, the key trajectory has seen the creation of increasingly large firms. These have been BC-based firms, and their growth has been an outcome of the withdrawal of many multinational corporations from BC's forest sector, and the amalgamation or acquisition of regional competitors. Such corporate concentration is not especially new, but the scope and scale is unprecedented with significant industry and forest land control now resting with a small number of firms.

A second key trajectory has been in production. Post-1980, increasing competition from low-cost producer regions has challenged market share and profitability. The industrial response has been an aggressive substitution of capital (especially computer-guided technology) for labor to decrease the per-unit costs of production. In general terms, while the scale of this change has been quantitatively different from earlier eras, the general processes of increasing efficiency via the adoption of the latest production technology is an old story in BC's central interior forest industry.

The implications of these first trajectories have been considerable. There are fewer workers within the industry, and this has hurt many small towns. Smaller and less efficient mills have been closed, and production has concentrated into a few super mills—again hurting the economies of many small towns. More generally, while companies "can shift their operations around the world relatively easily, towns—and the people who create lives and communities there—are not so mobile and closures can have traumatic impacts" (Halseth and Sullivan, 2002 p. 98). The strategy has been a success in terms of allowing the companies to remain competitive, viable, and a key contributor to the regional and provincial economies. That the industry has been cost competitive, especially in its key US market, has also initiated retaliatory trade complaints from various US lumber lobby organizations. A response by the emergent giants of BC's interior industry has been to purchase a number of sawmills in the southeast regions of the US.

A third trajectory involves the product range of the industry. By 1980, the four key product streams were already set: dimension lumber, pulp and paper, panel boards, and manufacturing residuals (chips for pulp, and sawdust and chips for panels and other manufactured boards). Post-1980, the industry is still reliant upon this limited product range. The application of computer-based manufacturing techniques has allowed for some degree of flexibility in matching product characteristics with consumer specifications. However, the only significant addition in recent years has been the transfer of some manufacturing residuals into energy production. In some cases, this has been partnership, or in joint venture, with pellet-producing firms to create a new export product. In other cases, it has involved the use of residuals as a biofuel within the manufacturing plants themselves to reduce energy consumption and net operating costs (and in some cases even generate electricity for retail sale). As noted above, there have been changes, but such changes have been within the industry's existing experience and product field.

A fourth key trajectory has been with respect to markets. The reliance upon the US market, especially the US housing market, remains, but there have been efforts to diversify into Asian markets, especially China. In this transition, the focus is upon dimension lumber exports. As noted, dimension lumber exports to

Asian countries have always played a role for BC's forest industry, but now the central interior firms are looking at the large market opportunities of China, and then India.

One of the threads running through the discussion of the change within BC's interior forest industry since the 1970s is that the more internal and external pressures seem to push for change, the more things seem to stay the same. There is more technology now, greater efficiency, but as one observer noted:

> I don't think there's a fundamental change in the products, really. More gets produced in the forest industry on the pulp and paper side, pulp and paper and newsprint, and... so the wood side tends to be lumber... but let's talk about the interior. The only slight variation from my perspective is in the approach in marketing. They still make dimension lumber, for the most part. And unfortunately, a really heavily reliance on the US; although, in recent years, that's changed a little bit, with more emphasis on China and other areas.
>
> (Participant P6, 2013)

In trying to situate these trajectories into a global-local nexus, it seems clear from the literature and corporate actions that increasing competition in the global economy has played a role in the imperative for firms to increase their scale as well as the efficiencies of their operations, in the absence of considerable investment in product diversification or value-added processing. Larger firms, more efficient production, and lower costs, together with a degree of product flexibility, have allowed BC's central interior firms to stay competitive. Specific competitive pressure in the US lumber market has also pushed the global diversification of markets for these producers. In this case, they are using liberalized trading agreements to their advantage and as a counter to how low-cost producers have used such to enter the continental North American market.

Local linkages for firms remain important as communities supply labor for production facilities. However, these local ties have become regional as industry continues to consolidate operations and the timber harvest areas that supply those operations. For local communities, there is less benefit as the workforces are reduced by efficiencies or closures.

The local and the global have come together in one corporate strategy—the purchase of sawmills in the southeast US. The global strategy is to overcome softwood lumber challenges by having production facilities within the US market. The local strategy is the same as above, securing a regional wood supply (fast-growing pine in this case) and homes for production workers.

The outcomes of the post-1980 changes are that today quantitative aspects of the industry have changed, but qualitatively much remains the same. The move into the US, and into new markets in China, has provided incremental resilience. However, longer-run threats remain and continue to create vulnerability. Included here are competition from low-cost producer regions and product substitution. The adjustments in the pulp sector to product substitution by emphasizing markets that require the long-fiber strength of our northern pulp speaks to an emerging opportunity in fiber and fiber residuals. In a geographic setting where we have relatively high costs in labor, taxation, and environmental protection, residuals are increasing in value. What are the biological, physical, and chemical attributes of our slow-growing northern trees that would create the future competitive advantage for the industry?

Staples theory and evolutionary economic geography assist in making sense of both the changes and the continuity described for BC's central interior forest industry since the 1970s. Staples theory describes a significant degree of lock-in or path-dependency within resource industries. Such lock-in or path-dependency is framed in terms of both products and markets (Innis, 1933, 1950; Barnes *et al.*, 2001). This is seen in the post-1980 development of the industry. Staples theory also describes a significant degree of dependence by producers on external market forces around demand and price (Marchak, 1989). Adjustment by the industry in both these areas has been the driver behind corporate concentration, production efficiency, market diversification, and even expansion into the US lumber producing sector. Staples theory also describes the process of truncated development, where limited up-stream processes or value-added production remains a hallmark of staples-producing regions. The emphasis, especially in the 1990s and 2000s, by firms refocusing on their core business in lumber, pulp/paper, and panel production fits expectations.

However, with respect to both lock-in and path-dependency, there have been shifts and adjustments. Evolutionary economic geography assists in understanding these (Boschma and Frenken, 2006; Martin, 2012). Writing from an evolutionary economic geography perspective, Edenhoffer and Hayter (2013b p. 140) describe that "how industrial evolution is shaped by place (and across space) is a central theme especially with regard to the changing competitiveness of industrial agglomerations or clusters over long periods of time."

While particular arrangements of social, economic, labor, investment, institutional, and infrastructure elements of established resource economies create relatively rigid techno-economic (and social-political) paradigms for different development eras, shocks in the market place can lead to adjustment (Hayter, 2008; Tonts *et al.*, 2012; Sheppard, 2013). The strategic decisions around the aforementioned corporate concentration, production efficiencies, market diversification, and US expansion are the manifest outcomes of adjustment to post-1980 shocks. That change is, therefore, bounded by a strong degree of continuity. As Halseth *et al.* (2014 p. 358) argue in another northern BC resource sector, "processes of change are both apparent but also highly circumscribed by path dependence."

References

Andersen, J. and Svensson, T. 2012. Struggles for recognition: A content analysis of messages posted on the Internet, *Journal of Multidisciplinary Healthcare* 5: 153–162.

Barnes, T. and Hayter, R. 1994. Economic restructuring, local development, and resource towns: Forest communities in coastal British Columbia, *Canadian Journal of Regional Science* XVII: 289–310.

Barnes, T. and Hayter, R. 1997. *Troubles in the rainforest: British Columbia's forest economy in transition.* Victoria, BC: Western Geographical Press.

Barnes, T., Hayter, R., and Hay, E. 2001. Stormy weather: Cyclones, Harold Innis, and Port Alberni, BC, *Environment and Planning A* 33(12): 2127–2147.

BC Ministry of Forests. 2014. *Water-borne exports of wood products 1913–1964.* Victoria, BC: BC Ministry of Forests. Available online at: www.for.gov.bc.ca/hfd/pubs/docs/mr/annual/MinForestsAnnualReportStatsOnHarvestAndManufacturing_v4.xls. Accessed February 29, 2016.

BC Stats. 2014a. *Exports of softwood lumber (440710) to the United States by province.* Victoria, BC: BC Stats. Available online at: www.bcstats.gov.bc.ca/StatisticsBySubject/ExportsImports/Data.aspx. Accessed March 4, 2014.

BC Stats. 2014b. *Annual data for BC exports with selected destination and commodity detail.* Victoria, BC: BC Stats. Available online at: www.bcstats.gov.bc.ca/StatisticsBySubject/ExportsImports/Data.aspx. Accessed March 4, 2014.

Bentley, P. 2012. *Canfor and the transformation of BC's forest industry: One family's journey.* Vancouver, BC: Douglas & McIntyre.

Bernsohn, K. 1981. *Cutting up the North: The history of the forest industry in the Northern Interior.* Vancouver, BC: Hancock House.

Boschma, R. and Frenken, K. 2006. Why is economic geography not an evolutionary science? Towards an evolutionary economic geography, *Journal of Economic Geography* 6(3): 273–302.

Bowles, P. 2013. 'Globalizing' northern British Columbia: What's in a word? *Globalizations* 10(2): 261–276.

Canfor. 2012a. *Annual report, 2012.* Vancouver, BC: Canadian Forest Product Ltd.

Canfor. 2012b. *Canfor: Our rich history.* Canfor. Available online at: www.canfor.com/our-company/our-rich-history#. Accessed March 4, 2014.

Canfor. 2013. *The Canfor connection,* Volume 10 (October). Vancouver, BC: Canadian Forest Product Ltd.

Canfor. 2014. *The Canfor connection,* Volume 11 (February). Vancouver, BC: Canadian Forest Product Ltd.

Drache, D. 1991. Harold Innis and Canadian capitalist development. In G. Laxer (ed.), *Perspectives on Canadian economic development: Class, staples, gender, and elites* (pp. 22–49). Don Mills, ON: Oxford University Press Canada.

Drushka, K. 1998. *Tie hackers to timber harvester: The history in British Columbia's Interior.* Madeira Park, BC: Harbour Publishing.

Edenhoffer, K. and Hayter, R. 2013a. Organizational restructuring in British Columbia's forest industries 1980–2010: The survival of a dinosaur, *Applied Geography* 45: 375–384.

Edenhoffer, K. and Hayter, R. 2013b. Restructuring on a vertiginous plateau: The evolutionary trajectories of British Columbia's forest industries 1980–2010, *Geoforum* 44: 139–151.

Farley, A. 1979. *Atlas of British Columbia: People, environment, and resource use.* Vancouver, BC: University of British Columbia Press.

Gunton, T. 2003. Natural resources and regional development: An assessment of dependency and comparative advantage paradigms, *Economic Geography* 79(1): 67–94.

Haley, B. 2011. From staples trap to carbon trap: Canada's peculiar form of carbon lock-in, *Studies in Political Economy* 88: 97–132.

Halseth, G. 1999. 'We came for the work': Situating employment migration in BC's small, resource-based communities, *Canadian Geographer* 43(4): 363–381.

Halseth, G. and Sullivan, L. 2002. *Building community in an instant town.* Prince George, BC: University of Northern British Columbia Press.

Halseth, G., Ryser, L., Markey, S., and Martin, A. 2014. Emergence, transition, and continuity: Resource commodity production pathways in northeastern British Columbia, Canada, *Journal of Rural Studies* 36: 350–361.

Halseth, G., Straussfogel, D., Parsons, S., and Wishart, A. 2004. Regional economic shifts in BC: Speculation from recent demographic evidence, *Canadian Journal of Regional Science* 27: 317–352.

Hayter, R. 1982. Truncation, the international firm, and regional policy, *Area 14*(14): 277–282.

Hayter, R. 1992. International trade relations and regional industrial adjustment: The implications of the 1982–86 Canadian–US softwood lumber dispute for British Columbia, *Environment and Planning A* 24: 153–170.

Hayter, R. 2000. *Flexible crossroads: The restructuring of British Columbia's forest economy.* Vancouver, BC: University of British Columbia Press.

Hayter, R. 2008. Environmental economic geography, *Geography Compass* 2(3): 831–850.

Hayter, R. and Barnes, T. 1997. Troubles in the rainforest: British Columbia's forest economy in transition. In T. Barnes and R. Hayter (eds.), *Troubles in the rainforest* (pp. 1–11). Victoria, BC: Western Geographical Press.

Hodgins, E., Wah, J., and Sauvé, S. 2006. *It's what's inside that counts: The story of West Fraser's first 50 years.* Vancouver, BC: West Fraser Timber Co. Ltd.

Hutton, T. 2002. *British Columbia at the crossroads.* Vancouver, BC: BC Progress Board.

Innis, H. 1933. *Problems of staple production in Canada.* Toronto, ON: Ryerson Press.

Innis, H. 1950. *Empire and communications.* Toronto, ON: University of Toronto Press.

Krippendorff, K. and Bock, M. (eds.). 2009. *The content analysis reader.* Thousand Oaks, CA: Sage Publications.

Mackenzie, S. and Norcliffe, G. 1997. Guest editors—restructuring in the Canadian newsprint industry, *The Canadian Geographer* 41: 2–6.

Marchak, P. 1983. *Green gold: The forest industry in British Columbia.* Vancouver, BC: University of British Columbia Press.

Marchak, P. 1989. History of a resource industry. In P. Roy (ed.), *A history of British Columbia: Selected readings* (pp. 109–128). Toronto, ON: Copp Clark Pitman.

Markey, S., Halseth, G., and Manson, D. 2012. *Investing in place: Economic renewal in Northern British Columbia.* Vancouver, BC: University of British Columbia Press.

Martin, R. 2012. Re(placing) path dependence: A response to the debate, *International Journal of Urban and Regional Research* 36(1): 179–192.

Mitchell, D. 1983. *WAC Bennett and the rise of British Columbia.* Vancouver, BC: Douglas & McIntyre.

Sheppard, E. 2013. Thinking through the Pilbara, *Australian Geographer* 44(3): 265–282.

Tonts, M., Plummer, P., and Lawrie, M. 2012. Socio-economic wellbeing in Australian mining towns: A comparative analysis, *Journal of Rural Studies* 28(3): 288–301.

Trade Union Research Bureau. 1974. *The Mackenzie story.* Vancouver, BC: Citizens Committee of Mackenzie.

Veemes, M. 1986. *Mackenzie BC turns twenty.* Prince George, BC: Spee-Dee Printers.

Walter, G. 1997. Staples, regional growth and community sustainability. In T. Barnes and R. Hayter (eds.), *Troubles in the rainforest* (pp. 287–303). Victoria, BC: Western Geographical Press.

West Fraser. 2014. Available on-line at: www.WestFraser.com. Accessed March 4, 2014.

Williston, E. and Keller, B. 1997. *Forests, power, and policy: The legacy of Ray Williston.* Prince George, BC: Caitlin Press.

4 Global-Local Links and Industrial Restructuring in a Resource Town in Finland

The Case of Lieksa

Markku Tykkyläinen, Eero Vatanen, Maija Halonen, and Juha Kotilainen

Introduction

Finland is a country whose national economy became essentially dependent on the extraction, processing, and export of local natural resources during the nineteenth and twentieth centuries. This dependence was a consequence of many conscious decisions. While minerals had some importance, it was mainly the forest sector, consisting of forestry and the forest industries, that were seen as a basis for the national economy before the information technology sector started to change the image of and ideas about the structure of the national economy. From the outset, the exploitation of resources was coupled with the evolving development of industrial technologies for their extraction and processing, leading to whole clusters created around the utilization of natural resources. Considering the importance of the forest cluster for the Finnish economy over the last century (Järvinen and Linnakangas, 2012), and especially the significance it had for exports and the income it brought, Finland can with reason be categorized as being part of the resource periphery that supplied the more central areas of Europe with wood and paper products.

In the chapters on Finland, we reflect on the position of rural areas in Finland as a resource periphery especially through a case study locality in the Finnish borderlands, where the rise and fall pulses of the resource sector can clearly be seen. The case study illustrates the transformation of the resource periphery from a North European perspective and highlights the structural transitions in industrial structures and relations in Finland. The case study town, Lieksa, is located in forested Fennoscandia, at the easternmost part of the European Union, about 500 kilometers northeast of Helsinki, the capital of Finland, and one and a quarter hours' drive from the regional center, Joensuu (Figure 4.1). The municipality covers 4,000 square kilometers of mostly forested areas. About 80 percent of its 12,000 inhabitants live in central core area (62°19′N, 30°01′E); the rest of the municipal area consists of small villages, forests managed for timber production, and wilderness. The sparsely populated hinterland is mainly covered by forests which are the resource on which the economy of the town was based for more than a century.

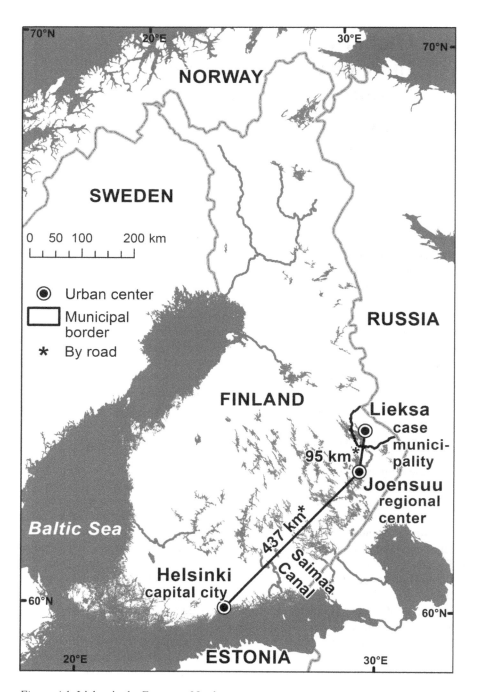

Figure 4.1 Lieksa in the European North.

The purpose of the chapters on the Finnish resource periphery is to show, by using the municipality of Lieksa as an example, how resource-based industries and their production cycles have impacted on the development of Finnish resource towns (see also Halonen *et al.*, 2015; Kotilainen *et al.*, 2015). As an example of the sparsely populated Nordic pattern of development (Gløersen *et al.*, 2005), the case study illustrates changes in industrial activities, employment, and population in the context of theory-building around cycles, resilience, and evolution.

From a Trade Place to a Mill Town

In the Middle Ages Lieksa was a fishing and trading place due to its location along a river (Mökkönen, 2003). The area was known as Pielisjärvi, from Lake Pielinen into which the Lieksa River flows. The river begins in the Republic of Karelia in Russia flowing from Lake Leksozero and Lake Tulos. The current land mass of Lieksa became part of Sweden in the Treaty of Stolbovo of 1617 when Sweden gained the province of Käkisalmi, southwest Karelia, and the province of Ingria. The area was gradually populated by slash-and-burn settlers, traders, and public servants. The town of Brahea was established on the estuary of the Lieksa River in 1653 to be a trading place for watershed lands and areas influenced by the White Sea (Mökkönen, 2003). The town was closed in 1681, as was possible during mercantilism, and the former town was incorporated into Pielisjärvi parish. Lieksa became more populated and started to industrialize in the late nineteenth century. The locality was a township from 1936 to 1972, and has been a town since 1973. The river's rapids and the board mills are located in the village of Pankakoski, which was incorporated into the town in 1973. The Pankakoski waterfall has been the main source of electricity for the area since 1912. An 11.8 m drop provided energy and made it possible to set up pulp production and sawmills.

The mill town developed step by step as described in Chapters 8 and 12. In 2016, the average population density of Lieksa was 3.5 inhabitants per square kilometer and with its large hinterland, Lieksa is considered a sparsely populated rural municipality. The main urban center of Lieksa fulfills all the criteria for a small town center in Finland; for preceding three years the average number of inhabitants was over 5,000, the urban population density over 400 inhabitants per square kilometer, the number of jobs more than 2,000 and their density high enough (Helminen *et al.*, 2014). The urban-rural fringe of this town is more densely populated than the remote hinterland, but the businesses are more rural-like than in the center with, for instance, active agricultural farms. Beyond the center and the commuter belt a very sparsely populated area begins and is mainly covered by forests—the resource on which the economy of this town was based for more than a century.

Resource Cycles, Industry Cycles, and Long Waves

We conceptualize local development processes as industry life-cycles (Peltoniemi, 2011; Potter and Watts, 2011; Edenhoffer and Hayter, 2013), which we associate with an evolutionary framework of development. In this context, techno-economic paradigms are seen to generate global-local conditions and modes of production for industry cycles (Perez, 2010). We include local, regional, and national responses and policy interventions in our analysis, and apply the concept of resilience to describe the turn of the local economy from one cycle to another (Simmie and Martin, 2010; Wilenius and Casti, 2015; see also Chapters 8 and 12 on the Finnish resource periphery in this book).

Since the 1930s, many scholars have developed the economic theory of 'long economic cycles' known also as long waves, supercycles, or Kondratieff waves. The best-known developer of the theory is Nikolai Kondratieff, whose observations of long cycles in the 1920s and 1930s gave the name to the theory (Daniels, 1984; Kondratieff, 1935; Perez, 2010). The impact of Schumpeter was to explain economic evolutions and these the long economic cycles by innovations (Schumpeter, 1939). This innovation-driven development was a central driver in society before the Industrial Age when agriculture was the source of livelihood. Its innovations released labor to other activities and made population growth possible (Smihula, 2009). Carlota Perez has extended the original thoughts of Kondratieff, which were rather technology oriented, to include more societal aspects by introducing the concept of a techno-economic paradigm to the theory (Freeman and Perez, 1988; Perez, 2010). In addition to suitable demand conditions, Perez concluded that the vehicle supporting decades-long growth cycles is the techno-economic paradigm, which consists of the best production practice of that time and an industry gradually emerging from practical industrial experience in applying a new, ascending technology. It represents the most effective and most profitable way of making use of the new innovative potential, including new infrastructures and public and private utilities. A new techno-economic paradigm reorganizes production together with the new technologies and generates a surge of development (Perez, 2010). Its influence extends from the expanding industries to societal values, norms, and structures, so that as its adoption advances, it becomes the shared common sense for decision-making in management, engineering, finance, trade, and consumption, and gradually also in the public sector. This new ascending production system and its capacity to increase efficiency shape institutional and social organizations, expectations, behaviors, and social networks.

Innovations and their industrial applications are seen more generally as a root cause of development providing a new set of associated generic technologies, infrastructures, and new organizational principles that can significantly increase the efficiency of industries and the economy. Progress takes place by both trial and error and learning, in interaction with many factors (Devezas and Corredine, 2001). In the explanation of global cycles, generic innovations and all-pervasive new technologies make it possible that new industries supersede the high employment effects of previously existing industries by introducing more efficient technologies leading to rationalization. This manifests itself as industry-specific crises of profitability and the resulting moves to substitute capital for labor. All industries from agriculture to high technology have experienced these rationalization phases. Because of economies of scale, production may concentrate geographically, which means that the number of production units declines, in turn leading to sporadic development as economic growth occurs only in some localities. This has been obvious in later cycles which have been less dependent of evenly distributed resources, such as land, wood, and water resources and waterways. Development is also temporally lagged and geographically selective as the geographical conditions for development are specific in each locality (Bond and Tykkyläinen, 1996; Tykkyläinen, 2015).

The capacity to transform other industries and activities stems from the influence of the associated new techno-economic paradigm. It is the most effective way of using new technologies within and beyond the new industries. While the new industries grow to become the engines of growth for a long period, the preexisting industries may face vast reorganization because of competition over resources, capital, and labor, and from shifts in demand. Combined with changes in demand, this transformation may powerfully change economic landscapes. If development takes place in the areas where production factors are underutilized or new resources emerge, the benefits may increase production, leading to better overall performance of the national economy.

High-volume production (Hudson, 1997), such as is found in forest industries, exploits low-cost inputs of natural resources, sources of energy, chemicals, and other high-volume intermediate products plus new infrastructure. Investments in infrastructure change the frontier and conditions of transportation—for products, people, energy, and information—by extending their reach, increasing their speed and reliability, and also reducing their cost. The construction of the dense network of forest roads is a good example. In terms of industrial structure, each new industry life-cycle includes a significant number of new intermediate products and new production technologies, consisting of a network of subcontractors and services. It can be conceptualized by the term 'forest cluster' (Hernesniemi *et al.*, 1996; Hyttinen *et al.*, 2002; Järvinen and Linnakangas, 2012). An industrial complex or cluster is an old concept used originally in depicting high-volume production systems (Isard and Vietorisz, 1955), but it was reinvented and modernized by Michael Porter (1990, 2000). A cluster is a networked group of interconnected companies, enterprises, and associated institutions in variable geographical scales in a particular field, linked by interindustry flows, reciprocal expertise, and untraded interdependencies. It benefits from interaction and scale economies from local to global. The geospatial scope of clusters ranges from a company town, a region, and a state to global networks of production. Many parts of these networks increasingly operate globally whereupon the local impacts from the high-end production activities of a long production chain may spring up from factories abroad.

Perez (2010) summarizes that a new industry life-cycle develops when it is possible to combine production factors in a profitable way so that the key input is cheap and getting cheaper, inexhaustible in the foreseeable future, all-pervasive in its applications in suitable locations, and capable of increasing the economic performance and decreasing the cost of industrial capital and labor. In what follows, we investigate how the ideas of Perez on the emergence of a new techno-economic paradigm can be interpreted in resource peripheries and their industry cycles in a mill town and its hinterland. However, as our main interest lies in the development and transformations caused by the forest sector, we first explore its evolution in Finland.

History and Transformation of the Forest Sector in Finland

The expansion of the forest sector (consisting of forestry and forest industries) in twentieth-century Finland was based on the position of the country in relation to the European and Russian markets; abundance of a raw material, timber, in the Finnish territory, that could be processed and the products exported to these markets (Kotilainen and Rytteri, 2011); as well as close connections between the industry, high-level political decision-making, and national financial mechanisms that helped fund investments and control the competitiveness of the industry (Ojala, 2008). The forest industries evolved in the Grand Duchy of Finland (that was a part of the Russian Empire until 1917) in the form of sawmills and paper production during the nineteenth century, but after the Russian revolution, independence of the Republic of Finland in 1917, and major shifts in European geopolitics in the aftermath of World War One, exports from Finland turned toward Western Europe, where demand was growing for roundwood, sawn timber, and paper products. Trade with Russia ceased almost completely in 1917 and the structure of exports changed from consumer goods to the products of the forest sector (Hjerppe, 1989). Western and Central Europe then became the most important market area for sawn timber, pulp, paper, and other forest-industry products, with Russian forests later serving for additional supply of timber to be utilized as raw material for paper production (Ojala, 2008).

At an increasing pace, the forest industries became a major vehicle for the development of the Finnish economy and society (Jensen-Eriksen, 2007). This goal was largely shared by industrialists and politicians, and the expansion of the forest industries became closely associated with rural development and industrialization policies. The progress of the forest industries required not only a steady supply of raw material, backed by the standardization and intensification of forest management methods on state and private lands (Virtanen, 2008; Kotilainen and Rytteri, 2011), it also necessitated the development of machinery for more efficient wood procurement and the production of advanced paper products (Sierilä, 2008). Together, the fields of forestry, paper production, and industrial engineering came to form a strong forest cluster that with its exports brought considerable revenues to the national economy. Forestry and the forest industries were substantial employers during the twentieth century, leading to adjustments in resource peripheries as a result of the significantly reduced workforce needs during the recent decades. We explore the employment effects of these transformations in more detail in the second chapter on the Finnish resource periphery (see Chapter 8).

National-scale government policies became a major tool for organizing the presence of the forest sector in the resource periphery. The emphasis of the Finnish industrial, development, and social policies was on mobilizing human resources to increase the exploitation of forests and cultivable land. These policies had the dual aim of connecting the rural areas to industrial production chains to increase the provision of raw materials, and industrializing the rural communities. As a part of these policies, timber resources in the more remote parts of the country were to be more intensively utilized to provide the growing industry with raw material (Kotilainen and Rytteri, 2011), but the aim was also to promote the development of remote rural areas, for which colonization by small landholders and natural resource-based industrialization was seen as suitable means. As a result, the twentieth century saw an increase in the number of forest-based production units flagshipped, by pulp mills in the eastern and northern parts of Finland, in effect pushing the spatial limits of the forest sector toward 'underutilized' timber and human resources (Figures 4.2 and 4.3).

From the perspective of national economic development in the last century, the resource and industrial policies seem to have been successful as forest industries increased wealth all over the country. The added value of the forest industries increased considerably for decades (Figure 4.4). The decrease in the very early 1990s reflects the severe economic recession that hit the national economy due to changes in geopolitics and demand in the export markets. In the pulp and paper industry, that recession turned soon to growth and high profits at the turn of the century (Official Statistics Finland, 2014). It is noteworthy that for many decades the value of paper production grew faster than the GDP (Figure 4.5). A notable exception is the last decade, which can be seen as a sign of structural problems in the industry. In the longer run, the industry cycle of the forest industries is maturing as other manufacturing industries and the service sectors have grown faster and thus the share of the forest industries within the GDP is also much lower now (*c.*2 percent) than it used to be in the high point in the 1950s (8.4 percent) (Figure 4.6). The national-scale economic indicators of course hide the much more diverse developments locally, something we explore in the following sections.

A crucial part of the story of the forest industries in Finland is the way the state took an active role in expanding and developing the industry for almost a century. As timber resources became better available by colonization and investments in rural infrastructure, new opportunities emerged, in turn, for developing the production chain further. From early on, the aim of the government was to create an economic niche for the production of Finnish producers and thereby secure the development of the young national economy.

One company of great importance especially for Lieksa was the originally Norwegian firm AB W. Gutzeit & Co that came under state ownership and was transformed into Enso-Gutzeit Oy AB (Figure 4.7). Over several decades during the twentieth century, Enso-Gutzeit Oy was in a decisive position in the development of the case study resource town, both through raw material procurement and establishment of industrial production plants. Later on, in the 1990s, it merged with the Swedish Stora AB to form Stora Enso Oyj. By 2000, Stora Enso had grown to become the world's second largest forest company after the North American International Paper, as measured in paper production capacity.

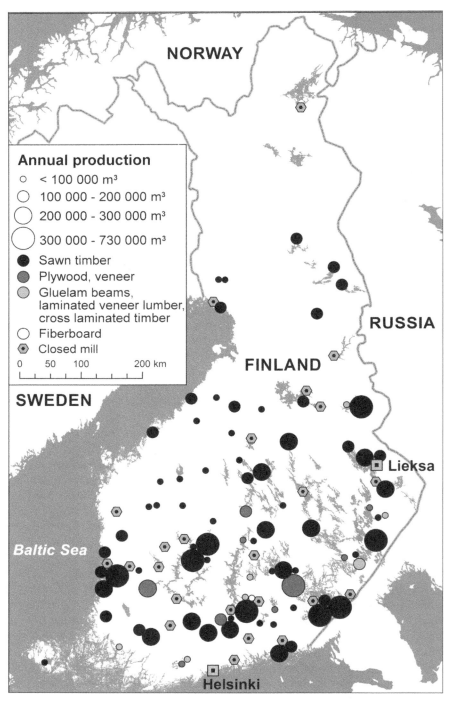

Figure 4.2 Annual Production in Mechanical Forest Industries by Production Unit in Finland in 2014.

Data sources: Finnish Forest Industries, 2015; Suomen Sahat, 2015.

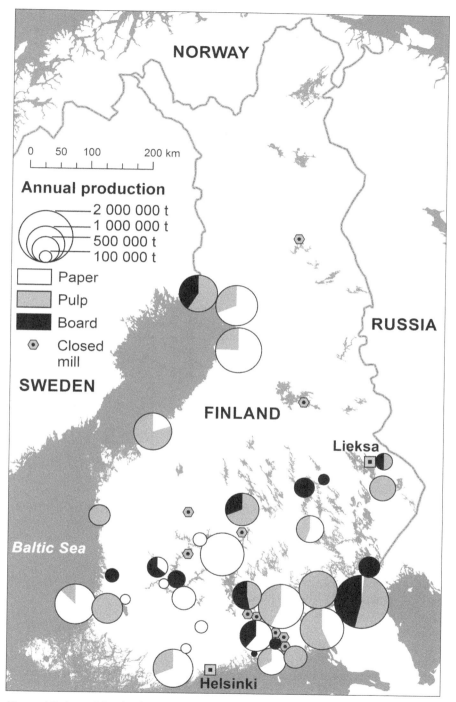

Figure 4.3 Annual Production in Pulp, Boards, and Paper Products by Production Unit in Finland in 2014.

Data source: Finnish Forest Industries, 2015.

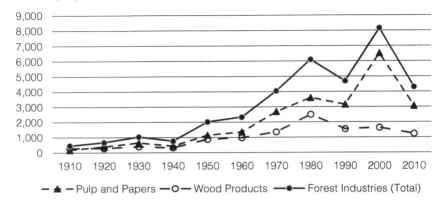

Figure 4.4 Value Added in the Forest Industries in Finland, 1910–2010 (million euros, 2010 value).
Data sources: Official Statistics Finland, 18 A, Industrial Statistics, various years; Official Statistics Finland, Finnish Statistical Yearbook of Forestry, various years.

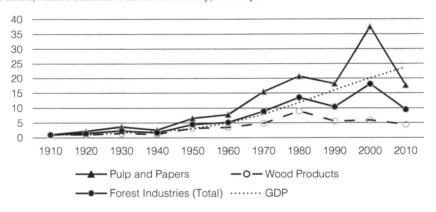

Figure 4.5 Forest Industries in Finland Compared to GDP in Real Prices (1910=1), 1910–2010.
Data sources: Official Statistics Finland, 18 A, Industrial Statistics, various years; Official Statistics Finland, Finnish Statistical Yearbook of Forestry, various years.

This is a considerable rise compared with Enso-Gutzeit's ranking as seventeenth in 1974 (Ojala, 2008). There was also a link to the Canadian forest industries with Enso-Gutzeit's Eurocan Pulp mill project in Kitimat, British Columbia, in 1965. This was an early, but unsuccessful, attempt at internationalization by the company, and that particular mill was later purchased by British Columbia-based West Fraser Timber. Much later, in the mid-1990s, several Finnish forest-industry companies introduced internationalization as an explicit growth strategy, which they enacted through supranational mergers (Enso-Gutzeit with Stora) and acquisitions in the United States, and by attempting to shift pulp production to

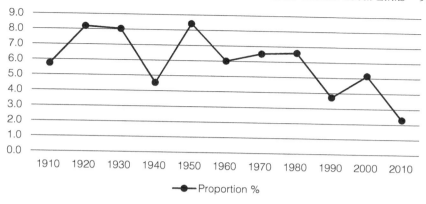

Figure 4.6 Share of the GDP of the Forest Industries in Finland, 1910–2010.
Data sources: Official Statistics Finland, 18 A, Industrial Statistics, various years; Official Statistics Finland, Finnish Statistical Yearbook of Forestry, various years.

Asia and South America to increase production capacity and reduce costs for raw materials and labor (Sajasalo, 2003; Ojala, 2008).

On the downside of this economic success, the environmental impacts of the forest industries were realized to be harmful to human health in the 1970s, with local air pollution from pulp mills and damage to water ecosystems from unpurified waste waters (Virtanen, 2008). The groundwood mill has always produced pulp mechanically in Lieksa and thus waste waters were not a problem at the scale of chemical pulp-making. The adaptation to new limitations took place mostly through new investments in production technology. The Finnish ministry of environment boosted this environmental transformation through regulations for cleaner environments, lower emissions, and closed processes. Supplying new production technology also became a competitive advantage for many machine works supplying machinery and automation processes to forest companies. Fuel-based greenhouse gas emissions decreased 39 percent from 1990 to 2012. Especially high was the decrease in sulfur emissions, at 91 percent (Official Statistics Finland, 2014). Biochemical oxygen demand (BOD7) decreased from 262,770 tonnes in 1980 to 88,851 tonnes in 1990 and to 9,066 tonnes in 2013—a decline of 97 percent within 33 years (Official Statistics Finland, 2014).

In the 1990s, forest biodiversity became an increasing concern due to the very intensive forest management methods. This concern was linked to the rise of sustainable development on the political agendas and sealed by the International Convention on Biological Diversity signed at the Rio Summit on Sustainable Development in 1992. The forest companies and forest owners were gradually obligated by both legislative changes and civil society pressure to integrate environmental and biodiversity policies into their forest management strategies (Kotilainen and Rytteri, 2011). The forest sector was pressured by civil society actors in the Central and Western European markets to make forestry less harmful for biodiversity. Forest certification was promoted as a means; however, in

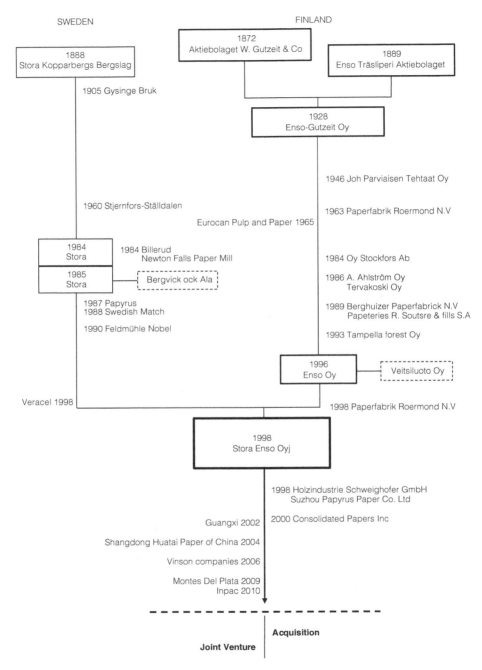

Figure 4.7 The Evolution of Forest Companies Leading to the Formation of the Finnish–
Swedish Stora Enso Oyj.

Source: Modified from Hoving (1961) and Stora Enso Oyj (2015).

Note: Joint ventures are shown on the left side on the vertical lines and acquisitions on the right.

Finland, voluntary third party certification schemes such as the FSC never found ground, and, instead, the process led to the adoption of the industry-led Programme for the Endorsement of Forest Certification (PEFC). Today, PEFC certificated forest cover about 90 percent of the forests outside the conservation areas in Finland (PEFC, 2015). As a reaction to this changing demand, legislation and forestry practices were also modified to support more sustainable forestry and to make the origin of the wood transparent to purchasers. The Finnish Forest Act (1996/2014) requires safeguarding the biodiversity of forests by protecting the characteristics of particular valuable habitats in forestry operations, leaving uncleared timber zones, and considering environmental protection objectives. According to Similä *et al.* (2014) there have been relatively few identified breaches regarding the habitat regulation aspects of the Forest Act. Uneven-aged forest management, in contrast to silviculture practices of nearly coeval cohort groups of trees, has been possible since the 2014 amendment in the forest legislation, which increases biodiversity and improves the use for forests for recreation.

With increasing internationalization of production and attempts at securing profits and competitiveness, the high revenues of the companies which provided wealth for the forest-dependent regions in Finland turned down in the early twenty-first century. By corollary, there were closures of many production lines and whole mills (Figures 4.2 and 4.3), resulting in massive layoffs accordingly. We next examine how our case study locality is linked to these national-scale developments in a global-local context.

Industry Life-Cycles and Long Waves in Lieksa

Competitiveness in mill towns and rural areas generally comprises assets such as abundant natural resources, access to non-urban resources, cheap land, place commitment, and natural amenities (Markey *et al.*, 2006). Physical properties of given areas, such as climate, soil, and accessibility impact economic performance and wealth (Sachs and Warner, 1997a, 1997b; Gallup *et al.*, 1999). In postindustrial economies, the legacy of resource dependence is a reason for a decline in jobs in hinterlands since the value added increasingly comes from high-order services (Gløersen *et al.*, 2005). The barriers to economic diversification include a stagnant economic base, a low level of education, an aging and declining population, and declining employment and thus many elements of competitiveness demanded by new, growing industries are poorly developed in rural settings (Mikkonen, 2002; Kitson *et al.*, 2004; Roto *et al.*, 2014). At a time when growth in jobs is concentrated in the largest cities, geographically marginal regions suffer the most in Europe as a result of their declining industries and more problematic locations (Espon Project 2.1.3, 2006). Economic wealth is geographically uneven as a result of stagnant or declining demand and poor competitiveness for economic diversification.

Growth in current global demand increasingly consists of technology-intensive manufactured consumer goods and services. In such economic circumstances, growth tends to constitute a series of cumulative, spatially centripetal processes generated by economies of scale and a relative decline in transportation costs.

Since production shifts relatively away from primary production and attached industries, place-bound initial advantages, such as hub location and knowledge (Krugman, 1991, 1993, 1998; Fujita and Krugman, 2004), are crucial for restructuring and growth. As we will show, growing demand for forest products, availability of energy, and the development of logistics were crucial factors in Lieksa. According to Krugman (1993), there is a strong accidental component in the upsurge of development. Increasingly some of the initial advantages, such as the concentration of human capital, emerge as a result of the policy measures of a constructed advantage (Cooke and Leydesdorff, 2006). Subsidies to investments and training, growth center policies, and the promoting of research and development related to particular industries can shape the economic landscape. As the focus was in new hi-tech industries which were not related to natural resources as a production factor and to the institutions and infrastructure associated with the resource sector, the impacts of growth focused on large, versatile urban agglomeration in main. That is to say, remote areas were uncompetitive for high-tech industries (Lehtonen, 2015). Gløersen *et al.* (2005) and Suorsa (2007) concluded that the measures of growth policies since the mid-1990s did not reach Finnish peripheral regions and even decreased their opportunities.

The two-century-long economic history of the municipality of Lieksa has rested on the utilization of ores, forests, and land for farming when its spatial dynamics have comprised phases of colonization boosted by the state and supralocal capital. The last half-century has been the era of population concentration and depopulation. Similarly with other resource-based areas, Lieksa has been strongly dependent on the global market. Mills have been part of global production chains and networks and, hence, a suitable location and the emergence of costs must be interpreted in relation to particular networks of their time (Garretsen and Martin, 2010; Kortelainen and Rannikko, 2015). Moreover, current growth, if any, in the boreal zone takes place outside the primary and traditional manufacturing sectors; an increasing part of value added is generated by the service sector and the production of new technologies and information in production systems. In many resource-based regions, the economy evolves in spatially uneven ways which indicates a changing demand and relative cost conditions globally in local industries impacting finally on factor compensations (wages, salaries, profits, and rents) and local living conditions (Lehtonen, 2015). The poor generation of jobs in forested areas in the current phase of industrial development in the boreal zone tends to be a result of industry life-cycles in their rationalization phases primarily reflecting the outcome of productivity growth.

Lieksa has faced five past industry life-cycles (Figure 4.8) from the early nineteenth century up until today (Halonen *et al.*, 2015). Now the town is in troubled times and puts much emphasis on new development directions, such as bioenergy (Huikuri and Okkonen, 2012) and tourism as the sixth wave shown in Figure 4.8. The past cycles reflect the rise and fall of the incumbent main industry as the source of wealth for the community and various policy-led development measures to improve the local industry and the provision of services in the town.

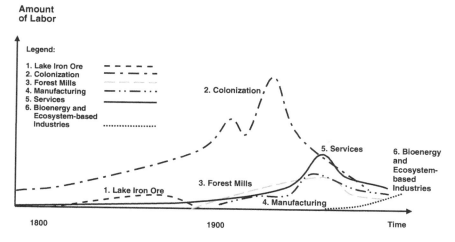

Figure 4.8 Industry Life-Cycles in Lieksa Since the Beginning of Industrialization.
Source: Modified from Halonen *et al.* 2015.

The town of Lieksa is located in a river estuary and close to the rapids of Pankakoski, and thus both the waterway and water power were the initial advantages to the setup of resource-based industrial activities. The waterway with canal locks all the way from the Baltic Sea to Lieksa was completed in 1879 and by 1910 Lieksa had been connected to Joensuu and other parts of the country by railroad. The long wave theory distinguishes similar infrastructural factors as the prerequisites for development (Freeman and Perez, 1988), but Lieksa lagged behind half of a century in development as the infrastructural preconditions of industrial evolution diffused step by step from core areas to the periphery.

The industrialization of Lieksa started from the production of pig iron from sedimentary deposits in the lakes leading to the first distinguishable industry life-cycle combining industrial capital and labor as an enterprise. The Lake Iron Ore resource cycle comprises the production of iron from limonite from the lakebed. This cycle lasted almost a century from the early nineteenth century as long as it was profitable.

Based on developing agricultural skills and market demand, the area of the present-day municipality of Lieksa was colonized as, first, agriculture and, later, forestry activities expanded. The rural population grew rapidly in the nineteenth century and various land reforms and colonization laws enacted in the first half of the twentieth century accelerated the growth of the population and enabled the utilization of forests for timber and pulp production. Primary production in small farms was labor intensive, which explains the strong impacts of the second industry cycle on employment. The double peak in the second cycle stems from major geopolitical incidences: first, the separation of the Finnish economy from the Russian economy and, second, World War Two leading to the need for food security, land reforms, and settlement of World War Two veterans and refugees from ceded territories. Hence, it is a specific episode which does not match the long wave theory but which had a significant impact on demography and infrastructure in remote areas in Finland.

The third cycle in Lieksa stems from the global demand for sawn timber and cardboard. It fits in the second and the third long waves of industrialization which utilized water power, electricity, machinery, and waterway and railway connections (Freeman and Perez, 1988). In Lieksa, the utilization of forest resources was the focus. Sawmills were established in the estuary and the cardboard factory was by the rapids, six kilometers east of the current town center. These industries reached a mature stage in the late 1960s, which meant rationalization and modernization of production, in turn leading to a loss of jobs in these production units since the early 1960s.

The upsurging manufacturing cycle in the 1970s was the Finnish government's response to declining employment in the primary production, abundant labor, and opening opportunities to supply consumer goods to growing foreign markets in Europe in the late 1960s and early 1970s. In the context of the fourth wave of long wave theory, it represents a mass-production stage based on relatively low-cost labor and consists of assembly-line production techniques (Freeman and Perez, 1988). In addition to domestic markets, the markets were in Europe and the Soviet Union. However, the expansion of this cycle was short-lived, as state regional policy support based on the infant industry argument waned and the heydays of low-cost mass production were over in Finland by the 1980s.

Rural decline, which plagued Finland in the late 1960s, was eased in the parallel development of the public service sector, the fifth wave which started in the 1970s and achieved its mature stage in the following decade. This wave of setting up public services is a unique Nordic sidetrack in industrial history. It was based on a political ideology of the welfare state and its ambition to provide equal opportunities for education, employment, and social security across the country. It was also based on the principles of equitable distribution of wealth and opportunities geographically. The central argument for the justification and wide political acceptance of this policy was that social equality reinforces and mobilizes human resources and leads to economic growth (Kettunen, 2001).

The school system was modernized and it was implemented by starting from the northern part of the country in 1972 and competed in the southern cities in 1977. The Primary Healthcare Act was passed in 1972 and reformed the entire healthcare system obliging each municipality alone or with neighboring municipalities to organize and co-finance doctors' practices, maternity clinics, dentistry, hospital wards, and school healthcare. Public healthcare centers were established and there were a considerable increase in public jobs in small towns and smaller centers where health services were underrepresented. Services were decentralized. As a result, the service sector expanded considerably outside the core areas, which is well illustrated by the case study municipality. There was also growth in private sector services including tourism, but most of the growth of the service sector is explained by the expansion of the public sector.

In the long wave theory, the age of information and telecommunications started in the early 1970s when microprocessors were developed and automatic data processing diffused to the economy and public use. Before the turn of the millennium, information and communication technology (ICT) industries became one of the leading industries in Finland alongside with the traditional metals and engineering industries, and forest industries (Rouvinen and Ylä-Anttila, 2003). The fifth global wave, however, passed by Lieksa although it brought about growth to many other rural localities due to smaller producers of parts and services in the ICT industrial network (Tykkyläinen, 2002).

Researches have widely concluded that five pervasive waves of industry cycles in industrializing economies with each representing the new modes of growth are to be identified since the Industrial Revolution in England (Freeman and Perez, 1988). The preconditions of each cycle were numerous innovations in production, power generation, and infrastructure which opened new windows of opportunity for profitable production. In Table 4.1, we match these cycles to the observed cycles in Lieksa and investigate how the global cycles diffused and fell on this locality to form different phases of industrial evolution in Lieksa.

Many scholars agree that we are in the dawn of the sixth long wave, but are rather reluctant to predict it because of the extreme sensitivity of socioeconomic systems to initial conditions and triggers in the learning processes and societal development (Devezas and Corredine, 2001; Wilenius and Casti, 2015). We probably live at the beginning of new global cycle which is emerging and financed by the kind of venture capital that demands high return on investment in the long run. The uncertainty stems from two facts. First, we are primarily unable to predict any future cycle as there is a significant random element, a random trigger, which picks a particular event out of the space of possibilities as being the one that becomes actually realized and enables the emergence of a new cycle (Wilenius and Casti, 2015). Uncertainty is more understandable if we look at what happens at the enterprise level, from the elements of which the cycle is made. This random outcome is comparable to the success of new companies in the leading edge of technology, the majority of which fail and only some survive and surge. Second, there are unknown processes which may lead to unexpected crises and outcomes. Many scholars failed to anticipate anything like the turmoil of the financial crises of 2008. For instance, many scholars imagined in the NATO Program for Security through Science a rather opposite development (Wilenius and Casti, 2015). Although the sixth cycle is still in its infancy, discussion is around nano- and biotechnologies, bioeconomy and biomaterials, robotization, and the need for the increase in technologies for better resource productivity (Wilenius and Casti, 2015).

In Finnish government policy, the bioeconomy and clean solutions are a focus for the coming years up to 2025 (Finland, 2015). One of the aims is that an increasing part of fossil fuel-based energy will be replaced by renewable domestic energy in the near future. Cleantech enterprises, the increase in the sustainable use of natural resources, rural enterprises, and an efficient circular economy are highlighted in government policy that seems to be less urban-centric than the former growth policies (Lehtonen, 2015). The policy promotes digitalization of services to improve productivity and industrial Internet applications are in focus. This vision is only a narrow slice of the entire spectrum of the industrial contents

Table 4.1 Long Waves and the Industry Life-Cycles of Lieksa

Long Waves of Advanced Economies	Industry Life-Cycles in Lieksa
Early mechanization lasted up to 1840s; it did not reach Lieksa, except iron production which commenced the early nineteenth century.	The lake iron ore cycle from the 1820s on developed as both domestic and global demand for iron ore grew, but there were no spin-offs as the locality was relatively poorly connected to global trade due to the undeveloped transport systems.
Steam power and railroads up to the 1890s; railroad connections to Lieksa were completed in 1911, a half-century later than the first railroad by the Finnish State Railways.	Colonization from the early twentieth century on, combined with the growth in rural population earlier, up to the mid-1960s was a specific industry cycle in Finland which did not exist in a large scale in Europe; the USA was an exception; it substantially improved the preconditions of the utilization of forests later.
Electrical and heavy engineering from the 1880s up to 1940s; this techno-economic paradigm was adopted with a short delay of two decades in Lieksa.	Forest mills were set up in the 1900s based on the development of electrical and heavy engineering, water power and waterway connections, the delayed railroad connections and the availability of wood and labor force both in mills and forestry.
Fordist mass production, from the 1930s up to the 1990s did not reach Lieksa before the 1970s.	The manufacturing cycle faced its strongest growth phase in the 1970s after which its employment effects waned; it was not able to significantly compensate job losses in the primary sector and in forest industries facing their mature stage.
The age of information and telecommunications, from the 1990s on, generated wealth for Finland but did not generate new industrial activities in Lieksa.	The surge of services started in the 1970s when several reforms in healthcare, social insurance, and education created a great number of jobs. The cycle started to wane due to the rationalization of the service sector and depopulation. The cycle based on the setup of the Nordic welfare state and was not linked to global long waves.
The proposed long wave of intelligent technologies, starting in the 2010s on, is ascending.	Bioenergy- and ecosystem-based industries have been propagated as the next new cycle in Lieksa, but so far with relatively poor results. Intelligent technologies will certainly be implemented but hardly produced.

Source: the global cycles are presented according to Freeman and Perez (1988), Wilenius and Casti (2015), and Wilenius (2015).

of the sixth wave (Smihula, 2009; Wilenius and Casti, 2015), but one must ask whether this vision is too narrow and risks the misallocation of resources although such an emphasis may fit well in the regions where forest resources play a central role. Relatively more significant than the selected industries are the aims of policy measures whose focus is in deregulation, structural reforms of a tax policy supporting work and employment, and employment-boosting reforms.

Intelligent technologies diffuse worldwide from innovative hubs and companies that change the patterns of human behavior and daily life. Thus, they seem to constitute a common denominator for a new cycle. People would be embraced by ubiquitous digital space where they operate globally, which creates opportunities for social and institutional innovations and new individual behaviors and identities. This emerging cycle caused by the long wave of intelligent technologies (Wilenius, 2015) summarizes the endeavors to improve productivity by applying intelligent technology widely in the economy and society, and it would lead to new industries developing and applying it in a new digitally structured global space. Thus, the name of the sixth wave would probably change in the course of time. However, its impacts on spatial structures and thus resource peripheries are very speculative.

Ownership Arrangements in Forest Industries in Lieksa

In order to understand transformations in the resource periphery in the boreal zone, our interest is primarily focused on the cycles caused by forestry and the forest industries as well as manufacturing. These were the cycles, after all, that have provided the primary incentive for industrial growth in Lieksa. The forest industries have exploited natural and labor resources, and they enabled an increase and fall in employment to be discussed in Chapter 8 in detail. The diverse forms of manufacturing were a consequence of past developments as they drew from the continuity of the labor force and industrial traditions in the town. Services— although under different circumstances they could have formed an independent line of development—have been mostly developing as a consequence of the existing population, government policy, and industries.

In Lieksa, the long industry life-cycle that started in 1903 is shown in the multiphase evolution of cardboard and plank production peaking from the 1960s to the 1980s. Figure 4.9 illustrates the internal transformation process of this cycle through the ownership changes of the major forest mills. They have faced several changes during their existence, and especially in the last 20 years. The first major turn took place in the early twentieth century, at the time when interest in paper and pulp production was raised and major forest companies, such as the Finnish Ahlström and the Norwegian-founded Gutzeit, were attracted by local mills located close to timber resources (Kuisma, 2006). Also, iron-ore producers began to invest in wood-processing industries. Such a development took place in Lieksa with investment by the local ironworks factory in groundwood pulp production. This led to the first demerger in the mills in Lieksa, as the sawmill producing planks in Kevätniemi diverged from the Pankakoski Groundwood Mill that produced groundwood pulp and cardboard. The decades-long era of state ownership began in 1909 with the state forest administration (*Metsähallitus*) beginning to operate the Kevätniemi sawmill with the purpose of producing construction material for railroads (Palokas, 2002).

Later on, the Norwegian shareholders of AB W. Gutzeit & Co were willing to sell their equity stake in a Finland that seemed politically unstable, under conditions of a civil war in 1918. As the state of Finland became the major shareholder in 1918, the Pankakoski Groundwood Mill became a part of the state-owned Enso-Gutzeit, at first as a separate unit and then as a merged unit of the parent company (Hoving, 1961; Näsi *et al.*, 2001). For the next six decades the ownership remained unchanged. In 1987, the factory producing packaging boxes was sold to Ahlström, while the rest of the production remained with Enso-Gutzeit. At the same time, new machinery for packaging was inaugurated and a production line was converted to produce plastic-based products (Luoma-aho and Strömberg, 2008; Kontiainen, 2010). The production process thereby shifted toward imported raw materials and more place-neutral manufacturing, and started diverging from the main operations of the board mill.

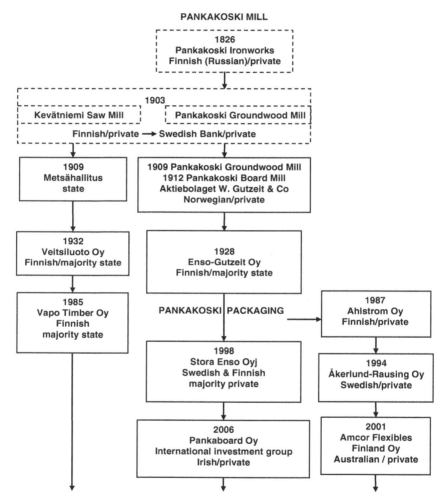

Figure 4.9 Changes in the Ownership of the Forest Industries (Earlier Iron Production) Mills in Lieksa.

Sources: Kontiainen, 2010; Luoma-aho and Strömberg, 2008; Oinonen-Edén, 1991; Palokas, 2002; Pankaboard, 2013; Pääkkönen, 2013; Stora Enso Oyj, 2015.

In the mid-1990s, Pankakoski Groundwood Mill faced major transformations in ownership. At first, there was the Nordic merger of Enso-Gutzeit Oyj with Stora AB. Soon the new company decided to sell the mill, and it was purchased by an Ireland-based investor in 2006. The several decades-long stable ownership situation was therefore changed into one with foreign investors taking an active role in the forest industries in Finland. This was new for the industry that had been built for decades on strong domestic networks connecting forest management, processing, machine-building, financing, and political support. Although it can be taken as a sign of globalization, the situation differed radically from the internationalization strategies of the major forest companies, as it was now an external investor penetrating the field of forestry products in Finland rather than a Finnish company aiming at global expansion.

Over the decades, industrial ownership changes in Lieksa have been frequent and they reflect the adaptations of the local economy to cope with crises and challenges from the market. The local producers have become tied to global production networks not only via exports, but increasingly as parts of global companies and investors. Without the ownership arrangements, many companies barely survived the changing conditions of competition. The timing of the arrangements reveals that they have been most frequent in the early phase of the cycle as well as in the phase when the production has reached its mature phase and faced pressures to restructure.

Conclusions

The case study of Lieksa unveiled five past industry life-cycles (Figure 4.8) from the early nineteenth century up until today. The first cycle emerged based on lake ore, the second on colonization waves generating small holdings and forestry, the third on the development and processing of the forest resources in mills, the fourth on light and assembly-type manufacturing by means of a strong nationwide regional policy, and the fifth on the services sector that expanded especially due to the implementation of the Nordic welfare-state model. Except for the growth of manufacturing and its decline and the heydays of the welfare and state service sector, the cycles have been long, varying from 50 to 80 years. The bell-shaped cycle of manufacturing is shorter and the service sector has been under restructuring. It remains to be seen what will happen to the industrial estate in the future—renewal and regrowth, stagnation or decline.

The long wave theory emphasizes the diffusion of all-pervasive technologies and institutions globally. Lieksa has been part of global pulses of trade and technology, but there have been various place-based and state-led factors which have impacted on local development. Thus, the industry life-cycles do not match long wave theory without place-specific and industry-specific interpretation. Industrial development has been the interplay between various factors in different geospatial scales and our research results indicate that there are limits to what could be done locally.

The local economy of the town of Lieksa, together with its rural hinterland, has been very dependent on exports during the cycles of its industrial evolution. The significance of local-global links has changed according to global demand, ownership changes in industries, and transformations of the national development policies. The national-scale governmental policies had a strong role earlier in the colonization of the wilderness areas and in resource-based industrialization, promoted as parts of larger scale nation- and region-building processes. However, the impact of the state on developing economic activities has diminished over time. The state has withdrawn from peripheries in the same way as in Canada (Markey *et al.*, 2008). Instead of a sign of development, currently the presence of the public sector in peripheries is largely due to the former growth in municipal services and a relatively large proportion of the population living on welfare.

In addition to the impacts of global demand, various policy measures have shaped economic landscapes in resource peripheries. In the Finnish economy, there were several crises and turning points that had local effects during the two centuries. Economic growth diffused to the peripheries in the late nineteenth century in part because of easy access to the Russian market, but this connection came to an end abruptly. The independence of the Republic of Finland from Russia in 1917 led to a closed border, an expansion of small-scale farming to marginal areas and the reorientation of exports of industrial products to the Western markets. The local economy was reoriented and renewed relatively successfully. The next major growth period took place after World War Two. Postwar colonization increased growth in the forestry sector as the state strived to mobilize the labor resources to work in the peripheries and intensified the use of forest resources in remote areas.

Overall, the driving forces since the mid-1960s for the increase in employment outside farming and forestry were a combination of global and local demand for consumer goods, the measures of national-scale policies and high supply of labor. Much of the manufacturing work was based on assembling work and, therefore, the shift to the global spatial division of labor along with trade liberalization had a significant restructuring impact on the local manufacturing sector. Much of its competiveness decreased in relative terms.

Several changes in the global economy have affected Lieksa in the last two decades. Because of changes since the early 1990s, such as the collapse of the economy of the Soviet Union, the opening up of China to the world economy and its low labor costs, and the advance of the Latin American forest sector, it has been hard to maintain production in this relatively remote part of Europe. During that time period Lieksa was too remote to benefit from the urban-centric growth policy and no footloose assembling company has located in Lieksa during the ICT boom as had occurred in many other small localities.

What could be the sixth industry life-cycle in Lieksa? The utilization of natural resources is stressed again in current development strategies of the town and the subregion, but with a new emphasis: forests as a resource for renewable energy, specialized agriculture as a resource for the food industry, and nature and wilderness as resources for tourism and other similar industries (PIKES, 2014).

Various bioenergy projects, such as a biorefinery and bioterminal, have been planned (Huikuri and Okkonen, 2012), the Koli national park is under constant development in order to fulfill the requirements for diversifying customers, and the food industry aims, for instance, to penetrate into the market of ready meals and specialized dairy products.

Many parallel economic processes exist in evolving localities. There have always been devolutionary processes in the existing local economies, meaning that some enterprises and industries vanish from a locality. Some organizations and occupations disappear, and development in that part of the economy is devolutionary pressurizing individuals and other actors to make choices of the ways to adapt (Tykkyläinen, 2015). During crisis periods enterprises face strong devolutionary processes which various adaptive processes such as cost savings attempt to relieve, but also evolutionary processes promoting and enhancing the emergence of new economic activities. The long-term results of such evolution are uncertain and unpredictable and vary by industry.

References

Bond, D. and Tykkyläinen, M. 1996. Northwestern Russia: A case study in pocket development, *European Business Review* 96(5): 54–60.

Cooke, P. and Leydesdorff, L. 2006. Regional development in the knowledge-based economy: The construction of advantage, *Journal of Technology* 31(1): 5–15.

Daniels, G. 1984. Translator's note. In N. Kondratieff, *The Long Wave Cycle* (pp. i–ii). New York: Richardson and Snyder.

Devezas, T.C. and Corredine, J.T. 2001. The biological determinants of long-wave behaviour in socioeconomic growth and development, *Technological Forecasting and Social Change* 68, 1–57.

Edenhoffer, K. and Hayter, R. 2013. Restructuring on a vertiginous plateau: The evolutionary trajectories of British Columbia's forest industries 1980–2010, *Geoforum* 44: 139–151.

Espon Project 2.1.3. 2006. *The territorial impact of CAP and rural development policy.* European Union, European Policy Development. Available online at: www.espon.eu/main/Menu_Projects/Menu_ESPON2006Projects/Menu_PolicyImpactProjects/capimpact.html. Accessed March 4, 2016.

Finland 2015. *Finland, a land of solutions: Strategic programme of Prime Minister Juha Sipilä's government.* Helsinki, Finland: Government Publications.

Finnish Forest Industries. 2015. Available online at: www.forestindustries.fi/statistics/. Accessed November 13, 2015.

Forest Act (1093/1996; amendments up to 567/2014). Available online at: https://www.finlex.fi/en/laki/kaannokset/1996/en19961093?search[type]=pika&search[pika]=forest%20act. Accessed November 13, 2015.

Freeman, C. and Perez, C. 1988. Structural crises of adjustment: Business cycles and investment behavior. In G. Dosi, C. Freeman, R. Nelson, G. Silverberg, and L. Soete (eds.), *Technical change and economic theory* (pp. 38–66). London/New York: Pinter Publishers.

Fujita, M. and Krugman, P. 2004. The new economic geography: Past, present and future, *Papers of Regional Science* 83(1): 139–164.

Gallup, J., Sachs, J., and Mellinger, A. 1999. Geography and economic development, *International Regional Science Review* 22(2): 179–232.

Garretsen, H. and Martin, R. 2010. Rethinking (new) economic geography models: Taking geography and history more seriously, *Spatial Economic Analysis* 5(2): 127–160.

Gløersen, E., Dubois, A., Copus, A., and Schürmann, C. 2005. *Nordregio Report 2005:4: Northern peripheral, sparsely populated regions in the European north.* Stockholm, Sweden: Sweden Ministry of Industry and the Finnish Ministry of Interior.

Halonen, M., Kotilainen, J., Tykkyläinen, M., and Vatanen, E. 2015. Industry life cycles of a resource town in Finland: The case of Lieksa, *European Countryside* 7(1): 16–41.

Helminen, V., Nurmio, K., Rehunen, A., Ristimäki, M., Oinonen, K., Tiitu, M., Kotavaara, O., Antikainen, H., and Rusanen, J. 2014. *Kaupunki-maaseutu- alueluokitus. Paikkatietoihin perustuvan alueluokituksen muodostamisperiaatteet.* Helsinki, Finland: Finland Environment Institute (SYKE) Suomen ympäristökeskuksen raportteja 25/2014.

Hernesniemi, H., Lammi, M., and Ylä-Anttila, P. 1996. *Advantage Finland: The future of Finnish industries.* Helsinki, Finland: Taloustieto, ETLA, Sarja A, 113.

Hjerppe, R. 1989. *The Finnish economy 1860–1985: Growth and structural change.* Helsinki, Finland: Bank of Finland, Government Printing Office.

Hoving, V. 1961. *Enso-Gutzeit Osakeyhtiö 1872–1958.* Vol. II. Helsinki: Frenckellin Kirjapaino Osakeyhtiö.

Hudson, R. 1997. Regional futures: Industrial restructuring, new high volume production concepts and spatial development strategies in the new Europe, *Regional Studies* 31(5): 467–478.

Huikuri, N. and Okkonen, L. 2012. *Bioenergiaa Pielisen Karjalaan.* Joensuu: Pohjois-Karjalan ammattikorkeakoulu. Available online at: www.pikes.fi/documents/812306/0/1_Bioenergiaa+Pielisen+Karjalaan+vuosiraportti+2012.pdf. Accessed November 13, 2015.

Hyttinen, P., Niskanen, A., Ottitsch, A., Tykkyläinen, M., and Väyrynen, J. 2002. *Forest Related Perspectives for Regional Development.* Leiden, Netherlands: Brill.

Isard, W. and Vietorisz, T. 1955. Industrial complex analysis and regional development, *Papers in Regional Science* 1(1): 227–247.

Järvinen, J. and Linnakangas, J. 2012. Firm capabilities in the Finnish forest cluster: Comparisons based on self-organizing map, *Silva Fennica* 46(1): 131–150.

Jensen-Eriksen, N. 2007. *Läpimurto. Metsäteollisuus kasvun, integraation ja kylmän sodan Euroopassa 1950–1973.* Jyväskylä, Finland: Suomalaisen Kirjallisuuden Seura.

Kettunen, P. 2001. The Nordic Welfare State in Finland, *Scandinavian Journal of History* 26(3): 225–247.

Kitson, M., Martin, R., and Tyler, P. 2004. Regional competitiveness: An elusive yet key concept? *Regional Studies* 38(9): 991–999.

Kondratieff, N. 1935. The long waves in economic life, *Review of Economic Statistics* 17(6): 105–115.

Kontiainen, H. 2010. Factory manager. Amcor Flexibles Lieksa. Interview August 17, 2010.

Kortelainen, J. and Rannikko, P. 2015. Positionality switch: Remapping resource communities in Russian borderlands, *Economic Geography* 91(1): 59–82.

Kotilainen, J. and Rytteri, T. 2011. Transformation of forest policy regimes in Finland since the 19th century, *Journal of Historical Geography* 37(4): 429–439.

Kotilainen, J., Eisto, I., and Vatanen, E. 2015. Uncovering mechanisms for resilience: Strategies to counter shrinkage in a peripheral city in Finland, *European Planning Studies* 23(1): 53–68.

Krugman, P. 1991. Increasing returns and economic geography, *Journal of Political Economy* 99(3): 483–499.

Krugman, P. 1993. First nature, second nature, and metropolitan location, *Journal of Regional Science* 33(2): 129–144.

Krugman, P. 1998. What's new about the new economic geography? *Oxford Review of Economic Policy* 14(2): 7–17.

Kuisma, M. 2006. *Metsäteollisuuden maa: Suomi, metsät ja kansainvälinen järjestelmä 1620–1920.* Helsinki, Finland: Suomalaisen Kirjallisuuden Seura.

Lehtonen, O. 2015. Space-time dependence in regional development: The geospatial approach to understanding the development processes in small-scale areas of Finland. Joensuu: dissertation in Social Sciences and Business Studies 105, University of Eastern Finland.

Luoma-aho, J. and Strömberg, H. 2008. Enso-Gutzeit oy, Pankakosken tehtaat. Available online at: http://elma.elka.fi/ArkHistory/E062.DOC. Accessed March 10, 2014.

Markey, S., Halseth, G., and Manson, D. 2006. The struggle to compete: From comparative to competitive advantage in northern British Columbia, *International Planning Studies* 11(1): 19–39.

Markey, S., Halseth, G., and Manson, D. 2008. Challenging the inevitability of rural decline: Advancing the policy of place in northern British Columbia, *Journal of Rural Studies* 24(4): 409–421.

Mikkonen, K. 2002. The competitive advantage of regions and small economic areas: The case of Finland. *Fennia-International Journal of Geography* 180(1/2): 191–198.

Mökkönen, T. 2003. *Brahea (1653–1681)—Nykyinen Lieksa.* Helsinki, Finland: National Board of Antiquities, Museoviraston rakennushistorian osaston arkisto (MV:RHOA).

Näsi, J., Lamberg, J-A., Ojala, P., and Sajasalo, P. 2001. *Metsäteollisuusyritysten strategiset kehityspolut: Kilpailu, keskittyminen ja kasvu pitkällä aikavälillä.* Helsinki, Finland: Metsäalan tutkimusohjelma Wood Wisdom.

Official Statistics Finland. *18 A: Industrial Statistics.* Years 1910 (Vol. 27), 1920 (Vol. 37), 1930 (Vol.47), 1940 (Vol. 56), 1950 (Vol. 66), 1960 (Vol. 76), 1970 (Vol. 86), 1980 (Vol. 96). Statistics Finland.

Official Statistics Finland. 2000. *Finnish statistical yearbook of forestry.* Available online at www.metla.fi/julkaisut/metsatilastollinenvsk/. Accessed August 31, 2015.

Official Statistics Finland. 2013. *Finnish statistical yearbook of forestry.* www.metla.fi/julkaisut/metsatilastollinenvsk/. Accessed August 31, 2015.

Official Statistics Finland. 2014. *Finnish statistical yearbook of forestry.* Available online at: www.metla.fi/julkaisut/metsatilastollinenvsk/. Accessed August 31, 2015.

Oinonen-Edén, E. 1991. *Pielisjärven ja Juuan historia 1811–1864. Pielisjärven historia III. Lieksan kaupunki, Juuan kunta: Pielisjärven ja Viekijärven seurakuntayhtymä.* Lieksa, Finland: Lieksan kaupunki, Juuan kunta: Pielisjärven ja Viekijärven seurakuntayhtymä.

Ojala, J. 2008. Pankkileireistä kansainvälisiin jättiyhtiöihin. In M. Kuisma (ed.), *Kriisi ja kumous. Metsäteollisuus ja maailmantalouden murros 1973–2008* (pp. 193–229). Keuruu, Finland: Suomalaisen Kirjallisuuden Seura.

Pääkkönen, E. 2013. *Ruukin aikaan: Pankakosken harkkohytin historia 1820–1911.* Tampere, Finland: Mediapinta.

Palokas, U. 2002. *Kevätniemen saha 100 vuotta: Kevätniemen saha 1902–2002*. Lieksa, Finland: Vapo Timber.

Pankaboard. 2013. History. Available online at www.pankaboard.com/about-us/history/. Accessed March 4, 2016.

PEFC Suomi. 2015. PEFC-sertifioitujen metsien määrä Suomessa kansainvälistä huippua. Available online at www.pefc.fi/media/Ajankohtaista/PEFC_Suomen_uutinen_04112015.pdf. Accessed November 13, 2015.

Peltoniemi, M. 2011. Reviewing industry life-cycle theory: Avenues for future research, *International Journal of Management Reviews* 13(4): 349–375.

Perez, C. 2010. Technological revolutions and techno-economic paradigms, *Cambridge Journal of Economics* 34: 185–202.

PIKES. 2014. *The economic development strategy of Pielinen Karelia 2014–2017*. Pielisen Karjalan Kehittämiskeskus Oy PIKES. Available online at: www.pikes.fi/documents/757708/1416317/Pielisen+Karjalan+Elinkeinostrategia+2014-2017_final.pdf/74ea804a-b6f6-47e6-8f03-d98fee4353c8. Accessed February 12, 2015.

Porter, M.E. 1990. *The competitive advantage of nations*. London: Macmillan.

Porter, M.E. 2000. Location, competition, and economic development: Local clusters in a global economy, *Economic Development Quarterly* 14(1): 15–20.

Potter, A. and Watts, H.D. 2011. Evolutionary agglomeration theory: Increasing returns, diminishing returns, and the industry life cycle, *Journal of Economic Geography* 11(3): 417–455.

Roto, J., Grunfelder, J., and Rispling, L. (eds.). 2014. *State of the Nordic Region 2013*. Stockholm, Sweden: Nordregio, Nordregio Report 2014:1.

Rouvinen, P. and Ylä-Anttila, P. 2003. Case study: Little Finland's transformation to a wireless giant. In S. Dutta, B. Lanvin, and F. Paua (eds.), *The global information technology report 2003–2004* (pp. 87–107). New York: Oxford University Press.

Sachs, J. and Warner, A. 1997a. Fundamental sources of long-run growth, *The American Economic Review* 87(2): 184–188.

Sachs, J. and Warner, A. 1997b. *Natural resource abundance and economic growth*. Cambridge, MA: Harvard University Center for International Development and Harvard Institute for International Development.

Sajasalo, P. 2003. *Strategies in transition: The internationalization of Finnish forest industry companies*. Jyväskylä Studies in Business and Economics 23. Jyväskylä, Finland: Jyväskylä University Printing House.

Schumpeter, J.A. 1939. *Business cycles: A theoretical, historical, and statistical analysis of the capitalist process*. New York/London: McGraw-Hill Book Company, Inc.

Sierilä, P. 2008. Metsäyritysten pysyvät ja muuttuvat strategiat. In M. Kuisma (ed.), *Kriisi ja kumous. Metsäteollisuus ja maailmantalouden murros 1973–2008* (pp. 230–260). Keuruu, Finland: Suomalaisen Kirjallisuuden Seura.

Similä, J., Pölönen, I., Fredrikson, J., Primmer, E., and Horne, P. 2014. Biodiversity protection in private forests: An analysis of compliance, *Journal of Environmental Law* 26: 83–103.

Simmie, J. and Martin, R. 2010. The economic resilience of regions: Towards an evolutionary approach, *Cambridge Journal of Regions, Economy and Society* 3(1): 27–43.

Smihula, D. 2009. The waves of the technological innovations, *Studia Politica Slovaca* 1/2009: 32–48.

Stora Enso Oyj. 2015. *Stora Enso history*. Available online at: www.storaenso.com/about/history. Accessed May 28, 2015.

Suomen Sahat. 2015. Available online at www.suomensahat.fi/. Accessed November 13, 2015.

Suorsa, K. 2007. Regionality, innovation policy and peripheral regions in Finland, Sweden and Norway, *Fennia-International Journal of Geography* 185(1): 15–29.

Tykkyläinen, M. 2002. Spatial turns of manufacturing since 1970, *Fennia-International Journal of Geography* 180(1/2): 213–226.

Tykkyläinen, M. 2015. Turmoil in rural communities as an extreme event exemplified by the cases of Hungary and the Russian North, *Geographische Zeitschrift* 103(1): 37–55.

Virtanen, S. 2008. Metsät ja ympäristö: pitkä linja. In M. Kuisma (ed.), *Kriisi ja kumous: Metsäteollisuus ja maailmantalouden murros 1973–2008* (pp. 304–343). Keuruu, Finland: Suomalaisen Kirjallisuuden Seura.

Wilenius, M. 2015. The next K-Wave and the challenge of global democracy, *Foresight* 17(1): 35–52.

Wilenius, M. and Casti, J. 2015. Seizing the X-events: The sixth K-wave and the shocks that may upend it, *Technological Forecasting and Social Change* 94: 335–349.

5 Restructuring of the New Zealand Economy

Global-Local Links and Evidence From the West Coast and Southland Regions

Sean Connelly and Etienne Nel

Introduction

The last three and a half decades (since the early 1980s) have witnessed fundamental changes in the New Zealand space economy directly associated with processes of globalization, national policy reform, and the shifting international market. These processes have catalyzed or exacerbated spatial unevenness with both regions and the localities within them benefiting or losing differentially in response to forces which are increasingly beyond local control. This exemplifies what Peck *et al.* (2009) refer to as the uneven development of neoliberalism. New Zealand's economy and society has transformed fundamentally from the 1970s when it had an overtly welfare state, enjoyed privileged access to the UK for its agricultural produce, and had high levels of state management and intervention which sought to reduce and compensate for regional disparities. By the early 1980s, this scenario had changed radically in the face of global economic crises, globalization forces, the entrenchment of neoliberalism, the loss of UK market access, sectoral shifts in the economy, and the New Zealand government's decision to rationalize the welfare state and embrace neoliberalism. The regional and local effects of these changes have been profound. The loss of state regional support and the closure of state primary industries had severe implications on local employment, particularly in more peripheral areas, while places more attuned to current market opportunities have reaped some rewards from these changes. In this context New Zealand has a distinctive political-economic history having swung from having had one of the most protected and controlled economies in the OECD and from being a champion of social democracy and the welfare state prior to the 1980s to one of the least interventionist countries in the world (Challies and Murray, 2008; Conradson and Pawson, 2009).

According to Peet (2012 p. 151) "New Zealand is a particularly interesting case because of its well-deserved reputation as a social democratic, welfare state that went neoliberal with a vengeance in the mid-1980s." It is important to note that state restructuring and the associated removal of trade barriers meant that from the mid-1980s the national economy and its regional sub-economies were severely influenced by both nationally driven economic policy changes and the parallel impact of globalization.

How localities have responded to these structural changes and the loss of state support makes New Zealand worthy of investigation for various reasons; these include the radical nature of the changes which took place, the country's deep-rooted embrace of neoliberalism, the vulnerability of its small economy to market forces and the reality that, compared with many other Western democracies, local government is almost wholly reliant on locally generated funds which reduces their capacity to respond to change. The preexisting regional development policy, particularly after World War Two, had attempted to influence the spatial location of economic activity. Though rather muted in focus and scale compared to interventions elsewhere, the rationalization of this policy from the 1970s left investment capital free to gravitate to and focus on the major centers of economic activity (Britton *et al.*, 1992). This chapter will first provide an overview of literature regarding current themes on economic restructuring and their impact on localities before moving on to outline the structural and policy changes which have taken place in the country since the 1970s. The chapter will then examine the national and subnational economic effects of these changes. Specific emphasis is placed on two regions, West Coast and Southland (see Figure 5.1).

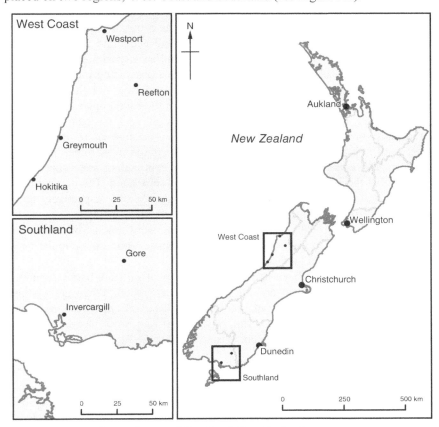

Figure 5.1 Map of West Coast and Southland, New Zealand.
Map credit: Chris Garden.

The West Coast is a sparsely populated region that stretches 600 km along the coast of the South Island of New Zealand, between the Southern Alps to the East and the Tasman Sea. It was first settled in the thirteenth century by Māori, who discovered pounamu (greenstone), which was then traded throughout the country. European settlers arrived en masse following the discovery of gold in the 1860s and the population rose from 500 to 28,700 between 1864 and 1867 (Simon, 2015). As gold production declined, the economy developed around coal mining, timber, and agriculture. The population peaked at 40,136 in 1936 and has fluctuated downward with the booms and busts of various resources ever since, with the 2013 population being 31,148, and with over half of the population located in the towns of Greymouth, Westport, and Hokitika. The decline of the forestry sector as a result of the ban on native-timber mining in the late 1990s and conversion of 84 percent of the land area into a conservation estate has been offset by the rapid growth in dairy production and tourism (Simon, 2015).

Southland is the southernmost region of New Zealand and accounts for 12.7 percent of the land area and 2 percent of the population of the country. Initial Māori settlements were located in coastal areas and the interior of the region was used for hunting and gathering in the summer months. European settlers followed the earlier sealing and whaling expeditions of the late 1700s, with the development of pastoral leases in the 1850s (Grant, 2015). The economic development of Southland was driven primarily by the agricultural sector, with sheep and beef farming on large estates and frozen-meat factories processing meat for export situated in Mataura and Bluff. As the number of farms and the volume of production increased in the early 1900s, so too did the rural population, and that of the smaller towns and the City of Invercargill. As agriculture became increasingly mechanized, Southland's population became more centered in Invercargill. Timber milling, coal mining, and fisheries were other important aspects of the economy in the 1900s. With the removal of state support for agriculture in the 1980s, the agricultural economy contracted. The population of the region and of Invercargill peaked at 108,000 and 53,000 respectively in the early 1980s before declining. Since 2000, the agricultural economy has rebounded on the strength of the dairy boom, with widespread conversion from sheep and beef farming to dairy (Grant, 2015). The 2013 census reports the population of Southland as 93,339 and Invercargill as 47,892.

Both of these regions have been highly dependent on state-based economic activity—primarily in the coal and forestry sectors and which, subsequently, have been exposed to the volatility of market forces which makes their resource-based economies vulnerable. This material provides a context to understand how localities have responded to these changes—which is the focus Chapter 13.

Uneven Landscapes of Neoliberalism

The themes of geographical unevenness and the differential impact of neoliberalism on local and regional spaces has become a key feature in recent academic discourse. Smith's (1986) exploration of the spatiality of the space economy and the emergence of uneven development in the face of capital expansion, was further developed in Chisholm's (1990) arguments about "regions in recession and resurgence," Harvey's (2006) recognition of geographically uneven development, and his argument that "capital moves its crisis tendencies around geographically as well as systematically" (Harvey, 2010 p. 12). These arguments help to clarify the reality and self-reinforcing nature of regional differences and the degree to which globalization does not create homogenization but rather in a situation in which regional and local economic advantages and disadvantages persist and can in turn be reinforced. The theme of geographical unevenness underlay the 2009 World Development Report (World Bank, 2009) and has been the focus of two recent special journal issues: *Tijdschrift voor Economische en Sociale Geografie* (TESG) (Büscher and Arsel, 2012) and *Urbani izziv* (Pallares-Barbera *et al.*, 2012). These authors draw attention to the extreme challenges faced by 'lagging regions' which occupy inferior positions in their national and now the increasingly global economy which they struggle to participate in and to benefit from. Themes of territorial competition, differential responses, broader aspatial processes of capital accumulation and expansion, and the uneven development of neoliberalism (Peck *et al.*, 2009) have profound effects on the ground and on local communities (Harvey, 2006; Büscher and Arsel, 2012).

Within this context the parallel forces of globalization and human agency are important, "the extremes of uneven social geographies in the context of an increasingly integrated world lurching from crisis to crisis juxtaposed with the implications of nature more and more transformed by human action" (Prudham and Heynen, 2011 p. 224). New rounds of capitalist investment and globalization build on each other leaving behind relic landscapes of economic activity impacted on by market loss in favor of more lucrative sites of accumulation and investment (Lawson, 2010). Profoundly this leads to a scenario in which "the restless remaking of space, or, more precisely, the spatial conditions of capitalist accumulation, challenges ideas that all people and places ultimately benefit from economic integration" (Lawson, 2010 p. 355).

The shift to an information economy from a resource-based one in Western countries perpetuates inequalities creating a "mosaic of economic marginalization contemporaneous with integration of rural areas into the new economy," in turn creating tensions between productivist and post-productivist spaces (Markey *et al.*, 2000 p. 428). The decline of rural economies dominated by a single industry or resource challenges the path-dependence of traditional resource-based economies. These export-oriented productivist landscapes that dominated historical development often conflict with attempts to diversify post-productivist rural economies based on tourism, knowledge, and information technology. In an era in which governments are less likely or less able to respond to challenges in terms of inequality, more localized, bottom-up responses are widely regarded as a way forward (Markey *et al.*, 2010). These bottom-up responses are highly dependent on the capacity and skills that exist in particular places, resulting in some communities being better able to access resources, draw on existing amenities and implement their own development initiatives. Others are less able to respond. This emergence of uneven development in New Zealand forms the focus of the rest of this chapter while locally driven responses, which tap into thinking on 'new regionalism,' will be further explored in subsequent chapters.

From the Keynesian to the Neoliberal State in New Zealand

Prior to the 1980s, Keynesian thinking dominated state economic policy in New Zealand. State control become a dominant feature of the economy after the Great Depression in the 1930s and was marked by high levels of state ownership of industry and resources, spatial interventions, and the regulation of individuals and firms (Roper, 2005). Trade and financial controls, centralized bargaining, state subsidies, control of strategic industries, and state welfare were hallmarks of the era. Under Keynesian thinking, "the principal objective of this mixed economy was to promote full employment by encouraging the domestic production of a wide range of goods, regardless of whether New Zealand had a comparative advantage in all cases" (Dalziel and Lattimore, 2004 p. 15). The economy relied on import substitution and the export of agricultural produce—largely to the then guaranteed UK market. Until the 1980s, New Zealand was regarded as "the triumph of social democracy" as it had had the fifth highest gross domestic product per capita (GDP pc) in the Organisation for Economic Co-operation and Development (OECD) in the 1960s and had been regarded as a world leader in social reform (Peet, 2012 p. 160). In terms of spatial policy, an extensive system of regional industrial development support, in parallel with that in other countries, known as the 'think big' program had been put in place after World War Two, anchored on concepts of building catalytic projects which could 'drive' regional growth be they infrastructural or industrial in focus (Abbott, 2007).

The period from 1945 to 1973 was regarded as the 'long boom' and the 'golden years,' marked by high levels of employment, guaranteed export markets, and a strong welfare state. However, by the 1970s structural crises were impacting New Zealand. Externally this included the loss of privileged access to the UK market when the latter entered the then European Economic Community (EEC), the oil price shocks, and a 30 percent fall in the terms of trade made change inevitable. Domestically, by the 1970s, stagnation, income decline, rising unemployment, and public debt had wrought their toll, laying a basis for subsequent restructuring (Peet, 2012). Other economic problems included: "overprotection of the economy, which led to a misallocation of resources away from internationally competitive export sectors" (Rudd and Roper, 1997 p. 8), a rigid labor market, excessive regulation of the financial market, a large and inefficient public sector, high tax rates, and excessive regulation of business. The growing domestic crisis promoted the government to announce in the late 1970s that it would need to cut its spending and devalue the dollar which would impact on living standards (Dalziel and Lattimore, 2004).

Dramatic change took place in 1985, when under the Labour government a neoliberal policy known locally as Rogernomics, named after the then Minister of Finance, was introduced. These changes, which were extended by the National (conservative) government after 1990, impacted on all aspects of the economy and its management. State-owned enterprises and control boards were replaced by policies of corporatization and then privatization, state services were trimmed in almost all sectors, and state expenditure was cut (Challies and Murray, 2008; Lewis, 2012). In parallel, industrial and agricultural subsidies and control boards were suspended, the currency was allowed to float, and more flexible labor market conditions, which did away with collective bargaining, were introduced (Lattimore and Eaqub, 2011). The efficiency and accountability of the civil service was enhanced through a performance-based system and the independence of the central bank was enshrined through a series of legislated Acts (Mascarenhas, 1993; Bale and Dale, 1998).

The effects of these changes were profound. State expenditure fell 25 percent, the New Zealand dollar was devalued 20 percent, manufacturing lost 30 percent of jobs, sheep production—the key export commodity—fell 30 percent, and unemployment rose from 2 percent to 11 percent by 1991 (Abbott, 2007; Challies and Murray, 2008; Lattimore and Eaqub, 2011). Thereafter, however, employment levels slowly rose and the country's non-tradeable sectors, which include construction, financial services, and retail, started to experience growth, and export diversification slowly came about with a movement into higher value industrial and agricultural products, primarily dairy (Abbot, 2007; Lattimore and Eaqub, 2011) (see Figures 5.2 and 5.3). While the economy did eventually recover, the 1980s was regarded as a traumatic period and many regions and small towns dependent on resource exploitation and, up until 2006, productivist farming, had not recovered (Abbott, 2007). For example, Figure 5.4 demonstrates the continued shift over the last decade in employment in primary production and manufacturing toward professional and service-related employment that is typically located in the larger urban centers. Despite the shift in jobs toward the service industry, the export economy is dominated by dairy produce that has grown significantly over the first decade of the twenty-first century, creating a contrast between the nature of the internal economic structure and the trading economy.

In terms of regional and local development, the move from a command and control economy to a market-based one was profound (Lattimore and Eaqub, 2011), with the "responsibility for regional futures often shifting from the level of central government to the level of the regions themselves" (Conradson and Pawson, 2009 p. 78). Regional policy was not totally abandoned but was rather significantly downscaled, in terms of focus and funding and by the 1990s had transformed from one driven by top-down intervention to one geared more toward support for local initiatives through the funding of a series of business development centers designed to support small businesses, with a focus on innovation and export potential. Parallel support was also provided through the Community Employment Development Unit to provide assistance for unemployed and disadvantaged groups (Scott and Pawson, 1999).

From the late 1990s the language of 'partnership' came to characterize regional thinking and emphasis was placed on multilevel collaborative arrangements between government, agencies, local institutions, and community and volunteer

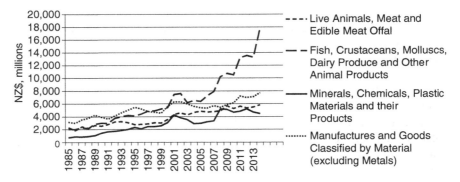

Figure 5.2 Export Value by Selected Sectors of the Economy.
Source: Statistics New Zealand (2014), EXP014AA.

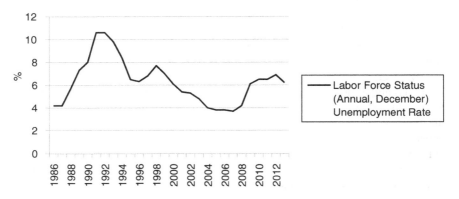

Figure 5.3 Annual Unemployment Rate.
Source: Statistics New Zealand (2014), HLF035AA.

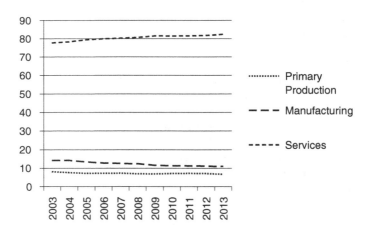

Figure 5.4 Employment by Sector Nationally as a Percentage of Total Jobs.
Source: Statistics New Zealand (2014), QEX016AA.

groups which entrenched neoliberal thinking at the local level (Larner and Butler, 2007). It was argued that neoliberalism was being used to achieve collaborative outcomes (Haggerty *et al.*, 2008). Moves to encourage regional partnerships, regional innovation through support for regional polytechnics, and local collaboration, however, tended to favor regions with the greatest capacity to mobilize partnership formation and project identification, with little progress being noted in the more marginal areas (Schöllman and Nischalke, 2005). By the earlier years of the present century these initiatives were scaled down.

Regional and Local Impacts of Change: Evidence From West Coast and Southland

With the introduction of austerity measures from the 1980s, at one level past regional development interventions were severely curtailed while at another the rationalization of state services, such as the railroads, the timber industry, and postal services took place. This in particular weakened the economic vitality of dozens of small towns (Wilson, 1995) and in some cases, whole regions, such as the West Coast of the South Island which had been heavily dependent on state-owned resource extraction activities (Britton *et al.*, 1992; Conradson and Pawson, 1997). The result of this policy shift, according to Pratt and Lowndes (2005 p. 139), was that "the market-focussed policies of government in the 1980s and 1990s meant New Zealand's provinces were largely left to shape their own economic destiny without central assistance or interference beyond the trickle-down effects of national policies." Since 2008, regional policy has been further downgraded, such that in 2013 the national budget for this policy was reduced from just under $4NZ million per annum to just $200,000NZ (NZ Treasury, 2013). All of this has led to a scenario in which state support for local level development has fallen. In this context, local governments often lack the resources or political will to engage in local level economic development, and civil society is obliged to play a greater role in terms of self-help (North, 2002).

Effects on the National Economy and the Regions

Attention now shifts to an examination of the effects of restructuring nationally and regionally. Key within the uneven geographies of change is the enhanced level of marginalization within which the more remote regions and small towns have found themselves. The combined effects of the embracing of neoliberalism, structural changes in the economy and its management, and parallel and associated processes of trade liberalization and globalization have impacted differentially on both people and places. At the national level, however, it is argued that "these structural changes occurred gradually but were accelerated by the reforms of the mid-1980s" (NZIER, 2009 p. ii). The initial impact was clearly dramatic. In 1985, the GDP growth rate was 1 percent per annum, by 1991 it had fallen to −1 percent; in the corresponding period unemployment rose from 4 percent to 16 percent and the consumer price index (CPI) rose above 16 percent after 1985 (Evans *et al.*, 1996).

The effects of market liberalization and reform on the primary sector were dramatic. Between 1973 and 2006, the primary sector's contribution to the GDP fell dramatically from 26 percent to 7 percent of the GDP, and non-food manufacturing fell from 19 percent to 11 percent as import tariffs were phased out, leading to the closure of 20 percent of manufacturing plants, including the once-important vehicle assembly industry in the 1990s. By contrast, in an era of deregulation, the service sector's contribution to the economy grew from 52 percent to 77 percent (Gibson and Harris, 1996; NZIER, 2009).

Employment was impacted by the changes, nationally and sectorally, with significant regional implications. Nationally total employment fell by approximately 4 percent between 1984 and 1999 (Fairweather, 1992). Though a relatively low fall, in certain sectors the loss was much more severe. Between 1987 and 1990, the state-owned coal corporation reduced its employment from 1,861 to 715 jobs; the state telecoms company cut its employment from 24,000 to 16,263, Electricorp (the state-owned electricity supply company) went from 5,999 to 3,690 employees, the railroads from 14,900 to 8,400, and NZ Post from 12,000 to 850 (Roper, 2005). As part of the switch in state economic policy the civil service was trimmed from 62,102 jobs to 34,505 between 1983 and 1994 (Rudd and Roper, 1997). Spatially in mining areas and those areas and towns once reliant on state employment, such as state forestry services and the railroads, the effect was particularly severe. In terms of postal services, 625 district post offices were closed, weakening rural service provision and employment (Wilson, 1995). Another outcome of these processes was the weakening of the power and size of trade unions. Union membership fell from 524,325 in 1991 to 385,538 in 2006 (Feinberg-Danieli and Lafferty, 2007).

On the positive side, despite the harsh impact of the restructuring in the 1980s and the easing of restrictions on trade, by the 1990s, at a national level the economy showed signs of recovery. By 1993 the economy growth rate had risen from −1 percent in 1991 to 6.4 percent in 1993 (Dalziel and Lattimore, 2004), the Consumer Price Index (CPI) fell to under 3 percent and unemployment fell from 10.5 percent to 6 percent (Evans *et al.*, 1996). Unemployment continued to fall to a low of 3.7 percent in 2007, before the 2008 recession resulted in an increase in unemployment (see Figures 5.5 and 5.6). Other positives included the significant improvement in the government fiscal balance from −6 percent in 1983 to +3 percent in 1995 (Evans *et al.*, 1996). While manufacturing jobs fell from 298,000 to 270,000 between 1977 and 1987, the service sector rose from 845,000 to 956,000 signifying a dramatic shift in the structure in the economy, which also saw a declining dependence on manual jobs (Economic Monitoring Group, 1989). The shift to higher levels of tertiary sector dependence benefited the larger urban centers but had little if any impact on more marginal areas.

Trade and Investment

The restructuring of the economy saw a fall in the level of import tariffs from 28 percent to 1981 to 6 percent in 1997, and by 1999 95 percent of imports were tariff

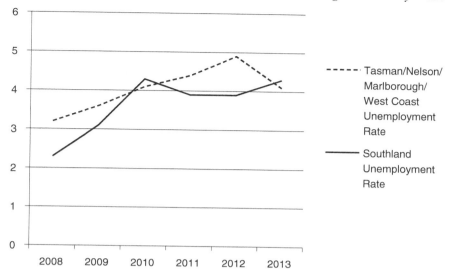

Figure 5.5 Unemployment Percentage for Southland and Tasman/Nelson/Marlborough/West Coast.
Source: Statistics New Zealand (2014), HLF191AA.

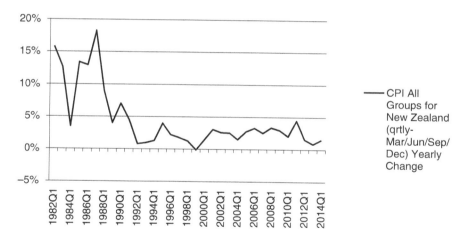

Figure 5.6 Consumer Price Index Annual Change.
Source: Statistics New Zealand (2014), CPI009AA.

free (Rudd and Roper, 1997). Foreign imports impacted negatively on local manufacturing, which was not well placed to compete internationally. The country has continued its significant dependence on the export of agricultural goods which accounted for 50 percent of exports by 1995 (Evans *et al.*, 1996). Key exports by value in 2007 were dairy products (23 percent), meat (13 percent), forestry (6 percent), oil (5 percent), and machinery and metal goods (8 percent) (Abbott,

2007). Despite government efforts to encourage export industries, dependence on a narrow band of primary sector exports, lack of broad level competitiveness in more advanced sectors, and the small size and isolation of the economy combined with the high exchange rate have meant that New Zealand is not in a strong position in terms of global trade (NZIER, 2009, 2012). The loss of the key UK market in the 1970s led to the encouragement of trade links with Australia and China in particular through the signing of free trade agreements (Abbot, 2007) (see Figure 5.7). For example, as of 2012, trade with China had grown by 160 percent since the signing of a free trade agreement in 2008 (Ministry of Business Innovation and Employment, 2012).

The key export success story in New Zealand is the country's only significant corporation, named Fonterra, which focuses on the export of dairy produce and which relies on the Asian market and international partnerships. This has encouraged the intensification of dairy production nationally (Gray and Le Heron, 2010). While the export of selected primary products has meant selective benefits accrue in the dairy-based rural economies of the Waikato and Southland in particular, limited value adding and the uncompetitive nature of many industrial subsectors has led to export dependence on a narrow range of products and the failure to create significant export-led employment in secondary industry (see Figure 5.2 above).

Recent government policy seeks to reinforce this trend, with government plans to double the value of primary sector exports by 2025 from $32NZ billion to $64NZ billion per year as part of the Government's Business Growth Agenda (Ministry of Business Innovation and Employment, 2013). As part of this ambitious target, the government has established the Primary Growth Partnership

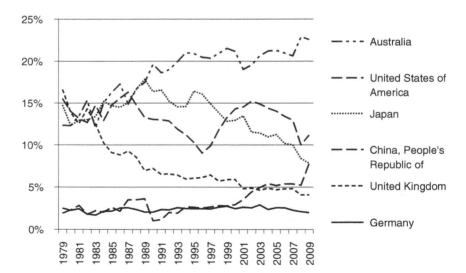

Figure 5.7 Overseas Exports as Percentage of Total Value.
Source: Statistics New Zealand (2014), LYM28207.

funding program that seeks to allocate $708NZ million for "business-led, market-driven-driven primary sector innovation" to increase both the volume and value of agricultural exports (MPI, 2014).

Foreign investment levels increased after government's privatization drive and through government encouragement. In 1978 foreign companies owned 35 percent of the country's productive assets, but by the mid-1990s this had risen to 51 percent of the top 40 companies (Rudd and Roper, 1997). Foreign investment as a percent of GDP rose from 7 percent in 1988 to 140 percent by 2003 which is regarded as very high by international standards (Dalziel and Lattimore, 2004). These processes have encouraged international financial flows and the takeover of key productive assets such as former state forests by foreign investors (Britton *et al.*, 1992). Foreign direct investment (FDI) in New Zealand was $92NZ billion in 2010 which is regarded as high by OECD standards while New Zealand investment overseas was only $21.4NZ billion (NZIER, 2011). Figure 5.8 demonstrates the gap between inward flows and outward flows of FDI as a percentage of GDP and the rapid rise in foreign investment in the post-1988 period. While this clearly reflects on a net flow of investment capital into the country, regional distribution was not a necessary outcome of this process.

Localized Effects of Restructuring and Job Loss

While the macroeconomic picture clearly improved in the 1990s following the painful transition of the 1980s, the same cannot be said about all local places and regions, with the effects of uneven regional development being an apparent outcome in the country (Smith and Montgomery, 2004). According to Dyer and Hurd (2011), the most negatively affected places were single-industry towns where either state disinvestment and/or the removal of trade tariffs led to the collapse or significant downscaling of the singe dominant industry often in the absence of significant alternatives. Examples include the mill town of Tokora,

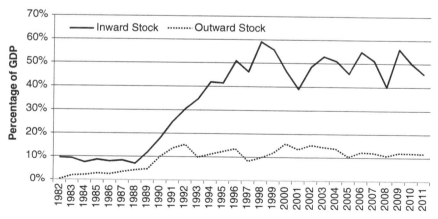

Figure 5.8 Changes to Foreign Direct Investment.
Source: based on Wilkinson (2013).

the forestry town of Kawerau, the coal mining town of Huntley, and the gold-mining town of Waihi. Regions with a particular resource-focused economy, such as the West Coast with its traditional reliance on mining and forestry (often state owned), witnessed significant job losses. In this region, for example, state mining jobs and state employment generally fell 60 percent between 1986 and 1991 (Pawson and Scott, 1992). In this area, towns such as Reefton experienced an 80 percent loss in the number of mining jobs, outmigration of young people, and increased reliance on the private sector (Conradson and Pawson, 1997, 2009). On the positive side, over time, there is evidence that some small towns which experienced the loss of former dominant industries have moved into postindustrial activities such as tourism (Conradson and Pawson, 2009).

Restructuring also had a severe impact on extensive parts of the agricultural economy with some areas losing up to 50 percent of their farming income. This, of course, had knock-on effects on local service centers, with towns such as Gore seeing the loss of agricultural processing jobs and farm services (Wilson, 1995; Johnsen, 1999). There is certainly evidence that rural economies have had to become more diversified and reliant on multiple job strategies to ensure that those who remain on the land can survive (Johnsen, 2003; Robertson et al., 2008). The amount of land cultivated has fallen as have sheep numbers, while in selected areas beef and dairy have increased in scale. Overall farm sizes have grown, labor numbers have fallen, but productivity levels have risen and corporatization is a growing reality anchored on niche market production and frequent links with the Fonterra operation (MacLeod and Moller, 2006; Conradson and Pawson, 2009).

Focus on West Coast and Southland Regions

The regions of West Coast and Southland are of particular interest in this analysis, given their historic, high levels of dependence on state support, their persistence reliance on resource production and export, and the associated increasing vulnerability to market shifts following the ending of state production, subsidies, and protective tariffs after the 1970s. As a result, more than other regions which could often shift into service sector operations and higher valued-added activity, these two regions have been particularly vulnerable to globalization pressures.

While the value of manufacturing and construction has increased in both the West Coast and Southland in real terms, they have declined as a percentage of total regional GDP, from 18 percent and 25 percent in 2007 for the West Coast and Southland respectively, to 16 percent and 20 percent by 2011 (the last year for which there is available regional data) (Statistics New Zealand, 2014). However, the regional economies of the West Coast and Southland are still far more dependent on primary production and manufacturing than the national economy as a whole. Figures 5.9 through 5.11 demonstrate the differences in regional economies relative to the national economies and clearly illustrate the dual nature of economic development involving a rural economy still heavily tied to the resource base and an urban/national economy dominated by the service sector. The relative growth of the primary sector in both the West Coast and in Southland are both driven by the relative weight the of primary production and manufacturing in these regions which stand apart from the national trends away from primary production and manufacturing.

The West Coast and Southland are heavily reliant on primary production, with the primary focus still being on mining, albeit it private and not state-run, in the West Coast and agricultural production in Southland. However, both of these sectors are highly dependent on global prices and the changes in GDP in these

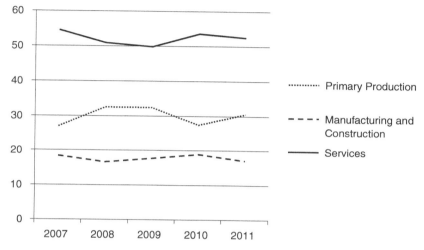

Figure 5.9   West Coast GDP by Sector as Percentage.
Source: Statistics New Zealand (2014), RNA001AA.

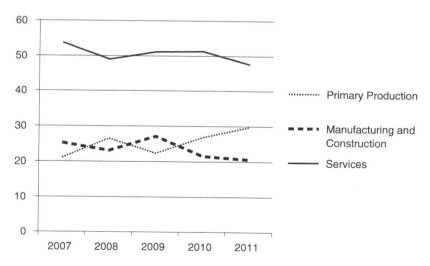

Figure 5.10 Southland GDP by Sector as Percentage.
Source: Statistics New Zealand (2014), RNA001AA.

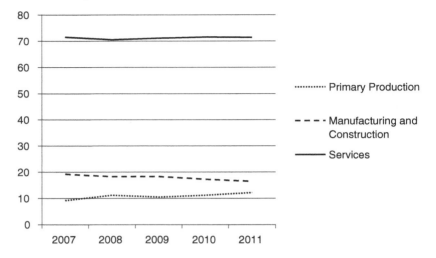

Figure 5.11 New Zealand GDP by Sector as Percentage.
Source: Statistics New Zealand (2014), RNA001AA.

regions can be linked to fluctuations in global commodity prices. For example, Tables 5.1 and 5.2 demonstrate the fluctuations in regional GDP for agriculture and forestry, fishing, and mining sectors for both the West Coast and Southland. In both regions, agriculture has become dominated by the dairy industry, while coal mining dominates the GDP figures in the West Coast, and Southland still has some forestry operations and coal mining (for both regions, commercial fishing is not a major economic activity). The volatility in mining on the West Coast is reflective of a rising global price for coal, which reached a high of $330NZ per tonne in 2011, leading to significant investment and reinvestment in coal mines, including the opening of the Pike River mine in 2009. The subsequent mining disaster at Pike River in 2010, which claimed the lives of 29 miners, resulted in the closure of the mine (and the loss of 150 jobs). Since that time, the price of coal has dropped dramatically, to a low of $120NZ per tonne in 2014 and has resulted in further mine closures, most prominently the 300 jobs lost at Solid Energy's Spring Creek mine in 2012 (Baxter *et al.*, 2014; IEA, 2014).

Table 5.1 West Coast GDP in $NZ millions

	Agriculture	*Forestry, Fishing, Mining*
2007	128	183
2008	220	218
2009	139	343
2010	185	209
2011	222	257

Source: Statistics New Zealand (2014), RNA001AA.

Table 5.2 Southland GDP in $NZ millions

	Agriculture	Forestry, Fishing, Mining
2007	510	238
2008	807	280
2009	669	283
2010	894	287
2011	1,086	323

Source Statistics New Zealand (2014), RNA001AA.

The boom–bust cycle of resource industries is something that is expected in the region and residents have adapted coping strategies, as one resident commented:

> after Solid Energy pulled out of Spring Creek here, after the Pike tragedy which has had its impact, you'd be surprised how many little mines are opened up ... the guys that are down the mine tend to be men that own diggers, they like diggers and they like doing other stuff, hell of a lot of them just, got their digger started up, and got the gold screen up, found a paddock up the back, and they're gone, they're gold mining again ... and so they employ two or three of their mates who also used to be down the mine ... so there's quite a lot of small mining going on.
>
> (Key Informant 1, personal communication, 2013)

> 'cause it is quite interesting, how many small, how many guys are going back round, into smaller mines, and are opening up or working on opening up some of it, that coal mining isn't as dead as we think, here. There's still a market for it, there's still a market for that coal, and the coal still in the ground. That's what they know.
>
> Key Informant 2, personal communication, 2013)

As two representatives from a community development organization explained, the job losses in the mining industry had an immediate impact in terms of employment, but there is faith in the community that the jobs will return once the price of coal rebounds:

> and they'll just be waiting for the next opportunity to go down the mine, because that's what they do, you know teaching at the school here, I remember 14, 15 year olds saying to me, I remember one in particular who I, I tried to teach fractions to, and he said "how much do you earn [teacher's name]," I said "why," he said "because I'm going down the mine next week, I'm gonna earn more than you next week, why do I need to learn fractions." And he's right, and he drives a BMW.
>
> (Key Informant 1, personal communication, 2013)

But, yeah, Greymouth [the town] is still sitting on the edge of its chair waiting for the larger mines to open up. This town certainly is feeling the impact now, you know a lot of the miners got paid out last Christmas [2012], have spent that money now and now they've really gotta make hard decisions, I think this Christmas is going to be rough.

(Key Informant 31, personal communication, 2013)

When asked about how these kinds of activities compare to the jobs, wages, and economic impact that the larger-scale mining contributes to the community, through the mining service industry, community development officers acknowledged the obvious difference in scale, but also commented on the greater percentage of spending that remains localized:

It doesn't compare to Pike River ... but it probably means that most of the profits if there are any, are getting reinvested here, it's all local ... and they might, they may not employ engineers themselves, but they might engage an engineer who is working for a bunch of different ones, doing other services around it and stuff like that, but yeah you'd never get, you'd have to have a hell of a lot of them to employ the 200 that Pike was employing or something and the, god knows how many hundred Solid Energy were employing.

(Key Informant 2, personal communication, 2013)

In Southland, the overall expansion of the dairy industry also reflects the global prices for milk products. Global dairy prices peaked in late 2007 at $1,691NZ per tonne based on the Global Dairy Trade index (which aggregates a range of milk product prices) and dropped to $573NZ per tonne in July 2009, before rising again to $1,419NZ in March 2011. The rapid expansion of dairying in the South Island (13 percent growth in cattle numbers in 2008/2009 alone) has resulted in large herd sizes (average of 564), and higher productivity per cow and per hectare (Tipples *et al.*, 2010). As a community development officer in Southland stated:

Dairy boom has injected a lot of wealth into local economies. But it is uneven and it creates resentment in some communities. The $2 billion payout to Fonterra member farmers [in 2013, based on a record farmgate price of $7.00/ kg of milksolids] is huge. We hope that a significant amount of that will trickle down to communities. But there are issues; a lot of the labour for dairy is migrant and transient labour. How do we create conditions that they might stay in the community?

(Key Informant 4, personal communication, 2014)

As a result of the expansion and labor requirements, dairy farms have become less reliant on family labor and more reliant on seasonal migrant workers, largely from the Philippines (Tipples *et al.*, 2010). While the dairy boom has injected significant amounts of money into communities across the country, this has been uneven. Similar to other resource-dependent communities, the local economies are heavily dependent on global commodity prices that are well beyond the control of local communities. In 2014, Fonterra, the farmer-owned cooperative cut its farmgate price to $6.00NZ/kg of milksolids, based on the rapid collapse of global dairy prices between June 2014 and August 2014 of 16 percent. In a news release to announce the cuts, the Fonterra chairman stated: "This drop in the forecast Farmgate Milk Price will have an impact on our farmers' cash flows. We continue to urge caution with on-farm budgets in light of the continuing volatility in international dairy markets" (Fonterra, 2014).

As a result of restructuring, the boom and bust cycles of resource based economies are magnified by the absence of regional development strategies and government support. As a result of the relative dominance of the primary sector of the economy, rural and regional economies are increasingly at the mercy of global commodity prices, and hence have little control over their future prosperity.

Tables 5.1 and 5.2 show the GDP (in $NZ) for agriculture and for forestry, fishing, and mining, for the years 2007 to 2011 inclusive for the West Coast and Southland regions. Figures 5.9 through 5.11 demonstrate the GDP growth rates annually for the period 2007–2011 for the West Coast, Southland, and New Zealand by sector of the economy. They clearly highlight the dependence of the regional economies of Southland and the West Coast on primary production and their exposure to global commodity prices. The bulk of the growth in this sector has been a result of the rapid expansion of dairy farming, as farms and pastures are converted from less-profitable sheep and beef operations into the more lucrative dairying.

Trade and investment has shifted dramatically in recent decades in the country. These moves have privileged certain sectors and their host areas such as the dairy, selected manufacturing activities only, and elements of the service sector, while other sectors and their host areas such as mining, other manufacturing and the non-dairy/meat areas and smaller towns have struggled to compete in this new environment.

The divergent economic prospects of the sheep and beef sector and the dairy industry provide a good example of restructuring and consolidation in an industrial sector. Beginning with the loss of privileged access to the UK market after 1973, the New Zealand economy has been obliged to become increasingly global in outlook (Le Heron and Pawson, 1996). As a low-cost producer for agricultural products and with a small internal market, New Zealand agricultural producers have relied on increased access to foreign markets through freer trade on the one hand and consolidation within agricultural sectors in search of economies of scale on the other (Tamasy *et al.*, 2008).

Previously, in the sheep and beef sector, government support for farmers and preferred access to the UK market had resulted in rapid livestock growth in the 1960s and 1970s (e.g. rising from 33 million sheep in 1950 to 68 million in 1980 (Statistics New Zealand, 2014). This growth in numbers prompted significant reinvestment in the meat-processing industry, with the establishment of new, and expansion of existing, meat works and processing facilities. From the 1980s, however, the loss of farmer supports and the decline in global meat prices in the led to a dramatic decline in sheep numbers (to under 40 million sheep in 2002), resulting in overcapacity in slaughterhouse space. Companies responded through consolidation and the closure of meat works plants. The Primary Producers Cooperative Society, a meat marketing cooperative owned by farmers in the South Island pursued a strategy of mergers, consolidation, and closure of meat plants with a purpose of gaining market share. Today, it has been renamed Silver Fern Farms, a cooperative owned by over 16,000 sheep-, cattle-, and deer-farmers throughout New Zealand. Their website proclaims their mission as being "to create the world's best red meat experiences... [by first] identifying consumer needs and then work with our farmers to grow animals and apply our expertise to create differentiated products specifically to meet those needs" (Silver Fern Farms, 2015). This greater attention to marketing and higher-value cuts of meat is a significant departure from the volume model of whole carcass sales that dominated the industry up until the 1990s (Britton *et al.*, 1992). Similar consolidation and restructuring of the dairy industry took place after 1980 (see Le Heron and Pawson, 1996; Tamasy *et al.*, 2008; Gray and Le Heron, 2010).

However, these national trends mask the significant impact that singular investments in particular places can have on rural regions. For example, Bathurst Resources, formerly a Perth-based coal-mining company purchased Christchurch-based L&M Coal and subsequently set up head offices in Wellington and listed on the New Zealand Stock Exchange (NZX) with a goal of extracting coking coal from the Denniston Plateau. They expected to invest $64NZ million to establish an open-pit coal mine that was estimated to create 225 jobs in the construction phase and 400 jobs when the mine was in full production throughout the expected 40-year life of the mine. Once in full production, Bathurst Resources anticipated exporting 1 million tonnes of coal per year to China and India through the Westport Port and Lyttleton Port (Christchurch). These activities generated significant optimism for the West Coast economy, with the *Greymouth Star* reporting celebrations in the street of Westport when the environmental consents were granted (*Greymouth Star*, 2013). However, by February 26, 2014, Bathurst had begun laying off staff and had delayed indefinitely the start-up of the Denniston Plateau mine as the international price for coking coal dropped from a high of over $300NZ per tonne in 2012 to $120NZ per tonne, reflecting the volatility of the market and ultimately the dependent and vulnerable nature of the regional economy (Radio NZ, 2014).

Similarly, the planned closure of the Holcim Cement Plant in Westport in 2016 will result in significant job loss as a result of a process of rationalization within the global company. Holcim NZ, a subsidiary of the Switzerland-based multinational Holcim Ltd., has decided to shift from domestic production of cement to importing it through a new import facility and distribution center. The Westport Plant currently produces 500,000 tonnes of cement per year, and the new import terminal will be able to accommodate 1 million tonnes. The spin-off effects are significant, as Holcim is the last commercial user of the port (Radio NZ, 2013).

Conclusion

This chapter has revealed the degree to which exposure to global economic pressures directly associated with the New Zealand government's decision to step back from a policy of regional support and intervention has impacted local regions in the country. As evidence from Southland and West Coast indicates, job loss and the loss of state services was dramatic. Despite this, resource-dependency still dominates these economies and they are increasingly at the mercy of fickle processes of shifting market demand and foreign direct investment. The retreat of the state in its pursuit of neoliberalism (Peet, 2012) has exacerbated 'uneven geographical' development (Harvey, 2006) which has enabled the wealthier, more urbanized regions to benefit from the move to a more service-dominated economy. By contrast more peripheral regions retain their historic dependence on resource-based activity, but in the absence of state support are vulnerable to market shifts, employment changes, and boom and bust cycles. Within this context the role of key corporates in the resources sector, particularly in terms of coal and dairy, as discussed above, is critical to the regional economy, employment, and global links, albeit that vulnerabilities are created through dependence on a narrow range of products and a limited number of corporates. The national and international investment and operational decisions made by these companies ensures both dependence and vulnerability in regions such as West Coast and Southland. The New Zealand government's encouragement of primary sector exports will perpetuate this vulnerable scenario for the foreseeable future, encouraging regional differentiation in a context in which regional authorities and local role-players are ill-placed to manage developments.

References

Abbott, M. 2007. *New Zealand and the global economy.* Wellington, New Zealand: Dumore.

Bale, M. and Dale, T. 1998. Public sector reform in New Zealand and its relevance to developing countries, *The World Bank Research Observer* 13(1): 103–121.

Baxter, C., Campbell, J., Eyre, R., Fitzsimons, J., Gillies, K., Downing, Z., Jones, T., and Penwarden, R. 2014. *Jobs after coal: A just transition for New Zealand communities.* New Zealand. Available online at: https://coalactionnetworkaotearoa.files.wordpress.com/2014/05/jobs_after_coal_may2104_lowres.pdf. Accessed September 20, 2015.

Britton, S., Le Heron, R., and Pawson, E. 1992. *Changing places in New Zealand: A geography of restructuring.* Christchurch, New Zealand: New Zealand Geographical Society.

Büscher, B. and Arsel, M. 2012. Introduction: Neoliberal conservation, uneven geographical development and the dynamics of contemporary capitalism, *Tijdschrift voor economische en sociale geografie* 103(2): 129–135.

Challies, E.R. and Murray, W.E. 2008. Towards post-neoliberalism? The comparative politico-economic transition of New Zealand and Chile, *Asia Pacific Viewpoint* 49(2): 228–243.

Chisholm, M. 1990. *Regions in recession and resurgence.* London: Unwin-Hyman.

Conradson, D. and Pawson, E. 1997. Reworking the geography of the long boom: The small town experience of restructuring in Reefton, New Zealand, *Environment and Planning A* 29(8): 1381–1397.

Conradson, D. and Pawson, E. 2009. New cultural economies of marginality: Revisiting the West Coast, South Island, New Zealand, *Journal of Rural Studies* 25: 77–86.

Dalziel, P. and Lattimore, R. 2004. *The New Zealand macroeconomy*, Melbourne, Australia: Oxford University Press.

Dyer, S. and Hurd, F. 2011. Gendered perceptions of corporate restructuring and community change in a single industry town, *New Zealand Society* 26(1): 68–88.

Economic Monitoring Group. 1989. *The economy in transition.* Wellington, New Zealand: New Zealand Planning Council.

Evans, L., Grimes, A., Wilkinson, B., and Teece, D. 1996. Economic reform in New Zealand 1984–95: The pursuit of efficiency, *Journal of Economic Literature* 34: 1856–1902.

Fairweather, J.R. 1992. *Agrarian restructuring in New Zealand.* Lincoln, New Zealand: Research Report No. 213, Agribusiness and Economics Research Unit, Lincoln University.

Feinberg-Danieli, G. and Lafferty, G. 2007. Unions and union membership in New Zealand: Annual review for 2006, *New Zealand Journal of Employment Relations* 32(3): 31–39.

Fonterra. 2014. Fonterra revises forecast farmgate milk price for 2014/15 season and announces estimated dividend. Available online at: https://www.fonterra.com/wps/wcm/connect/Fonterra_NewZealand_en/Fonterra/Hub%20Sites/News%20and%20Media/Media%20Releases/FONTERRA%20REVISES%20FORECAST%20FARMGATE%20MILK%20PRICE%20FOR%20201415%20SEASON%20AND%20ANNOUNCES%20ESTIMATED%20DIVIDEND. Accessed March 8, 2016.

Gibson, J.K. and Harris, R.I. 1996. Trade liberalisation and plant exit in New Zealand manufacturing, *The Review of Economics and Statistics* 78(3): 521–529.

Grant, D. 2015. Southland Region, *Te Ara—The encyclopedia of New Zealand*. Available online at: www.TeAra.govt.nz/en/southland-region. Accessed December 12, 2015.

Gray, S. and Le Heron, R. 2010. Globalising New Zealand: Fonterra Co-operative Group, and shaping the future, *New Zealand Geographer* 66(1): 1–13.

Greymouth Star. 2013. Westport celebrates mine. Available online at: www.greystar.co.nz/content/westport-celebrates-mine. Accessed August 9, 2013.

Haggerty, J., Campbell, H., and Morris, C. 2008. Keeping the stress off the sheep? Agricultural intensification, neoliberalism and 'good' farming in New Zealand, *Geoforum* 40: 767–777.

Harvey, D. 2006. *Spaces of global capitalism: Towards a theory of uneven geographical development*. London: Verso.

Harvey, D. 2010. Roepke Lecture in Economic Geography—Crises, geographical disruptions and the uneven development of political responses, *Economic Geography* 87(1): 1–22.

IEA (International Energy Agency). 2014. *Coal information 2014*. Paris: OECD/IEA.

Johnsen, S. 1999. Agricultural restructuring and responses: Inter-relationships between farm adjustment strategies in Waihemo, 1984–1997, *New Zealand Geographer* 55(1): 25–34.

Johnsen, S. 2003. Contingency revealed: New Zealand farmers' experiences of agricultural restructuring, *Sociologia Ruralis* 43(2): 128–153.

Larner, W. and Butler, M. 2007. The places, people, and politics of partnership. In H. Leitner, J. Peck, and E. Sheppard (eds.), *Contesting neoliberalism: Urban frontiers* (pp. 71–81). New York: Guilford Press.

Lattimore, R. and Eaqub, S. 2011. *The New Zealand economy.* Auckland, New Zealand: Auckland University Press.

Lawson, V. 2010. Reshaping economic geography? Producing spaces of inclusive development, *Economic Geography* 86(4): 351–360.

Le Heron, R. and Pawson, E. 1996. *Changing places: New Zealand in the nineties.* Auckland, New Zealand: Addison-Wesley Longman.

Lewis, N. 2012. Splitting a northern account of New Zealand's neoliberalism, *New Zealand Geographer* 68(3): 168–174.

MacLeod, C.J. and Moller, H. 2006. Intensification and diversification in NZ agriculture since 1960, *Agriculture Ecosystems and Environment* 115: 201–218.

Markey, S., Connelly, S., and Roseland, M. 2010. 'Back of the envelope': Pragmatic planning for sustainable rural community development, *Planning Practice & Research* 25(1): 1–23.

Markey, S., Pierce, J.T., and Vodden, K. 2000. Resources, people and the environment: A regional analysis of the evolution of resource policy in Canada, *Canadian Journal of Regional Science* 23(3): 427–454.

Mascarenhas, R.C. 1993. Building an enterprise culture in the public sector: Reform of the public sector in Australia, Britain, and New Zealand, *Public Administration Review* 53(4): 319–328.

Ministry of Business Innovation and Employment. 2012. *Building export markets.* Auckland, New Zealand: Ministry of Business Innovation and Employment. Formerly available at: www.mbie.govt.nz/pdf-library/what-we-do/business-growth-agenda/bga-reports/building-export-markets-bga-progress-report-august-2012.pdf. Accessed April 30, 2015. See: http://web.archive.org/web/20140423213126/http://www.mbie.govt.nz/pdf-library/what-we-do/business-growth-agenda/bga-reports/building-export-markets-bga-progress-report-august-2012.pdf.

Ministry of Business Innovation and Employment. 2013. *Business Growth Agenda.* Auckland, New Zealand: Ministry of Business, Innovation and Employment. Available online at: www.mbie.govt.nz/info-services/business/business-growth-agenda/2013/?searchterm=business%20growth%20agenda*. Accessed March 8, 2016.

MPI. 2014. *Primary Growth Partnership: For business-led, market-driven primary sector innovation.* Auckland, New Zealand: Ministry of Primary Industries. Formerly available at: www.mpi.govt.nz/agriculture/funding-programmes/primary-growth-partnership.aspx. Accessed June 15, 2014. See: http://web.archive.org/web/20140605102946/http://mpi.govt.nz/agriculture/funding-programmes/primary-growth-partnership.aspx.

North, P. 2002. LETS in a cold climate: Green dollars, self-help and neoliberal welfare in New Zealand, *Policy & Politics* 30(4): 483–499.

NZ Treasury. 2013. *Estimates of appropriations 2012 vote economic development.* Auckland, New Zealand: NZ Treasury. Available online at: www.treasury.govt.nz/budget/2013/estimates/est13ecodev.pdf. Accessed June 16, 2013.

NZIER (New Zealand Institute of Economic Research). 2009. *Economic progress and puzzles: long-term structural change in the New Zealand economy, 1953–2006.* Wellington, New Zealand: Working paper 2009/6, New Zealand Institute of Economic Research.

NZIER (New Zealand Institute of Economic Research). 2011. *Foreign direct investment.* Wellington, New Zealand: New Zealand Institute of Economic Research.

134   *S. Connelly and E. Nel*

NZIER (New Zealand Institute of Economic Research). 2012. *Lifting export performance.* Wellington, New Zealand: New Zealand Institute of Economic Research.

Pallares-Barbera, M., Le Heron, R., Suau-Sanchez, P., and Fromhold-Eisebith, M. 2012. Globalising economic spaces, uneven development and regional challenges: Introduction to the special issue, *Urbani izziv* 23(2): 2–10.

Pawson, E. and Scott, G. 1992. The regional consequences of economic restructuring: The West Coast, New Zealand (1984–1991), *Journal of Rural Studies* 8(4): 373–386.

Peck, J., Theodore, N., and Brenner, N. 2009. Neoliberal urbanism: Models, moments, mutations, *SAIS Review of International Affairs* 29(1): 49–66.

Peet, R. 2012. Comparative policy analysis: Neoliberalising New Zealand, *New Zealand Geographer* 68(3): 151–167.

Pratt, M. and Lowndes, T. 2005. Regional economic development and sustainability. In J.E. Rowe (ed.), *Economic development in New Zealand* (pp. 127–147). Aldershot: Ashgate.

Prudham, S. and Heynen, N. 2011. Uneven development 25 years on: Space, nature and the geographies of capitalism, *New Political Economy* 16(2): 223–232.

Radio NZ. 2013. *Holcim to shut Westport cement plant.* Radio NZ. Available online at: www.radionz.co.nz/news/national/215923/holcim-to-shut-westport-cement-plant. Accessed November 11, 2014.

Radio NZ. 2014. *Jobs cut, mine delayed as price slumps.* Radio NZ. Available online at: www.radionz.co.nz/news/national/237204/jobs-cut,-mine-delayed-as-price-slumps. Accessed November 11, 2014.

Robertson, N., Perkins, H.C., and Taylor, N. 2008. Multiple job holding: Interpreting economic, labour market and social change in rural communities, *Sociologia Ruralis* 48(4): 331–350.

Roper, B.S. 2005. *Prosperity for all: Economic, social and political change in New Zealand since 1935.* Auckland, New Zealand: Thomson.

Rudd, C. and Roper, B. 1997. *The political economy of New Zealand.* Melbourne, Australia: Oxford University Press.

Schöllman, A. and Nischalke, T. 2005. Central government and regional development policy. In J.E. Rowe (ed.), *Economic development in New Zealand* (pp. 47–68). Aldershot: Ashgate.

Scott, G. and Pawson, E. 1999. Local development initiatives and unemployment in New Zealand, *Tijdschrift voor Economische en Sociale Geografie* 90(2): 184–195.

Silver Fern Farms. 2015. *Our vision & strategy.* Available online at: www.silverfernfarms. co.nz/our-co-operative/our-vision. Accessed February 28, 2015.

Simon, N. 2015. Story: West Coast region—Overview, *Te Ara—The Encyclopedia of New Zealand.* Available at: www.TeAra.govt.nz/en/interactive/21051/west-coast-region-and-town-populations-1863-2013. Accessed December 12, 2015.

Smith, N. 1986. Gentrification, the frontier and the restructuring of urban space. In N. Smith and P. Williams (eds.), *Gentrification of the City* (pp. 15–34). Boston, MA: Allen and Unwin.

Smith, W. and Montgomery, H. 2004. Revolution or evolution? New Zealand agriculture since 1984, *GeoJournal* 59(2): 107–118.

Statistics New Zealand. 2014. *Group: Agriculture—AGR001AA.* Available online at: www.stats.govt.nz. Accessed December 12, 2015.

Tamasy, C., Stringer, C., and Le Heron, R. 2008. Knowledge transfer in a globalising world economy: Fonterra's management of its mobile work force, *Geographische Zeitschrift* 96(3): 140–157.

Tipples, R., Trafford, S., and Callister, P. 2010. *The factors which have resulted in migrant workers being 'essential' workers on New Zealand dairy farms.* Wellington, New Zealand: Proceedings of the Labour, Employment and Work Conference 2010, Victoria University, Wellington.

Wilkinson, B. 2013. *New Zealand's Global Links: Foreign ownership and the status of New Zealand's net international investment.* Wellington, New Zealand: New Zealand Initiative. Available online at: www.nzinitiative.org.nz/site/nzinitiative/files/publications/global%20links.pdf. Accessed November 11, 2014.

Wilson, O.J. 1995. Rural restructuring and agriculture-rural economy linkages, *Journal of Rural Studies* 11(4): 417–431.

World Bank. 2009. *World Development Report 2009: Reshaping economic geography.* Washington, DC: World Bank.

Part II

Labor and Employment Perspectives on Restructuring

Introduction

Jobs and Labor Power Under Threat

Roger Hayter

Export-led resource booms are generators of plentiful well-paid jobs in peripheries. In this stage of the resource cycle, labor supply is often problematical. While nineteenth century resource exploitation in the New World countries of Australia, Canada, and New Zealand depended on significant inflows of labor, the opening up of new remote resource spaces continued to pose problems for attracting a workforce. In Mackenzie's case, to obtain employees for the start-up of its new pulp mill in 1973 that provided the main economic base of the new community, the controlling forest product corporation embarked on a recruitment tour that focused on established forest towns across Canada. In order to obtain a skilled workforce that would not be prone to quit, the firm wanted to hire labor from other small remote towns, and who were working in pulp mills. These characteristics were deemed vital for a productive, stable labor force and for a stable community; interestingly Mackenzie's founding firm chose to hire from many different communities rather than from just a few to avoid accusations of raiding and community dislocation. However, the onset of restructuring has meant problems of labor demand for all case study communities, underlined by job loss, unemployment, low incomes, and out-migration

As Halseth et al. document, Mackenzie's workforce in pulp and sawmills was unionized and organized by established collective bargains that emphasized seniority and job demarcation, the long-lasting implications of these principles reinforcing the company's investments in recruitment. Mackenzie originated not only as a planned industry town (with one dominant company) but as a union town with workers represented by locals that were part of province-wide industry unions. More generally, unions have been a powerful presence in resource sectors, and they have been well established in the forestry and mining activities of Lieksa and the Southland and West coast communities (as well as Mackenzie) and perhaps more surprisingly in the agriculture activities of the Northern Tablelands. Yet, as Part II reveals, the evolution of labor power differs among the case study communities. In Mackenzie, employee relations developed around a resolutely adversarial model, in a province and country where levels of unionization at their peak were between 40 percent and 50 percent. Similar comments can be made in relation to the forest and mining operations in the New Zealand case study communities. In contrast, as Halonen et al. note, Lieksa's employees are part of a

Scandinavian-wide union culture where peak levels of national unionization exceeded 80 percent and union bargains are part of broader social bargains. Meanwhile farming communities are more entrepreneur-oriented in nature, although they are related to union contexts by their own powerful organization of Central Union of Agricultural Producers and Forest Owners (MTK) in Finland. Argent's analysis of the Tablelands, however, reveals that across Australia, traditionally strong unions and supportive national legislation (along with protection for manufacturing) did occur in farming and meant unusually high wages that encouraged capital substitution of labor decades ago, with surplus labor resulting in out-migration from the Tablelands by the early 1970s. Ironically, a seasonal labor supply problem emerged that has only been addressed through the hiring of temporary immigrant workers, made possible by various new forms of national legislation.

Contemporary unionized labor conflict has been especially evident in Mackenzie, and focused on the issue of demands for more flexible forms of workplace arrangements. After all, flexibility imperatives of team work and merit-based promotion are direct challenges to job demarcation and seniority, principles legally endorsed in collective bargains. While new mills that hire a brand-new workforce can now readily create flexible collective bargains, as Mackenzie's experience demonstrates, attempts to flexibilize existing contracts are deeply contentious. Contracting out production jobs (e.g. logging) or service jobs (e.g. first aid, security, cleaning, catering) as part of corporate restructuring can also be an issue for unions, although such activities typically remain local.

The most insistent, important cause of job loss in resource communities among the case study communities stems from technological change, and the substitution of capital for labor, as firms strive to increase efficiency in the face of increased competition from elsewhere. For unions and employment in the resource industries of Lieksa, Southlands, West Coast, Mackenzie, and the Tablelands, the restructuring of mature industry life cycles has meant relentless job loss, even if in some cases production capacities have been maintained. However, as is especially evident in the bigger peripheries of Southlands and West Coast, New Zealand and Tablelands, New South Wales, intra-regional patterns of employment (and related income) change have been highly uneven with consolidation and growth occurring in a few more accessible centers and declines occurring elsewhere (see Chapters 5 and 2 respectively in Part I). Restructuring has also involved both corporate and union consolidation that has typically involved merger with larger units, and the creation of new bargaining partners. In Mackenzie's case, a new regionally based bargaining institution has been created, while in the New Zealand communities union voices have become similarly more local but with less regional coordination.

Possibilities for the rejuvenation of employment within mature resource sectors by promoting small-scale operations and adding value are touted among the case study communities. In Lieksa, for example, efforts to promote bioenergy, specialized forms of agriculture, and tourism have been recognized, as they have to varying degrees in Mackenzie and the New Zealand case studies. Yet even in Lieksa, such possibilities are limited by various factors such as high cost and intense competition from elsewhere, while value-added processing activities tend to be drawn to major markets. In the New Zealand case study communities, neoliberal policies that have encouraged raw material exports and narrow specialization have further limited such possibilities. In the Tablelands, neoliberal policies have similarly not been empathetic to regional support programs and the region seems to have adjusted to its labor market situation of declining permanent demands with seasonal spikes by relying on a combination of youth out-migration and seasonal inflows of migrant workers. Lieksa has experimented with the traditional regional policy solution of diversifying employment by attracting branch plants in secondary manufacturing, but this strategy has not proven sustainable. Costs are lower elsewhere, and local multiplier effects were limited. Indeed, it is hard to compensate for the large-scale losses of well-paid jobs that occur when major resource facilities are closed down with multiple small-scale alternatives. Moreover, specialized union workers are not well prepared to become 'entrepreneurial' and their retraining is problematic, especially when there is no guarantee of employment.

In practice, the decline in well-paid union jobs in large-scale resource-based operations has occurred in the case study communities, and, especially in the New Zealand, Australian, and British Columbian cases, labor power has declined significantly. Service sector jobs have grown, but these are typically less well paid, non-union, and female-oriented, albeit with caveats to the experience of Armidale, Northern Tablelands. Community incomes have fallen, income dependency has increased, in many cases populations have declined, while pension funding has become an issue in Mackenzie. Until recently, Mackenzie workers have been able to find alternative high incomes in the oil and gas sector in British Columbia and neighboring Alberta, but the sharp decline in oil prices during 2015 has reduced if not eliminated this alternative. If all the communities, now mature, have aging populations, employment generation is a major problem that must be increasingly addressed at the local level.

6 Labor/Capital Relations and Sustainable Development in the New South Wales' Northern Tablelands

Neil Argent

Introduction

In rural development circles, one of the most fundamental concerns is the retention and/or growth of local populations so as to better ensure the long-term social and economic viability of towns and their hinterlands. Often central to this objective is the capacity of the region and its constituent towns and hinterlands to provide sufficient employment opportunities for its own denizens and for those it seeks to recruit. In regions such as our case study area of the New South Wales (NSW) Northern Tablelands, Australia, this task has been rendered problematic by, inter alia, the seemingly inexorable competitive drive within the dominant industry sectors for ever more technologically sophisticated and capital intensive means of production, and the labor 'saving' consequences of this pressure. Yet, as numerous regions around Australia have realized, solving this dilemma is vital for their long-term futures for at least two key reasons. First, of course, rural towns and regions desire the economic and sociocultural multiplier effects associated with population growth, especially that driven by labor in-migration. The recruitment of the 'economically active' population serves, at least in part, to replace the young adult cohorts that have been leaving all categories of rural regions in large numbers for the cities (Argent and Walmsley, 2008). New labor in-migrants also provide an important boost to local economies through their consumption behaviors along with their contribution to sheer factor expansion. Second, and notwithstanding the observations above regarding the onward drive for labor- and cost-saving technological applications, human labor (and ingenuity) is still fundamental to the success, or otherwise, of the major industries of the Northern Statistical Division (Northern SD) and, therefore, to the broader economic, social, and demographic prospects of the region.

Chapter 2 established that the case study region of the Northern SD of NSW had, over the period of a century or so, developed a particular path dependence on pastoral livestock and broadacre farming. The development of this dependence was attributed to a range of political, historical, geographical, economic, and biophysical factors that, depending on the era studied, involved different geographical scales. One conclusion from Chapter 2's analysis was that, via Australia's progressive adoption of neoliberal approaches to state management and consequent deregulation of key elements of what were once regarded as the 'national economy,' the Northern SD had been more-or-less fully integrated into global economic flows. This process of integration has had positive *and* negative effects for the Northern Tablelands, producing both economic 'winners' and 'losers.' Another important finding from Chapter 2 was that the Northern SD's 'propulsive sector'—agriculture—had undergone a traumatic process of adaptation to these multiscalar processes of change, shedding many individual farm operators and workers over the 1980s to the present day. Shift/share analysis confirmed that farming is both a structural weakness and a strategic, competitive strength of the Northern SD in employment terms. Insights from staples theory, geographical political economy, and evolutionary economic geography lead us to understand that, in the staples-dependent regional economy, the cyclonic gales of economic restructuring have destructive effects on employment, sweeping away redundant labor and their families and precipitating demographic decline.

This chapter explores the key dynamics in the regional and local labor markets of the Northern SD and, in particular, the changing organization and management of labor in a broader national and, indeed, global context of heightened labor mobility and 'flexibilization' of industrial relations and migration policy. In doing so, the conceptual insights developed in Chapter 2 are carried through the analysis, and brought to focus explicitly on the role of key institutions and their evolution. The remainder of this chapter is organized as follows. First, a brief review of the temporal and spatial evolution of the Australian industrial relations system is provided so as to set the national regulatory context for the remainder of the chapter. Second, given agriculture's centrality to the economic base of the Northern SD, together with the structural forces driving employment decline in this sector (outlined in Chapter 2), an outline of recent national trends in the demand for and supply of farm labor is given. Third, the development of new international migration programs in Australia to tackle farm labor market shortages are discussed in the broader context of major philosophical shifts in the nation's immigration policy. Fourth, the use of at least of some of these new visa programs by businesses in the Northern SD are discussed, focusing specifically on the Costa Group's use of the Pacific Seasonal Workers Scheme (PSWS) at its tomato farm in the small Northern SD town of Guyra. The chapter ends with some summary points.

The Rise and Decline of a Working Man's Paradise? Labor/Capital Relations in Nineteenth- and Twentieth-Century Australia

As has been noted elsewhere, for much of its late nineteenth- and early twentieth-century history, Australia was known nationally and internationally as a 'working man's paradise' and an advanced laboratory for the application of socially progressive ideas in public policy (McIntyre, 2009). Through the arrival—forced or voluntary—of prominent dissenting individuals and formally and informally organized groups, contemporary questions of social equity and class were debated actively and publicly via, inter alia, a robust and diverse press (Bowden, 2011). Inspired by memories of the poor treatment and conditions meted out to workers in the old 'Mother Country,' together with the recognition of the practical exigencies resulting from a shortage of qualified crafts- and tradespeople at the time, employers and workers frequently agreed on the need for fairer wages and working conditions in the new colonies (Bowden, 2011). Australia became the first country in the industrialized world (as we know it now) to formally register and, equally, to elect to government a party representing the interests of labor (de Garis, 1974). Australia also pioneered the formal institution of the eight-hour day, together with the notion of the 'living wage' for a worker and *his* family via the 1907 Harvester judgment (Crowley, 1974; Irving, 1974; Clark, 1993). The male pronouns in the passage above are used advisedly as an explicit acknowledgement of the patriarchal nature of society at that time. The Australian labor movement's highly selective stance on fairness is further evidenced in its xenophobic campaigns against the occasional influxes of Chinese or other non-white workers into Australia during the nineteenth century (Clark, 1993). Therefore, the nineteenth and early twentieth century Australian labor movement's concern for fairness was a strictly qualified one, restricted to the brotherhood of white Anglo-Saxon men. Nonetheless, via the Constitution's stipulation that labor market affairs and regulation be the responsibility of an independent statutory body, and governments' commitment to arbitration, together with an apparently abiding concern with social justice, a somewhat progressive system for industrial relations and labor market management and regulation was established (Dabscheck, 1994; Bowden, 2011). These same arrangements helped install unions as central players in the national (and colonial/state) industrial relations system, at least until the final decades of the twentieth century.

For much of the twentieth century, industry-specific awards were decided upon and regulated by the central umpire in the Australian industrial relations system, the Commonwealth Court of Conciliation and Arbitration (renamed the Australian Conciliation and Arbitration Commission in 1973 until 1996) (Dabscheck, 1994). For much of the productivist, 'long boom' era, and notwithstanding the points just made above regarding the formal separation of powers between the State and Commonwealth governments on one side, and the various conciliation and arbitration commissions on the other, relations between employers, workers, and the state have often been characterized as corporatist. The generally buoyant economic climate of the 1950s, 1960s, and 1970s provided the conditions for a particularly Keynesian compromise between all three groups that both reflected the times as well as helping to perpetuate them (Fagan and Webber, 1999; O'Neill and Argent, 2005). High levels of protection via tariffs and quotas were introduced in the post-World War Two era to allow the domestic manufacturing sector to establish itself as a major industry sector and employer (Linge, 1988; Fagan and Webber, 1999). This loose compact, referred to somewhat disparagingly as 'protection-all-round' (Fagan and Webber, 1999) worked as long as economic conditions permitted. Ongoing rapid economic growth and industrial expansion, reflective of Commonwealth and state governments' firm commitment to develop an independent, import substitution manufacturing sector and to grow the national population, helped feed a virtuous circle of development in which high immigration intakes, a post-World War Two marriage and baby 'boom' and rapid rates of household formation flowed into rising levels of demand and employment. Freed from the straitjacket of wartime rationing, consumer demand escalated.

Organized labor demands for better pay and conditions, though never given carte blanche by either the various employer lobby groups or government, tended to be acceded to. For employers, the higher wages bill was tolerable as long as protection was maintained: the increased costs of production could simply be incorporated in the sales price of the goods and services. In spite of the various concessions and subsidies provided to the farm sector during the productivist era, tensions emerged between it, the manufacturing sector, organized labor, and governments over these seemingly cozy arrangements. For farmers, high manufacturing-sector tariffs and quotas increased their costs of production through higher machinery, automobile, and other key farm input costs, making them increasingly uncompetitive on international markets. Due to the strongly centralized nature of industry award (wages) setting, farmers also often found themselves on the wrong side of wage cases in which, for instance, pastoral workers campaigned for 'cost-of-living' increases that related to national-scale average increases in the cost of the standard basket of goods rather than that pertaining in rural areas. And yet, the farm sector saw itself, quite rightly for a substantial part of the 'long boom,' as a vital source of the nation's income and a (temporary) solution to the nation's chronic balance-of-payments problems and, thus deserving of some protection from such 'flow-on' wage increases. Such was the dual structure of the Australian economy at this time (Linge, 1988; Emy and Hughes, 1991).

This is not the place for a detailed examination of union membership among Australian rural workers over the twentieth century. Nevertheless, some key points are pertinent to this chapter's focus. First, rural workers—especially shearers—played a lead role in the development of an organized labor movement in the last decades of the nineteenth century and in the later development of the Australian Labor Party (Clark, 1993; McIntyre, 2009). Union representation among shearers and other blue-collar rural workers was relatively high up until the end of World War Two. The increased mechanization of farm work after this time saw employment and union membership decline (Bowden, 2011). This said, particular industries and occupations tended to have higher levels of union coverage, regardless of location. For instance, until recently mining workers have exhibited relatively high levels of unionization, in spite of persistent and concerted campaigns by particular mining corporations to break down union representation of workers in key mine sites (Ellem, 2003). Overall, though, from the late 1970s onward union representation among farm workers—including most employed in the shearing industry—was comparatively low and declining. This is hardly surprising given the often small numbers of workers on each farm, the broader context of substantial labor shedding in the industry, and the frequent physically and socially isolated nature of the work (see Chapter 2).

As with many other long-standing social and economic institutions built up over the Keynesian–Fordist era of the post-World War Two boom, Australia's centralized industrial relations system underwent ongoing and substantial 'reform' during the 1980s, 1990s, and 2000s. Consistent with the nation's drive for global free trade, consecutive federal and state governments over this era, regardless of political stripe, embraced an agenda of macroeconomic reform that would putatively raise the competitiveness and productivity of every branch of industry and government. New institutions, such as the Productivity Commission and National Competition Council were formed to drive this agenda and ensure adherence to it by public and private sector players alike. In the arena of industrial relations, the old corporatist arrangements between state, capital, and labor were maintained under the Hawke–Keating Federal Labor Governments (1983–1996) but the various 'Accords' negotiated between the parties concerning wages and conditions also contained the need for ongoing increases in worker productivity as a trade-off for continued improvements in the welfare safety net and wages growth. A key element of this productivity drive that emerged over the various Accords was 'enterprise bargaining'—the negotiation of wages and conditions between business owners and workers at the scale of the individual business. Theoretically, at least, this approach was a boon for employers for it would allow for the better matching of wage levels and worker productivity than that provided by the hitherto centralized arbitration and conciliation process (Dabscheck, 1994). The conservative Howard-led Coalition Federal Government (1996–2007) attempted more radical reform of the industrial relations system, seeking to further remove the influence of labor unions in workplace representation while encouraging greater flexibility in bargaining arrangements (Fagan and Webber, 1999; Ellem, 2006). In the context of these institutional changes, amid other far-reaching changes in Australian society and economy, union representation has gradually but consistently declined. Between 1990 and 2009, levels of union representation in Australian workplaces approximately halved from just over 40 percent to 20 percent (ABS, 2010a).

While the above-noted changes have no doubt affected the organization of farm work, other equally, if not more, dramatic structural forces operating in rural Australia have impacted on the availability of work and who performs it. It is to these forces, their effects on Australian agriculture, and the various solutions to these impacts, that this chapter now turns.

Victims of Their Own Success? Farm Structural Change, Demographic Shifts, and Employment Crises in Australian Agriculture

As noted in Chapter 2, although farming remained the largest single industry of employment in the Northern SD until the most recent census in 2011, both its aggregate employment numbers and share of overall employment declined dramatically from the 1960s to the present. The reasons for this decline have been covered in great depth by many researchers before, and also touched on in that chapter. To summarize briefly, though, the seemingly inbuilt drive for individual farmers to achieve greater economies of scale so as to lift turnover and incomes and to help relieve the drudgery of some farm tasks saw on-farm investment in plant and machinery increase substantially during the productivist years. Correspondingly, farm employment levels declined over the same period. Not surprisingly, in the drier, more remote rural regions with economic bases dominated by broadacre farming and extensive pastoralism, redundant farm workers—many of whom comprised an extremely valuable floating 'pool' of labor that could once be drawn upon for a wide range of seasonal farm tasks—moved away to regions where their skills and abilities were more in demand. Cumulatively, from the 1970s onward, this migratory process began to take its toll on the demographic and economic structures and sociocultural functions of affected rural communities, creating the pathway for something of a looming crisis in the supply of agricultural labor.

Given the sheer demographic dominance of the capital city regions over the remainder of the Australian settlement system, although numbers of out-migrants from inland rural regions have been and remain comparatively small, the cumulative effect of this always selective process has been significant in the drier, more remote and agriculturally dependent regions of Australia (Bell, 1996). Young people, defined here as those aged 15–24 years, have consistently exhibited the highest mobility of all Australian cohorts and have tended to be overrepresented in out-migration flows from Australian rural areas. For example, three-quarters of all women, and over half of all young men, aged 15 to 24 years from the broadacre farming zone of the Upper Great Southern SD of Western Australia moved out between 1996 and 2001 (Argent and Walmsley, 2008). Figure 6.1 shows clearly that it has overwhelmingly been teenagers and young adults—the "future leaders, small business owners and entrepreneurs and community drivers" of inland communities (Alston cited in Lewis, 2005 p. 26)—that account for most of inland Australia's net migration losses since the 1970s. The contemporary high mobility of young rural people is underscored by the finding that over three-quarters of a group of former high school students from the NSW New England Tablelands and Mid-North Coast had moved from their 'home town' in the 13 years since they had completed their studies. However, a further 13 percent were categorized as 'returners' in that they had moved away from the former home town but then returned to live (Dufty-Jones *et al.*, 2014).

Youth net migration loss has implications that spread across many of the economic, demographic, and social functions of rural regions and communities. On top of the very direct effects that youth out-migration has on the viability of sporting clubs and social organizations (Tonts and Atherley, 2005) and the direct consumption of services (Walmsley *et al.*, 2006; Argent and Walmsley, 2008) the phenomenon can also negatively affect the present and future labor markets of a rural region in two main ways. First, protracted and/or heavy net migration losses of young men and women reduces the aggregate number of potential workers in a region and, often, deprives a regional workforce of some of its most physically and intellectually able potential employees (and entrepreneurs). Second, as this group comprises the cohorts who would otherwise bear and raise succeeding generations—though the peak age of fertility has steadily risen in Australia over the past couple of decades, including in rural regions (ABS, 2010b)—not only

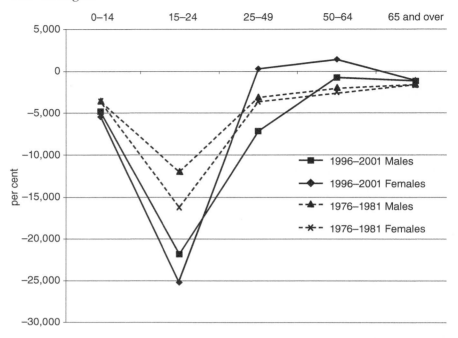

Figure 6.1 Age- and Sex-Specific Net Migration Rates: Australian Inland Statistical
   Division, 1976–1981 and 1996–2001.
Walmsley *et al.* (2006).

does youth net migration loss directly lead to smaller cohort sizes but also produces
older local population structures with reduced natural reproduction potential. At
the other (older) end of the population pyramid, this situation accelerates structural
aging and increases the aged dependency ratio (Davies and James, 2011; Argent
et al., 2015). Recent research on rural aging processes reveals that the age structure
of the population of the lower reaches of the Murray–Darling Basin, Australia's
major 'food bowl,' had shifted from being very much younger than the national
average at the time of the 1981 census, to very much older, in relative terms, by
2011. The chief driving forces for this change were, in order of most importance:
youth net migration loss; retiree in-migration to selected river-adjacent regional
centers; and slowly declining regional fertility trends (Argent *et al.*, 2015).

   The cumulative impact of these age-selective migration trends has become
increasingly evident in the Australian agricultural labor force. A 2008 report on
labor shortages in rural Australia emphasized that one of the major challenges
facing the industry is the loss of the 'prime age' workforce and the limited entry
of young workers into agriculture (DAFF, 2009). This same report further noted
that the agricultural sector faced critical skilled and general labor shortages that
are linked primarily to a combination of out-migration and the inability to compete
with other sectors for labor. The median age of Australian farmers reached 53
years at the 2011 census; 13 years older than the national average for all workers

(ABS, 2012a). Due in part to the out-migration of children from farming households in order to pursue non-agricultural (and non-local) jobs and careers as farms become larger and increasingly mechanized, the average age of Australian farmers increased by nine years between 1981 and 2011: for all other occupations the mean age grew by six years (ABS, 2012a).

One of the major drivers of the current demographic shape and trajectory of the Australian farm workforce is its declining capacity to recruit staff relative to other industry sector. Some evidence suggests that at the height of Australia's recent mining boom farmers found it very difficult to recruit permanent and seasonal labor due to the out-migration of many young men and women to the key sites of 'the boom,' drawn in by the extremely high wages offered by mining companies (Davies *et al.*, 2009). Severe seasonal conditions have also seen agriculture shed labor. The Department of Agriculture, Fisheries and Forestry (DAFF, 2009) estimated that between 1998 and 2008 the agricultural labor force fell from 463,700 to 373,800; a decrease of nearly 15 percent (nearly 1.5 percent/annum). While 'structural adjustment' was acknowledged as an important contributor to this decline, environmental factors are also important. Recent severe droughts, together with regulatory and cost-related constraints on farmers' access to irrigation water, have also resulted in farm employment losses. Affected workers (and their families) frequently migrate to other regions. Typically, as conditions improve and new jobs are created, farmers struggle to attract back or replace those people who had been lost from the industry.

It is this combination of demographic, economic, social, and environmental forces that have seen farmers look to new and hitherto unexpected sources for workers—the global labor market (Argent and Tonts, 2015).

International Migration and Australia's Agricultural Workforce: Bridging a Divide?

It is something of a cliché to say that Australia is a nation of immigrants—apart from the nation's Indigenous peoples—yet that statement remains fundamentally correct. From very early in its post-1788 history, colonial (later state and national) governments formed the philosophical stance that the rapid growth and wide distribution of the population was necessary to secure the country's economic, demographic, and strategic future. To those ends, until the late 1990s, permanent migration formed the central pillar of Australian immigration policy (Burnley, 2001; Hugo, 2008). While the Commonwealth government did use immigration occasionally to deal with temporary shortages of labor in different industries and parts of the nation, this was always coupled with the expectation that those accepted would become permanent members of Australian society and national citizens. This, of course, is in direct contrast to the guest-worker schemes used in many western European nations after the conclusion of World War Two in which workers were recruited from their respective colonies and/or Mediterranean nations to form the industrial labor force needed to rebuild war-ravaged economies (Castles and Miller, 2009).

The mid-1990s saw a dramatic rethink of Australia's immigration program (Hugo, 2008). While permanent settlement continued to form a central plank of immigration policy, sporadic but severe labor shortages in select industries saw the introduction of a range of temporary visas aimed primarily at the recruitment of both skilled and unskilled labor. As a consequence, the skilled component of the immigration program has expanded to comprise up to two-thirds of the overall annual settler intake since 2005/2006 (DIAC, 2012), which itself had been running at historic highs over the same period (McGuirk and Argent, 2011; DIAC, 2012).

However, as might be expected in a nation that has so avidly pursued global free trade and, true to Woods' (2007) notion of the 'global countryside,' it is also important to consider the dynamic global labor market context in which Australia increasingly operates. Two factors are centrally important here. First, according to Castles and Miller (2009, p. 1), much of the world has entered an "era of transnational revolution" in which long-standing physical and categorical barriers between migrant-sending and -receiving nations have been effectively eradicated. Similarly, Australia has entered a 'new age of migration' in which unprecedentedly large flows of migrants, originating primarily from lesser-developed nations, are attracted to it as an economically and politically secure destination (Hugo, 2008; Castles and Miller, 2009). With a substantial and growing 'beach head' Asian population built up from previous waves of immigration—commencing from the immediate post-Vietnam War period—Australia has become inexorably bound into an extensive and expanding Asian migration network and, thereby more strongly linked to its geopolitical 'home' region. For Hugo (1996 p. 36) this development "has the potential to increase economic, social and political linkages, and transactions and alliances with the rapidly growing economics and changing societies of the Asian region."

The second factor relates to demographic structural change, though this time at the societal level. Many Western developed nations have entered a phase of long-term structural (and numerical) aging. Equally, many of these self-same countries face worsening aged dependency ratios, where the proportion of the economically active population relative to that in the post-retirement years declines, indicating a potentially dwindling labor force (Australian Government, 2010). It is in this context that the so-called 'minority' world's increased interest in the cheap and abundant sources of labor available in the lesser-developed 'majority' world needs to be interpreted (Castles and Miller, 2009). In the case of Australia, the ongoing aging of its population—driven by the combined processes of long-term fertility decline and the movement of the large cohort of post-World War Two baby boomers into the post-retirement years—means that labor force recruitment over the coming decades will be progressively challenged. Federal government population projections suggest that approximately 23 percent of the population will be in the post-retirement cohorts by 2050 (Australian Government, 2010). As I have attempted to demonstrate above, though, aging is not a spatially homogenous process. Broad national-scale measures of aging primarily reflect the attributes of metropolitan populations because of the latter's dominant share of the population. The dynamics of structural aging operate very differently at the subregional scale, with often the highest levels and rates of aging seen in small, isolated rural towns and regions (Stockdale, 2011; Argent *et al.*, 2015). As already noted, in the productivist zones of inland Australia, decades of youth out-migration and net migration loss have greatly diminished the stocks of young adults capable of entering the workforce. Further, the deficit in the local population structure that this process creates has been compounded by the 'knock-on' effect of reduced fertility (Argent *et al.*, 2015). In these areas, the combination of small resident populations, challenging environmental conditions, and the absence of any 'reserve army of unemployed' means that local labor demands are often difficult to fill (Davies *et al.*, 2009).

Over the past two decades new permanent and temporary visa categories have been introduced by the federal government to fill just such gaps in regional labor markets. Five key subcategories of the revised skilled migration program relate directly to regional migration and agricultural employment (Hugo, 2008; Phillips and Spinks, 2012); two are focused on permanent migration and three on temporary migration, but all fall within the skilled migration stream of the nation's immigration program (Argent and Tonts, 2015; see Figure 6.2). In numerous respects the permanent visa categories—the State Specific and Regional Migration Scheme (SSRM) and the Regional Sponsored Migration Scheme (RSMS)—could be seen as a concession to state government and regional development agency calls for a fairer share of the nation's immigration intake. While the nation's immigration intake has overwhelmingly favored the major capital cities due to the historical concentration of population and industry located therein, over recent decades the proportion of the immigration intake locating in non-metropolitan areas has declined substantially relative to the levels seen in the post-World War Two 'long boom' era. In 2006, just over one-third of Australians lived in the nation's two largest cities, Melbourne and Sydney, yet over half of the overseas born population resided there (Hugo, 2008).

In terms of process, in consultation with domestic employers, the Federal Department of Industry develops lists of occupational vacancies that Australian employers have demonstrated difficulties filling. These lists then form a central component of the temporary worker visa program (DIBP, 2014a). For any nominated target occupation, employers are required to demonstrate that they have made a reasonable attempt at recruiting Australian workers (e.g. provision of copies of advertisements in local media). Nonetheless, these visa programs—particularly the Temporary Business (Long Stay) Visa category 457 visa—has met with controversy, with labor unions, among others, repeatedly alleging that the temporary migration scheme is being used by employers as a 'cheap fix' for short-term structural mismatches in the labor market, and to undercut Australian award pay and conditions (Azarias *et al.*, 2014). Irrespective of such claims and counter-claims, these visa programs now form a central element of the restructured immigration program (see Figure 6.2).

Agriculture and related processing businesses (e.g. abattoirs) were among one of the key sectors to experience severe and chronic labor shortfalls from the 1980s. Alongside the new temporary migration schemes outlined above, other programs

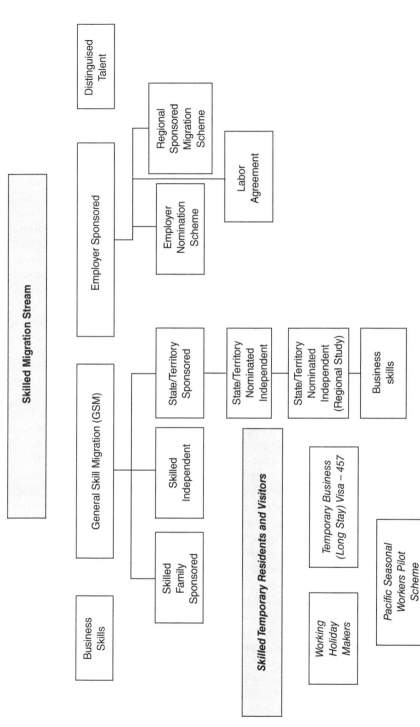

Figure 6.2 Selected Components of the Australian Skilled Migration Stream, 2011.
Source: Argent and Tonts (2015).

were introduced that explicitly directed immigration into rural areas. The number of settlers arriving under both the State Specific and Regional Migration Scheme (SSRM) and the Regional Sponsored Migration Scheme (RSMS) has expanded dramatically since 2004 but has fluctuated somewhat more recently. The SSRM intake grew from a little over 4,000 in 2004 to 47,733 in 2012, but then dropped to 42,183 in 2014/15. The number of workers recruited via the RSMS increased from 2,183 to 16,471 in 2012, but declined to 12,380 by 2014/2015 (DIAC, 2012; DIBP, 2014b).

Three other temporary visa programs facilitate the entry of foreign workers into rural areas, primarily to fill short-term labor shortages. Two of these—the 457 and Working Holiday Maker (WHM) visa programs—are not 'regionally specific' per se but nonetheless play a critical role in bolstering the rural labor force (Hanson and Bell, 2007; Tan and Lester, 2012). The 457 visa allows employers to sponsor skilled foreign workers for a period of between three months and four years. This program has been widely used to fill skilled labor market gaps in agriculture, mining, tourism, and manufacturing (Davies *et al.*, 2009), with 90 percent of all visas granted in 2010/2011 for farm work. The WHM visa permits young people aged 18–30 to travel, work, and study in Australia for up to 12 months. Following major revisions to the WHM program in 2005, visa holders are permitted a second visa providing they undertake specific work in a rural area for at least three months during their first visa. The 'specific work' is broadly categorized as involvement in plant and animal cultivation, fishing and pearling, tree farming and felling, mining, and construction (Tan and Lester, 2012). In 2013/2014, a total of 239,592 WHM visas were granted; over double the 2005/2006 level (DIBP, 2014b). In the context of the long-term evaporation of most rural regions' 'floating pools' of agricultural labor, WHM visa holders have come to form a vital component of Australia's seasonal fruit and vegetable harvest workforce (Hanson and Bell, 2007). The Australian farmers' peak organization, the National Farmers Federation (NFF), has praised the WHM program for enabling farmers to harvest food and fiber commodities in a timely manner (NFF, 2011).

Arguably, though, Australian farmers' increasing dependence on the WHM has effectively counteracted the development of a more reliable and robustly regulated temporary agricultural laborer migration scheme: one that meets domestic farmers' needs for an inexpensive and reliable means of harvesting crops *and* safeguards workers' rights and conditions regardless of the variety of places they undertake employment (Hugo, 2009). In spite of the undoubted success of the WHM scheme, seasonal labor shortages are a persistent (if sporadic) feature of many horticultural regions in Australia. As an indication of the underlying strength of labor demand in the industry, horticultural sector employment grew by 40 percent between 1993 and 2003 to reach 68,000 (Ball, 2010 p. 118). Partly in response to this ongoing structural (spatial) labor market mismatch, and partly in response to persistent Pacific Island nation demands for freer access to such work in Australia and New Zealand, a Pacific Seasonal Workers Pilot Scheme (PSWPS) was introduced for Australia in 2009.

The PSWPS was substantially modelled on the generally well-credentialed New Zealand Recognised Seasonal Employer Scheme (RSE) (Hammond and Connell, 2009; Hugo, 2009). The PSWPS emerged following the signing of the Pacific Islands Countries Trade Agreement (PICTA) (Ball, 2010) and marked something of a 'sea change' in Australia's diplomatic and economic engagement with a neighboring region; one which it had long been accused of treating with contempt at worst and, at best, benign neglect (Hawksley, 2009). At its philosophical core, the PSWPS aimed to facilitate the economic and social development of both the labor-receiving regions and the labor-sending communities and regions. Initially, the scheme envisaged the recruitment of up to 2,500 Pacific Islanders (i.e. residents of Tonga, Vanuatu, Kiribati, and Papua New Guinea) to work as fruit pickers and pruners in Australian orchards and vineyards between mid-2009 to mid-2012 (Ball, 2010). The capacity of the PSWPS to help achieve UN Millennium Goals in labor-donor regions and communities is underscored by UN development data on Tonga, the nation that accounted for the vast majority of PSWPS visas (Gibson and McKenzie, 2011). In 2009, just under a quarter of the country's population was living below the basic needs poverty line, with approximately half of national GDP attributable to remittances (UNDP, 2010). As discussed below, Tongan migrants now form a vital component of the workforce at Costa's tomato glasshouse facility in Guyra.

The Emergent Multiscalar Labor Geographies of the Northern Statistical Division

In this penultimate section, the discussion focuses on the emerging interlinkages between the changing shape and size of the rural labor force, on the one hand, and dramatic changes in the regulation of industrial relations and in Australia's immigration program, on the other, in the case study of the NSW Northern SD. This discussion moves through a brief consideration of on-farm labor dynamics in the Northern SD before outlining the changing level of international labor migration into the region following the reformulation of the national immigration program. The region's own experiences of the PSWP are then considered via an examination of the Costa Group's involvement in this scheme.

In the NSW Northern Tablelands' transition from the productivist era to that of the multifunctional countryside (Holmes, 2006) on the average employment per farm changed remarkably little, fluctuating over the early 1960s to the early 1990s from just over two workers—including, in most cases, an owner/manager—to just over one-and-a-half workers (in 1991). Of course, the stability of this ratio was affected by the ongoing drop in farm numbers which occurred over the three decades. Research conducted on the changing economic and social relationships between Northern SD (specifically Inverell and Guyra) farmers during the mid-2000s (see Pritchard *et al.*, 2012) revealed that in 2006/2007 paid external labor comprised about one-third of all farm labor inputs. While Inverell and Guyra farmers' use of paid employees had increased over the previous five years, with the number of full-time paid employees doubling, most farms relied primarily on family labor, chiefly the owner(s). The increased use of paid workers on the case study farms was largely attributable to the rapid aging of farm owners and managers and their consequent need for younger and more physically able bodies to manage day-to-day farm tasks.

However, as highlighted in Chapter 2, agriculture is no longer the dominant employer in the Northern SD. Other industries in the region have also experienced periodic labor shortages and forced (or permitted at least) local businesses to source skilled migrants via the temporary and permanent components of the skilled migration program. Figure 6.3 shows the number of temporary labor visa applications supported by employers (and state government) in the Northern SD for the period 2007–2014. An obvious feature of Figure 6.3 is the dramatic fluctuation in numbers following the rapid growth from 2007 to 2010. By and large, these are explained by the tightening of eligibility conditions by the Federal Department. Visa applications were to a variety of skilled migration programs though employer and state government nominated and RSMS categories account for the vast majority (RDA— NI, 2015). While not all applications result in actual skilled worker arrivals in the region, over 2013–2014 approximately three-quarters of applicants join the Northern SD workforce (RDA—NI, 2015). Migrants come from a diverse set of mainly non-English speaking countries, including India, Brazil, Philippines, Japan, and Korea. The occupations that these migrants are recruited to fill are also quite varied. Metal trades and basic farm work categories are dominant though services sector occupations (e.g. chefs, hairdressers) have also been nominated in relatively large numbers (RDA—NI, 2012; Argent and Tonts, 2015). However, it is important not to overstate the likely potential economic, demographic, and sociocultural impact of these inflows: the aggregate number of labor immigrants since 2007 amounts to just over 1 percent of the region's total labor force.

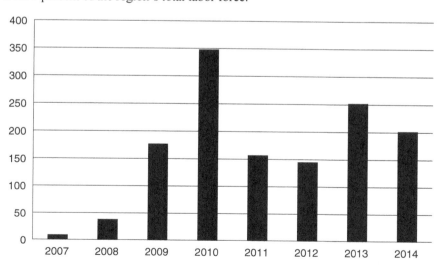

Figure 6.3 Temporary Labor Visa Applications, Northern Statistical Division, 2007–2014.
Source: RDA—NI (2012, 2015).

The Pacific Islands Seasonal Worker Scheme (PSWS), discussed above, has proved to be a further important source of international workers for the Northern SD, specifically Costa's fresh tomato production facility at Guyra. With 30 hectares of production under glass—the largest facility of its type in the southern hemisphere—Costa grows three different types of tomato at Guyra, supplying the major Australian supermarket chains of Woolworths, Coles, and Aldi. Just as the Guyra operations have rapidly expanded spatially (from five hectares in 2009) and in production terms (Argent *et al.*, 2010), so its demand for labor has also grown. From a workforce of 70 in 2009, the newly expanded facility currently employs 600 staff though levels do fluctuate from due to production cycles. Historically heavily dependent on wool production and livestock grazing, Guyra experienced a series of economic and demographic crises during the 1990s, from the withdrawal of the wool reserve floor price scheme to the closure of the local abattoir (Argent *et al.*, 2010). Therefore, Costa's arrival and ongoing growth has been a tremendous boon for the town. However, even with a minimum employment of 350 workers, 40 percent of whom are local Guyra residents (interview with current general manager, 2015), the local and broader regional labor market has struggled to meet Costa's labor requirements, even with the University of New England and its relatively large student population lying only 30 kilometers to the south of Guyra. It was in this context that Costa chose to become involved in the PSWS for its Guyra operations in 2013 (interview with former Costa Guyra production facility manager, 2014).

For seven months of each year since joining the PSWS, Costa at Guyra host between 70 and 100 Tongan men and women to work in the tomato glasshouses in the manual tasks of, inter alia, training and harvesting tomatoes. A local Guyra employment agency, Speedie Staff Solutions, has the responsibility of managing the recruitment of the Tongan workers, including organizing airfares, housing, and remuneration (*The Guyra Argus*, 2013; interview with former Costa Guyra production facility manager, 2014). In a town (and a region) well renowned for its frosty winters and still strong Anglo-Celtic cultural heritage (93 percent of Guyra residents were born in Australia or other mainly English-speaking countries at the 2011 census (ABS, 2012b)), the social and cultural settlement of this group in the community has been of utmost importance (interview with former Costa Guyra production facility manager, 2014). By and large, the settlement process, including work satisfaction, could be seen as a success, with 90 percent of workers returning the following year (interview with current general manager, 2015). This is also importantly economically for Costa as each returned worker is money saved on training.

Conclusion

This chapter has charted the substantial shifts in the Australian rural workforce and labor market over the twentieth and twenty-first centuries in the context of ongoing changes in important national institutions. Continual reform of the national and state industrial relations systems as part of the uneven process of neoliberalization has irrevocably changed the ground rules for the establishment of pay and conditions in Australian workplaces in spite of the ongoing Constitutional requirement for an independent central 'umpire' to provide arbitration. Over this period of reform, other changes in the national economy and society have seen levels of unionization decline markedly. As noted in this chapter, though, collective labor representative arrangements have had only a fairly meagre presence and influence on workplaces in rural Australia since the 1970s even though levels of representation are higher in some industry sectors than in others.

A key argument of this chapter has been that Australian and Northern SD farmers' embrace of technology as part of the inbuilt drive for greater economies of scale has helped create something of a structural crisis in the supply of rural labor, and in the social and economic viability of rural communities more broadly. Like many other inland, (somewhat) agriculturally dependent regions, the Northern SD has experienced demographic decline over recent decades as young people have left for brighter futures elsewhere. The aging communities left behind have consequently struggled to both create and fill employment. As also noted, though, similar structural problems exist in other regions and industries and a radically reformed immigration policy—with a far greater emphasis on temporary labor migration—has been one of the solutions. The advent of a guest worker-type scheme—the first of its kind in Australia—was developed in 2012 in recognition of the specific problems faced by Australian farmers at harvest time. Northern SD businesses have availed themselves of these programs in order to maintain or even grow their operations. Debate continues throughout Australian society over the relative merits of training 'born-and-bred' local residents for emerging job vacancies as against hiring suitably trained and experienced temporary foreign labor. In the case of Guyra and Costa's tomato production facility, itself a remarkable success story in an otherwise declining community, labor mobility has been used as a tool for enhanced local rural development in both labor-sending and labor-receiving regions.

References

ABS (Australian Bureau of Statistics). 2010a. *Labour market statistics, July 2010*, Cat. No. 6105.0. Belconnen, Australia: Australian Bureau of Statistics.

ABS (Australian Bureau of Statistics). 2010b. One for the country: Recent trends in fertility. *Australian social trends*, Cat. No. 4102.0. Belconnen, Australia: Australian Bureau of Statistics.

ABS (Australian Bureau of Statistics). 2012a. Australian farming and farmers, *Australian social trends December 2012*, Cat. No, 4102.0. Belconnen, Australia: Australian Bureau of Statistics.

ABS (Australian Bureau of Statistics). 2012b. *2011 census of population and housing-time series profile, Guyra*, Cat. No, 2003.0. Belconnen, Australia: Australian Bureau of Statistics.

Argent, N. and Tonts, M. 2015. A multicultural and multifunctional countryside? International labour migration and Australia's productivist heartlands, *Population, Space and Place* 21: 140–156.

Argent, N. and Walmsley, D. 2008. Rural youth migration trends in Australia: An overview of recent trends and two inland case studies, *Geographical Research* 46: 139–152.

Argent, N., Smailes, P., and Griffin, T. 2015. Migration and ageing processes in non-metropolitan Australia: An analysis of thirty years of dramatic change. In T. Wilson, E. Charles-Edwards, and M. Bell (eds.), *Demography for planning and policy: Australian case studies* (pp. 133–154). Dordrecht: Springer.

Argent, N., Walmsley, D., and Sorensen, A. 2010. Something old, something new, something borrowed, something…? Rediscovering the comparative advantage of the 'new' pastoral economies of northern New South Wales, Australia. In G. Halseth, S. Markey, and W. Reimer (eds.), *The next rural economies: Constructing rural place in global economies* (pp. 17–31). Wallingford: CABI Publishing.

Australian Government. 2010. *Australia to 2050: Future challenges* (the 2010 Intergenerational Report). Canberra, Australia: Parliament of Australia. Downloadable from: www.treasury.gov.au/igr/.

Azarias, J., Lambert, J., McDonald, P., and Malyon, K. 2014. *Robust new foundations: A streamlined, transparent and responsive system for the 457 programme.* Canberra, Australia: Department of Immigration and Border Protection.

Ball, R. 2010. Australia's Pacific Seasonal Worker Pilot Scheme and its interface with the Australian horticultural labour market: Is it time to refine the policy? *Pacific Economic Bulletin* 25: 114–130.

Bell, M. 1996. *Understanding internal migration.* Canberra, Australia: Bureau of Immigration, Multicultural and Population Research Monograph, AGPS.

Bowden, B. 2011. The rise and decline of Australian unionism: A history of industrial labour from the 1820s to 2010, *Labour History* 100: 51–82.

Burnley, I. 2001. *The impact of immigration on Australia: A demographic approach.* Melbourne, Australia: Oxford University Press.

Castles, S. and Miller, M. 2009. *The age of migration: International population movements in the modern world.* 4th edition. Basingstoke: Palgrave Macmillan.

Clark, M. 1993. *Manning Clark's history of Australia*, abr. M. Cathcart. Carlton South, Australia: Melbourne University Press.

Crowley, F. 1974. 1901–14. In F. Crowley (ed.), *A new history of Australia* (pp. 261–311). Richmond, Australia: William Heinemann Australia.

Dabscheck, B. 1994. The arbitration system since 1967. In B. Head and S. Bell (eds.), *State, economy and public policy in Australia* (pp. 142–168). Richmond, Australia: Heinemann Australia.

DAFF (Department of Agriculture, Fisheries and Forestry). 2009. Workforce, training and skills issues in agriculture. A report to the Primary Industries Ministerial Council by the Industries Development Committee Workforce, Training and Skills Working Group. Canberra, Australia: Department of Agriculture, Fisheries and Forestry.

Davies, A. and James, A. 2011. *Geographies of ageing: Social processes and the spatial unevenness of ageing.* Farnham: Ashgate Publishing.

Davies, A., Tonts, M., Troy, L., and Pelusey, H. 2009. *Australia's rural workforce: An analysis of labour shortages in rural Australia.* Canberra, Australia: Rural Industries Research and Development Corporation.

de Garis, B. 1974. 1890–1900. In F. Crowley (ed.), *A new history of Australia* (pp. 216–259). Richmond: William Heinemann Australia.

DIAC (Department of Immigration and Citizenship). 2012. *Population flows: Immigration aspects, 2010–2011*. Belconnen, Australia: Department of Immigration and Citizenship.

DIBP (Department of Immigration and Border Protection). 2014a. *Discussion paper: Reviewing the skilled migration and 400 series visa programmes*. Belconnen, Australia: Department of Immigration and Border Protection.

DIBP (Department of Immigration and Border Protection). 2014b. *Australia's migration trends, 2013–14*. Belconnen, Australia: Department of Immigration and Border Protection.

Dufty-Jones, R., Argent, N., Walmsley, D., and Rolley, F. 2014. The role of gender in the migration practices and aspirations of Australian rural youth. In J. Connell and R. Dufty-Jones (eds.), *Rural change in Australia* (pp. 25–41). Farnham: Ashgate Publishing.

Ellem, B. 2003. New unionism in the old economy: Community and collectivism in the Pilbara's mining towns, *The Journal of Industrial Relations* 45: 423–441.

Ellem, B. 2006. Scaling labour: Australian unions and global mining, *Work, Employment and Society* 20: 369–387.

Emy, H. and Hughes, O. 1991. *Australian politics: Realities in conflict*, 2nd edition. South Melbourne, Australia: Macmillan.

Fagan, R. and Webber, M. 1999. *Global restructuring: The Australian experience*, 2nd edition. South Melbourne, Australia: Oxford University Press.

Gibson, J. and McKenzie, D. 2011. Australia's Pacific Seasonal Worker Pilot Scheme (PSWPS): Development impacts in the first two years, *Working Paper in Economics* 09/011. Hamilton, New Zealand: Department of Economics, University of Waikato.

Hammond, J. and Connell, J. 2009. The new blackbirds? Vanuatu guestworkers in New Zealand, *New Zealand Geographer* 65: 201–210.

Hanson, J. and Bell, M. 2007. Harvest trails in Australia: Patterns of seasonal migration in the fruit and the vegetable industry, *Journal of Rural Studies* 23: 101–117.

Hawksley, C. 2009. Australia's aid diplomacy and the Pacific Islands: Change and continuity in middle power foreign policy, *Global Change, Peace and Security* 21: 115–130.

Holmes, J. 2006. Impulses towards a multifunctional transition in rural Australia: Gaps in the research agenda, *Journal of Rural Studies* 22: 142–160.

Hugo, G. 1996. Global mobility. In P. Newton and M. Bell (eds.), *Population shift: Mobility and change in Australia* (pp. 24–38). Canberra, Australia: Australian Government Publishing Service.

Hugo, G. 2008. Immigrant settlement outside of Australia's capital cities, *Population, Space and Place* 14: 553–571.

Hugo, G. 2009. Best practice in temporary labour migration for development: A perspective from Asia and the Pacific, *International Migration* 47: 23–74.

Irving, T. 1974. 1850–70. In F. Crowley (ed.), *A new history of Australia* (pp. 124–164). Richmond, Australia: William Heinemann Australia.

Lewis, D. 2005. Greener pastures, *Sydney Morning Herald* (pp. 21, 26), October 1.

Linge, G. 1988. Australian space and global space. In R. Heathcote and J. Mabbut (eds.), *Land, water and people: Geographical essays in Australian resource management* (pp. 239–260). Sydney, Australia: Allen and Unwin.

McGuirk, P. and Argent, N. 2011. Population growth and change: Implications for Australia's cities and regions, *Geographical Research* 49: 317–335.

McIntyre, S. 2009. *A concise history of Australia*, 3rd edition. Cambridge: Cambridge University Press.

National Farmers' Federation. 2011. *Pacific Island seasonal workers scheme achieves permanency, Media Release*, December 19. Canberra, Australia: National Farmers' Federation.

O'Neill, P. and Argent, N. 2005. Neoliberalism in antipodean spaces and times: An introduction to the special themed issue, *Geographical Research* 43: 2–8.

Phillips, J. and Spinks, H. 2012. *Skilled migration: Temporary and permanent flows to Australia*, Background note. Canberra, Australia: Department of Parliamentary Services, Parliament of Australia.

Pritchard, W., Argent, N., Baum, S., Bourke, L., Martin, J., McManus, P., Sorensen, A., and Walmsley, D. 2012. Local-if-possible: How the spatial networking of economic relations amongst farm enterprises aids small town survival in rural Australia, *Regional Studies* 46: 539–557.

RDA—NI (Regional Development Australia—Northern Inland). 2012. Confidential regional labour migration data report. Armidale, Australia: RDA—NI.

RDA—NI (Regional Development Australia—Northern Inland). 2015. Confidential regional labour migration data report. Armidale, Australia: RDA—NI.

Stockdale, A. 2011. A review of demographic ageing in the UK: Opportunities for rural research, *Population, Space and Place* 17: 204–221.

Tan, Y. and Lester, L. 2012. Labour market and economic impacts of international working holiday temporary migrants to Australia, *Population, Space and Place* 18: 359–383.

The Guyra Argus. 2013 Jobs contract put local focus on workers' needs, *The Guyra Argus*, February 14 2013. Available online at: www.guyraargus.com.au/story/1308935/jobs-contract-put-local-focus-on-workers-needs/. Accessed December 21, 2015.

Tonts, M. and Atherley, K. 2005. Rural restructuring and the changing geography of competitive sport, *Australian Geographer* 36: 125–144.

UNDP (United Nations Development Programme). 2010. *Second national millennium development goals report: Tonga*. Ministry of Finance and National Planning.

Walmsley, D., Argent, N., Rolley, F., and Tonts, M. 2006. Inland Australia. Paper presented at the Academy of the Social Sciences in Australian Symposium Australians on the Move: Internal Migration in Australia, December 2006.

Woods, M. 2007. Engaging the global countryside: Globalization, hybridity and the reconstitution of rural place, *Progress in Human Geography* 31: 485–507.

7 Contentious Flexibility

Job Losses in Labor Restructuring in Mackenzie, British Columbia

Greg Halseth, Laura Ryser, and Sean Markey

Introduction

Just as the forest industry in British Columbia's central interior has been changing over the past 40 years, so too has the organization of labor. This chapter explores how new labor arrangements are being put in place across the region. After this introduction, the first section explores changing employment levels, especially the pattern of job losses following the early 1980s global economic recession. The next section explores changing industrial relations and the transformation of union representation. The third section provides a case study of Mackenzie with special attention to a significant strike in the late 1990s over the question of job flexibility. The chapter wraps up with a contemporary look at the competition for labor in the natural resource sector.

As noted in Chapter 3, in order to explore the restructuring of the central interior forest industry, we conducted key informant interviews with 14 people who had extensive experience in the region's forest industry dating back to the 1970s. Interviews were recorded and transcribed, and the transcripts were checked by participants for accuracy and clarity. Latent and manifest content analysis was then used to compile themes from the data (Krippendorff and Bock, 2009; Andersen and Svensson, 2012).

Employment

Through much of its postwar history, the forest industry has provided tremendous employment opportunities. Markey *et al.* (2012 p. 87) describe how industrial expansion and an emphasis on low-skill manual labor created attractive conditions for new immigrants and other workers:

> Through the 1950s and 1960s, the provincial government followed a coordinated public policy approach based on a model of industrial resource development (Williston and Keller, 1997). This led to twenty-five to thirty years of rapid economic and community growth across the region (Halseth *et al.*, 2004). New communities and high quality local infrastructure were the backbone of industrial centres drawing from the province's rich resource base

(Horne and Penner, 1992). This resource industry growth was instrumental in creating a wealthy province and in transforming BC's urban and rural economies alike.

Prior to this period of civic and industrial investment, BC was a 'have-not' province within the Canadian federation, meaning that the province relied on the federal government for transfer payments to meet basic public service requirements. The boom created by the demand for resources during World War Two was an exception; prior to the war, the economic status of the province suffered because of its small and relatively inefficient resource sector. While being quite entrepreneurial, the resource sector (mainly forestry) lacked scale, generated few secondary and support industries, and contributed relatively little wealth (that was subject to wide fluctuations) to provincial coffers (Marchak, 1983; Hayter, 2000). In its hinterland regions, the province had poorly developed community and industrial infrastructure and, as a result, was not experiencing either economic or population growth.

More than 40 years later, these interior and northern hinterland regions are undergoing a second round of transformation. Since the 1980s, pressures from social, economic, and political restructuring have changed the way resource industries operate, and these changes have affected the demographic structure of non-metropolitan BC (Halseth *et al.*, 2004). Hayter (2000) describes how pressures from environmental debates, consumer demands for more specialized products, continuing demands for low-cost products, international trade disputes, increasing relative labor costs, and increasing competition from low-cost global competitors are pushing forest companies to focus on progressively leaner production techniques. While technological innovation in the forest sector has always been a factor in downward employment pressure, the intensification of competitive pressures after the 1980s recession accelerated the substitution of capital for labor as the industry made increasing efficiency the driver of change.

Background

In the BC central interior, the industrial expansion of the 1960s and 1970s created opportunities for young workers who were part of the baby-boom generation, and who were just starting to graduate from high school. As one participant told us:

> Basically it was pretty good when I got in, that's why people got in and it kept getting better because there was huge competition for labor back in the '70s and early '80s. The wages, the benefits, that sort of stuff, they were good. And the other good thing is it wasn't a camp job. You got home every day and you saw your wife and kids. If your wife didn't want to work, she didn't have to. You could make enough money and you could buy a house and buy a car and have some toys and stuff like that, on a single income. It was good.
>
> (Participant P1, 2013)

Even within management, people were pursuing opportunities that seemed to set the stage for long-term careers within the same company. Length of tenure was one of the hallmarks for companies that recognized the value of good workers to support reliable operations. This was reinforced by one participant who explained:

> There's a board of directors who are responsible to the shareholders. There weren't too many companies like that in the start of the 1970s. In the lumber business, most of them were family companies. They would have a logging manager, for instance, and had some crews of their own. Sometimes, they had a combination of some crews of their own and some contractors. And generally, though, that logging manager probably worked with that company for twenty years. Might have been his whole working career. So I think there was quite a bit of stability.

> (Participant P2, 2013)

In the period leading up to the 1980s economic recession, job growth and new construction of industrial mills was the norm for BC's forest industry. Young workers flocked to the region and its many opportunities to build a livelihood and career. Single workers, however, often changed jobs quite routinely in this 'job rich' environment. This negatively impacted the efficiency of harvesting and processing operations. As a result, industry turned to recruiting young married workers as part of strategy to bring stability to their labor force—and in turn, to the local community.

Capital Investment and Job Losses

The 1980s recession, however, turned around the industry's employment trajectories. As described by Hayter (2000 p. 264), the growth in jobs for young workers was now replaced by "the problem of forced layoffs of older, married workers and managers with families." In 1979, the BC forest products industry employed approximately 97,000 people. By 1982, that employment had fallen to approximately 75,000 people (Hayter, 2000). In the years since, the industry has never significantly recovered employment growth. Additional production has been met through increased automation and other production efficiencies. The adoption of flat management structures have also resulted in significant job losses on the nonproduction side of the forest industry.

Tables 7.1 and 7.2 track the long-run impacts of labor changes over time (1950 to 1995). Table 7.1 includes harvest and employment data from 1950 to 1995. The increasing efficiency of the industry over time is readily apparent. Over the 45-year period, the forest harvest increased from 23.4 million m³ to 76.5 million m³, a growth of 227 percent. Over the same period, employment in wood products manufacturing only increased from 34,000 to 41,000 workers (or 20.6 percent). In the pulp and paper sector, employment increased from 6,000 to 17,000 workers (183.3 percent). This growth is less remarkable when one considers the significant number of new pulp and paper mills added in the late 1960s and early 1970s in the interior of the province.

Overall, the employment picture is more bleak. In 1965, total forest industry employment was about 73,000; in 1980, it had reached 96,000. The global economic recession of the early 1980s, and the efficiency and job cutting efforts that came afterward, had the workforce back to 77,000 in 1995.

Table 7.2 uses the same data as Table 7.1, only the employment numbers are converted to a ratio of the number of employees per 1,000 m³ of forest harvest. The drive toward industry efficiency is clearly seen. Even though the harvest in 1995 was just about double the harvest in the early 1960s, it produced only 1.01 jobs per 1,000 m³ compared to 1.69 jobs 30 years earlier.

Table 7.1 Employment in the British Columbia Forest Industry (Numbers of Employees)

| Year | Harvest | | | | |
	('000 m³)[1]	*Logging[2]*	*Wood[3]*	*P & A[4]*	*Total*
1950	23,408	n/a	34,439	6,155	n/a
1955	29,280	n/a	41,434	8,640	n/a
1960	33,975	n/a	37,202	10,409	n/a
1965	43,413	18,746	40,499	14,176	73,421
1970	54,726	18,581	38,329	17,089	73,999
1975	50,077	18,046	38,655	20,225	76,926
1980	74,654	24,784	49,708	21,540	96,032
1985	76,868	21,870	39,603	16,850	78,323
1990	78,316	19,753	40,312	18,427	78,492
1995	76,471	18,655	41,068	17,631	77,354

Source: BC Ministry of Forests (2014a, 2014b).

Notes
1 m³ = cubic meters.
2 Employment for logging includes working owners and partners for the years 1975 and later.
3 Wood = wood industries.
4 P & A = paper and allied industries.

Table 7.2 Employment in the Forest Industry in British Columbia (Employees/1,000 m³)

| Year | Harvest | | | | |
	('000 m³)[1]	*Logging[2]*	*Wood[3]*	*P & A[4]*	*Total*
1950	23,408	n/a	1.47	0.26	n/a
1955	29,280	n/a	1.42	0.30	n/a
1960	33,975	n/a	1.09	0.31	n/a
1965	43,413	0.43	0.93	0.33	1.69
1970	54,726	0.34	0.70	0.31	1.35
1975	50,077	0.36	0.77	0.40	1.54
1980	74,654	0.33	0.67	0.29	1.29
1985	76,868	0.28	0.52	0.22	1.02
1990	78,316	0.25	0.51	0.24	1.00
1995	76,471	0.24	0.54	0.23	1.01

Source: BC Ministry of Forests (2014a, 2014b).

Notes:
1 m³ = cubic meters.
2 Employment for logging includes working owners and partners for the years 1975 and later.
3 Wood = wood industries.
4 P & A = paper and allied industries.

If we look at employment by sector, the logging sector shifted from 0.43 jobs per 1,000 m³ in 1960 to 0.24 in 1995. Just as dramatic efficiency gains were seen in the wood products manufacturing sector, where employment went from 1.47 jobs per 1,000 m³ in 1950 to 0.54 in 1995. With fluctuations, only the pulp and paper sector had not seen significant employment efficiencies from 1950 to 1995. Such efficiencies would await the application of computer-based monitoring and management systems in the late 1990s and the early 2000s.

Changes in technology and infrastructure have been a significant part of the industry's history. A number of interviewees noted that this increased after 1980. Automation was the key, especially automated saw adjustments for different size logs. When linked to computers, the mill could also be tasked to maximize particularly high-value lumber sizes depending upon changing market conditions. Interviewees noted:

> The employment? Well of course, the way technology has developed, people are just way more productive, whether they're working in the office, or working in planning, doing mapping, it's all done by computers now. If you're on a machine harvesting logs, your essential equipment's run by a computer in the machine. It's so much more productive now. When forestry started, and the railroad came in, and workers came in the hundreds around 1914 to Prince George … and everything was labor. You'd cut the trees by hand, you'd skid them out of the forest, you'd lift them into the sawmill, you'd lift the lumber by hand onto the truck … it was all manual. And that's a long time ago, but it kind of evolved from that, but the advent of computers in the workplace, it's just so much more efficient.
>
> (Participant P5, 2013)

> They are making a whole lot more wood with a whole lot fewer people. So they're good paying jobs and that sort of stuff, but in terms of numbers, it's not like it used to be.
>
> (Participant P1, 2013)

The post-1980 period saw an intensified substitution of capital for labor. In addition to the market pressures driving this transformation, industry was positioned to take advantage of the increasing application of computer-based technologies. As two different participants explained:

> Some of the retrofits of the equipment posed quite a challenge to employees who were used to much more simplistic processes. But they tend to catch on. I'll give you an example. There used to be in the primary breakdown part of the sawmill was what was called a chip'n saw, and they'd take the log and basically, orient it the same way, and feed it through the machine in a manner that wasn't always sophisticated … by size settings and stripped a certain amount of the log based on a visual perception on what was optimal. Now all

that is done from scanners and optimization computers, so that there is a high value extracted out of every log.

(Participant P6, 2013)

In the late 1990s, the mills embarked on a huge modernization. We put in a whole new control system. We went from old pneumatic controls, to all electronic, and the computers started running the mills. And of course, the production went up, quality went up. But [we needed fewer] operators, they became overseers. We reconfigured ourselves. Between the two mills, we took out 36 positions of operators, which was unheard of. And then in 2000, we went into the maintenance department and downsized it by doing it smarter, learning from other people on how to maintain things better instead of being in a kind of break down mode, or emergency thing. It had become planned and predicted maintenance and cost control, and better purchasing. So everything began to be looked at, and in the end, it was 30 percent of the workforce.

(Participant P14, 2013)

More recently, the mountain pine beetle infestation is having an impact on employment levels. The mountain pine beetle is a bark beetle endemic to BC's Lodgepole pine forests. Its natural growth and regeneration cycle is usually held in check by cold winter temperatures. Traditionally, the beetles attack over-matured pine and kill the trees as they eat the layers that move nutrients between the roots and the needles. As will be detailed below, the mountain pine beetle infestation is resulting in a long-term reduction in the volume of forest harvest. Plant closures mean job losses. In late 2013, the central interior's two largest companies, Canfor and West Fraser, closed competing sawmills in two small towns and transferred their timber harvesting rights around those towns to the other company. Reducing from two firms and two mills in each town leaves some opportunity for the remaining firm and mill to be viable:

"The timber availability in the Quesnel region following the mountain pine beetle infestation unfortunately leaves us unable to continue operation of our Quesnel sawmill," said Don Kayne, President and CEO of Canfor Corporation. "The additional fibre we have been able to secure in the exchange agreement with West Fraser enhances the fibre requirements for our Houston facility."

(Canfor, 2013)

Labor Relations

The transformation of employment occurred against the backdrop of transformation in labor relations. By the 1970s, the majority of forest product manufacturing was under the direction of large companies. Within these companies, two general approaches to labor management were common practice. For harvesting and log transportation, the industry relied upon the use of contractors. This created a degree of flexibility and also competition between contractors to assist with managing costs. On the manufacturing side, in the sawmills, pulp mills, and other plants, labor was organized by industrial unions.

Industry

On the corporate side, one of the ongoing challenges around labor relations and labor negotiations concerns how to account for the unique circumstances of individual operations within a broader framework where workers will move between companies and sectors if they perceive a significant difference in wages and benefits. One of the results has been the creation of industry bargaining associations (Bernsohn, 1981). While there has always been some sectoral organization to such bargaining associations; at different times, these associations have been province-wide while at other times they have been more regional.

Master contract negotiations:

> were standard practice between industry and woodworkers through FIR [Forest Industrial Relations], and between industry and pulp unions through the Pulp Bureau. FIR bargained for all coastal employers in the logging and wood-product sectors with a capable staff of negotiators and researchers. The organization comprised an executive committee made up of CEOs of both large and small companies, and a caucus of industrial relations experts from the industry. Parallel structure existed of the Pulp Bureau, a provincial body for all the pulp mills in the province. Similar regional organizations provided support for the BC Interior.
>
> (Bentley, 2012 p. 231–232)

One such regional organization was the Council of Northern Interior Forest Employment Relations (Conifer). Conifer is a non-profit society established in 1985. It was formerly known as the North Cariboo Forest Labour Relations Association. That association was formed in 1972:

> Conifer originated here in the early 1970s. Formerly, it had been a division of what was called the Northern Interior Lumberman's Association, which is now COFI [Council of Forest Industries]. The mandate of Conifer is a voluntary association, what is called a non-accredited association. It basically works for a number of companies at their request to support a negotiation of collective agreements on their behalf and the administration of those agreements, and that really hasn't changed.
>
> (Participant P6, 2013)

Conifer is a central interior forest industry based organization. In addition to supporting labor relations and collective bargaining processes, Conifer also administers employment benefits plans that are part of the industry collective agreements with organized labor. In 2014, full membership companies included Ainsworth, Bid Construction, Carrier Lumber, Conifex, Dunkley Lumber, Excel

Transportation, Hampton Affiliates, Lakeland Mills, Northern Engineered Wood Products, Pacific BioEnergy, Parallel Wood Products, Tolko Industries, Stella-Jones, and West Fraser (Conifer, 2014). The collective agreements for these member companies involved about 2,500 unionized workers.

The 1970s and the 1980s were particularly difficult labor negotiations periods. The emphasis during these decades was primarily on wage rates and productivity. A significant set of strikes in the early 1980s, coincident with the global economic recession, was a critical part of the transformation of the industry. Drawing upon what had happened elsewhere, and a bit earlier, across other regions of Canada, the industry began to focus more upon job flexibility.

The tenor of negotiations very much reflected the personalities of the individuals at the bargaining table. In his biography of the company, longtime Canfor CEO Peter Bentley (2012 p. 226) describes his company's take on labor relations:

> We forged a working relationship over the years with the Canadian branch of the IWA, but our dealings with the pulp side of things were different. Two unions represented pulp and paper workers: The PPWC (Pulp, Paper and Woodworkers of Canada) and the CPU (Canadian Paperworkers Union), and they varied markedly in their respective leadership style and philosophy.

He also describes the honest and respectful working relationship he and Canfor came to develop with longtime IWA leader Jack Munro. Bentley (2012 p. 232) describes Munro as "an excellent negotiator, a likable guy, and a decent person."

The impact of what was going on elsewhere in their competitive environments also forced companies to look at a different approach to collective bargaining:

> I think in terms of the industry side, and the management side, collective bargaining, I think there's an increased sensitivity with respect to the competitive environment. That may have been to some degree, a reflection of the industry; but more recently, there's been an increased concern about what is really going on elsewhere in order to make appropriate decisions in collective bargaining in order to be competitive, especially with mining, the oil sands, oil and gas.
>
> (Participant P6, 2013)

Linked to the process of industrial restructuring, flexibility implies several key changes. The first is that the workforce receives wider training across a number of skill areas. The idea is that workers can do a wider range of jobs when they are on the shift. A second key change is that the shop floor is reorganized from assembly-line type job descriptions and work into a more team-based approach to production. As had already been seen earlier in the pulp and paper sector across Canada (Mackenzie and Norcliffe, 1997), the imposition of flexible wage agreements would mean job losses as companies sought to marry the efficiencies of computer-directed manufacturing processes with a smaller supporting workforce. As noted above, these changes happened coincident with the increasing application of new industrial technologies and set in place a long period where the industry reduced its workforce over time.

As a high-wage industry, with a relatively large workforce and making a significant contribution to the provincial economy, human-resource debates turned to issues of benefits and retention of highly skilled workers. As one participant noted:

> The benefits have become more complex. That's something that you can really comment about that's fundamentally changed in three decades to the point where benefits were almost unheard of. They were very limited back in the late 1970s, early 1980s, and now they're quite complex in their nature and their scope. The overall value that they bring to the employment relationship with respect to the employee is a lot more involved.
>
> (Participant P6, 2013)

As Bentley (2012 p. 238) describes, the industrial relations scene has "shifted dramatically with two major adjustments. One, we now bargain alone as a company rather than on an industry-wide basis. And two, we had moved away from annual negotiations and now tend to make multi-year contracts."

Labor Unions

In BC's single industry towns, both labor and capital are juxtaposed in close proximity and the workplace has been the principal site for conflict and contention (Marchak, 1983; Wilson, 1998). Historically, large companies tended to dominate all aspects of community life and there is a well-documented legacy of company town labor relations (Bedics and Doelker, 1992). For example, Mouat (1995) describes the early struggle for unionization within BC's Kootenay mining region during the 1895 to 1901 period. With capital and labor locked in a fight over who would control the terms of work, unions organized strike actions and owners hired strike-breakers. For both sides, success had a different calculus. Owners were content with a return on their investment and this was accomplished by bringing the mines back into production. The unions achieved legislative changes to limit the use of strike-breakers. In more remote places such as the copper mine and smelter complex at Anyox, on BC's north coast, the company responded to unionization drives and strike talk with violence backed by provincial constables (Loudon, 1992).

In many respects, the organization of labor with BC's forest industry had followed the wider North American story of labor organization. As Halseth and Sullivan suggest (2002 p. 104) "just as companies require a larger base of operations and support, so too are workers relying upon larger collective voices to assist them in negotiations for fair wage and benefits settlements." Hak (2007) provides an overview of labor organizing in the BC forest industry from 1934 to 1974. It is a story of capital and labor that also links places with the global economy. He describes in detail how the: "The history of the forest industry was worked out in the context of the ongoing interaction between capital and labour, which created and sustained a web of economic, social, and ideological relationships" (Hak, 2007 p. 4).

Through these relationships:

> Owners, workers, and managers were located in the impressive systems that link to the forests and towns of the province to markets and consumers around the globe. Complex institutions—corporations, unions, and markets— situated people in relationships with each other and with machines.
>
> (Hak, 2007 p. 2)

The interior industry, "which came into production in the Kootenays in the 1880s with the arrival of the Canadian Pacific Railway, and in the Northern Interior with the arrival of the Grand Trunk Pacific just before the First World War" (Hak, 2007 p. 34), was more difficult than the coastal industry to organize. Hak (2007 p. 32) describes how the "Interior did not have the geographic and economic cohesion of the coastal region, where the sea linked logging and milling centres. The Interior was divided into a number of subregions, each dominated by a few milling centres." In the central interior, geography presented even more acute challenges:

> Distance and transportation were problems. Mills and logging camps were strung out along the Canadian National Railway line for 200 kilometres to the east of Prince George. There was no road to these camps and communities, and in 1946 the train went each way only three days per week. For a worker attending a regional meeting in Prince George, this would mean the loss of two days of work.
>
> (Hak, 2007 p. 89)

But through the early years, there were many laborers, in the woods and in the mills. The emphasis upon labor was due to the relatively unsophisticated harvesting and production technologies of the day. In the woods, falling and bucking was done by axe or handsaw. Logs were moved by horse teams. In the mills, lumber was moved by hand. It was sorted, stacked for drying, unstacked, resorted, and then loaded onto railcars—all by hand. One interviewee recounted how he came to Prince George in the late 1950s,

> at the end of an era when horses still played a part in the sawmill and logging industry, and where many of the workers in the woods were farmers from the Prairies who arrived in the fall and returned in the spring.
>
> (Participant P15, 1999)

In these early years, two battles for the hearts and minds of labor were underway. The first was between organized labor and employers. The second was between rival labor unions. Bernsohn (1981) argues that World War Two was really the 'father' of unionization in BC's central interior forest sector. The significant growth in activity, and the demands for labor that the increased activity created, brought many to debate working conditions in both the woods and the mills:

> The hot stove league in the camps debated solutions to the problems of low wages and bad working conditions. Socialists, communists, new worlders, freethinkers, apprentice capitalists, and representatives from every other viewpoint had their say. This wasn't new, but the war brought a new mood: the bull sessions ended and the serious debate began. ... By 1944 the question wasn't whether the workers in the northern mills wanted a union, but which union they wanted.
>
> (Bernsohn, 1981 p. 51–52)

Against that backdrop, the International Woodworkers of America (IWA) sent representatives to the area. It was during the high employment years of World War Two that "both the IWA and the pulp and paper unions stepped up organizational activities, attempting to bring more workers into the fold. Second, unions, especially the IWA, sought an improved industrial relations act" (Hak, 2007 p. 75). While strength of numbers, and better legislation governing working conditions, strengthen the bargaining position of unions, the struggles were not easy. A significant strike covering most of the interior forest industry occurred in 1953–1954 (Bernsohn, 1981). In this showdown, Hak (2007 p. 67) describes how "employers wanted to crush the union, and the union, the International Woodworkers of America (IWA), was fighting for its life in the region."

But such conflicts have hidden a more fundamental tie between labor and capital:

> Dramatic strikes and lockouts too often represent the point of contact between capital and labour, obscuring the ongoing relations that bind them together in the production system. In the Fordist era, collective agreements formalized and structured relationships, but tension remained. In large companies, special industrial relations and personnel departments dealt with employee concerns, while smaller firms relied on persuasion and goodwill to maintain productive work sites.
>
> (Hak, 2007 p. 124)

Those immediate post-World War Two years also saw rivalries between labor unions and among the leadership of individual unions. As described by Hak (2007 p. 95):

> There were constant struggles between unions and within unions in the British Columbia forest industry. Best known is the battle to wrench control of the International Woodworkers of America (IWA) from its communist leadership in the late 1940s, but the resolution of this dispute did not end political dissension in the IWA. ... Raids induced workers to leave one union to join another.

Technological change accelerated after 1980, and especially after 2000.

> The main response of forest industry unions was to get more money for workers in the new jobs: "The generally accepted principle was that workers' earnings on new automated jobs must exceed those on their old jobs because of the increased productivity of the operation."
>
> (Hak, 2007 p. 166)

Another trend was for the unions to become increasingly focused within the mills themselves as logging and trucking operations continued a long trend toward the use of independent contractors. A one participant noted, "that was a big thing in terms of evolution of the union, it got more plant based and got out of the woods" (Participant P5, 2013). In the following sections, we continue our discussion of labor, focusing on workforce trends, negotiations, and how the scaling-up of companies in response to global competition resulted in corresponding changes to labor organizations.

Workforce Trends

The acceleration of earlier corporate concentration and production efficiency trends into the post-1980 period has had two significant implications for the workforce. The first is the obvious resulting reduction in the number of employees as detailed earlier. The second is workforce aging.

Workforce aging is a result of several structural processes acting together over time. To start, the very rapid expansion of the central interior forest industry during the post-World War Two period, and especially during the 1960s and 1970s, created a large demand for labor. Young workers flocked to these new opportunities. This relatively young workforce became engaged in wood manufacturing sectors that featured high levels of unionization. In addition to wages and benefits, unions also provided measures around job protection. A key protective feature practice in job protection is that if layoffs occurred, they would occur in reverse seniority order. In colloquial terms, the 'last hired would be the first fired.' As the industry has increased efficiencies and reduced the size of its workforce, older and experienced workers remained in place while younger entrants to the industry were often the ones laid off. The result has been that the workforce has been aging in place (Hanlon and Halseth, 2005).

Using information from the 2012 annual report on the IWA-Forest Industry Pension Plan, we can see some of the implications of past workforce trends. Table 7.3 shows the age distribution of unionized workers currently active in the industry and members of the pension plan. Only 11 percent of the workforce is under 25 years of age, and only 25 percent is under 34 years of age. This is the complete opposite of what was seen in the 1960s and 1970s era of rapid expansion:

> The biggest change: demographics. When I came to town, I was a senior citizen. I was 28 years old. Seriously. I was working for guys 3–5 years

younger than me. Now, it used to be that if you saw grey hair, there was some grandparents in town. Now I would say the average age of the workforce in that pulp mill is probably pushing 50.

(Participant P1, 2013)

In the 2012 report, just over 58 percent of the workforce is 45 years or older, and 26 percent is 55 years or older.

Within the pension plan, particular attention is paid to the balance between working members and those on pension. As with all pension plans, viability over time depends upon the balance of past and current investments into the plan relative to current and future withdrawals. Table 7.4 lists approximate membership numbers for the IWA-Forest Industry Pension Plan between 1992 and 2012. The impacts of longer-term workforce trends are clearly seen. Active workers in the pension plan declined from approximately 38,000 in 1992 to 15,000 in 2012 (−60.5 percent). Over the same period, pensioners and beneficiaries increased from 20,000 to 25,000 (25 percent). There was also considerable growth in those eligible for a future pension, but no longer active in the industry.

Put more starkly, the 2012 IWA-Forest Industry Pension Plan report also shows the ratio of active-to-retired members (Table 7.5). The change in the ratio is quite dramatic. In 1992, annual pension plan payments amounted to about $95 million. In 2012, such payments amounted to about $215 million.

Table 7.3 Active Members by Age, 2012

Age	Percentage
Under age 25	11.0
Age 25–34	14.0
Age 35–44	16.5
Age 45–54	32.0
Age 55–64	25.0
Over age 64	1.5

Source: IWA-Forest Industry Pension Plan (2012).

Table 7.4 Approximate Membership Breakdown, IWA-Forest Industry Pension Plan, 1992–2012

Membership Type	1992	2002	2012
Active members	38,600	30,000	15,100
Pensioners and beneficiaries	15,000	20,000	25,300
Inactive members	18,000	24,000	29,200
Total	71,600	74,000	69,600

Source: IWA-Forest Industry Pension Plan (2012).

Table 7.5 Ratio of Active-to-Retired Members

Year	Ratio
1980	18 to 1
1990	3.5 to 1
2012	0.75 to 1

Source: IWA-Forest Industry Pension Plan (2012).

Negotiations

As the industry worked through significant restructuring, the approach to labor negotiations also changed. During the years of growth in the 1960s and 1970s, when there was still secure and dominant market access to the United States, one of the key tools that unions had in collective bargaining would be the withdrawal of their labor. If a strike action could have a significant impact upon corporate profitability or market share, companies would have a very real and immediate enticement to resolve contract negotiations.

However, the same global competitive pressures that were challenging companies were also being recognized by organized labor. Job losses, company bankruptcies, and continued uncertainty over market access to the United States all contributed to a rethinking of the relationship between organized labor and companies. This transformation from a sometimes combative to a more collaborative approach that recognizes the needs of both companies and labor, and that their successful future destinies are in fact intimately intertwined, was reflected in the observations from a number of interviewees:

> I think the unions understood that here's what's happening in the world and in our business. And we may not like it, but if we want to keep working we're going to have to do some things a little differently. The good point is, we haven't had a strike at the mills now since 1998 or something was the last strike they had. At one time, it was—for sure we had a strike every three years.
>
> (Participant P14, 2013)

> I think that there were some nasty strikes back in the early days. I think that it's really matured. There's no point in killing the goose that lays the golden egg, and the way things are now, all these big companies, all the major firms are public companies, and you know what's happening, so the ministries have been sitting down with unions negotiating these days, and they had a pretty good idea of what the business is doing and how it's doing.
>
> (Participant P5, 2013)

Scaling Up

As described in Chapter 3, one response to global competitive pressures was that companies worked to get bigger. They did this by purchasing competitors both within their region and in other strategic market areas. The pressures of restructuring worked a similar set of changes in labor organization. Two of the biggest transformations in BC's central interior involve the wood workers union and the pulp sector unions.

For decades during the growth era of BCs forest sector, the IWA was the labor power house in the wood products manufacturing sector. As described by Drushka (1998):

> The postwar labour shortage dramatically affected all the forest industries, perhaps more than other economic sectors. The entire economy was booming and there were jobs everywhere, so loggers and mill operators face stiff competition for workers. The situation had two immediate consequences for the industry. The first was the migration of the woods union, the International Woodworkers of America (IWA), into the BC Interior (p.129) … The second consequence of the postwar labour shortage was the mechanization of logging.
>
> (p.133)

As noted above, labor organization then concentrated, in the decades following, in the manufacturing facilities rather than the woods.

After the recession of the early 1980s, the industry downsized its labor force. Despite increasing harvest and production levels, efficiencies through the introduction of computer-managed manufacturing led to significant job losses through the existing unions. As a solution, they sought amalgamation with brother unions. In BC, the most dramatic change came when the IWA merged with the United Steelworkers Union (Steelworkers).

A sense of the scale of the contemporary Steelworkers union, and the rationale for scaling up labor organizations, are included in the union's history:

> The United Steelworkers at the beginning of the 21st Century barely resembles the mostly-male industrial union of the 1930s, '40s and '50s. But the increasing diversity of the membership has only strengthened the basic principles on which the union was founded. Workers employed in the steel industry and in mining—two of the union's traditional jurisdictions—total about 65,000, out of a total membership in Canada of 225,000. Steelworker members can be found in every sector of the economy—from factories to offices, to hospitals, university campuses, hotels, warehouses, bakeries, banks, transportation and communication workers and many more. More than 20 per cent of Steelworkers now are women, and there is a growing membership among visible minority workers.
>
> (United Steelworkers of Canada, 2014)

Of course, any transformation of the scale, whether it is on the corporate or the labor side, means adjustments—in terms of operations, politically, and even mentally. As one participant told us:

The biggest change, and the most powerful unions as far as the forest industry goes, is the IWA. And in 2004, and I would never have predicted it, they merged with the Steelworkers, and they became part of the Steelworkers. It's a huge adjustment. I mean even if you think about it, even the term steelworkers, for people involved in the manufacturing of wood products, it's a tough linkage. It's a big adjustment for them I think, and it's resulted in some degree of repercussions in the forest industry, adjusting to this new entity.

(Participant P6, 2013)

A similar process occurred with the pulp unions. One of the most dramatic changes has been with amalgamations surrounding the Communications, Energy, and Paperworkers Union of Canada (CEP). As shown in Figure 7.1, successive rounds of union amalgamation came together over time to form the CEP. In 1992, these processes of amalgamation culminated in the Canadian Paperworkers Union (CPU), the Communications and Electrical Workers of Canada, and the Energy and Chemical Workers Union joining together in the CEP.

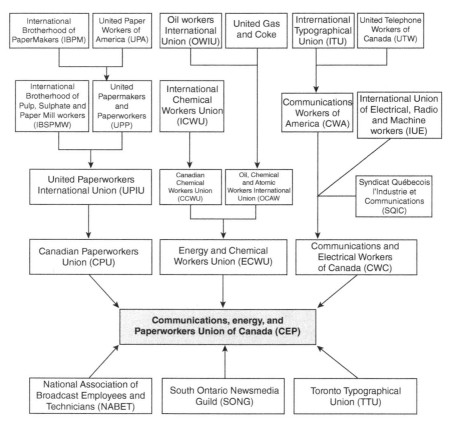

Figure 7.1 Growth of CEP and its Parent Unions.
Source: McCrostie, 1996.

The rationale for the CEP is described in an early document that charges their pathway to their partnership:

> The CEP held its founding convention in November, 1992. The Canadian Paperworkers Union, the Communications and Electrical Workers of Canada and the Energy and Chemical Workers Union joined forces after a year of discussion. The new CEP membership of more than 140,000 made it the eighth largest union in the Canadian Labour Congress and the fourth largest private sector union in Canada.
>
> For the first time, three strong unions agreed to give up their independence. Although the workplaces the three unions organized may appear to have little in common, the similarities among the unions outweighed the differences. The three parent unions were set up after breaking away from internationals. The unions had similar democratic structures, with representatives from the rank and file on the national executive. The constitution of the new union carries on these democratic structures and guarantees a balance of power so that no one branch can dominate.
>
> The new CEP offers several advantages. A larger union means a larger strike fund and more money to research increasingly complex contract issues and to fund educational programmes. A diversified union offers the opportunity to launch industry-wide campaigns. Many collective agreements with different expiration dates means the union does not have to worry about having most of its members on strike at one time.
>
> The most important advantage is the strength that comes from numbers. The CEP gives its members a stronger political voice and the ability to play a greater role in shaping Canadian society.
>
> (McCrostie, 1996 p. 1)

Table 7.6 lists the major unions organizing labor within Mackenzie's forest sector. Between 2000 and 2014, there was significant change in the ownership structure of these operations. The Slocan operations were taken over by Canfor, Paper Excellence eventually became the owners of the Pope and Talbot pulp mill, and the bankrupt Abitibi-Consolidated complex is now being operated by Conifex.

The structure of union representation remained quite stable between these periods and these ownership changes. Local 18 of the Pulp, Paper, and Woodworkers of Canada Union represented sawmill workers at Slocan/Canfor. Local 1092 of the Communications, Energy, and Paperworkers Union of Canada represented pulp mill workers at Pope and Talbot/Paper Excellence. When Conifex took over the Abitibi-Consolidated complex, they only restarted the sawmill operations. As result, the Communications, Energy, and Paperworkers Union representation was replaced by the United Steelworkers Local 1-424.

Changing union representation in Mackenzie raises the question of how union rights and obligations transferred between owners and between periods of closure. These were important matters in Mackenzie, and they unfolded during the closure of the Abitibi pulp- and sawmill complex and the subsequent purchase by Conifex:

Table 7.6 Labor Organization: Major Employers and Union Locals, 2000 and 2014

2000
Slocan Forest Products
Pulp and Paper Workers of Canada Union (PPWC), Local 18
Pope and Talbot
Communications Energy and Paperworkers Union of Canada (CEP), Local 1092
Abitibi-Consolidated
Communications Energy and Paperworkers Union of Canada (CEP), Local 1092

2014
Canfor Forest Products Ltd.
Pulp, Paper and Woodworkers of Canada (PPWC), Local 18
Paper Excellence
Communications, Energy, and Paperworkers Union of Canada (CEP), Local 1092
Conifex Timber Inc.
United Steelworkers (USW), Local 1–424

Source: authors.

Well Conifex acquiring Abitibi is what's called successorship in the collective agreement and [workers] had to a large degree recall rights to employment there. Of course Conifex Mackenzie only runs a fraction of what used to be the lumber activity.

(Participant P6, 2013)

Well, both Conifex operations they acquired had shutdown prior and so there was interactions between the company and the union to resolve a host of concerns from the perspective of Conifex and the union before the final decision was made to resume operations. So there was a memorandum of understanding about Fort St. James initially and then Mackenzie. They weren't that comprehensive in scope, there were some small concerns that the union brought forward and the company brought forward, ultimately in very rapid manner to reach a resolution. It was very cooperative.

(Participant P6, 2013)

The challenges associated with these adjustments were described by a number of interviewees:

The unions have gone one of two ways. They have either become smaller and less relevant, or they become like the CEP and become a huge tent that has a fair bit of ability to support a labor dispute; but again, because you represent so many diverse groups of organized labor, it's harder for your local's voice to be heard.

(Participant P1, 2013)

When I first got involved in negotiations, it was a joint PPWC/CPU negotiation. And there was always bickering between the two unions, so they stopped negotiating together when they went from provincial bargaining to local bargaining. But they also tried to maintain the same contract. So in Prince George you'd have the pulp and paper mills negotiating with CEP. And the CEP originally, when they were the CPU, was fairly answerable to the locals. But once they became CEP, they were more diverse and, therefore, they weren't solely represented by the pulp and paper industry. They were representing everything. And they got bigger and I don't necessarily think bigger is better. But now they are merging with the CAW.

(Participant P3, 2013)

And changes continue. Most recently, the CEP in negotiations with the Canadian Auto Workers Union, officially formed in 2013 the new union under the title Unifor.

The challenges facing labor, and organized labor in particular, together with the opportunities that arise from scaling up labor representation, were described in an early mission statement:

Unifor was officially formed on August 31, 2013, at a founding convention in Toronto, Ontario. It marked the coming together of the Canadian Auto Workers Union (CAW) and the Communications, Energy and Paperworkers Union of Canada (CEP)—two of Canada's largest and most influential labour unions. ...

For decades, union membership (as a share of total employment) had been in steady decline—particularly in the private sector. Running parallel to this decline in union density had been a sharp rise in income inequality, growing threats to retirement security, chronic unemployment and underemployment (particularly for young people) and a noticeable rise in insecure, precarious forms of work, especially among newcomers. The decline of union influence coincided with the rise of grossly imbalanced business-friendly policies, starting in the 1980s, that included tax cuts, labor market deregulation and corporate-led free trade deals.

Unifor was a bold answer to the question: "How do Canadian unions respond to the changing economy and these challenging times?"

(Unifor, 2014)

Organized labor and the forest industry share a long history in BC. From early struggles to organize workers, the labor movement has adjusted over time to changing workforce trends, increasing corporate consolidation, and even the changing size of its own parent union organizations. Together with these historical trends and changes, the next section looks at some of the new realities facing labor.

The New Realities of Labor

To this point, the chapter has dealt with the employment and labor relations transitions that affected BC's central interior forest industry since the 1970s. This section looks at some of the current challenges associated with labor recruitment and retention within the industry. The aging of the workforce, together with competition for skilled labor from other industrial sectors, has changed again the landscape for labor recruitment.

Competition for Labor

The growth phase of industrial forest development across the interior of BC coincided with the postwar baby-boom generation entering the workforce. When combined with international immigration, there was a steady flow of young workers able to enter this relatively stable, well-paid, expanding industry. That the skill requirements for entrance into employment were relatively low further encouraged a sense that the industry provided opportunity and the foundation for a career.

Following the global economic recession of the early 1980s, the industry then entered a phase of significant employment downsizing. For much of the next 30 years, little attention was paid to human-resource issues within the sector. The attention that was paid focused upon the new skill sets required to handle increasingly sophisticated production operations.

At the start of the 2010s, the industry faced four human resource challenges. The first was that they had not focused upon ways to grow the pool of labor eligible to work in the industry. The second was that a long period of job reductions, plant closures, and corporate takeovers had created an image that this was a sunset sector within the economy. If news coverage wasn't difficult enough, many commentators describe the post-1980s period as involving the rise of the information and service economy. The third was that other natural resources actors, specifically oil and gas, were entering an expansion phase of their own and were aggressively developing human resource policies together with recruitment and retention strategies. The fourth included that the current workforce in many production facilities had been employed for many years, and would soon be retiring in large numbers. Such mass retirements will significantly disrupt production efficiencies and increase training costs.

In general terms, many of the experienced industry observers we spoke with noted:

> It's a bit more challenging to recruit even entry level, unskilled labor. I noticed an ad in the paper by companies advertising for entry level labor positions in sawmills across the northern interior. You didn't see that even ten years ago. They wouldn't even have to advertise, they'd have them just knocking at the door. That's how they used to meet their needs. Now, they are having to be a lot more creative, put more energy into recruiting and retention, especially in the trades' area where there's more competition.
>
> (Participant P6, 2013)

Everybody is competing for skilled labor now. And if you've got a ticket and you haven't blown up your reputation, you can get a job. The job you want where you want it? That's a little tougher. But there's a lot of guys leaving the pulp industry.

(Participant P1, 2013)

In the interim, the workforces are aging, and older workers are being enticed back to continue to fill positions vital to the operation of the manufacturing facilities. As noted by one longtime forest industry participant:

Well, one of the ways we're meeting the demand is old guys like me are still working, and that's happening, some people have a lot of institutional knowledge and all that. So as long as you're filling a shortage, that's fine. But a danger I guess would be that it's eliminating progress of younger people. And right now I don't see that as an issue, because we're short of people. But the workforce is getting older.

(Participant P5, 2013)

Competition From the Oil and Gas Sector

As noted, the forest industry is in a competition with other natural resource sectors for skilled workers. One of the key competitors, and one that significantly influences the ability to attract and retain skilled workers in BC's central interior, is the Canadian oil and gas sector. Opportunities in Alberta, and in northeastern BC, have been growing and are poised for significant future growth. As part of its competition strategy for labor, the oil and gas sector is able to pay significantly higher wages than other natural resource sectors. In addition, they actively promote a team-based working environment, workplace health and safety issues as a daily component of all workplace activity, and considerable interest in continuous skills development and training.

Competition from the oil and gas sector, was noted by several interviewees as a critical challenge to workforce retention and recruitment in BC's central interior forest sector:

The biggest one for the industry is the fact that there is so much development going on in the Peace Region. Never mind Alberta, the Peace Region—they're looking at $39 billion worth of investment. Potentially, we're looking at up to eight natural gas pipelines and possibly one oil. And the people in those industries are going to be the same people we need for the forest industry. The equipment operators, welders, engineers, electricians, they'll all be involved in that. The forest industry is not paying the kind of money they are.

(Participant P3, 2013)

The key challenge is the difficulty the mill is having in hiring skilled trades workers and keeping those skilled trades workers. One reason is the wage differential between the forest sector and its competitors in the mining and oil and gas sector. It is not unreasonable that people might earn double their salary doing similar work, such as being a power engineer in the oil and gas sector. A second challenge about pay rates was that when the mill was in negotiations to restart after its long shutdown with its new owners, the union negotiated a start-up contract that had upward of a 10% wage cut. While that might be good for the company in terms of lowering its operating costs, it further exacerbated the wage differential between forestry and the other sectors.

(Participant P7, 2013)

In many cases, the wage rate differential was staggering:

A friend of mine is a second-class power engineer. The first year that the mill shut down, he went to Alberta and he made $300,000 that year. And all he did was work. And he changed employers three times. That was a huge jump for him. Guys that were fourth-class engineers that I was working with… I was making $60,000 here and they were making $120,000 there. So that's going to be the big problem in the future.

(Participant P3, 2013)

No, they didn't come back. They were making $70,000–$80,000 here, and in Fort McMurray they were making $120,000 or $160,000.

(Participant P3, 2013)

Forestry and Employment in Mackenzie, BC—A Case Study

Background

Employment in BC's central interior forest industry has typically been governed by two factors. The first has to do with the technical capacity and efficiency with which wood can be harvested and processed. The second has to do with the volume of wood available for processing. In this section, we examine the connection between employment levels and volume of wood available for harvesting.

The town of Mackenzie is located two hours north of Prince George in BC's central interior. Founded in the 1970s to be the processing center for a new regional forest industry, Mackenzie's economy is dominated by large forestry firms. In 1995, the province's Ministry of Forests conducted a timber supply review in the area. It found that the town's economy was "overwhelmingly dominated by forestry. Over 70% of the region's employment is either directly or indirectly dependent on the harvesting and milling of wood products" (BC Ministry of Forests, 1995 p. i).

The industrial base in Mackenzie is impressive. Until the 2008 global economic recession, Mackenzie's industrial facilities included four major sawmills, a pulp mill, and a pulp and newsprint mill, together with several smaller producers of woodchips (for the pulp sector) and some value-added wood products.

The forest base in the Mackenzie timber supply area (TSA) is composed of spruce, Lodgepole pine, and balsam fir. As with other forest regions in BC, there is a considerable volume and range of deciduous trees within the supply area as well. However, "virtually no volume has been utilized" in industrial production to date (BC Ministry of Forests, 1995 p. ii). In the mid-1990s, the annual allowable cut (AAC) in the Mackenzie timber supply area was set at approximately 2.95 million m³. Of this forest harvest, 90.2 percent was controlled by the two largest firms operating in the area.

Through the 1990s, Mackenzie had a population of about 5,800 people. The workforce was estimated to be about 3,200 people. About 61 percent of this workforce was male. Incomes in Mackenzie were high as the unionized forest sector paid good wages. The Ministry of Forests reported in 1995, that Mackenzie's average income is in the order of $61,000, "which is roughly $8000 higher than the provincial average. Over ⅓ of all families had incomes which exceeded $70,000" (BC Ministry of Forests, 1995 p. 14).

Based on its 1995 data, the Ministry of Forests estimated that direct employment in forestry and forest products manufacturing involved approximately 1,500 workers. Indirect or induced employment connected with forestry and the production of forest products added another approximately 650 workers. The total employment generated by the forest and forest products sectors was approximately 2,100 workers, accounting for about 71 percent of all employment in Mackenzie.

In its 1995 timber supply review, the BC Ministry of Forest estimated that very little change is anticipated with respect to the area's annual allowable cut. It forecast a:

> continuation of the harvest level at 2,951,121 m³ per year for three decades. In the fourth decade the harvest is reduced to 2,796,000 m³ per year and in the fifth to the tenth decade to 2,640,000 m³ per year. After that the harvest level will rebound to 2,810,000 m³ over the next 200 years.
>
> (BC Ministry of Forests, 1995 p. 35)

A further timber supply review in 2001 also forecast stable, if not growing, forest industry opportunities in the area. It was identified "that short-term harvests can be maintained at the current AAC (2,997,363 cubic metres per year). The medium- and long-term harvests could be increased to 3,305,000 cubic metres and maintained at that level over the analysis period (250 years)" (BC Ministry of Forests, Lands, and Natural Resource Operations, 2001, iv). The analysis also indicated that strong market demand at the time of the study now supported approximately 1,559 direct jobs and 566 indirect and induced jobs.

The Ministry again highlighted how the community is dependent upon, and vulnerable to changes in, the forest economy. They reported that the:

economy of Mackenzie depends on the forest sector for 65% of its employment and 71% of its total income. The community was built for and continues to rely heavily on timber harvested and milled in the area. Any sizable reduction in the harvest level or shift in processing location would have a large impact on the local economy. Given the current review of the timber supply, this scenario is unlikely, at least in the foreseeable future.

(BC Ministry of Forests, Lands, and Natural Resource Operations, 2001 p. 69)

By the time of the 2012–2013 timber supply review, however, conditions had changed dramatically. In the decade between the two timber supply reviews, three key issues had interceded. The first was connected with the longer-term restructuring of the industry and involve the changes and conflicts over labor flexibility as we have articulated above. The second involved the 2008 global economic recession that significantly affected markets—especially the key US housing market. The third, and longest lasting factor, was the mountain pine beetle infestation.

The 2008 economic recession was critically important in Mackenzie. For more than a year, all major forest industry operations (sawmills and pulp and paper mills) in the community (Hoekstra, 2010). The Ministry of Forest review reported that Mackenzie:

is the most heavily dependent TSA in BC. Between 2006 and 2011, the population decreased from 4,539 to 3,507 or by about 23 percent. During the recent economic downturn, local lumber manufacturing plants either ran at reduced harvest volumes or were temporarily closed. One paper manufacturing facility closed permanently, resulting in the loss of about 804 full-time employees.

(BC Ministry of Forests, Lands, and Natural Resource Operations, Forest Analysis and Inventory Branch, 2013 p. 6)

Markey *et al.* (2015) found that up to 27 percent of local forest sector families chose to engage in long-distance labor commuting (LDLC). LDLC describes a situation where the workplace is isolated at a distance of more than 200 kilometers from the worker's home community (Öhman and Lindgren, 2003). This labor practice has significant implications for the 'home' communities. In Mackenzie, this loss of jobs resulted in a restructuring of household responsibilities as the remaining spouse assumed more responsibility for childcare and household duties. LDLC families also had less time to spend with friends and neighbors, and less time to invest in community groups and organizations.

As noted earlier, all of BC has been impacted since the 1990s by a significant mountain pine beetle infestation. In Mackenzie, much of the forest base is far enough north to use natural temperature levels to control beetle populations. Nevertheless, the beetle has had an impact on the Mackenzie timber supply area. The BC Ministry of Forest 2013 (p. 2) timber supply review discussion paper identifies that as of 2004, the "mountain pine beetle has impacted about 75 percent of the Lodgepole pine forest or about 37 percent of the THLB [timber harvesting land base]."

The problem with the mountain pine beetle is that once trees are dead, they begin to deteriorate. Depending on local climate and site conditions, they may only be valuable for lumber or pulp production for a limited number of years. The short growing season means the forest may take 70 to 100 years in the central interior to grow into harvestable mature forests. The Ministry's 2013 discussion paper suggests that the Mackenzie timber supply area's annual allowable cut of approximately 3.05 million m³ per year may be viable for the next 10 to 15 years. After that point, the fall-down impacts from the mountain pine beetle damage will impact harvest levels. The base case is a reduction to 2.58 million m³ per year for up to an additional 80 or 90 years. This 15 percent reduction in available timber would result in additional mill closures and job losses.

Conflict Over Flexibility

Hayter's (2003) treatment rethinking the place of resource peripheries in economic geography detailed a 'contested remapping' of power and control through iterative global-local dynamics. The 'local' consequences of this remapping also needs to direct attention to labor–capital relations. The ongoing restructuring of the industry through the adoption of flexible regimes of production is affecting these labor–capital relations. The concept of job flexibility is well understood by labor:

> The company had the right to assign duties as they saw fit. There was some discussions on who did what, but again when they accepted the flexibility agreement, all the boundaries were basically lost ... back when I first started there, if you were a pipefitter you did all the pipefitting. If you were a welder, you didn't do pipefitting.
>
> (Participant P3, 2013)

Contestation over labor flexibility clearly manifested itself in Mackenzie, BC. In May 1998, a nine-month strike ended at Fletcher Challenge Canada Ltd. (FCCL). The strike, which was bitter and centered on a company plan to introduce flexible job classifications, was resolved through use of an external arbitrator. Both the company and the union stated they were not pleased with the arbitrator's final recommendation and the period after operations resumed was marked by a renewed contest between the company and the union. The strike, and the continuing contestation between capital and labor puts into sharp relief that as capital becomes increasingly mobile, labor remains relatively less mobile, has fewer local options, and is disadvantaged in local disputes.

In 1980, British Columbia Forest Products was taken over by New Zealand-based Fletcher Challenge. Over the next few years, a number of labor disputes arose. Into the 1990s, FCCL operations continued to see job action. As part of the run-up to the 1997 strike, local news coverage reported that "if the strike goes ahead as scheduled, it will be the third at Fletcher Challenge in BC over the past five years" (Bernsohn, 1997).

1997–1998 Strike

At the time of the strike, FCCL operated three pulp mill facilities in BC. One is at Mackenzie while the other two were in Campbell River and Crofton (on Vancouver Island in southern BC). Employees at the Mackenzie mill are represented by the Communications, Energy, and Paperworkers Union (CEP) and the Pulp, Paper, and Woodworkers of Canada Union (PPWC). During the spring of 1997 negotiations over a new collective agreement got underway. The company's opening offer included an eight-year contract, a 365-day per year operating schedule, elimination of overtime hour banking for future time off, and complete flexibility across all job classifications. The unions were interested in a two- or three-year contract, maintenance of the three-day Christmas period shutdown, continued overtime banking, and no job flexibility (Hoekstra, 1997). The only proposal common to both the company and union opening positions was inflation-level pay increases (Bernsohn, 1997).

Job flexibility was to be the key issue for both the company and the workers. For the company, job flexibility meant that "any employee could do any job they're capable of doing safely" (Hoekstra, 1997). It also means reducing costs, increasing opportunities for profit, and being more responsive to market changes.

The push for flexibility by capital "is interpreted by workers as a direct attack on the basic union principles of job demarcation and seniority which are there to provide dignity and stability in the workplace" (Hayter and Holmes, 2001 p. 145). Job flexibility also means layoffs and job losses as fewer employees are typically required under this management regime. As described by Leach and Winson (1995 p. 345), flexibility is "a euphemism for cutting the wage bill." Research on flexible employment contracts at Canadian pulp and paper plants showed job losses between 18 percent and 59 percent (Mackenzie and Norcliffe, 1997). Other research (Grass and Hayter, 1989; Barnes and Hayter, 1994; Hayter, 1996) also trace that job flexibility pathways have led to significant job losses in BC's sawmill sector.

With little in the way of progress being made in negotiations, the union membership voted 96 percent in favor of a strike (Hoekstra, 1997). This vote came in response to an ultimatum issued by the company that the union must agree to demands for downsizing through full flexibility of work practices (*Mackenzie Times*, 1997a). What was to become a nine-month long battle of attrition began on July 14, 1997 (Trick, 1997). From the start, it was clear that both sides were prepared for a long dispute. Over the fall and through the winter, the FCCL mill at Mackenzie remained idle. To combat the winter snows and temperatures which could go down to −40°C, workers on the Mackenzie picket lines erected a sturdy shelter, complete with wood heating units, at the mill's entrance gate.

The union's firm stance was bolstered by long local experience with economic booms and busts. When confronted with company calls for the need to increase profitability in a difficult and changing market, labor's response, often supported by local attitudes and past experiences was simply to wait for the next boom (Hayter, 2000). For Reed (2003), such reliance upon past experience creates an 'occupational community' constructed, and embedded, within place-bound social and geographic relations. And workers knew that times had changed. Through the 1950 to 1980 period, "most lay-offs during recessions were temporary, limited to 'blue-collar' workers, and organized on the basis of seniority ... [but after 1980] job losses in the big union mills were permanent and affected all segments of the labour force" (Hayter, 1996 p. 112).

Other consequences of changing times followed as the strike unfolded. Tensions rose when the company hired a private security firm to protect the homes of mill managers and executives. The union local president argued that this would not only alter the way people interacted in town, but that the move was unnecessary since no incidents of trouble had occurred during at least the past five strikes (Forbes, 1997). While the union brought in representatives from other locals and held picnics to show collective support (*Mackenzie Times*, 1997b, 1997c), the company was watching its return to shareholders. Barely three months into the strike, FCCL sold its Minnesota-based paper operations for US$650 million, a sale that netted a US$300 million after taxes (*Mackenzie Times*, 1997d). About seven months into the strike FCCL announced that it was in negotiations to acquire Trust International Paper Corp., the largest newsprint producer in the Philippines, to meet its customer's needs (*Mackenzie Times*, 1998b, 1998c).

The following spring, the provincial government appointed a mediator to resolve the dispute (*Mackenzie Times*, 1998a; *Prince George Citizen*, 1998). After two attempts, an agreement was reached in April 1998 (Canadian Press, 1998b, 1998c). Typical of mediated settlements, the final agreement took a middle ground between negotiating positions. A five-year term would see wage increases in the order of 2 percent per year in the last four years and improvements to the pension plan. On job flexibility, the agreement granted the company language on flexible work practices, while giving the unions a new "grievance protection on job flexibility and no job losses from work flexibility" (Canadian Press, 1998b). This last point has proved very difficult to track for grievance purposes, as any retirement or employment quit can be used as an opportunity to implement flexibility.

The tenor of the strike had been bitter and its legacy would carry forward. When the agreement was put to the union membership for ratification, only 59.3 percent of all FCCL employees voted in favor (Canadian Press, 1998a). In Mackenzie, "68 percent of workers there voted *against* the deal" (emphasis added) (Canadian Press, 1998a, p. 3).

Continuing 'Discourses' of Conflict

The FCCL pulp mill in Mackenzie renewed operations in May of 1998. The end of the strike did not, however, signal the end of the struggle between the workers and the company—which now moved to the shop floor. As the debate shifted to the shop floor, at least two discourses were underway, a corporate discourse and a countervail discourse by workers.

On September 17, 1998, FCCL issued a statement to the effect that production at the pulp mill must reach 580 tonnes per day or the mill would close for six months (Benton, 1998c). The company claimed that production had been averaging only 440 tonnes per day since the strike ended. This occurred despite that the mill has a normal operating capacity of 600 tonnes per day. Given world market prices for pulp, the company argued that it was losing money through low productivity and that if the trend was not reversed, the mill would be closed (Hoekstra, 1998b). According to the FCCL pulp mill manager, after the "nine month strike workers returned to work in May and ... May, June, July, August, and September have not been good" (Benton, 1998c).

The editor of the local newspaper captured the community's angst at the thought of a further mill closure: "both the management and the union said 580 tonnes per day is attainable, both parties have to now figure out how they can attain this amount and keep the mill running" (Benton, 1998c). The President of the Mackenzie Chamber of Commerce reiterated the local need to keep the FCCL mill operating: "[i]f Fletcher decides to close those doors ... it's going to be bad. The way the whole economy is now. Mackenzie is hurting as it is" (Hoekstra, 1998b).

A Corporate Discourse

Within a week of the statement threatening to close the facility, the company reported that production levels at the FCCL mill had increased dramatically. As reported by the company, "during the past four to five days production has exceeded capacity of 600 tonnes a day to about 700 tonnes a day ... [while] the mill had been producing about 440 tonnes a day when the ultimatum was issued" (Hoekstra, 1998a). A spokesman for FCCL stated that "it's obvious from the past few days, when people put their hearts and minds to it, they can make that mill run." The news release ended with the ominous warning that the company hoped the production "can be sustained so we don't have to worry about a shutdown" (Hoekstra, 1998a).

The good production news continued and the following weeks were filled with reports of further production successes. Near the end of October 1998, it was reported that the mill was averaging 677 tonnes per day of production, well above the company's baseline requirement of 580 tonnes (Benton, 1998a). The mill went on to set weekly, monthly, and quarterly production records. Not to leave a 'victory' as sufficient, the company reiterated the lingering threat that,

> the bottom line is that the company has to stay in a cash positive position in order for it to stay open ... with pulp mill markets down and not expected to recover till the spring of 1999, Fletcher Challenge could face some tough times.
>
> (Benton, 1998b)

A Labor Discourse

Against this corporate discourse, the workers offered a counter discourse in which they claimed success. They blamed the low production levels on the company and then claimed the production increase success for themselves:

> the article paints a picture of an unco-operative work force that faced with losing their jobs suddenly pulled together and started producing pulp. This is absolutely not the case! The hourly employees are doing nothing differently than they have done for five months. There was never any sabotage, work slow-downs, or refusals to work. We have all been trying to run the mill since coming back to work. Our jobs and our futures depend on it.
>
> Why the sudden production increase? Fletcher has performed some much needed repairs to equipment and has changed their approach allowing the operators to operate the way their experience has shown is most effective.
>
> (Kroeker, 1998)

Another worker confirmed that production had increased "because operators were allowed to make the decisions" (Hoekstra, 1998a). The message was simple, if management got out of the way, the workers could make the nearly 35-year-old mill run at top capacity.

One of the outcomes of the discourse of resistance is that worker morale was boosted. Not only was there pride in what they had accomplished (increasing production), but there was also pride in having defeated the company ultimatum. As noted by one employee: "[w]orker morale has gone up, said Berry, a machinist with 19 years experience. 'It's pride. If they're going to shut us down, it's not going to be our fault' " (Hoekstra, 1998a).

Epilogue

While both sides in the conflict went on with statements through which they claimed victory, the production successes at the plant continued. In July, the local newspaper reported that the FCCL mill had established a new quarterly production record of "639 tonnes per day! This breaks the previous record of 631 that stood for ten and a half years" (Boughner, 1999).

Success followed success, as "a new production record was set at Fletcher Challenge Pulpmill the week of July 26—August 1, 1999, when over 725 tonnes [per day] were produced" (Benton, 1999). The workers claimed to have pulled the mill out of trouble. When built,

> Mackenzie Pulp was a world class performer. The start up had been excellent, the quality was second to none and the operational reliability was exceptional. About ten years ago, something happened and the mill went into a downhill slide. I don't know what happened, but there is still a lot of pride and capability in our people here. That's why the turnaround has been so quick: we're

getting back to being as good as the good old days and capturing the advantage of improvements that had been made along the way. The way you control your destiny is to act like you are in control.

(Benton, 1999)

At the close of the production level debate it became clear that this piece of the conflict puzzle had an intensely personal and human connection. Much of the public dialogue over low production levels and worker responses had been carried out between the FCCL mill manager and the union local presidents. In a sense, they came to embody the local representation of the larger struggle between capital and labor. Labor argued that the struggle was over control of the mill and how it was to be run. The reorganization of work affects daily rhythms and the application of flexibility will mean jobs losses, out-migration, and population decline.

The need for contract flexibility, and the production conflict which followed the end of the strike, all centered on company demands for profitability. Yet, operational profitability may never really have been the real question. In April of 1999, forest products companies in British Columbia began to post quarterly profits. FCCL reported profits of $12 million on sales of $270 million (Hoekstra, 1999). These profits occurred during a period of very poor pulp prices and were a significant improvement over the same period the previous year. In that year, FCCL lost $11.4 million at a time when most other forest products companies in the province were also mired in red ink (Hoekstra, 1999). Yet the minor profits recorded after more than two years of poor market performance paled in comparison to the revelation in July that FCCL was indeed cash rich, and had over $700 million "in the bank" (*Prince George Citizen*, 1999). The revelation came out when it was announced that FCCL would use that bankroll to purchase the debt-ridden paper-making assets of its parent Fletcher Challenge Limited of New Zealand. The profits generated from its Canadian mills and activities would now be transferred overseas to their parent company via the acquisition agreement. Concerns raised about the transparency of this fiscal transfer to a parent company meant that the plan did not proceed.

Unable to proceed with the takeover of Fletcher Challenge New Zealand's assets, FCCL looked elsewhere. Production increases and the introduction of a flexible work structure and job classification scheme had added value to FCCL shares. In April 2000, it was announced that FCCL was to sell its pulp and paper division to Norwegian-based Norske Skog ASA for $3.6 billion. At the time of the sale, Fletcher Challenge New Zealand was the parent company, and majority stockholder, of FCCL. As a result, the profits and value generated by production levels and contract concessions were now effectively transferred overseas. Throughout the 1997–1998 strike, and the crisis in production which followed, FCCL was not preparing for operational profitability. Instead, it was preparing for merger and takeover actions.

In Mackenzie BC, the nine-month strike, and its aftermath, at FCCL's pulp mill identifies one way by which place-bound labor is at a disadvantage under globalization. The company succeeded in gaining the introduction of contract flexibility, under threat it achieved increased production levels, and both of these actions raised the market value of the company. This was soon parlayed into a $3.6 million 'cash-out' through the sale of FCCL assets—most of which was transferred to its New Zealand-based parent. Labor, in contrast, lost the flexibility struggle and, after working hard to increase production levels, found itself 'rewarded' by the uncertainty of successive corporate takeovers.

Discussion

This chapter has explored a number of issues concerning the changing organization of labor in BC's central interior forest industry since the 1970s. In general, and not surprising, outcome from increasing production efficiency has been a reduction in the number of workers in the sector. Just as companies have scaled up to meet the challenges of the global economy, so too has organized labor also scaled up. One of the consequences is that neither corporate offices nor union headquarters are as closely linked to the place of production and labor as they have been in the past. These impacts, and the contestation between capital and labor over broader transformations in the industry, are highlighted in the case study focused upon a significant strike over job flexibility. Through the case study the increasing global mobility of capital poignantly highlighted the vulnerability of local-bounded labor. After nearly 40 years of transformation, however, the forest industry now finds itself in a new competition for labor. The replacement of an aging forest sector workforce, together with the growth of workforce demands in the mining and energy sectors, suggests that forestry is now in a difficult competitive position for skilled labor. As Halseth and Sullivan (2002 p. 122) summarize: "the opportunities of work have defined the community in the past; pressures on the workplace will define the community into the future."

References

Andersen, J. and Svensson, T. 2012. Struggles for recognition: A content analysis of messages posted on the Internet, *Journal of Multidisciplinary Healthcare* 5: 153–162.
Barnes, T. and Hayter, R. 1994. Economic restructuring, local development, and resource towns: Forest communities in coastal British Columbia, *Canadian Journal of Regional Science* XVII: 289–310.
BC Ministry of Forests. 1995. *Mackenzie timber supply analysis: Socio-economic analysis.* Victoria, BC: Economics and Trades Branch, BC Ministry of Forests.
BC Ministry of Forests. 2014a. *Employment in the forest industry in BC.* Available online at: www.for.gov.bc.ca/hfp/publications/00001/3-2g-can-employ.htm. Accessed March 4, 2014.
BC Ministry of Forests. 2014b. Harvest data—Ministry of Forests, harvest database system. Employment Data—Statistics Canada, Annual Survey of Manufactures & Logging Industry Catalogue 25-201-XPB.
BC Ministry of Forests, Lands, and Natural Resource Operations. 2001. *Mackenzie timber supply area analysis report.* Victoria, BC: BC Ministry of Forests, Lands, and Natural Resource Operations.

BC Ministry of Forests, Lands, and Natural Resource Operations, Forest Analysis and Inventory Branch. 2013. *Mackenzie TSA timber supply analysis: Public discussion paper*. Victoria, BC: BC Ministry of Forests, Lands, and Natural Resource Operations.

Bedics, B. and Doelker, R. 1992. Company town: Beyond the legacy, *Human Services in the Rural Environment* 16: 20–24.

Bentley, P. 2012. *Canfor and the transformation of BC's forest industry: One family's journey*. Vancouver, BC: Douglas & McIntyre.

Benton, J. 1998a. Fletcher Pulp continues to meet target. *Mackenzie Times* October 27: 1.

Benton, J. 1998b. Pulpmill meets target. *Mackenzie Times* October 13: 1.

Benton, J. 1998c. Serious problem at Fletcher Pulp. *Mackenzie Times* September 22: 1.

Benton, J. 1999. Fletcher Challenge sets new production record. *Mackenzie Times* August 10: 1.

Bernsohn, K. 1981. *Cutting up the North: The history of the forest industry in the Northern Interior*. Vancouver, BC: Hancock House.

Bernsohn, K. 1997. Pulp mill faces strike Monday in Mackenzie. *Prince George Citizen* July 9: 1.

Boughner, T. 1999. Fletcher Challenge pulp breaks record. *Mackenzie Times* July 6: 1.

Canadian Press. 1998a. Fewer than 60% of pulp workers in favor of deal. *Prince George Citizen* April 20: 3.

Canadian Press. 1998b. Tentative deal reached in pulp strike. *Prince George Citizen* April 15: 1.

Canadian Press. 1998c. Top mediator tries again to end pulp strike. *Prince George Citizen* April 14: 1.

Canfor. 2013. *Canfor Corporation announces the closure of Quesnel sawmill and tenure exchange agreement with West Fraser*. Vancouver, BC: Marketwired October 24, 2013. www.marketwired.com/press-release/canfor-corporation-announces-closure-quesnel-sawmill-tenure-exchange-agreement-with-tsx-cfp-1844842.htm. Accessed October 10, 2014.

Conifer. 2014. Member and Associate Member List. Available online at: www.conifer.ca/index.php/about/member-and-associate-member-list/. Accessed March 17, 2014.

Drushka, K. 1998. *Tie hackers to timber harvester: The history in British Columbia's interior*. Madeira Park, BC: Harbour Publishing.

Forbes, D. 1997. Letter to the editor—My concerns. *Mackenzie Times* August 5: 4.

Grass, E. and Hayter, R. 1989. Employment change during recession: The experience of forest product manufacturing plants in British Columbia, 1981–1985, *The Canadian Geographer* 33: 240–252.

Hak, G. 2007. *Capital and labour: In British Columbia forest industry, 1934–74*. Vancouver, BC: University of British Columbia Press.

Halseth, G. and Sullivan, L. 2002. *Building community in an instant town*. Prince George, BC: University of Northern British Columbia Press.

Halseth, G., Straussfogel, D., Parsons, S., and Wishart, A. 2004. Regional economic shifts in BC: Speculation from recent demographic evidence, *Canadian Journal of Regional Science* 27: 317–352.

Hanlon, N. and Halseth, G. 2005. The greying of resource communities in northern British Columbia: Implications for health care delivery in already-underserviced communities. *The Canadian Geographer* 49(1): 1–24.

Hayter, R. 1996. Technological imperatives in resource sectors: forest products. In J.N.H. Britton (ed.), *Canada and the global economy: The geography of structural and technological change* (pp. 101–122). Montreal and Kingston: McGill-Queen's University Press.

Hayter, R. 2000. *Flexible crossroads: The restructuring of British Columbia's forest economy*. Vancouver, BC: University of British Columbia Press.

Hayter, R. 2003. 'The war in the woods': Post-Fordist restructuring, globalization, and the contested remapping of British Columbia's forest economy, *Annals of the Association of American Geographers* 93: 706–729.

Hayter, R. and Holmes, J. 2001. The Canadian forest industry: The impacts of globalization and technological change. In M. Howlett (ed.), *Canadian forest policy: adapting to change* (pp. 127–156). Toronto, ON: University of Toronto Press.

Hoekstra, G. 1997. Stage is set for pulp bargaining. *Prince George Citizen* June 25: 1.

Hoekstra, G. 1998a. Pulp mill closure averted: Mackenzie workers answer ultimatum with big production hike. *Prince George Citizen* September 23: 1.

Hoekstra, G. 1998b. Mackenzie fears pulp mill closure. *Prince George Citizen* September 19: 1.

Hoekstra, G. 1999. West Fraser, Fletcher join forest firms in profit picture. *Prince George Citizen* April 29: 1.

Hoekstra, G. 2010. Mine by them; local government, First Nation back Mount Milligan. *Prince George Citizen*, April 24: 1.

IWA-Forest Industry Pension Plan. 2012. *IWA-forest industry pension plan annual report 2012*. Prince George, BC: IWA-Forest Industry Pension Plan.

Krippendorff, K. and Bock, M. (eds.). 2009. *The content analysis reader*. Thousand Oaks, CA: Sage Publications.

Kroeker, J. 1998. Pulp mill closure still a threat. *Prince George Citizen* September 25: 4, Letter to the editor.

Leach, B. and Winson, A. 1995. Bringing 'globalization' down to earth: Restructuring and labour in rural communities, *Journal of the Canadian Regional Science Association* 32: 341–364.

Loudon, P. 1992. Gone but not forgotten, *Canadian Geographic* January/February: 61–64, 66.

Mackenzie Times. 1997a. Strike notice served for July 14th, 1997. July 15: 8.

Mackenzie Times. 1997b. Picnic for Mackenzie Union—CEP Local 1092. August 26: 1.

Mackenzie Times. 1997c. Support from down under. September 30: 1.

Mackenzie Times. 1997d. Fletcher Challenge sells Blandin Paper Company. October 7: 7.

Mackenzie Times. 1998a. Inquiry Commissioner to examine pulp dispute. January 13: 1.

Mackenzie Times. 1998b. Fletcher products would be 'unfair' unions warn. April 7: 1.

Mackenzie Times. 1998c. Fletcher Challenge Canada moving forward on Philippines paper company acquisition. April 7: 12.

Mackenzie, S. and Norcliffe, G. 1997. Guest editors—restructuring in the Canadian newsprint industry, *The Canadian Geographer* 41: 2–6.

Marchak, P. 1983. Green gold: The forest industry in British Columbia. Vancouver, BC: University of British Columbia Press.

Markey, S., Halseth, G., and Manson, D. 2012. *Investing in place: Economic renewal in northern British Columbia*. Vancouver, BC: University of British Columbia Press.

Markey, S., Ryser, L., and Halseth, G. 2015 'We're in this all together': Community impacts of long-distance labour commuting, *Rural Society* 24(2): 131–153.

McCrostie, J. 1996. *Just the beginning! The Communications, Energy and Paperworkers Union of Canada*. Edited and designed by Rosemarie J. Bahr. Ottawa: Communications, Energy and Paperworkers Union of Canada. Formerly available at: www.cep.ca/sites/

cep.ca/files/docs/en/beginning-e.pdf. Accessed March 12, 2014. See: https://web. archive.org/web/20140313042917/http://www.cep.ca/sites/cep.ca/files/docs/en/ beginning-e.pdf.

Mouat, J. 1995. *Roaring days: Rossland and the history of mining in British Columbia.* Vancouver, BC: University of British Columbia Press.

Öhman, M. and Lindgren, U. 2003. Who is the long distance commuter? Patterns and driving forces in Sweden, *Cybergeo: European Journal of Geography* 243: 1–33.

Prince George Citizen. 1998. Pulp strike breakthrough? April 9: 1.

Prince George Citizen. 1999. Fletcher Challenge deal doubles pulp, paper capacity. July 13: 5.

Reed, M. 2003. Marginality and gender at work in forestry communities of British Columbia, Canada, *Journal of Rural Studies* 19: 373–389.

Trick, B. 1997. Strikers gear for long haul in Mackenzie. *Prince George Citizen* August 15: 1.

Unifor. 2014. *History and mission.* Available online at: www.unifor.org/en/about-unifor/ history-mission. Accessed March 12, 2014.

United Steelworkers of Canada. 2014. *The United Steelworkers in Canada: A story of struggle, growth, and evolution.* Formerly available at: www.usw.ca/union/who/ history?id=0002. Accessed March 12, 2014. See: https://web.archive.org/web/2015 0312162224/http://www.usw.ca/union/who/history?id=0002.

Wilson, J. 1998. *Talk and log: Wilderness politics in British Columbia, 1965–96.* Vancouver, BC: University of British Columbia Press.

8 Industrial Labor in a Resource Town in Finland

The Case of Lieksa

*Maija Halonen, Eero Vatanen, Markku Tykkyläinen,
and Juha Kotilainen*

Introduction

Economic growth and restructuring, especially in robust urban areas and their
commuting zones, have attracted labor from less-productive sectors and areas in
Finland for decades (Kangasharju and Pekkala, 2004; Tervo, 2009; Lehtonen and
Tykkyläinen, 2010a). Similarly, rural areas close to the largest cities in Canada
have succeeded better than other rural areas in compensating for employment
losses in the primary industries, as they have benefited from commuting to the
regional cores (Polèse and Shearmur, 2004; Partridge *et al.*, 2007). At the local
level, the transformation to an urban-centric knowledge economy is the most
problematic in remote rural places. For resource-dependent municipalities like
Lieksa local job creation is crucial as the municipality is located outside the
commuting area of the nearest regional center (Halonen *et al.*, 2015) and lagging
behind due to costs related to distance (Lehtonen, 2015).

As the central source of income and wealth, one common characteristic of
small mill and mining towns and their hinterlands is their reliance on resource-
based production. Global demand maintains cyclic growth and this pressures
resource-based industries to restructure. In some areas, such as Finland, the
resource sector has sustained relatively high rural populations. As labor
productivity has increased, reducing above all the amount of work required in
forests and mills, jobs in forestry, first, and then in the forest industries have
diminished in Finland since the 1960s. Moreover, a wave of mine closures in the
1980s and mill closures especially in the early 2000s (Johansson *et al.*, 1992;
Kotilainen and Rytteri, 2011) have affected the structure of the population and
economic development in the resource towns and rural areas of Finland. The
increase in labor productivity as well as closures of mills and mines have led to
high unemployment, reflecting the local formation of surplus labor and lack of
opportunities for economic diversification.

The case of Lieksa exemplifies the problems of economic restructuring in
peripheral rural localities from the economic dominance of agriculture and the
production chains originating from forestry to other economies (see Chapter 4 for
an introduction to Lieksa). The first cycle of lake iron ore production was quite
common in Finland but has disappeared in full as shown in Chapter 4. In the

second cycle, the majority of jobs in agriculture have disappeared since the 1960s. Similarly, the forestry sector, from logging to final production, has been strongly rationalized and restructured several times in order to gain adaptive resilience in changing market situations, and thus to avoid from falling on an adverse path of devolution. However, economic transformation of a region or locality does not guarantee a return to vitality as there is always the risk of failure in each stage of adaptation. In particular, when the region remains unattractive to new industries, industrial resilience in the form of reorientation or renewal is beyond the bounds of possibility (Martin, 2012). In this chapter, we investigate the changes in labor force of these industry cycles in Lieksa and analyze the reasons for the growth and decline of different cycles of development. Moreover, we discuss the potential for development which would support the emergence of the sixth cycle of development in Lieksa.

Labor Shifts in Industry Waves

In the long run, the content, skills, and organization of labor in society and enterprises change fundamentally. It happens in each industry and between industries as new industries emerge and mature industries vanish (see Chapter 4). Changes in employment reflect the success of communities revealing how various production factors have been combined. In resource communities, the role of natural resources varies according to demand for products and changes in the techno-economic paradigm impacting on labor. As society develops, industrial and regional policy regimes create mechanisms which attempt to balance the labor market. Their role is especially significant in economic, industrial, and company-based crises to pave the way from one cycle to another. The use of local natural resources in scattered rural settlements in the nineteenth century—whether for local consumption or for the export-dominated Finnish peripheries—linked labor to the land, in the form of small-scale agriculture, and to the forests rather more than to industrialized centers. The first mills tied labor to unionization and labor movement. Corporatism in industrial relations developed (Bergholm, 2009), creating a foothold for various policy measures to mitigate crises and to create policy ensembles that were often reinforced by legislation which emphasized industrial diversification and allocation of funds to research and development (Sippola, 2011).

Land for cultivation and forests were initial advantages in the emergence of resource-based activities in Finland, but their expansion and diffusion to peripheral border areas was boosted by government measures, such as tax reductions during the Swedish times and the giving of land since independence (Westerholm, 2002). The most diversified economies in Finland exist in places with temperate climatic conditions in the south and on the coast, as forestry and smaller-scale agriculture prevail in less advantageous, colder inland environments. Although the climate in Lieksa is more favorable than in Kainuu and Lapland, Lieksa is the most landlocked town in Fennoscandia. Production and housing preferences have changed dramatically since the times of resource frontier expansion and traditional industries have undergone restructuring and job losses for a long time. Then the question arises of how economically successful the new businesses—which are necessarily built not only on the basis of former economic tradition but other qualifications—can be in the long run.

Finnish regional policy has focused on investments, labor costs, and research and development (Sippola, 2011). Nascent enterprises have been supported based on the 'infant industry' argument until they reach a profitable level of production. As this policy has not been able to restrain rural decline, place-based approaches have received much notice. The place-based argument implies that more balanced regional development can only be achieved by more clearly taking into consideration the variability of local assets and local capabilities (Markey *et al.*, 2008; Barca *et al.*, 2012; Huggins and Thompson, 2015; Lehtonen, 2015). Apart from what policies have been outlined, there have been lively discussions on the importance of exploiting immobile or at least less-mobile amenity assets related either with the physical environmental resources such as scenic nature, or production chains built up around the place, or social resources like traditions of skilled specialists and crafts (Bryden and Munro, 2000; Wiggins and Proctor, 2001). Such inputs should lead to offering and pricing goods or services so that they are competitive with the prices of comparable products produced elsewhere. Wiggins and Proctor (2001) pay attention also to low wages and off-season work as competitive factors. Some find new possibilities in the footloose industries such as the production of high-tech products or services with no transportation costs outside the core areas (Oakey and Cooper, 1989; Gillespie and Richardson, 2000). According to Johnson and Rasker (1995), the entrepreneurs in a survey considered the quality of the environment including scenic beauty, the proximity of public land, and the recreational opportunities more important locational factors than tax structure and the low costs of doing business or values related to opportunities for knowledge-building like the proximity of a university. Rural depopulation, however, indicates that there are a few rural areas that have thrived. Natural conditions and amenities facilitate migration to places endowed with high levels of natural amenities, low living costs, and good economic opportunities (Deller *et al.*, 2001; Partridge, 2010), but counterurbanization seems to be only a minor backwash in migration.

Development is evolutionary and thus there is not much a priori evidence about which economic structure would lead to the most resilient economy. Both specialized and diversified economies can lead to local success as seen in the economic history of Lieksa—at least for short periods. In place-neutral theory, the clustering networks of firms, relying not only on physical but on social resources, specialization, well-functioning distribution channels, and, above all, true technological innovations, have played a key role in really changing the paradigm and improving old processes or product development (Glasmeier, 1994; Terluin, 2003; Perez, 2009). These conditions are extremely difficult to achieve in a periphery. For instance, the reaching of relevant human capital is difficult in the distant peripheries (Lehtonen, 2015), as the lack of skilled labor is obvious and the legacy of formerly booming industries more or less maintains old institutions and traditions, known as path dependence (Devezas and Corredine, 2001; Martin and Sunley, 2006), in the economy. Lieksa has coped with crises several times and, therefore, this chapter is intended to show how new production alternatives have emerged and how the labor force has adapted to the changing situations.

Economic Restructuring and Organizing Labor in Finland

The current rural decline in the forested parts of Finland is primarily the outcome of labor productivity growth related to technical process development and economies of scale. The roots of the decline lie in the 1960s when resource peripheries of this kind faced a fundamental restructuring, not only because of a general change from an agrarian society to first an industrial and later a knowledge society, but very much because of advances in mechanization and the subsequent reorganization of forestry work (Kotilainen *et al.*, 2015). For employment, process innovations tend to reduce the number of jobs (Goddard *et al.*, 1986). The change can be seen well in the case of Lieksa where both the total population and proportion of labor force fell rapidly after the long period of growth (Figure 8.1).

The long-run job loss of remote areas due to productivity increases in primary industries is global but their impacts on the population vary to some extent. Industry mix, competitive positions, and business cycles play a role. For instance, the findings in earlier studies from Canada have often revealed the regressive impacts of primarily logging-based forestry dominance on economic well-being, including high poverty rates and high unemployment (Freudenburg and Gramling,

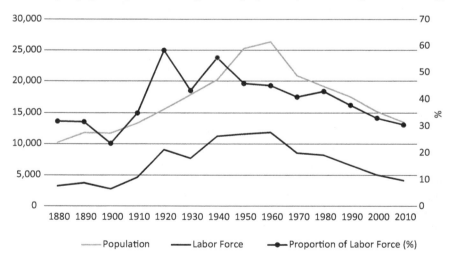

Figure 8.1 Population, Labor Force,[1] and the Proportion of Labor Force to the Total Population in Lieksa.

Sources: Official Statistics Finland (1979, 2014).

Note

1 Labor force (economically active) is defined as comprising both employed and unemployed people (Official Statistics Finland, 2015a).

1994; Overdevest and Green, 1995; Stedman *et al.*, 2004, 2005; Patriquin *et al.*, 2007). As Leake *et al.* (2006) found, forest dependence in Canadian communities had a significant positive correlation with the unemployment rate and an increase in the poverty of households over the period 1986–1996. In Finland, the relationship between unemployment and poverty in mill communities seems to be more complex than that.

When industrial production of forestry became competitive, resource-based towns such as Lieksa gained wealth compared with the surrounding localities. The wages in pulp and paper industries in particular have been remarkably higher than the average of wages in the manufacturing sector in Finland. For instance, in 1975 the wages were 25 percent higher, and since then the gap between the average wages has widened, being 44 percent higher in the pulp and paper industries than in all manufacturing in 2003 (Kujala, 2008). Thus, higher income pockets still exist (Lehtonen and Tykkyläinen, 2010b), in pulp and paper communities especially but not as much in other localities under the influence of forestry or even other forest industries, where the wages are typically lower than in pulp and paper operations (Table 8.1).

Relatively high incomes are mainly gained through successful local labor agreements, such as improvements in wages along with the economic boom, rationalization, and regular wage supplements, which are still more common in the pulp and paper industries than the most of other industries or services in Finland (Uhmavaara, 2002). In addition, as other organized employees in Finland, the employees of the forest industries have benefited from earnings-related unemployment allowance and other social benefits that have guaranteed a relatively good level of security against unemployment and temporary layoffs. The key principle of the labor market system in Finland, as in other Nordic countries, has been based on the ideology of corporatism, having an economic tripartite negotiation system between the state and both employers' and labor organizations, thus affecting not only the position of the employees but also the employers' opportunities to respond to the development of industries.

Corporatism has its roots in the abolition of mercantilism. Professional associations were established to replace the old guild system when the legislation of economic freedom was set up in Finland in 1868. Their successors, professional associations, started to negotiate with employers aimed at reaching agreements to regulate working conditions (Figure 8.2). Thereafter, industrial movements became more frequent and the first collective agreements were negotiated.

Table 8.1 Average Hourly Earnings (€) of Forestry Workers and Forest Industries

Year	Manual Forestry Work (Silvicultural Work)	Mechanized Harvesting (Average)	Wood-Products Industry	Pulp and Paper Industries
2000	8.60	9.05	10.14	14.06
2010	12.71	13.52	15.07	20.39

Source: Official Statistics Finland (2013a).

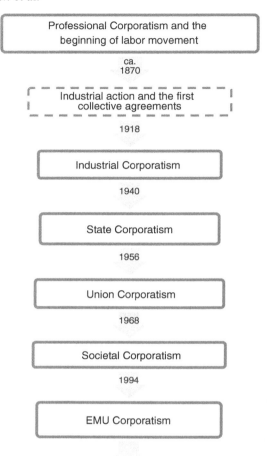

Figure 8.2 Stages of Labor Market Corporatism in Finland.
Source: Kauppinen (2005).

Kauppinen (2005) points out, however, that the first contemporary era of corporatism with the increasingly common industrial labor agreements (industrial corporatism) took place in the early days of independent Finland when the Finnish government, local trade union branches, and single companies became bargaining parties. Since the 1940s the negotiations have become more centralized as the local parties have been replaced with the nationwide organizations of both employees and employers. At first, negotiations were more state-led, while later on unions strengthened their power. Even though these previous eras included centralized and widely collective elements, the culmination point was achieved during societal corporatism that aimed at consensus policy between the bargaining parties, and had a close connection with the other wide-ranging economic, employment, and social policies.

The form and the power relationships of corporatism have varied over the last 150 years but the system has, together with other societal changes, affected the industrial peace, the overall security of the employees, and the ability of businesses to react to changing demands as well as to stay competitive in the markets. For a long time, this Keynesian-managed capitalism based on negotiations and contracts strengthened the power of labor unions compared with more market-oriented capitalism in countries such as the United States and United Kingdom (Kevätsalo, 1999; Schmidt, 2003; Heiskala and Luhtakallio, 2006). Since the 1970s, the security gained from the generally binding agreements has been seen as beneficial, especially by labor unions. Moreover, the wage negotiations of unions in forest industries were successful, especially in the boom times (Kujala, 2008). Due to successful agreements and the chance of earnings-related unemployment benefits, the labor union density has been much higher than in OECD countries in total or in the three other case studies in this book, Australia, Canada, and New Zealand (Figure 8.3). Furthermore, employment security has been a characteristic of industries dominated by middle-aged, unionized males (Soininen, 2015), which industries dominated in Lieksa for a long time.

Corporatism has been operated with a close connection to the implementation of state-led economic, employment, and social policies. In this way, the competitiveness of the export industries has been considered to be supported by various measures such as public spending on research and development, investment in infrastructure, and the devaluations of the former national currency

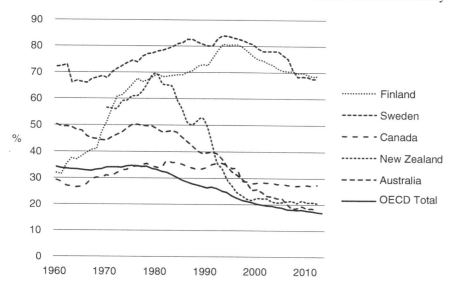

Figure 8.3 Labor Union Density[1] (%) in Selected Countries.
Source: OECD (2015a).

Note

1 Labor union density corresponds to the ratio of wage and salary earners that are trade union members, divided by the total number of wage and salary earners (OECD, 2015b).

(Kuusterä, 1997; Alho, 2002; Kauppinen, 2005). Compared with less-unionized countries, the labor market and the state policies under corporatism have been described as relatively inflexible to respond to external changes in the globalized markets and caused pressures to change the forms of corporatism (Kiander, 1998; Uusitalo, 2000; Molina and Rhodes, 2002).

After joining the EMU (Economic and Monetary Union) and finally after the introduction of euro, Finland has lost its ability to influence industrial price competitiveness by devaluating the currency after wage inflation. Adaptation then requires, on the one hand, more restriction of internal wage competition and, on the other hand, more flexibility and adaptability from the labor market system to confront external shocks (Holm *et al.*, 1998). The generally binding agreements have been criticized as being too inflexible to adapt to the volatile demand of global markets and, therefore, demands for more local factory- or company-based wage negotiations agreements have increased to broaden the adaptation capacity of companies and improve competitiveness locally (Uusitalo, 2000). In forest industries, wages have been negotiated by the union and the employers' association, taking in the account the conditions in each factory, but especially in economic busts when low wage-rise policies, demands for wage cuts, and outsourcing have caused industrial dispute (Kujala, 2008).

Limited labor arrangements at the company level have become more frequent but the modes and prevalence vary by the subject of flexibility. As Uhmavaara's (2008) findings show, wage-related local amendments commonly meant only improvements compared with the centralized agreements. Productivity-related flexibility normally has applied as a basis for bonus payments but actual impairment of wages is very rare as are flexible wage solutions related to business cycles. Especially in industries where continual full-time vacancies are typical and the rate of unionization is high, adaptation to economic pressure and intensification is more common via temporary layoffs or complete dismissals, which apply only to a part of the labor force, than through wage and salary cuts which are directed at a wider range of employees (Kevätsalo, 1999; Holm, 2000). In the forest industry, where the basic labor contracts are still in principle the same across the country, and locally gained improvements of salaries and wages are not flexible downward, the pressure is for an increase in productivity and a decrease in the number of jobs.

In this way, however, the income level has remained higher in mill communities than in their surrounding areas for decades and the outcome of restructuring has been only a relative decline of well-being compared with the neighboring remote rural areas of the towns (Lehtonen and Tykkyläinen, 2010b). Nevertheless, the peculiarities of organizing and securing labor in Finland rather explains the relationships between efficiency and labor costs as well as unemployment and relative well-being—i.e. people's opportunities to stay to some extent at the remote and less successful locations—than the actual causes of job creation which is more connected with the techno-economic paradigms and product innovations.

Labor-Force Changes in Lieksa

The Rise and Fall of the Labor Force in Farming and Forestry

Lieksa is located along the old trade route from Russia as the Lieksa River rises within Russia. This is not a common situation in the Finnish border area. Since 1617, it was a trading place colonized by Finns and was part of Sweden. The second industry cycle, named as colonization in the earlier Chapter 4 on Finland, started in the nineteenth century because of growing trade with Russia. Later, during several colonization periods up to the mid-1960s, Lieksa was a labor-absorbing municipality, but when the state support for settling population for the cultivation of the land and forests ended, rural depopulation started and has continued since.

Generally, much of the rural job loss in Finland is explained by growing labor productivity in resource-based sectors, where the same or a larger output is obtained by fewer workers. For instance, commercial roundwood removals have almost doubled since the 1950s. As the competitive advantage of remote, resource-based peripheries is limited to the use of local natural resources, the localities are usually uncompetitive for the growth of other industrial activities without government support (Polèse and Shearmur, 2006; Lehtonen and Tykkyläinen, 2010c). Reactions to the crises have included the shift of labor from one sector to another and gradual depopulation leading to a decline in towns and rural areas as the inevitable outcome when the dominant industries weaken as a result of poor adaptive capacity. In Lieksa, reorientation toward a more diversified economy (Figure 8.4) was the main response at the national and local scales to the end of the latest colonization period from 1945 to 1965 and to increasing rural unemployment.

The Industry Cycle of Wood Processing

In Lieksa, the third long industry life-cycle started in 1903 and is shown in the evolution of cardboard and plank production which peaked from the 1960s to the 1980s (see Figure 4.8 in the first chapter on Finland in this book). It originated from the investments of the past local iron producers and the state forest administration. Since the 1920s, it was a result of nation-scale industrialization policies concerning the forestry sector as an important basis for the national economy (Kotilainen and Rytteri, 2011). The export opportunities emerged because of a growth in demand for sawn timber and cardboard. After political separation through independence in 1917 from Russia, and from the Russian consumer markets, exports from Finland had oriented to western markets and became even more raw material intensive (Hjerppe, 1989). The importance of raw materials, especially timber, increased in the national and local economies.

As described in Chapter 4, the factories and mills faced several changes in their ownership structure, but the production of these industries continued to operate in the same locations, beside the Pankakoski rapids and along the shore of Lake Pielinen. Only the offshoot of packaging production started elsewhere, in the industrial park of Lieksa in the 1970s. The cycle related to forest products has been the longest in the industrial history of Lieksa—longer than a century and it still continues.

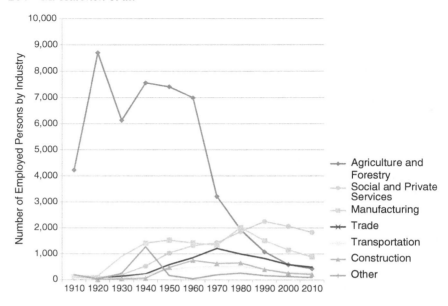

Figure 8.4 The Employment[1] Impact of the Resource Cycles From the Second Cycle of Agriculture and Forestry[2] to the Fifth Life Cycle of the Service Sector in Lieksa.

Sources: Official Statistics Finland (1979, 2013b).

Notes
1 Employment covers all persons—both employees and self-employed—engaged in some productive activity (Official Statistics Finland, 2015b).
2 The Finnish statistical system aggregates agriculture and forestry, so separating them is not easy on an exact level; however, assumptions are made on the basis of known developments within these sectors. It is also assumed that the agricultural and forestry employment in 1910 has been underestimated and in 1920 overestimated in the original statistical data due to the changes of classification.

After the heyday of the third quarter of the twentieth century, employment fell as a result of renewing wood-processing industries to be more cost-efficient. The downturn in labor was nationwide (Figure 8.5) and indicates that job losses originate from global demand and rationalization measures. Expensive labor was substituted by modernized machines in the early 1980s. The job loss in this part of the forest-industry cycle coincides with the stage when the fourth cycle in Lieksa, light manufacturing, became mature and jobs in manufacturing turned to decline.

The Rise and Fall of the Fourth and Fifth Cycles: Light Manufacturing and the Service Sector

The era of strong regional policy from the mid-1960s was seen as a way to overcome the decline in jobs in agriculture and forestry. The opening of Finnish economy to EFTA (European Free Trade Association) and Comecon/ SEV (The Council for Mutual Economic Assistance/Sovet Ekonomicheskoy

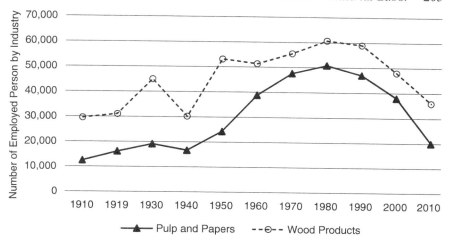

Figure 8.5 Employment of Finnish Forest Industries, 1910–2010.
Source: Official Statistics Finland (1910–1980, 2000, 2013a).

Vzaimopomoshchi) trade combined with regional policy measures led to the growth of non-forestry-related light industries in Lieksa. This era of new manufacturing and assembling industries remained very short since the production that commenced in the 1970s turned into a decline in the 1980s. The decline was accelerated by closures of the most footloose plants following the depression of the early 1990s. Similar to the forest-industry cycle, the manufacturing cycle of the 1970s still continues although its contribution to local employment has declined significantly. The ICT (information and communications technology) boom, in the age of information and telecommunications, from the 1990s onward generated wealth to Finland and to the commuting zone of the regional center within a distance of less than one and a half hours' drive, but did not bring new industrial activities to Lieksa.

Job developments in manufacturing differed by industry (Figure 8.6). The export-intensive industries survived moderately through the recession compared with the industries that were more dependent on domestic markets (Vuorenmaa, 2003). The most severe crisis in manufacturing fell on the clothing sector, which lost 81 percent of its employment in the 1990s. It was an example of too small production which was closed due to unprofitability and overcapacity, and production was relocated to countries of lower labor costs (Henttinen, 2007). Similarly, the sawmill and the cardboard sectors increased labor productivity and as a consequence, many workers were laid off. Cost savings and upgrading continued after Stora Enso sold its cardboard factory to an international investment group in 2006 (Lieksa, 2013; Pankaboard, 2013), but also the process of outsourcing specific work and tasks reduced the number of employees in cardboard production. Nevertheless, most jobs remained in the local economy since the outsourcing of the overhaul and maintenance works of the Pankaboard factory only relocated the jobs from the wood-processing industry to the metal products industry (Maintpartner, 2008; Regional Council of North Karelia, 2009).

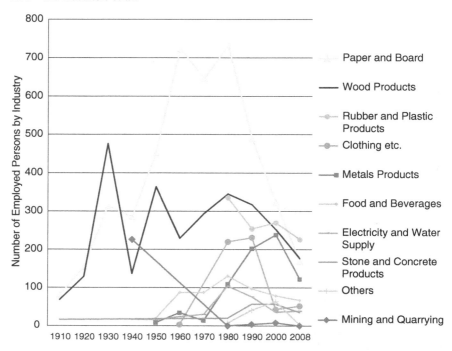

Figure 8.6 Development of Employment in Manufacturing and Mining in Lieksa.
Sources: Regional Council of North Karelia (2009); Vatanen (1986).

As forest industries outsourced parts of their operations, from maintenance work to the manufacturing of metal products, the increased number of jobs in this industry in the early 2000s is thus only partially explained by the actual increase in jobs. Several SMEs (small and medium enterprises) were active, and prospects for local companies seemed fairly good inasmuch as the metal products industry was regionally recognized as an essential target for promoting its operation and investments (Vuorenmaa, 2003). The development of the metal products industry in the whole of North Karelia confronted a setback when a major company at the regional center suspended its production and operations were transferred abroad closer to the growing markets (Hirvonen, 2009). In spite of the development efforts and the recovery of revenues in the metal products industry, the number of jobs stayed at a lower level than in the peak years (TE-centre of North Karelia, 2008).

The constant endeavors toward cost-efficiency and improvements in production also reduced the number of employees in the manufacturing of rubber and plastic products (Figure 8.6). Unlike in the more diverse yet fragmented local metal products industry, jobs in the production of rubber and plastic products were mainly dependent on three main companies (Regional Council of North Karelia, 2009). Ownership changes and the invention of new products were used as strategies to stay in the market for these products. For instance, the production of heavy inner tubes, bicycle tires, and shoe soles remained in Lieksa when the nationwide companies sold their branch businesses to a smaller local company in Lieksa (Nokian Renkaat, 2004; Taloussanomat, 2004; Suomen Kumitehdas, 2014). Processes in production lines were constructed so that their production could complement each other if one production line was out of operation. Nevertheless, in spite of increasing competitiveness, the total number of employees has kept on falling in these industries (YLE, 2009; Taloussanomat, 2014).

Jobs in the service sector grew continuously from the 1920s to around 1990. Until the mid-1960s, population growth and the expansion of the resource-based production increased the demand for services. The era of the intensive construction of the welfare state since the early 1970s generated the services of basic education, public healthcare, and social work that were administrated, produced, and financed by the municipalities, but additional financial government support was provided on demand (Kortelainen, 2010). In Lieksa, this reform demanded for new educated employees, especially in the healthcare sector, and without the simultaneously created system of state subsidies, these wide-ranging reforms would not have been possible (Lieksa, 1975, 1976). As Figure 8.4 shows, about 1,000 jobs were created. After that, due to considerable rationalization measures the decline of jobs has been significant. Hence, neither manufacturing nor the service sector grew enough to maintain population.

Point of No Return?

Lieksa came to a turning point in 1990. Since then, employment has grown neither in the main manufacturing industries nor in services. In most industries there were no abrupt collapses, but steady ongoing trends in the reduction in employment. Several simultaneous economic disturbances deepened the job loss further. The most affecting economic shock was the nationwide recession in the early 1990s. It was caused by several factors which were mainly the result of excessive foreign indebtedness combined with the simultaneous devaluation of the Finnish currency; it eventually led to a plunge in demand in the domestic market and the cutting of public spending (Kiander, 2001). At the same time exports to the Soviet market came to an end. As a result, the unemployment rate in Lieksa surged to 30 percent (Figure 8.7).

The case reveals how the restructuring of companies, changes in state policy, and the tight links with the global economy have impacted on the local industry life-cycles and on the reorganizing of public employment. The early 1990s recession hit most severely enterprises in the private sector, but the decline in employment seems to have been more persistent and long-standing in the non-private sector (Figure 8.8). The cutting of public spending in the 1990s fell upon the whole country but especially on municipalities with net migration deficits as the rationalization of services caused job losses in peripheries (Kangasharju and Pekkala, 2004). In order to gain better productivity, the interests of development policy have mainly turned to the southern part of Finland or other growth centers.

The new focus of rationalization in the early 1990s was the service sector. One of the pioneers was the postal service, which reduced its small offices. As a later

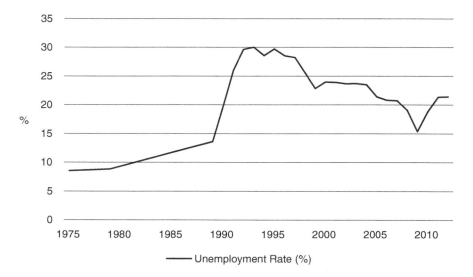

Figure 8.7 Unemployment Rate in Lieksa[1] (%).
Sources: Lieksa (1980); Official Statistics Finland (1982, 2014).

Note
1 Unemployment rate is the proportion of the unemployed people to the active population (labor force) (Official Statistic Finland 2015c).

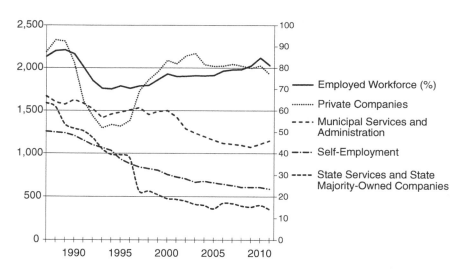

Figure 8.8 Employment Change by the Sector of Employer (Number of Employees) and Employed Labor Force (as Percentage of Total Labor Force) in Lieksa.
Source: Official Statistics Finland (2013b, 2014).

cutback, the Finnish Border Guard, for instance, closed down two of its border guard stations by the end of the 2010 (Finnish Border Guard, 2010), which had a direct impact on the services in the peripheral border town of Lieksa. The same occurred with the cutbacks in the state-owned forest administration (*Metsähallitus*) that reduced employment in the primary sector. These redundancies have been central in the job losses from the service sector although the job loss revealed by the statistics also contains the shifts of activities from one industry to another (Figure 8.8).

Changes in company ownerships and simultaneous layoffs in state majority-owned companies also had considerable impact. For instance, between the years 1996 and 1997 the government reduced its shares of Enso Oyj, the predecessor of Stora Enso Oyj, which changed the company's employment category from the state-based to private-based employment class (Enso Oyj, 1997). As a result, over 300 employees of the local cardboard company changed over from the public to the private sector in Lieksa (Pankakoski Board Mill, 1996). These changes in ownership emphasize the growing importance of private companies as employers although the significance of the municipality as a public employer cannot be ignored.

In spite of the major shrinkages, some of the ten biggest employers in Lieksa show signs that companies have tried to react and adapt to pressures by ownership changes and by changing the fields of business or resource use (Table 8.2). The largest single employer, with over 750 full-time employees, is still the town of Lieksa which as the local public employer, provides services, and is fully dependent on the development of the local population. The second biggest employer, Pankaboard, with over 150 employees, represents the private manufacturing sector which continues the legacy of the forest mill and invests in improvements in production processes and product development.

Since three of the main employers in manufacturing (Pankaboard, Anaika, and Vapo) are based on forest resources, and the number of their employees is over half of the total amount of jobs in the main manufacturing companies (Table 8.2), the legacy of wood processing is strong. All the main manufacturing companies have focused on the development of their products, including the substantial use of imported raw materials. Three companies (Joptek, Amcor, and Reino & Aino Kotikenkä) continuing the legacy of manufacturing and assembling are not linked to natural resources by production, but they have also benefited from the legacy of the former regional and development policies which constructed premises, trained labor, and created the industrial path dependencies in industrial culture. Companies have confronted a major change from the original production to another by product development and specialization.

State social insurance institution Kela set up a nationwide public call-center which could be described as a new kind of footloose service that is based on a change created by information technology and vacant labor in Lieksa. From this perspective, small-scale diversification exists in the town though that industrial structure is fragile and very much reliant on some core actors. What is notable is that the only cluster-like economic activity has been created around the original resource. While this tightened a dependence on forest resources on the one hand, it also helped

Table 8.2 The Largest Employers of Lieksa in 2013

Employer	Industry	Main Product/Service	Workforce
Lieksa municipality	Public social services	Health, education, public utilities	752 + 47 part-time
Pankaboard Oy, Maintpartner Oy	Manufacturing of paper and board products	Boards for packaging and graphical end uses	160 + 34
Kela (State social insurance service)	Social security	Nationwide customer guidance (call-center)	95
Joptek Oy Composites	Manufacturing of rubber and plastic products	Lightweight construction and composite construction systems	85
Anaika Wood Ltd Oy, Anaika Lieksa Oy, Lieksa Timber Ltd	Manufacturing of wood products	Sawn timber and glulam	54 + 12 + 10
Amcor Flexibles Finland Oy	Manufacturing of rubber and plastic products	Flexible packaging products	76
Pielisen OP and OP Kiinteistökeskus Oy	Financial services and real estate agencies	Banking and real estate services	73
Metsähallitus (State Forest Service)	Silviculture and logging	Forestry and park services on state-owned lands	51
Reino & Aino Kotikenkä Oy	Manufacturing of footwear	Slippers	50
Vapo Timber Oy Kevätniemi	Manufacturing of wood products	Sawn timber	42 + 15 contractors

Modified from Lieksa (2013).

to avoid the total drifting into a staples trap of single company communities, which for instance Rytteri (2010) found as the fragile feature of the Canadian case from Pine Falls, Manitoba compared with the forest industry community of Kemijärvi in Finland with its more plural economic links to the global forest industry.

Can Local Natural Resources Re-emerge as a Source for Employment?

The utilization of natural resources is stressed again in the development strategies of Lieksa municipality and the subregion to which Lieksa belongs. Only the emphasis of a saleable resource has developed: specialized agriculture as a resource for the food industry, nature and wilderness as resources for tourism, and forests as a resource for renewable energy (Lieksa, 2014; PIKES, 2014). These all could be placed under the sixth industry life-cycle in Lieksa, called bioenergy and ecosystem-based industries (presented in Chapter 4, Figure 4.8) which mostly highlights various ways of how existing branches or renewable natural resources can be turned into more saleable and value-added products under the concept of bioeconomy (cf. Staffas *et al.*, 2013; The Finnish Bioeconomy Strategy, 2014). Most of these new bioproducts or bioservices are mostly improvements based on something old or already existing, such as developing the Koli national park further as a place of nature tourism, or creating specialized products for the ready-meal or dairy markets. Some new investments have been made and new SMEs have begun to operate but as these actions have much been reliant on a few entrepreneurs and their willingness to renew their businesses, these have had a minor impact on the local employment as a whole. The entrepreneurs and their improvements, however, compensate other jobs that have been lost, and above all, regenerate the ground for the future's place-based policy measures by increasing the variability of local assets and capabilities through their own actions.

New forest-based bioenergy plans make exceptions to the pattern and are clearly linked with wider strategic planning and targeted impacts—not only from the perspective of the local community and its surrounding region but also the provincial- and-national scale policies (The Finnish Bioeconomy Strategy, 2014; Regional Program of North Karelia, 2014). The shift from the conventional forest production toward bioenergy is an example of a changing techno-economic paradigm as renewal through bioenergy requires both the introduction of new technology and amalgamation with other socioeconomic policies at various scales as well as access to the raw material. Technological solutions are necessary but not sufficient conditions for success, as key barriers in adopting bioenergy are socio-technical rather than merely technical (Åkerman *et al.*, 2010). In the subregion of Pielinen Karelia, two forest-based bioenergy projects are under consideration: one in the case town Lieksa and the other in the neighboring municipality of Nurmes. Lehtonen and Okkonen (2016) pointed out that both of them can benefit the local forest resources as in Lieksa where a fast pyrolysis plant (biorefinery) could use the by-products of the forest industries and in Nurmes a biochar factory could mostly utilize the surplus of the current local energy wood supply; and both plants are also planned to be constructed nearby the existing facilities to benefit from localization economies. Their case study shows that new ways of using natural resources create new jobs and bring incomes to Pielinen Karelia. Nevertheless, in order to gain a solid basis for new businesses and to reduce unemployment, not only additional similar local initiatives are sufficient but the local resources need to be combined with the external inputs, for instance, through partnerships or cooperation.

In Lieksa, the biorefinery project aims to reassert the local forest cluster and its competitiveness by linking the new initiatives with current forest-based industries. For instance, the biorefinery plant is planned to be located next to the Kevätniemi sawmill, and alongside the refinery a new bioterminal would serve the logistics of both the biorefinery and other forest industries in the area (Kevätniemen biojalostamo- ja bioterminaalihankkeen ympäristövaikutusten arviointiohjelma, 2014). Since the bioprocessing also requires new kinds of knowhow and technologies, the local vocational school has begun to develop related training programs and acquired test equipment and machinery with the cooperation of the

University of Eastern Finland (North Karelia Municipal Education and Training Consortium, 2015). For the remote rural community, which has faced more downsizing than job creation, improvements in knowledge and working skills with the university are necessary for the renewal of local human capital.

This shift back to local resources is not a new one in development policy. The revitalization of resource-based development of various kinds in development planning instead of favoring manufacturing was a reaction in the early 1980s to the slowing development of the industrial estate in Lieksa (Korhonen and Tykkyläinen, 1983). Although resources exist, it turned out be difficult to create profitable production and new jobs at a significant scale with small greenfield investments in various sectors, from agriculture to tourism. There were several development projects which promoted, for instance, hunting tourism and fishing, but their employment impacts were scanty.

The estimated employment impacts of biorefining are still small compared with job losses. If all jobs related to agriculture are counted, the estimated employment effect is 250 which shows that the new jobs would not even be able to replace the number of farms lost during the past 20 years (1990 = 542, 2010 = 191) (Vatanen *et al.*, 2012; Tike, 2013). Similarly, although Lieksa comprises Koli national park and Ruunaa hiking area and hundreds of square kilometers of waters and even more in forested lands, low employment effects are to be expected from tourism businesses that seek to utilize natural landscapes as attractions (Vatanen *et al.*, 2012). Contrary to Lapland in the north (Lehtonen and Tykkyläinen, 2014; Vatanen *et al.*, 2014), agro-forest areas in Eastern Finland have not attracted significant numbers of tourists, and their attractions are not very suitable for mass tourism which would be necessary to bring profits in the high-cost area. Hence, there is no evidence that the total number of employment effects in tourism and related services would grow much over 200 that was recently estimated (Vatanen *et al.*, 2012).

The forest-based industries will probably have the largest employment effect on the community in the future. The estimated employment effect of the conventional forest industry is 550–600 and the harvest for the bioreserve is 30–40 (Vatanen, 2010). In addition, the biorefinery project is expected to be the largest single investment whose employment effect alone would improve employment in the town and in forested areas significantly. The most optimistic forecasts begin with hundreds of new jobs (Huikuri and Okkonen, 2012), but the more careful calculation anticipates that the number of new local jobs in the production phase would be less than 130 (Okkonen and Lehtonen, 2014), and the toughest calculation predicts only 30 employees for the whole production chain of bioenergy (Vatanen, 2010).

Growth in the use of local natural resources is hardly a sufficient panacea as the new industries relying on the extraction and utilization of local natural resources, most importantly bioenergy production, do not seem to provide enough jobs for the locals and correct the curve of unemployment. It seems evident that there are no strong epoch-making market demands for the industries in Lieksa in sight, no new significant initial advantages emerging, and no financial resources from the state or the EU (European Union) for creating new constructed advantages. Hence, Lieksa, as a town in a declining resource region, is struggling to maintain any form of resilience.

Conclusions

As this chapter has illustrated, communities attempt to be resilient in the economic transition phase when ways to tackle external and internal pressures had to be found. The regional policy measures of setting up a constructed advantage have not created a sustainable booming new economy. Economic diversification faced cost-adjustment problems after the adaptation phase when various support measures, such as regional policy funding, ceased. As a result, jobs were lost.

Although Lieksa's economy diversified in the 1970s, transformation rested on one expanding local production factor only. Namely, there was no other new initial advantage than the postwar baby-boom generation which entered into the labor market. Even if the local industrial tradition provided the labor for new activities, the resilience at the time was essentially dependent on national-scale policy measures, as well as assets and capacities brought to the local scale from supralocal sources. The policy measures can be seen as partially successful at the time, as they brought about a regrowth in the number of jobs. The problem for the local economy, however, was that the policy measures from above did not last long, and without the national support the new industries were not able to maintain competitiveness. Hence a new crisis emerged rather soon. As the forest industries were further modernized and the diversification of the local industrial basis could not compensate for job losses, depopulation has been the way for local adaptation, with the population in Lieksa declining to the same level as in the early twentieth century.

The industry cycle of the service sector could under certain circumstances be seen as a form of renewal of the local economy. From the case study presented in this chapter the conclusion must be, however, that this is not to be. The services have been mostly a result of policies designed and implemented at the scale of the nation-state and provided at the local scale being thus dependent on the size of the population. For the locality, they may appear to be entirely exogenous in origin, but they are based on the expansion of the Nordic welfare state model. Most importantly, the original aim of the welfare services was not to substitute the declining forestry and manufacturing industries, but to provide healthcare and other well-being services for the existing populations. Therefore, even if there are some private sector services that have been designed for tourists, the bulk of the employment positions in services cannot be understood as leading to a renewal of the local economy as the main aim of this policy has not been to diversify the local industrial structure but rather to add a component to the existing structure that supports the local population in getting welfare services.

The case of Lieksa shows that competitiveness in forest-based towns and their rural hinterlands is still greatly dependent on their natural assets, such as natural resources, access to non-urban resources, cheap land, place commitment, and natural amenities. In high-volume resource processing production, especially, decisions are made in global production chains and networks and hence locational choices and profitability are considered in relation to particular networks all the time. In a global context, the short cycle of manufacturing indicates that peripheries in advanced economies are too expensive to generate growth in the great majority of manufacturing industries. Hence, forest-based towns and their rural hinterlands had to find new clever production alternatives and adapt to the situation.

References

Åkerman, M., Kilpiö, A., and Peltola, T. 2010. Institutional change from the margins of natural resource use: The emergence of small-scale bioenergy production within industrial forestry in Finland, *Forest Policy and Economics* 12: 181–188.

Alho, K.E. 2002. *Kannattaako tulopolitiikkaa jatkaa?* ETLA Discussion Papers No. 837. Helsinki, Finland: The Research Institute of the Finnish Economy (ETLA).

Barca, F., McCann, P., and Rodriguez-Pose, A. 2012. The case for regional development intervention: place-based versus place-neutral approaches, *Journal of Regional Science* 52(2): 134–152.

Bergholm, T. 2009. The making of the Finnish model, *Scandinavian Journal of History* 34(1): 29–48.

Bryden, J. and Munro, G. 2000. New approaches to economic development in peripheral rural regions, *The Scottish Geographical Magazine* 116(2): 111–124.

Deller, S., Tsai, T.H., Marcouiller, D., and English, D. 2001. The role of amenities and quality of life in rural economic growth, *American Journal of Agricultural Economics* 83(2): 352–365.

Devezas, T.C. and Corredine, J.T. 2001. The biological determinants of long-wave behaviour in socioeconomic growth and development, *Technological Forecasting and Social Change* 68: 1–57.

Enso Oyj. 1997. *Annual Report, 1997.* Helsinki, Finland: ENSO Group. Available online at: http://web.lib.hse.fi/FI/yrityspalvelin/pdf/1997/eenso.pdf. Accessed December 19, 2013.

Finnish Border Guard. 2010. *Annual Report 2010.* Helsinki, Finland: Finnish Border Guard. Available online at: http://live.grano.fi/tuotanto/r/rajavartiolaitos_2010/. Accessed November 1, 2010.

Freudenburg, W. and Gramling, R. 1994. Natural resources and rural poverty: A closer look. *Society & Natural Resources* 7(1): 5–22.

Gillespie, A.E. and Richardson, R. 2000. Call centre periphery: Teleservices and economic development in rural Scotland / Centres d'appel et développement économique en Ecosse rurale. *Géocarrefour* 75(1): 79–86.

Glasmeier, A. 1994. Flexible districts, flexible regions? The institutional and cultural limits to districts in an era of globalization and technological paradigm shifts. In A. Amin and N. Thrift (eds.), *Globalization, institutions, and regional development in Europe* (pp. 118–146). New York: Oxford University Press.

Goddard, J., Thwaites, A., and Gibbs, D. 1986. The regional dimension to technological change in Great Britain. In A. Amin and J. Goddard (eds.), *Technological change, industrial restructuring and regional development* (pp. 140–156). London: Allen and Unwin.

Halonen, M., Kotilainen, J., Tykkyläinen, M., and Vatanen, E. 2015. Industry life cycles of a resource town in Finland: The case of Lieksa, *European Countryside* 7(1): 16–41.

Heiskala, R. and Luhtakallio, E. 2006. Suunnittelutaloudesta kilpailutalouteen. In R. Heiskala and E. Huhtakallio (eds.), *Uusi Jako—Miten Suomesta Tuli Kilpailukyky-yhteiskunta?* (pp. 14–42). Helsinki, Finland: Gaudeamus Helsinki University Press.

Henttinen, A. 2007. *Moderni suomalainen—Luhdan ensimmäiset sata vuotta.* Lahti, Finland: L-Fashion Group.

Hirvonen, T. 2009. *Joensuun seudun sopeutuminen Perloksen tuotannon lopettamiseen.* Spatial Centre for Regional Research, Reports 1. Available online at: https://www.uef. fi/documents/1145887/1146339/rap2009_1.pdf/defc5877-c264-4676-a5f8-f6114b0ad539. Accessed March 10, 2014.

Hjerppe, R. 1989. *The Finnish economy 1860–1985: Growth and structural change.* Helsinki, Finland: Bank of Finland. Government Printing Office.

Holm, P. 2000. Työehtosopimusten kattavuus, palkat ja työllisyys. *Finnish Economic Journal* 2: 365–377.

Holm, P., Kiander, J., and Tossavainen, P. 1998. Työmarkkinoiden toiminta ja sopeutuminen EMUssa, *Kansantaloudellinen Aikakauskirja* 1: 21–36.

Huggins, R. and Thompson, P. 2015. Culture and place-based development: A socio-economic analysis, *Regional Studies* 49(1): 130–159.

Huikuri, N. and Okkonen, L. 2012. *Bioenergiaa Pielisen Karjalaan.* Joensuu, Finland: Pohjois-Karjalan ammattikorkeakoulu. Available online at: www.pikes.fi/ documents/812306/0/1_Bioenergiaa+Pielisen+Karjalaan+vuosiraportti+2012.pdf. Accessed March 10, 2014.

Johansson, M., Talman, P., Tykkyläinen, M., and Eikeland, S. 1992. Metal mining and mine closure in Sweden, Finland and Norway. In C. Neil, M. Tykkyläinen, and J. Bradbury (eds.), *Coping with closure: An international comparison of mine town experiences* (pp. 44–65). London/New York: Routledge.

Johnson, J. and Rasker, R. 1995. The role of economic and quality of life values in rural business location, *Journal of Rural Studies* 11(4): 405–416.

Kangasharju, A. and Pekkala, S. 2004. Increasing regional disparities in the 1990s: The Finnish experience, *Regional Studies* 38(3): 255–267.

Kauppinen, T. 2005. *Suomen Työmarkkinamalli.* Helsinki, Finland: Werner Södeström Osakeyhtiö.

Kevätniemen biojalostamo- ja bioterminaalihankkeen ympäristövaikutusten arviointiohjelma.2014.Availableonlineat:www.lieksada.fi/sivut/userfiles/file/L1-YVA-ohjelma_Kevatniemi_web.pdf. Accessed November 20, 2015.

Kevätsalo, K. 1999. *Jäykät Joustot ja Tuhlatut Resurssit.* Tampere, Finland: Osuuskunta Vastapaino.

Kiander, J. 1998. *Työmarkkinainstituutiot ja joustavuus: Suomi verrattuna muihin OECD-maihin. Valtion taloudellinen tutkimuskeskus.* Government Institute for Economic Research, Discussion Papers No. 162. Helsinki, Finland: Government Institute for Economic Research.

Kiander, J. 2001. *Laman opetukset: Suomen 1990-luvun kriisin syyt ja seuraukset.* Government Institute for Economic Research, Discussion Papers No. 27(5). Helsinki, Finland: Government Institute for Economic Research.

Korhonen, M. and Tykkyläinen, M. 1983. *Lieksan luonnonvaroista ja niiden hyödyntämismahdollisuuksista.* Lieksan kaupunki, Finland: Luonnonvarojen hyödyntämisprojektin julkaisuja 1.

Kortelainen, J. 2010. Aluepolitiikka. In: P. Niemelä (ed.), *Hyvinvointipolitiikka* (pp. 346–366). Helsinki, Finland: WSOYpro Oy.

Kotilainen, J. and Rytteri, T. 2011. Transformation of forest policy regimes in Finland since the 19th century, *Journal of Historical Geography* 37(4): 429–439.

Kotilainen, J., Eisto, I., and Vatanen, E. 2015. Uncovering mechanisms for resilience: Strategies to counter shrinkage in a peripheral city in Finland, *European Planning Studies* 23(1): 53–68.

Kujala, A. 2008. Työmarkkinapolitiikan murros: Paperiliitto ry erityisaseman ryhmiä, työehtosopimusneuvottelut politiikkaa. In M. Kuisma (ed.), *Kriisi ja kumous. Metsäteollisuus ja maailmantalouden murros 1973–2008* (pp. 261–303). Helsinki, Finland: Suomalaisen Kirjallisuuden Seura.

Kuusterä, A. 1997. Markan matkassa: Suomen rahajärjestelmän historiaa 1840–1997, *Kansantaloudellinen Aikakauskirja* 2 (pp. 285–305). Helsinki, Finland: Valtioneuvoston kanslia.

Leake, N., Adamowicz, W., and Boxall, P. 2006. An econometric analysis of the effect of forest dependence on the economic well-being of Canadian communities, *Forest Science* 52(5): 595–604.

Lehtonen, O. 2015. Space-time dependence in regional development: The geospatial approach to understanding the development processes in small-scale areas of Finland. Joensuu, Finland: dissertation in Social Sciences and Business Studies 105. University of Eastern Finland.

Lehtonen, O. and Okkonen, L. 2016. Socio-economic impacts of a local bioenergy-based development strategy: The case of Pielinen Karelia, Finland, *Renewable Energy* 85: 610–619.

Lehtonen, O. and Tykkyläinen, M. 2010a. Self-reinforcing spatial clusters of migration and socio-economic conditions in Finland in 1998–2006, *Journal of Rural Studies* 26(4): 361–373.

Lehtonen, O. and Tykkyläinen, M. 2010b. Tulotason spatiaalinen kaksoispolarisaatio Pohjois-Karjalassa 1996–2003, *Terra* 122(2): 63–74.

Lehtonen, O. and Tykkyläinen, M. 2010c. Kuinka väestö sijoittuu siirryttäessä tietoyhteiskuntaan?—esimerkkinä Itä-Suomi, *Yhteiskuntapolitiikka* 75(5): 500–518.

Lehtonen, O. and Tykkyläinen, M. 2014. Potential job creation and resource dependence in rural Finland, *European Countryside* 6(3): 202–224.

Lieksa. 1975. *Municipal report of Lieksa 1974 I.* Lieksa, Finland: Lieksan kirjapaino.

Lieksa. 1976. *Municipal report of Lieksa 1974 II.* Lieksa, Finland: Lieksan kirjapaino.

Lieksa. 1980. *Municipal report of Lieksa 1979.* Lieksa, Finland: Lieksan kirjapaino.

Lieksa. 2013. *Lieksa—pocket facts 2013–2014.* Lieksa, Finland: Lieksan kirjapaino. Formerly available online: www.lieksa.fi/documents/752511/1071630/Tietoa+ Taskuun+2013-2014+englanti/023c32b5-d565-48d7-b451-891549c41ec4. Accessed June 20, 2015. See: http://web.archive.org/web/20160307142611/http://www.lieksa.fi/ documents/752511/1071630/Tietoa+Taskuun+2013-2014+englanti/023c32b5-d565-48d7-b451-891549c41ec4

Lieksa. 2014. *Lieksan kaupunki strategia 2020.* Lieksa, Finland: Lieksan kirjapaino. Available online at: www.lieksa.fi/documents/752511/1071430/Lieksan+kaupungin+st rategia+2020/dcaf9ea2-8be4-4cb4-8ce9-7ed680e16aec. Accessed March 10, 2016.

Maintpartner. 2008. Pankaboard ja Maintpartner allekirjoittivat kunnossapidon kumppanuussopimuksen. Maintpartner. Available online at: www.maintpartner.fi/fi/ uutisia/uutiset-ja-tiedotteet/356/pankaboard-ja-maintpartner-allekirjoittivat-kunnossapidon-kumppanuussopimuksen.html. Accessed March 19, 2014.

Markey, S., Halseth, G., and Manson, D. 2008. Challenging the inevitability of rural decline: Advancing the policy of place in northern British Columbia, *Journal of Rural Studies* 24(4): 409–421.

Martin, R. 2012. Regional economic resilience, hysteresis and recessionary shocks, *Journal of Economic Geography* 12(1): 1–32.

Martin, R. and Sunley, P. 2006. Path dependence and regional economic evolution, *Journal of Economic Geography* 6: 395–437.

Molina, O. and Rhodes, M. 2002. Corporatism: The past, present, and future of a concept, *Annual Review of Political Science* 5(1): 305–331.

Nokian Renkaat. 2004. Nokian Renkaat Oyj myymässä polkupyöränrenkaat-liiketoimintansa. Available online at: www.nokianrenkaat.fi/tiedote?id=10340933. Accessed March 2, 2014.

North Karelia Municipal Education and Training Consortium. 2015. Pohjois-Karjalan ammattiopisto Lieksa kehittää alueen biotalouden osaamista ja koulutusta. Available online at: www.pkky.fi/pkky/ajankohtaista/Sivut/biotalous.aspx. Accessed February 5, 2015.

Oakey, R. and Cooper, S. 1989. High technology industry, agglomeration and the potential for peripherally sited small firms, *Regional Studies* 23(4): 347–360.

OECD. 2015a. Trade union density: Table. OECD StatExtracts. Available online at: https://stats.oecd.org/Index.aspx?DataSetCode=UN_DEN#. Accessed June 27, 2015.

OECD. 2015b. Trade union density: Key statistical concept. OECD StatExtracts. Available online from the expansion button at: https://stats.oecd.org/Index.aspx?DataSetCode=UN_DEN#. Accessed June 27, 2015.

Official Statistics Finland. 1910–1980. *Industrial Statistics*. Volume 18. Decennial publication.

Official Statistics Finland. 1979. *Väestön elinkeino: Väestö elinkeinon mukaan kunnittain 1880–1975*, Tilastollisia tiedonantoja 63.

Official Statistics Finland. 1982. 201—Population over 15 years by sex and belonging to labour force 1980. Unpublished data system printout.

Official Statistics Finland. 2000. *Finnish Statistical Yearbook of Forestry 2000*. Vantaa, Finland: Finnish Forest Research Institute.

Official Statistics Finland. 2013a. *Finnish Statistical Yearbook of Forestry 2013*. Vantaa, Finland: Finnish Forest Research Institute.

Official Statistics Finland. 2013b. 050—Employed workforce in area (workplaces) by area, employer sector, occupational status and sex 1987–2011. Available online at: http://pxnet2.stat.fi/PXWeb/pxweb/en/StatFin/StatFin__vrm__tyokay/050_tyokay_tau_105.px/?rxid=19e35825-1df7-4dca-908c-351c64dad149. Accessed March 10, 2016.

Official Statistics Finland. 2014. 010—Population by area, main type of activity, sex, age and year 1987–2013. Available online at: http://pxnet2.stat.fi/PXWeb/pxweb/en/StatFin/StatFin__vrm__tyokay/010_tyokay_tau_101.px/?rxid=19e35825-1df7-4dca-908c-351c64dad149. Accessed March 10, 2016.

Official Statistics Finland. 2015a. Concept and definitions: Economic activity (labour force). Available online at: http://tilastokeskus.fi/meta/kas/amm_toimi_en.html. Accessed February 10, 2015.

Official Statistics Finland. 2015b. *Concept and definitions: Employment*. Available online at: http://stat.fi/meta/kas/tyollisyys_en.html. Accessed February 17, 2015.

Official Statistics Finland. 2015c. *Concept and definitions: Unemployment rate*. Available online at: http://tilastokeskus.fi/meta/kas/tyottomyysaste_en.html. Accessed February 11, 2015.

Okkonen, L. and Lehtonen, O. 2014. Bioenergian aluetalousvaikutukset Pielisen Karjalassa. Available online at: http://bioenergia.pikes.fi/documents/812306/2713655/Lasse+Okkonen_Lieksa+2.12.2014.pdf/d033868a-7d6d-4c70-bf14-8b43e45c283a. Accessed November 20, 2015.

Overdevest, C. and Green, G. 1995. Forest dependence and community well-being: A segmented market approach, *Society & Natural Resources* 8(2): 111–131.

Pankaboard. 2013. *History*. Pankaboard. Available online at: www.pankaboard.com/about-us/history/. Accessed March 7, 2016.

Pankakoski Board Mill. 1996. The number of employees. Enso-Gutzeit Oy, Employee statistics. Central Archives for Finnish Business Records.

Partridge, M. 2010. The duelling models: NEG vs amenity migration in explaining US engines of growth, *Papers in Regional Science* 89(3): 513–536.

Partridge, M., Bollman, R., Olfert, M., and Alasia, A. 2007. Riding the wave of urban growth in the countryside: spread, backwash, or stagnation? *Land Economics* 83(2): 128–152.

Patriquin, M., Parkins, J., and Stedman, R. 2007. Socio-economic status of boreal communities in Canada, *Forestry* 80(3): 279–291.

Perez, C. 2009. Technological revolutions and techno-economic paradigms, *Cambridge Journal of Economics* 34: 185–202.

PIKES. 2014. *The economic development strategy of Pielinen Karelia 2014–2017*. Pielisen Karjalan Kehittämiskeskus Oy PIKES. Available online at: www.pikes.fi/documents/757708/1416317/Pielisen+Karjalan+Elinkeinostrategia+2014-2017_final.pdf/74ea804a-b6f6-47e6-8f03-d98fee4353c8. Accessed February 12, 2015.

Polèse, M. and Shearmur, R. 2004. Is distance really dead? Comparing industrial location patterns over time in Canada, *International Regional Science Review* 27(4): 431–457.

Polèse, M. and Shearmur, R. 2006. Why some regions will decline: A Canadian case study with thoughts on local development strategies, *Papers in Regional Science* 85(1): 23–46.

Regional Council of North Karelia. 2009. Database of industry 1980–2008. Unpublished summary table.

Regional Program of North Karelia. 2014. POKAT 2017—Työtä, elinvoimaa ja hyvinvointia kestävästi Pohjois-Karjalaan. Regional Council of North Karelia, Publication 169. Available online at: http://pohjois-karjala.fi/documents/557926/99266 7/169+POKAT+2017/aad6c2b7-9ac3-4c24-97d4-3de4cd144528. Accessed November 10, 2015.

Rytteri, T. 2010. Tehdasyhdyskunnat ja metsäteollisuuden rakennemuutos: vertailukohteina Kemijärvi, Suomi ja Pine Falls, Kanada, *Alue ja Ympäristö* 39(2): 3–15.

Schmidt, V. 2003. French capitalism transformed, yet still a third variety of capitalism, *Economy and Society* 32(4): 526–554.

Sippola, M. 2011. *Kehitysalueista aluekehitykseen. Suomen virallisen aluepolitiikan 30 ensimmäistä vuotta 1966–1995*. Työ- ja elinkeinoministeriön julkaisuja, Alueiden kehittäminen 31/2011.

Soininen, T. 2015. Changing expectations and realities of employment stability: Longitudinal analysis of tenures in Finland. Joensuu, Finland: Dissertations in Social Sciences and Business Studies 102, University of Eastern Finland.

Staffas, L., Gustavsson, M., and McCormick, K. 2013. Strategies and policies for the bioeconomy and bio-based economy: An analysis of official national approaches, *Sustainability* 5(6): 2751–2769.

Stedman, R., Parkins, J., and Beckley, T. 2004. Resource dependence and community well-being in rural Canada, *Rural Sociology* 69(2): 213–234.

Stedman, R., Parkins, J., and Beckley, T. 2005. Forest dependence and community well-being in rural Canada: Variation by forest sector and region, *Canadian Journal of Forest Research* 35(1): 215–220.

Suomen Kumitehdas. 2014. *Yli 80 vuotta Reinojen historiaa.* Suomen Kumitehdas. Available online at: www.reinokauppa.fi/contact.php. Accessed March 2, 2014.

Taloussanomat. 2004. Nokian polkupyöränrenkaat ja saapastehdas samaan yhtiöön. Availableonlineat:www.taloussanomat.fi/arkisto/2004/10/02/nokian-polkupyoranrenkaat-ja-saapastehdas-samaan-yhtioon/200430181/12. Accessed March 2, 2014.

Taloussanomat. 2014. Suomen Rengastehdas Oy. Available online at: http://yritys.taloussanomat.fi/y/suomen-rengastehdas-oy/lieksa/1920725-5/. Accessed February 7, 2014.

TE-centre of North Karelia. 2008. *Pohjois-Karjala talouskatsaus 1/2008.* Available online at: www.josek.fi/files/file/Talouskatsaus_1_2008.pdf. Accessed March 10, 2014.

Terluin, I. 2003. Differences in economic development in rural regions of advanced countries: An overview and critical analysis of theories, *Journal of Rural Studies* 19(3): 327–344.

Tervo, H. 2009. Centres and peripheries in Finland: Granger causality tests using panel data, *Spatial Economic Analysis* 4(4): 377–390.

The Finnish Bioeconomy Strategy. 2014. *Sustainable growth from bioeconomy.* The Ministry of Employment and the Economy. Available online at: http://biotalous.fi/wp-content/uploads/2014/08/The_Finnish_Bioeconomy_Strategy_110620141.pdf. Accessed November 10, 2015.

Tike. 2013. Statistics of active farms in Lieksa 1990–2010. Agricultural Statistics, Farm Register. Helsinki, Finland: Information Centre of the Ministry of Agriculture and Forestry.

Uhmavaara, H. 2002. Paikallisen sopimisen uudet kehityssuunnat: Toimialakohtaisia tuloksia paikallisesta sopimisesta työelämässä. Turku, Finland: University of Turku, Summary Report of the Field of Businesses.

Uhmavaara, H. 2008. *Paikallinen sopiminen empiirisen tutkimuksen valossa. Paikallinen Sopiminen Yksityisellä Sektorilla.* Turku, Finland: Turun yliopiston oikeustieteellisen tiedekunnan julkaisuja, Yksityisoikeuden sarja, A:121.

Uusitalo, R. 2000. *Paikallinen sopiminen ja yritysten työvoiman kysyntä.* VATT, Research Reports No. 62. Helsinki, Finland: Government Institute for Economic Research.

Vatanen, E. 1986. Pohjois-Karjalan teollisuus 1910–1982. Unpublished research archive material.

Vatanen, E. 2010. Lieksa—luonnonvaroista riippuvainen kaupunki. In: J. Kotilainen and I. Eisto (eds.), *Luonnonvarayhdyskunnat ja muuttuva ympäristö—resilienssitutkimuksen näkökulmia Itä-Suomeen, Joensu, 2* (pp. 41–54). Joensuu: Finland: Reports and Studies in Social Sciences and Business Studies: Publications of the University of Eastern Finland.

Vatanen, E., Eisto, I., and Rannikko, P. 2012. Luontopalvelut ja matkailu syrjäisen maaseudun elinkeinojen uudistajana: tapaus Lieksa, *Kunnallistieteellinen aikakauskirja* 2: 89–113.

Vatanen, E., Ovaskainen, V., and Hyppönen, M. 2014. Luontomatkailu alue- ja paikallistaloudessa. In L. Tyrväinen., M. Kurttila., T. Sievänen, and S. Tuulentie (eds.), *Hyvinvointia metsästä* (pp. 153–162). Helsinki: Suomalaisen Kirjallisuuden Seura.

Vuorenmaa, R. 2003. *30 vuotta: Lieksan Teollisuuskylä Oy*, Lieksa, Finland: Lieksa Development Agency.

Westerholm, J. 2002. Populating Finland, *Fennia* 180(1/2): 123–140.

Wiggins, S. and Proctor, S. 2001. How special are rural areas? The economic implications of location for rural development, *Development Policy Review* 19(4): 427–436.

YLE. 2009. *Aino ja Reino pitävät Kumitehtaan pinnalla*. Helsinki, Finland: Finnish Broadcasting Company. Available online at: http://yle.fi/uutiset/aino_ja_reino_pitavat_kumitehtaan_pinnalla/5283684. Accessed March 2, 2014.

9 Employment and Labor in New Zealand

Recent Trends and Reflections on Developments in the West Coast and Southland Regions

Sean Connelly and Etienne Nel

Introduction

Late nineteenth and early twentieth century New Zealand was characterized by profound social changes, not least among these the entrenchment of a strong culture of unions, labor protection, and social welfare. Mining and harbor unions led the way in successfully pioneering the realization of employment and industrial agreements (Maunder, 2012). In parallel with changes in social welfare provision, this led to the creation of one of the Organisation of Economic Co-operation and Development's (OECD's) most egalitarian states by the post-World War Two era (Stanford in Cooke *et al.*, 2014). In parallel, by the 1970s the country had one of the most controlled economies in the OECD. This was not, however, sustained and from the 1980s a series of drastic steps was initiated by government which effectively 'neoliberalized' all aspects of government, society, and the economy. This was done with the encouragement of the business sector which argued for greater labor market flexibility leading to a situation where the economy rapidly evolved from one based on 'control' to one based on market forces (Roper, 2005; Lattimore and Eaqub, 2011). The net result has been the progressive erosion of the social welfare system, the loss of job protection, the significant weakening of unions, withdrawal of the state from many aspects of the economy and society, and am increased dependence on market forces. The impact of these changes have been felt most strongly in the regions of the country which are either physical isolated from the economic mainstream and/or which depend on a single dominant economic sector and were characterized by the presence of strong, unionized labor movements. In this regard, mining, timber, and manufacturing towns in regions such as Southland and West Coast, which are examined in this chapter, have suffered from the combined effects of the loss of state support, erosion of social welfare, dependence on global market prices, and the weakening or even disappearance of the role which unions played in those towns.

This chapter examines key employment and economic shifts which have taken place in New Zealand, before turning attention to how changes in the employment and labor environment have impacted on issues such as job security and unionization nationally. The focus then shifts to an examination of recent economic and employment trends in two regions, West Coast and Southland, which are used as exemplars of nationally and internationally driven economic and employment changes and the localized effects of such changes, including the weakening of unions and labor protection particularly on mono-economy towns.

Economic and Employment Changes

Over the course of the twentieth and into the twenty-first century the New Zealand economy has experienced the growing tertiarization of the economy typical of the rest of the OECD (Le Heron and Pawson, 1996; Knox *et al.*, 2014), though perhaps somewhat delayed as a result of the significant and continued dependence on primary-sector activities. While this shift from primary production to services is pronounced and amplified by an increasingly urbanized population, complex global dynamics have impacts on both rural and urban spaces (McCarthy, 2005). Table 9.1 reflects this shift, with the tertiary sector rising from 40 percent of GDP in 1936 to 70 percent in 2010, in parallel the primary sector fell nearly three fourths in its value and the secondary sector fell one fourth of GDP over the same time period. At one level, these trends in economic activity can be discussed in terms of a shift from productivist to post-productivist economies; however, such analysis fails to account for the diverse, complex, and multifunctional nature of rural regional economies (Wilson, 2001). As the regions of West Coast and Southland demonstrate (as discussed in Chapter 5), broad shifts in economic activity and rural development are driven both by fluctuating global commodity prices that shift the focus of rural production (primarily from mining to dairy), while at the same time respond to local (and beyond) attempts to diversify economic activity, address demands for amenity, heritage, and cultural protection, and maintain ecological integrity.

National employment (see Table 9.2) reflects a broadly similar shift which shows a major loss in primary-sector employment which fell from 24 percent to 7 percent of all jobs, while the secondary sector has also declined, and the tertiary

Table 9.1 Sectoral Percentage Contribution to National GDP

Sector	1936	1953	2006	2010
Primary	34%	26%	7%	6.3%
Secondary	25%	22%	16%	18.3%
Tertiary	40%	52%	77%	70%
Unclassified	–	–	–	4.3%

Source: Hawke (1985); NZIER (2009); Infometrics (2012a).

Table 9.2 Sectoral Percentage Contribution to National Employment

Sector	1936	1976	2010
Primary	24%	10%	7%
Secondary	26%	35%	19%
Tertiary	50%	55%	74%

Source: Hawke (1985); NZIER (2009); Infometrics (2012a).

sector has risen from 50 percent to 74 percent of all jobs. These shifts are closely related to the agglomeration effect of Auckland, which accounts for 33.4 percent of New Zealand's population and 35.3 percent of national GDP (Statistics New Zealand, 2013). Likewise, Auckland and, to a lesser degree, Wellington lead the country in all measures of labor productivity, with significantly higher levels of labor income and wage rates (Lewis and Stillman, 2005), resulting in reference to the 'two economies' of New Zealand—Auckland and the regions (Eaqub and Stephenson, 2014).

This shift, while inevitable, was, according to New Zealand Institute of Economic Research (NZIER) (2009) accelerated by the structural reforms initiated in the 1980s, which, as discussed in Chapter 5, precipitated significant changes in the economy and employment in the country. Most notable in this regard were: the significant reduction in state involvement and employment in forestry and mining; the axing of agricultural support and the resultant rationalization of farming operations and employment; and the reduction in regional service provision to the detriment of rural communities. Between 1987 and 1984, employment in state-owned enterprises fell from 66,070 to 25,569 (Le Heron and Pawson, 1996). The net result, particularly in regions and communities reliant on primary-sector activity has been their increased vulnerability to fluctuations in the international economy which has impacted directly on local employment prospects, economic opportunities, and ultimately the viability of many small town and rural communities. Parallel urbanization trends in the country, rising levels of average wealth (albeit sectorally and spatially selective) and the growth of new sectors such as tourism have created a fundamentally different employment and economic structure over the last 50 years.

A key change, which will be discussed below, involved concerted efforts on the part of the state and established business to erode the power of the once-powerful unions and to shift employment into a more flexible, and by implication, more vulnerable, position which has since become the norm. Changes in the system of employment contracts and the operation of unions has led to deunionization in traditional stalwarts of the union movement, with mining being the most obvious, where after a century of operating with extremely powerful unions, the transition has taken place to a situation in which the casualization of labor has become the norm (Gallin, 2001; Feinberg-Danieli and Lafferty, 2007). These moves have accelerated employment loss in the primary industrial sectors. The net result of these changes and the removal of state or labor protection measures to reduce regional and local inequalities has been the very real emergence of a scenario which characterizes what Chisholm (1990) referred as a space economy characterized by 'regions of recession' and 'regions of resurgence,' which, as Harvey (2006) argues, are important in the reproduction of capitalism which relies on the persistence of uneven geographical development for its existence.

The Neoliberalization of Labor Relations and Employment

As discussed in Chapter 5, New Zealand is regarded as an exceptional case because of the degree and the tenacity to which the government neoliberalized the economy and society from the 1980s (Cox, 2006; Peet, 2012). The state's significant withdrawal from many aspects of the economy and its privatization drive spilled over into issues of labor regulation and employment. In a country such as New Zealand, which had a long social democratic tradition, a strong welfare state, and is one in which labor unions played a key role in industrial relations and the negotiation of workers' rights for over 100 years, the transformation was profound. In areas such as the West Coast, with its important mining base, the national labor movement had some of its key roots with a series of strikes and associated industrial negotiations on the region's mines helping to shape labor and employment conditions nationally for much of the late nineteenth and twentieth centuries (Maunder, 2012). The neoliberal reforms introduced from the 1980s led to the scenario in which "as economic protection was dismantled, and competitive pressures grew throughout the economy, … the government … moved to strip away the forms of protection built into the system" as government came to regard the existing labor system as a barrier to the efficient operation of the economy (Walsh in Rudd and Roper, 1993 p. 177). In parallel, employers sought reform of the existing arbitration system and successfully pressured the state to introduce labor arrangements that were more favorable to their perceived needs. This led to a situation which Roper (2005) describes as a 'triumph' of neoliberalism and the ruling class over working-class resistance.

The role of corporate influence on the restructuring of the economy in relation to labor is telling. While the first wave of reforms was brought in in the mid-1980s under a labor government, organized labor was excluded from the development of government policy (Cox, 2006). In contrast, the Business Roundtable (BRT) was successful in advancing the interests of the major corporations in New Zealand and was instrumental in providing a climate for liberalization through policy reports, submissions to government, dominance in media commentary, and direct ties with government bureaucracy (Goldfinch, 2000). The first of the new legal provisions after the start of the neoliberal reforms in the mid-1980s was the Labour Relations Act of 1987 which moved the country's employment practice away from a system of nationally binding awards to one anchored on in-house or single employer agreements, thus weakening the union's former strength of being able to exercise national bargaining power. On the positive side, the Act brought in minimum wage rates and rules round working conditions. This Act also forced unions with less than 1,000 members to merge, with the net result that the number of unions had fallen from 227 to 115 by 1989 (Birks and Chatterjee, 2001).

The next key step in the renegotiation of the labor environment was the Employment Contracts Act (ECA). The ECA, introduced in 1991, reduced statutory regulation in matters of arbitration and moved the focus of agreements between employer and employees from collective to individually determined ones and weakened the right to strike (Le Heron and Pawson, 1996). The Act represented "a comprehensive demolition of the 100-year-old institution of arbitration on which New Zealand's class compromise had been premised" (Cox, 2006 p. 112). In addition, it made union membership voluntary thus significantly weakening the bargaining and representational position the unions had once exercised. According to McAloon (2013 p. 211) the Act "deprived unions of much of their legal status, completely decentralized the bargaining process and was intended to drive wages down." The Act was introduced despite mass protests action involving over 300,000 people in 1991 (Roper, 2005). The ECA reflected the corporate takeover of industrial relations legislation. Key aspects of the ECA, including the removal of collective bargaining, were directly linked to submissions and policy reports developed by the BRT which were actively supported and disseminated by media (Cox, 2006).

In a seeming partial retreat, the Employment Relation Act 2000 was introduced to facilitate a return to collective bargaining, but it also reduced the compulsion on individuals to join unions and it facilitated greater access to mediation (Birks and Chatterjee, 2001; Dalziel and Lattimore, 2004). The Act also allowed for the emergence of smaller unions, and by implication weaker unions, which have often lacked power and served more as a conduit to allow members to access collective agreement mechanisms (Barry and Walsh, 2007). A net result of the preceding Acts has been the weakening of the bargaining power of unions and the overall protection of labor, with the "shift to individualised and workplace based employment relations" and a scenario in which "the majority of employers have negative attitudes towards collective bargaining and they seek more employer determined flexibility" (Rasmussen *et al.*, 2013 p. 1).

Changing union membership serves as a surrogate indicator of the degree to which labor relations have weakened in the country. In 1991 there were 603,118 union members (Barry and Walsh, 2007); by 2008 union membership had fallen to 384,777 (Blumenfeld and Ryall, 2010). Only 18 percent of the workforce was unionized in 2000 and the number of work stoppages fell from 383 in 1985 to 32 in 1999. The numbers of workers involved in work stoppages fell from 182,100 to 10,700 (Birks and Chatterjee, 2001). This represents a significant reduction in the role played by organized labor in an increasingly neoliberalized economy and one in which the rights of employers had become paramount in pursuit of the government's overt support for this group and of 'economic efficiency.'

Figure 9.1 demonstrates the impact these changes created in terms of greater stability and flexibility from an employer's perspective. Lost production as measured by person days of work lost due to labor conflicts was reduced from 1,329,054 in 1986 to 330,923 in 1991 and only 6,285 in 2010. The increased labor certainty from an employer perspective also contributed to what one union organizer referred to as "the demolition of unions, resulting in a generation gap about the role of unions and the value of collective activities" (Key Informant 5, personal communication, 2015). Anecdotally, in the few remaining West Coast mines, what little union activity remains today has been significantly diluted by new labor arrangements which include contract employment, fly-in-fly-out arrangements, and outsourcing (Key Informant 6, personal communication, 2015).

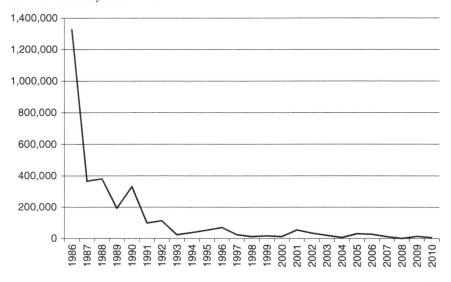

Figure 9.1 Strikes, Stoppages, and Lockouts, 1986–2010.
Source: Statistics New Zealand (2013), INS003AA.

As a result, unions have changed their approach and reconsidered their role in an attempt to reestablish their relevance. Unions have responded to a more flexible working environment through: amalgamation of many smaller unions; greater involvement in health and safety training on a contract basis for employers; taking on greater community service roles; and blending the trades and service unions. However, the underground coal mines of the West Coast have maintained their strong union culture and an unexpected consequence of employment restructuring and the loss of mining jobs is that miners that have been made redundant are getting jobs in other related industries (particularly in construction) and are bringing the union culture with them. As a result, union membership in contracting and construction is starting to increase (Key Informant 6, personal communication, 2015).

According to Thomas (in Cooke *et al.*, 2014 p. 11) the effects of labor reform were profound:

> the effect of the neoliberal revolution on working people has been devastating and savage. Arbitration, compulsory unionism, and the award system of bargaining with employers was swept away. Collective bargaining was shelved in favor of individual contracts between employer and employee. Successive governments have whittled away the workers' rights … the power of trade unions … has been decimated. Wages have stagnated and working conditions have become increasingly harsh. Profits have been put ahead of safety.

The weakening of workers' rights, their bargaining position, and overall employment security, and the economic well-being in the country, is reflected in the finding of the OECD (2014) that by 2012 New Zealand, along with Turkey, had the largest growth in income inequality in the OECD between 1985 and 2011, which, according to the OECD, has directly impacted on economic growth. The OECD also established that since 1985 the distribution of earnings in the country widened by 22 percent compared with an average rise of 15 percent across the OECD (OECD, 2008).

According to Stanford (in Cooke *et al.*, 2014), New Zealand now has some of the weakest employment protection systems in the OECD, the worst rate of deunionization, and the fifth lowest level of bargaining coverage in the OECD. The net outcome has not been the stimulation of employment. By 2014, employment rates (in percentage terms) were actually slightly lower than they were in the mid-1980s and the percentage of the working-age population actually employed fell to the mid-range of the OECD scores. A parallel outcome of the 2008 global financial crisis was the disproportionate loss of employment opportunities for the young, low-waged, and those with low levels of job tenure and job protection in a largely deunionized economy (Fabling and Mare, 2012). Another indicator of change in labor protection and the move to more flexible labor relations stemmed from the increased percentage of the workforce employed on a part-time basis. This rose from 9.7 percent to 22.7 percent between 1970 and 2003 (Dalziel and Lattimore, 2004), reflecting an economy which, according to Perry (in Spoonley *et al.*, 2004), is increasingly characterized by down-sizing, outsourcing, and privatization.

These changes to employment relations extend beyond workers, employers, and unions. The weakening of the unions and the breakdown of the historic relationship between mines and the local mining settlements by these arrangements has weakened local communities economically and socially.

West Coast and Southland

An examination of the two regions selected for particular investigation in this study, namely West Coast and Southland (see Figures 9.2 and 9.3 and as discussed in Chapter 5), reveals similarities and differences from the changing national employment and economic profiles and from the effects of changes in labor conditions. While tertiary economic activities have grown in parallel with national trends, both regions are characterized by a traditional and to some degree continued higher level of dependence on primary-sector activities such as farming, fishing, timber, and mining, and are impacted by their physical isolation from the main economic centers in the country.

Key impacts on the employment base in the West Coast and Southland regions over the last 50 years have included loss of state employment in forestry and mining, the suspension of the logging of indigenous forests, depletion of fishing stock, reductions in farm subsidies, and volatility in the mining economy. In the case of the West Coast, the subsequent designation of 80 percent of the region as reserve or national park land has curbed the scope for future resource exploitation and restricted associated employment prospects (Maunder, 2012). Coal mining

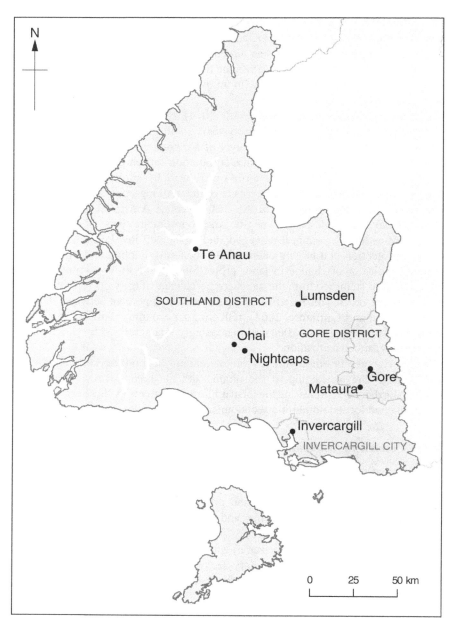

Figure 9.2 Southland.
Map credit: Chris Garden.

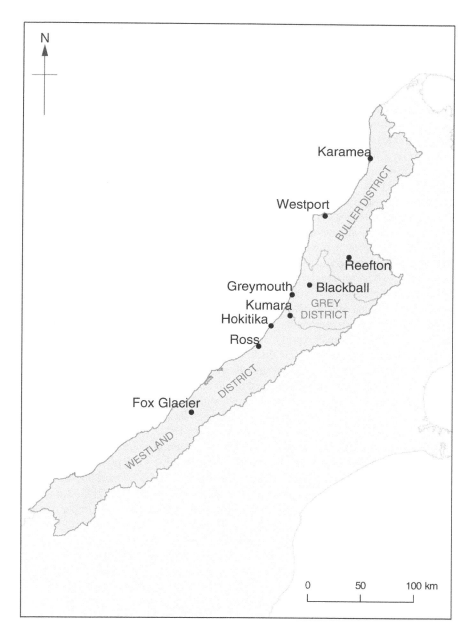

Figure 9.3 West Coast.
Map credit: Chris Garden.

had been the traditional mainstay of the regional economy of the West Coast and had been associated with the rise of a strong union movement which had played a key role in achieving social reform nationally, until the position of mining and miners was significantly reduced by state withdrawal from the mining industry, market fluctuations, and restrictions on union activity (Wright, 2014). The West Coast has experienced cycles of booms and busts as mining and employment is at the mercy of international demand, leading to successive rounds of employment growth and loss, and the reality that the region, according to Maunder (2012 p. 14), exists as a virtual "third world" province. The region's dependence on a limited range of raw material products, relative isolation, and difficulties experienced with trying to diversify its economy led to the government regarding the West Coast as a 'problem' region (Britton *et al.*, 1992; Conradson and Pawson, 2009). The difficult economic situation is exemplified by the reality that in 1984 one third of the region's employment was in primary-sector activities and 49 percent of all full-time jobs were in the state or local government sectors, making the region extremely vulnerable to both state-led economic restructuring and shifts in the global market (Pawson and Scott, 1992). A strong regional sense of identity and resentment against state cuts led to a series of popular protests in the 1980s in the region, but this had no effect on the process of restructuring (Britton *et al.*, 1992).

Agriculture in both regions has benefited from the opportunities which the dairy industry and international exports have provided for much of the last 30 years, but once again this has perpetuated these regions' dependence on externally driven market opportunities (Conradson and Pawson, 2009). The extent to which the conversion to dairying has taken over the agricultural sector is evident in Tables 9.3a and 9.3b. In a general sense, in both regions, we see a decline in the total number of farms and a significant shift from sheep farming into dairy in response to the restructuring of the rural economy. Farmers responded to the pressures of restructuring and the 'corporatization' of agriculture through strategies ranging from intensification to getting out of farming altogether (Joseph *et al.*, 2001). In Southland, the number of farm holdings declined from 5,379 in 1990 to 3,540 in 2013 while the total area of farms stayed relatively constant (1.271 million ha in 1990 to 1.171 million ha in 2013). During that same period the total number of dairy cattle increased from 37,772 to 615,428 and sheep declined from 8.9 million to 4.3 million. In the West Coast, an area with considerably less land suitable for agriculture, similar shifts are apparent. The number of farms declined from 1,288 to 684 from 1990 to 2013, the total area of farms declined from 447,381 ha to 196,407 ha while sheep numbers declined from 8.931 million to 4.390 million. Over the same period, total dairy cattle numbers grew from 37,772 in 1990 to 670,581 from 1990 to 2013. The intensification of agriculture, focused predominantly on dairy farming, resulted in fewer people working more land, decreasing on-farm employment and having flow-on effects for the consolidation of agricultural services in fewer towns (Joseph *et al.*, 2001).

These changes were also related to the restructuring of the processing of agricultural products. Throughout the 1990s, sheep and beef processing plants were rationalized to address plant overcapacity in the context of declining sheep numbers.

As a result, processing capacity in New Zealand had fallen 25 percent and employment by 40 percent in the decade prior to 1996 with flow-on effects on rural communities (Le Heron and Pawson, 1996). In contrast, the shift to dairy, particularly since 2000, has seen rapid expansion of milk processing plants. The Fonterra plant in Edendale, Southland, has the peak capacity to process up to 15 million liters of milk per day, employs 600 people and has a fleet of 65 tanker trucks that collect milk from throughout Southland and Otago (Fonterra, 2015). Likewise, the Westland milk products plant in Hokitika has undergone considerable expansion, with production increasing from nearly 400 million liters to 753 million liters (160 million liters of which is brought in by train from Canterbury). The Hokitika plant has 400 employees and has a fleet of 100 tanker trucks (Westland Milk, personal communication, June 12, 2015). However, with the continued decline in global dairy prices, the incomes of South Island dairy farmers are expected to drop by $3NZ billion from their peak of two years ago (Steeman, 2015). The trickle-down impacts of that loss of income will be felt in rural communities as farmers cut back on farm spending, inputs, equipment, and retail spending.

Table 9.3a Southland Farm Type and Size

	Number of Farm Holdings	Total Area of Farms	Total Dairy Cattle (Including Bobby Calves)	Total Beef Cattle	Total Sheep
1990	5,379	1,271,986	37,772	186,533	8,931,881
1991	5,375	1,265,545	43,956	181,037	8,453,558
1992	5,211	1,227,266	52,762	171,851	8,040,856
1993	5,282	1,242,020	70,910	174,537	7,806,683
1994	4,575	1,256,402	114,378	202,538	7,850,791
1995	4,493	1,269,141	125,806	214,326	7,687,777
1996	4,368	1,237,550	137,552	204,107	7,457,393
1997	–	–	–	–	–
1998	–	–	–	–	–
1999	4,791	–	232,966	229,830	6,738,097
2000	–	–	–	–	–
2001	–	–	–	–	–
2002	4,376	1,198,388	356,220	203,670	5,950,657
2003	4,137	1,186,760	347,793	220,042	5,855,296
2004	4,072	1,326,091	349,021	216,523	5,966,919
2005	4,089	1,275,630	348,075	202,326	5,950,627
2006	4,045	1,178,523	375,911	204,632	5,928,761
2007	3,947	1,178,136	432,642	207,588	5,662,387
2008	3,791	1,144,688	495,971	190,562	4,739,003
2009	3,693	1,201,607	589,184	214,927	4,556,206
2010	3,660	1,188,251	599,198	186,157	4,597,335
2011	3,660	1,124,553	614,648	173,798	4,112,930
2012	3,699	1,201,569	670,581	172,150	4,356,427
2013	3,540	1,171,571	615,428	168,031	4,390,785

Source: Statistics New Zealand (2014), AGR003AA.

Table 9.3b West Coast Farm Type and Size

	Number of Farm Holdings	Total Area of Farms	Total Dairy Cattle (Including Bobby Calves)	Total Beef Cattle	Total Sheep
1990	1,288	447,381	64,499	73,491	313,543
1991	1,277	443,589	65,518	72,511	260,195
1992	1,265	437,629	66,079	70,030	246,500
1993	1,284	464,595	70,212	70,148	237,449
1994	881	370,622	79,251	67,733	216,544
1995	890	406,940	85,156	65,975	221,246
1996	858	385,746	91,022	59,931	172,864
1997	–	–	–	–	–
1998	–	–	–	–	–
1999	1,287	–	120,992	52,364	103,837
2000	–	–	–	–	–
2001	–	–	–	–	–
2002	837	225,454	124,640	38,908	92,508
2003	756	–	122,572	36,968	83,978
2004	835	222,340	141,401	31,274	81,941
2005	770	228,915	142,370	32,275	74,988
2006	794	227,421	148,730	37,097	78,067
2007	823	200,126	152,481	30,275	54,094
2008	785	206,924	152,869	34,713	43,156
2009	777	228,987	179,416	35,892	42,889
2010	759	196,290	160,791	31,816	41,523
2011	732	195,573	179,308	29,531	34,778
2012	735	196,635	173,651	29,002	58,085
2013	684	196,407	178,907	26,242	32,876

Source: Statistics New Zealand (2014), AGR003AA.

The net result, if one examines Table 9.4, is that while both regions parallel the national shift to the tertiary sector as the dominant employment category, there is a very real time lag in this transition, and in the case of the primary sector in Southland there has even been a slight recovery between 2001 and 2010 in primary-sector employment, associated with the strengthening of the dairy industry. In the West Coast region, which once employed thousands of coal and gold miners, falling demand has significantly altered the traditional employment base. The decline in the secondary sector in both regions parallels national trends and broadly reflects closure of local timber mills and manufacturing as a result of loss of access to indigenous forests, free-trade policies, loss of subsidies, and market rationalization. Distinctive in both areas has been not only the decline in primary-sector jobs but also the parallel weakening of the labor movement, which has lost ground in the face of: declines in the mining, timber, and meat packing economies nationally; moves to casualize mining operations; and significant changes in employment legislation, as discussed above, which has weakened the role and place of unions. Associated with these changes has been the direct impact on once-important mining, timber, and manufacturing towns as is detailed below.

Table 9.4 Percentage Contribution to New Zealand (NZ), West Coast (WC), and Southland (SL) Employment

Sector	1966			1986			2001			2010		
	NZ	WC	SL	NZ	WC	SL	NZ	WC	SL	NZ	WC	SL
Primary	14	24	18	11	22	22	8	19	15	7	19	18
Secondary[1]	36	30	34	28	27	29	21	18	24	19	19	22
Tertiary	50	46	48	61	51	49	61	63	61	74	62	60

Source: Statistics New Zealand (1966, 1986, 2001); Infometrics (2012a, 2012b).
Note:
1 Secondary = manufacturing, construction and electricity (Infometrics, 2012a).

Localized Impacts of Change

The economic and settlement geography of the West Coast and Southland vividly reflect the dramatic impacts which economic change has had on the viability and future of large numbers of settlements. While larger settlements, which rely increasingly on service sector employment, have generally held their own in terms of employment and population levels the same cannot be said of smaller towns once reliant on single economic sectors—with the most obvious casualties being mining, timber, and industrial towns. According to Pawson and Scott (1992), as a result of the significant withdrawal of the state from direct involvement in resource sectors and the regions, state employment on the West Coast fell from 2,371 in 1986 to 917 in 1991. At a national level Perry (in Spoonley *et al.*, 2004) notes that by 2003, 70 percent of all the country's jobs were centralized in the seven largest urban centers following the decline in regional/rural employment levels.

The continuing marginalized position of the West Coast and Southland regions is reflected in data which indicate that they are two of only three regions in the country which experienced population decline in 2013. In addition, they shared the position for the highest decline in employment—with both regions losing 2 percent of their full-time equivalent positions. In economic terms, Southland had the lowest GDP growth rate of the country's 13 regions and West Coast the sixth lowest (BERL, 2014). In the case of the West Coast, this follows a brief period of employment and economic growth consequent upon a temporary surge in the mining industry which ended in 2014 following mine closure and associated job losses.

These regional economic trends are also reflected in median household incomes in both the West Coast (Figure 9.4) and Southland (Figure 9.5). With the exception of Southland District (as opposed to the whole Southland region), all districts lag behind the New Zealand average over the period 2001–2013. At the district level, median household incomes have converged in the $67,800NZ (for Invercargill) to $75,500NZ (for Southland District) bracket. However, when median household incomes are examined at a subdistrict level, greater unevenness is apparent.

If we look at median household incomes in select communities on the West Coast (Figure 9.6), we see the major centers of Hokitika and Greymouth following similar trends to the national average. Median household incomes in Westport,

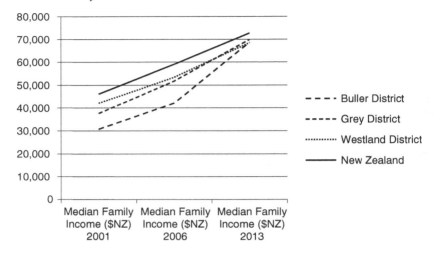

Figure 9.4 Median Household Income, West Coast Districts.
Source: Statistics New Zealand (2001, 2006, 2013).

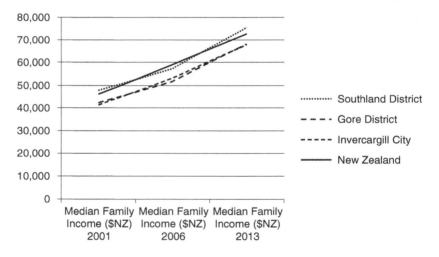

Figure 9.5 Median Household Income, Southland Districts.
Source: Statistics New Zealand (2001, 2006, 2013).

started from a lower base but grew quite rapidly in the 2006–2013 period in tandem with major expansion in coal mining. Solid Energy's Stockton open-pit coal mine, located just north of Westport, was one example of this temporary expansion. The site has been mined since 1886, and it has an estimated potential production capacity of 2 million tonnes per year through to 2028. Annual production at Stockton had risen from 500,000 tonnes per year in 1987, to 1 million tonnes in 1995 to 2 million tonnes per year in 2009. During that period, direct employment grew from 210 to 800 (Solid Energy, 2011), with production dropping back down to 1 million tonnes in 2015 when layoffs and redundancies brought the workforce down to 243 (O'Connor, 2015). The smaller towns of Blackball and Kumara's incomes lag between $20,000–$25,000NZ behind the national level. Reefton is another good example of dependence on a resource-based economy. Median family incomes in Reefton in 2001 and 2006 were on par with those of Blackball and Kumara, before the opening of the OceanaGold open-pit gold mine in 2007 that saw median family incomes soar from $39,200NZ to $67,900NZ in 2013. The Reefton gold mine reached peak production in 2009 but it is slated to close in 2016, which will lead to the loss of 240 direct jobs (OceanaGold, n.d.).

In Southland, median family incomes (Figure 9.7) tell a story of a two-track economy. In this case, the major service centers of Invercargill and Gore and tourist towns like Te Anau closely follow the national average while smaller, formerly forestry and mining towns, were lagging behind.

If we examine the percentage of households that rely on some form of benefit as a source of income (pension, unemployment, sickness, student allowance, etc.), we see similar patterns emerge. In both the West Coast and in Southland, the smaller, formerly mono-economy towns of Blackball, Kumara, Ohai, Nightcaps, and Mataura have greater percentages of families that rely on some form of benefit than either the regional or national averages (see Tables 9.5a and 9.5b). Meanwhile, towns that benefited from recent resource booms such as Reefton and Westport, or from an increase in tourism and recreational spending such as Te Anau, had much lower reliance on benefits. These trends are also reflected in population changes over time.

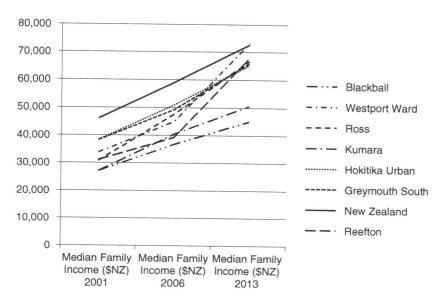

Figure 9.6 Median Family Incomes, Select West Coast Towns.
Source: Statistics New Zealand (2001, 2006, 2013).

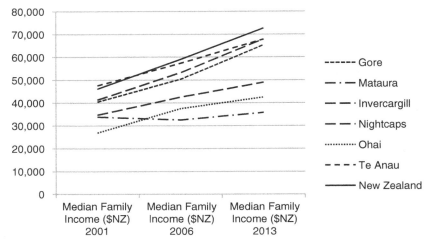

Figure 9.7 Median Family Incomes, Select Southland Towns.
Source: Statistics New Zealand (2001, 2006, 2013).

Table 9.5a Welfare Benefits and Families, Southland

	Total Families	Total Benefits	% of Families Relying on Some Sort of Benefit[1]
Gore			
2001	2,019	1,209	59.9
2006	2,022	1,101	54.5
2013	1,977	1,089	55.1
Mataura			
2001	465	315	67.7
2006	399	282	70.7
2013	402	261	64.9
Invercargill			
2001	13,116	8,157	62.2
2006	13,509	7,437	55.1
2013	13,878	7,725	55.7
Nightcaps			
2001	84	66	78.6
2006	81	54	66.7
2013	78	54	69.2
Ohai			
2001	93	75	80.7
2006	87	69	79.3
2013	66	60	90.9
Te Anau			
2001	744	264	35.5
2006	825	261	31.6
2013	957	372	38.9
Southland			
2001	24,171	13,197	54.6
2006	24,666	12,063	48.9
2013	25,434	12,699	49.9
New Zealand			
2001	1,294,047	846,306	65.4
2006	1,397,238	803,541	57.5
2013	1,478,703	811,850	54.9

Source: Statistics New Zealand (2001, 2006, 2013).

Note

1 Accident Compensation Corporation, Pension, Unemployment, Sickness, Domestic Purposes, Invalids, etc.

Table 9.5b Welfare Benefits and Families, West Coast

	Total Families	Total Benefits	% of Families Relying on Some Sort of Benefit[1]
Blackball			
2001	81	66	81.5
2006	81	57	70.4
2013	75	45	60.0
Westport			
2001	1,455	942	64.7
2006	1,611	894	55.5
2013	1,824	915	50.2
Ross			
2001	87	51	58.6
2006	81	42	51.9
2013	93	39	41.9
Kumara			
2001	84	69	82.1
2006	93	54	58.1
2013	81	54	66.7
Hokitika			
2001	744	486	65.3
2006	804	435	54.1
2013	786	417	53.1
Greymouth			
2001	1,623	1,032	63.6
2006	1,704	942	55.3
2013	1,587	891	56.1
Reefton			
2001	240	153	63.8
2006	249	132	53.0
2013	252	108	42.9
New Zealand			
2001	1,294,047	846,306	65.4
2006	1,397,238	803,541	57.5
2013	1,478,703	811,850	54.9
West Coast			
2001	7,677	4,560	59.4
2006	8,208	4,140	50.4
2013	8,445	4,062	48.1

Source: Statistics New Zealand (2001, 2006, 2013).

Note

1 Accident Compensation Corporation, Pension, Unemployment, Sickness, Domestic Purposes, Invalids, etc.

Table 9.6 reflects population change in towns which traditionally have relied on a single primary industry in both regions. Across the board decline, except in the tourism towns of Te Anau and Fox Glacier, are strikingly obvious.

In farming service centers such as Winton and Gore in Southland, the population rose by 27 percent and 29 percent respectively from 1966 to 2013, albeit that growth rates have fallen after 2011, which reflects the continued importance of

Table 9.6 Population Change in Mono-Economy Towns in Southland and West Coast

Town	Dominant Sector	1966 Population[1]	2013 Population	% Change
Southland				
Nightcaps	Mining	654	294	−55
Ohai	Mining	939	303	−41
Tuatapere	Timber	954	555	−25
Tapanui	Timber	844	723	−18
Mataura	Manufacturing	2,629	1,509	−43
Te Anau	Tourism	961	1,914	+99
West Coast				
Reefton	Mining	1,783	1,029	−42
Blackball	Mining	852	288	−66
Fox Glacier	Tourism	163	306	+88

Source: Statistics New Zealand (1966, 2013).

Note

1 The 1956 figures is used for West Coast due to incomplete census data for 1966.

farming and meeting its requirements from the key service towns. Regional centers such as Invercargill in Southland and Greymouth and Westport in West Coast have not kept pace with national population growth, only increasing by 12 percent and 14 percent in the first two cases in 47 years while Westport fell by 23 percent as a result of loss of manufacturing in the town and mining in the hinterland. Coal mining towns such as Blackball have been particularly hard hit with mine closure eroding the population, infrastructure, and community of the town (Maunder, 2012).

Discussion and Conclusion

The experience of the West Coast and Southland regions and their labor forces and communities reveals that dramatic processes of change have taken place in the last 30 years which reflect the overlay of multiple global, national, and local processes which have negatively impacted on employment levels and regional, local, and community well-being. Exposure to global competition, the neoliberalization of the economy, the scaled-down power of the unions, the increasing tertiarization of the economy, and the persistent marginalization of these regions have wrought their toll on local employment levels and the well-being of many small communities. This reality is reflected in the relatively static demographic position of both regions, relative to national trends, and the evident level of welfare dependence which economic change and associated losses have catalyzed. While overall regional economies have experienced some gain from the recent dairy industry boom, volatility in mining, the loss of manufacturing industry, rationalization of farm operations, and the sluggish performance of the general economies of both regions is evident.

At a macro level, we see regional economies that are heavily dependent on major national and international forces that shape economic activity and the quality of life in communities. The structure of the national and global economy determines the success or failure of these rural and regional economies and there is little scope for local stakeholders to intervene at a regional level to change prospects (Matthews, 1983). In this sense, we can see the prospects of regions such as the West Coast and Southland as reacting to the boom–bust cycles of global prices for coal or milk powder, or the restructuring of employment relations and state services. With improved mobility and flexibility, people and jobs will come and go in response to economic conditions and the best that local communities can hope for is to make the most of the booms and cope with the busts. This is, however, a functionalist view of the region which exists to develop resources for exchange through a linked system of regions, but such a view fails to account for community agency, culture, and capacity, essentially those things that make regions unique and provide for regional identity (Paasi, 2013) which can shape outcomes.

In Chapter 13, we shift our attention to how communities and rural places have responded to these challenges. Our discussion and analysis will shift from the functional impacts of rural restructuring discussed above to an approach that emphasizes the practice and relationships between people, place, and territory, and the characteristics that make these rural places and regions unique (Markey *et al.*, 2008).

References

Barry, M. and Walsh, P. 2007. State intervention and trade unions in New Zealand, *Labor Studies Journal* 31(4): 55–78.

BERL (Business and Economic Research Limited). 2014. *Regional rankings 2013: BERL regional rankings series.* Wellington, New Zealand: Business and Economic Research Limited.

Birks, S. and Chatterjee, S. 2001. *The New Zealand economy: Issues and policies.* Palmerston North, New Zealand: Dunmore Press.

Blumenfeld, S. and Ryall, S. 2010. Union membership in New Zealand: Annual review for 2008, *New Zealand Journal of Employment Relations* 35(3): 84–96.

Britton, S., Le Heron, R., and Pawson, E. 1992. *Changing places in New Zealand: A geography of restructuring.* Christchurch, New Zealand: New Zealand Geographical Society.

Chisholm, M. 1990. *Regions in recession and resurgence.* London: Unwin-Hyman.

Conradson, D. and Pawson, E. 2009. New cultural economies of marginality: Revisiting the West Coast, South Island, New Zealand, *Journal of Rural Studies* 25: 77–86.

Cooke, D., Hill, C., Baskett, P., and Irwin, R. (eds.). 2014. *Beyond the free market: Rebuilding a just society in New Zealand,* Auckland, New Zealand: Dunmore Publishing.

Cox, L. 2006. The Antipodean social laboratory, labour and the transformation of the welfare state, *Journal of Sociology* 42(2): 107–124.

Dalziel, P. and Lattimore, R. 2004. *The New Zealand macroeconomy.* Melbourne, Australia: Oxford University Press.

Eaqub, S. and Stephenson, J. 2014. *Regional economies: Shape, performance and drivers.* Wellington, New Zealand: New Zealand Institute of Economic Research, Working paper 2014/03.

Fabling, R. and Mare, D.C. 2012. *Cyclical labour market adjustment in New Zealand.* Auckland, New Zealand: Motu Working Paper No. 12-04, Motu Economic and Public Policy Research.

Feinberg-Danieli, G. and Lafferty, G. 2007. Unions and union membership in New Zealand: Annual review for 2006, *New Zealand Journal of Employment Relations* 32(3): 31–39.

Fonterra. 2015. *Edendale.* Available online at: www.fonterra.com/nz/en/about/our+locations/newzealand/edendale/edendale. Accessed August 2, 2015.

Gallin, D. 2001. Propositions on trade unions and informal employment in times of globalisation, *Antipode* 33(3): 531–549.

Goldfinch, S. 2000. Paradigms, economic ideas and institutions in economic policy change: The case of New Zealand, *Political Science* 52(1): 1–21.

Harvey, D. 2006. *Spaces of global capitalism: Towards a theory of uneven geographical development.* London: Verso.

Hawke, G.R. 1985. *The making of New Zealand: An economic history.* Cambridge: Cambridge University Press.

Infometrics. 2012a. *Labour market and economic profile: West Coast.* Wellington, New Zealand: Infometrics.

Infometrics. 2012b. *Labour market and economic profile: Southland.* Wellington, New Zealand: Infometrics.

Joseph, A., Udgard, J.M., and Bedford, R. 2001. Dealing with ambiguity: On the interdependence of change in agriculture and rural communities, *New Zealand Geographer* 57(1): 16–26.

Knox, P., Agnew, J., and McCarthy, L. 2014. *The geography of the world economy.* London: Routledge.

Lattimore, R. and Eaqub, S. 2011. *The New Zealand economy.* Auckland, New Zealand: Auckland University Press.

Le Heron, R. and Pawson, E. 1996. *Changing places: New Zealand in the nineties.* Auckland, New Zealand: Addison-Wesley Longman.

Lewis, G. and Stillman, S. 2005. *Regional Economic Performance in New Zealand: How does Auckland compare?* Wellington, New Zealand: New Zealand Treasury.

McAloon, J. 2013. *Judgements of all kinds: Economic policy making in New Zealand 1945–1984.* Wellington, New Zealand: Victoria University Press.

McCarthy, J. 2005. Rural geography: Multifunctional rural geographies: Reactionary or radical? *Progress in Human Geography* 29(6): 773–782.

Markey, S., Halseth, G., and Manson, D. 2008. Challenging the inevitability of rural decline: Advancing the policy of place in northern British Columbia, *Journal of Rural Studies* 24(4): 409–421.

Matthews, R. 1983. *The creation of regional dependency.* Toronto, Canada: University of Toronto Press.

Maunder, P. 2012. *Coal and the Coast,* Christchurch, New Zealand: Canterbury University Press.

NZIER (New Zealand Institute of Economic Research). 2009. *Economic progress and puzzles: long-term structural change in the New Zealand economy, 1953–2006.* Wellington, New Zealand: Working paper 2009/6, New Zealand Institute of Economic Research.

O'Connor, S.J. 2015. More West Coast jobs to go as OceanaGold mine closes. Available online at: www.stuff.co.nz/business/industries/70584778/more-west-coast-jobs-to-go-as-oceanagold-mine-closes. Accessed August 2, 2015.

OceanaGold. (n.d.) *Reefton open pit.* Available online at: www.oceanagold.com/our-business/new-zealand/reefton-open-pit/. Accessed March 9, 2016.

OECD (Organisation for Economic Co-operation and Development). 2008. *Growing unequal? Income distribution and poverty in OECD countries.* Paris: OECD. Available online at: www.oecd.org/els/social/inequality. Accessed January 23, 2015.

OECD (Organisation for Economic Co-operation and Development). 2014. *Does income inequality hurt economic growth? OECD Focus on Inequality and Growth.* Paris: OECD Directorate for Employment, Labour and Social Affairs.

Paasi, A. 2013. Regional planning and the mobilization of 'regional identity': From bounded spaces to relational complexity, *Regional Studies* 47(8): 1206–1219.

Pawson, E. and Scott, G. 1992. The regional consequences of economic restructuring: The West Coast, New Zealand, New Zealand (1984–1991), *Journal of Rural Studies* 8(4): 373–386.

Peet, R. 2012. Comparative policy analysis: Neoliberalising New Zealand, *New Zealand Geographer* 68(3): 151–167.

Rasmussen, E., Foster, B., and Coetzee, D. 2013. Transforming New Zealand employment relations: The role played by employer strategies, behaviours and attitudes. Auckland, New Zealand: unpublished paper, Auckland University of Technology.

Roper, B.S. 2005. *Prosperity for all: Economic, social and political change in New Zealand since 1935.* Auckland, New Zealand: Thomson.

Rudd, C. and Roper, B. 1993. *State and economy in New Zealand,* Auckland, New Zealand: Oxford University Press:

Solid Energy. 2011. *Stockton Mine.* Available online at: www.solidenergy.co.nz/operations/stockton-mine/. Accessed August 10, 2015.

Spoonley, P., Dupuis, A., and de Bruin, A. (eds.). 2004. *Work and working in twenty-first century New Zealand.* Palmerston North, New Zealand: Dunmore Press.

Statistics New Zealand. 1966. *New Zealand census of population.* Wellington, New Zealand: Statistics New Zealand

Statistics New Zealand. 1986. *New Zealand census of population.* Wellington, New Zealand: Statistics New Zealand.

Statistics New Zealand. 2001. *New Zealand census of population 2001.* Wellington, New Zealand: Statistics New Zealand.

Statistics New Zealand. 2006. *New Zealand census of population 2006.* Wellington, New Zealand: Statistics New Zealand.

Statistics New Zealand. 2013. *New Zealand census of population 2013.* Wellington, New Zealand: Statistics New Zealand. Available online at: www.stats.govt.nz/Census/2013-census.aspx. Accessed February 23, 2014.

Statistics New Zealand. 2014. *Infoshare Table AGR003AA,* Wellington, New Zealand: Statistics New Zealand. Available online at: www.stats.govt.nz/infoshare/Default.aspx. Accessed February 20, 2014.

Steeman, M. 2015. Failing dairy incomes will hurt the South Island economy. Available online at: www.stuff.co.nz/business/farming/dairy/70941412/falling-dairy-incomes-will-hurt-the-south-island-economy. Accessed August 8, 2015.

Wilson, G.A. 2001. From productivism to post-productivism…and back again? Exploring the (un)changed natural and mental landscapes of European agriculture, *Transactions of the Institute of British Geographers* 26(1): 77–102.

Wright, M. 2014. *Coal: The rise and fall of King Coal in New Zealand.* Auckland, New Zealand: David Bateman.

Part III
Community Implications

Introduction

"Whatever You Can Do at Ocean Falls You Can Do Better Somewhere Else"

Roger Hayter

This statement, offered in an interview in 1972, by a senior corporate executive of the multinational corporation (MNC) controlling the newsprint mill and sole economic base of Ocean Falls, located on the remote northwestern coast of British Columbia (BC), may be brutal but it underscores the vulnerability of resource communities. Ocean Falls was created to house the workforce for a new newsprint mill that opened in 1917 at the end of a fjord to access water and hydropower, local fiber supplies, and distant markets via ocean transportation. But by the 1950s, the MNC chose to develop a more accessible coastal site on Vancouver Island for a much bigger pulp and paper mill in the more accessible community of Campbell River with more amenities and much less rainfall than at Ocean Falls; as this mill was progressively expanded, Ocean Falls was gradually run down, before being purchased (for virtually nothing) by the provincial government in 1973, and soon after finally closed. Ocean Falls is now a virtual ghost town, still without road or rail access, and a handful of (jobless) residents barely connected by small, occasional ferries to the outside world. Campbell River's pulp and paper mill is now closed too, but the community has moved on as a relatively diversified, accessible, service and tourism center.

As Part III ascertains in the discussions of Mackenzie by Halseth *et al.*, Lieksa by Kotilainen *et al.*, the various communities in New Zealand's Southlands and West Coast regions by Connelly and Nel, and Armidale in the Northern Tablelands by Sorensen, resource communities seek to maintain themselves as workplaces and home places, admittedly with varying degrees of success. If the specter of ghost towns casts a large shadow in the literature, implying that busting will win out over booming, it is not inevitable. While resource cycles even in renewable resource contexts typically pose inexorable trends that sooner or later threaten community stability, resource communities are often remarkably resilient and able to adapt to changing circumstances. Lieksa, for example, has already adjusted to several resource cycles since the eighteenth century, helped by supportive national governments and empathetic social bargains in the past 70 years or so, and Kotilainen *et al.*'s explicit reference to the next (sixth) Kondratiev wave both recognizes challenges to, and optimism for, present restructuring. However, for Mackenzie and the mining towns of New Zealand's Southlands and West Coast, restructuring is more threatening, and staple traps are hard to escape. Several communities in the New Zealand regions are small and isolated, and if Mackenzie's population once exceeded 5,000 it is nevertheless located on a (highway) cul-de-sac, and its population is smaller now. Moreover, neoliberal policies, especially in New Zealand, Australia, and more erratically in BC, have complicated the challenges of community restructuring; in these places efforts to create local social bargains (among local actors) have been confounded by ambiguous mixes of national and regional policies. Yet, if the general picture is daunting, even gloomy, Armidale offers itself as a beacon of hope for resource communities that wish to reinvent themselves as vibrant, diversified, and proactive centers.

From a community perspective the challenge of local economic development often only becomes apparent in the mature and decline stages of resource cycles. Initially, and during booms, local government is a passive actor, providing local services and facilitating resource exploitation that is often orchestrated by outside interests. In Mackenzie's case, the mill and town was established in a 'top-down' way as a node within global space, created by outside capital, labor, and equipment to serve global markets. Even the town's design and governance was implanted. While jobs were plentiful there was no local interest in diversification. Now as large-scale mills have closed or downsized, Mackenzie and other communities in the region have actively engaged in promoting local economic development. In Halseth et al.'s terms, Mackenzie's challenge is to shift from being a subservient supply node within global space to a more engaged place that is seeking to shape its future from within. The same challenge confronts the New Zealand communities while Lieksa has more experience in this regard.

For the case study resource communities, established resident populations with strong place-based attachments provides the impetus for seeking new activities to replace downsized resource sectors. Indeed, the attractiveness of the case study communities is further intimated by the arrival of newcomers, whether for recreational reasons, retirement, or some other purpose. Yet, the community populations under investigation are generally aging, small, or very small, and dependencies on structured workforces and resource exports impose cognitive restraints on thinking outside the box. Moreover, in New Zealand and BC, senior governments have downloaded responsibilities to local governments without providing additional support (or much power), trends that for smaller resource communities have been especially problematic. New Zealand's national social support system has been reduced and the implications are left to communities, while in BC the removal of appurtenancy has undermined local access to the forest resource and increased corporate discretion over its allocation. Also, in BC, Australia, and New Zealand, environmental concerns have increased and are creating new demands for conservation, while opposing resource commodification. In BC, Indigenous peoples who have been formerly excluded from resource allocations and from conventional community life have become much more active, strengthened by court decisions supporting Aboriginal rights and demands for new treaties. In New Zealand, similar debates over Māori rights have been more structured, rooted in the (1840) National Treaty of Waitangi (for which there is no Canadian parallel). In general, in Mackenzie and nearby communities, and in the Southlands and West coast regions, local government has faced two new sets of responsibilities. First, local governments have needed to shift, in Halseth *et al.*'s words, from a managerial to an entrepreneurial mode actively seeking development and, second, to embrace a more diverse range of stakeholders with differing views of the industrial and nonindustrial values of resources.

As the following chapters document, the case study communities are shaping restructuring processes according to local experiences, priorities, and decision-making processes that are democratic and embrace a variety of different perspectives. If these contemplations are not autonomous, in one way or another influenced by senior governments, the initiatives are locally flavored and highly varied. In Lieksa, where governance structures are well established and links to national programs important, since the 1980s new ventures have focused on adding value in wood processing, developing tourism as a cottage industry, and adding several health and education services. Even so, for the most part, the new jobs are fewer than the old jobs lost, while successful local development depends crucially on institution building and leadership. In the Southland and Westcoast communities, institutional building to help promote development has been a major focus, especially in light of the lack of state support. Development West Coast and Venture Southland are regional bodies, only established in the mid-2000s, that have helped identify and fund developments, most successfully in Invercargill, a larger community led by a charismatic mayor. Some local development corporations have provided support and there are many local initiatives building on local history, arts, and related products. Again, however, new jobs have not compensated for the old ones lost in terms of numbers or income. Mackenzie's efforts are similar while illustrating the importance of perseverance for communities seeking to become entrepreneurial and inclusive. In the 1990s, initial local development plans were mainly formed by outsiders and they remained locked into old attitudes. However, following a further crisis in its forestry sector base, the community created its Mackenzie-in-Motion Plan. This Plan involved immediate response to the threatened closure of mills that linked tax relief with employment, and an energetic engagement with development planning that featured extensive local dialogue, strong local municipal leadership, and key collaborations with regional partners, notably local Indigenous peoples, and the provincial government. A community forest, tourism additions, and more self-belief within the community suggest Mackenzie-in-Motion may be just that.

But it is Armidale, now a thriving center of over 23,000 people that features strong relations between a local university, high-tech activities, and business start-ups, that provides the most radical, innovative model of community diversification. For Sorensen, an important key to Armidale's local development is the mutually supportive activities of "clusters of [local] people" (rather than clusters of economic activities themselves) with a shared entrepreneurial culture and ability to cooperate and build upon local amenities and educational expertise. More generally, Armidale has been able to re-envision itself as an integral part of the ICT industry, as a community that is an active part of the shift toward creative or resurgent cities, rather than as a remote space responding to, and controlled by, the needs of cores. Admittedly, the extent to which the Armidale model can be replicated elsewhere is not obvious. Few small resource communities can have a university, many do not have the amenity values of Armidale, entrepreneurship is not a mechanical activity, and local organizations and governance can become sclerotic rather than visionary. Yet bearing in mind its origins in an remote, inland region within the world's most remote continent, Armidale's experience indicates that even (still remote) resource towns can diversify and gain significant autonomy as places within the global system.

Located on the geographic margins of global economic activity, the case study communities seek to provide homes and workplaces for residents who desire to live there, even as their global roles have changed. That they should be successful is not only important locally but globally in terms of providing industrial and recreational goods and services, and for contributions to ecological, cultural, and lifestyle diversity. But the restructuring of resource communities implies rethinking their global roles as they seek to become more flexible in new, often highly nuanced ways and sometimes more radically. In an age of globalization, does this mean resource communities are becoming more differentiated, internally and among themselves? The case study chapters provide fascinating insights into such trends.

10 Community Development in an Age of Mounting Uncertainty
Armidale, Australia

Anthony Sorensen

"If you don't think about the future, you cannot have one."
John Galsworthy (1867–1933), Nobel Prize Winner in Literature

"The best way to predict the future is to invent it."
Theodore Hook (1788–1841)

"The future has a way of arriving unannounced."
George Will (1941–)

"The future always arrives too fast... and in the wrong order."
Alvin Toffler (1928–)

"If the rate of change on the outside exceeds the rate of change on the inside, the end is near."
Jack Welch (1935–), former CEO General Electric

"Tomorrow, and tomorrow, and tomorrow, creeps in this petty pace from day to day, to the last syllable of recorded time; and all our yesterdays have lighted fools the way to dusty death."
William Shakespeare (1564–1616), *Macbeth*

Introduction

Considered collectively, these quotations aptly signpost this chapter's contents and philosophy. At the start of what Brynjolfsson and McAfee (2014) call the second machine age (2MA), which parallels in many respects Rifkin's (2011) Third Industrial Revolution (TIR), much of rural Australia is potentially perched on an economic and social precipice. Such imagery may seem overly melodramatic, but is not misplaced because several monumental and complexly intersecting forces for change are likely reshape Australia's rural economy and society comprehensively over the next quarter century. Our task here is to explore how an expanding raft of rampant and essentially uncontrollable technologies could reshape rural society at the same time as processes of globalization, increasing loss of national sovereignty, ever greater social fragmentation, rising political complexity, and an age of budgetary austerity are conspiring to reduce public capacity to plan for the future constructively. In such an environment, the task of local development will likely fall increasingly to regional and local communities and will entail psychological reorientation (Sorensen, 2010) through exploratory self-help to deliver stable adaptation (Sorensen and Epps, 2005). In this way, communities may become more outward looking and future oriented, risk accepting, less fearful of change, and able to seize the development initiative.

However, the lessons of earlier industrial revolutions strongly suggest that losses of industries and jobs, and their subsequent replacements, are unlikely to be colocated, thereby brightening the development prospects of some communities, while simultaneously blighting those of others—depending on local portfolios of physical resources, finance, social and human capital, and quality of infrastructure. Moreover, Australian rural communities typically have little accumulated knowledge of how to accomplish psychological reorientation effectively, which is the main focus of this chapter. To make this task more difficult, experiences are likely to be spatially variable depending on local geography. Thus, documenting such experiences, in line with de Montaigne's (1580) philosophy of experience, may become a key element in explaining to community leaders potential sound paths for their communities to take in navigating the future. We therefore focus here, via participant experience, on how one region and a key city within it, namely the Northern Inland (NI) of New South Wales (NSW) and the city of Armidale, are coping with the hazards of inventing the future from a behavioral perspective. The town is fortunate to have a sizable coterie of technological activists who are collectively working to signpost the future drawing on commercial cultures prevalent in such business start-up capitals as Silicon Valley and Tel Aviv. I am part of that group, being a member of the Northern Inland region's Digital Economy Taskforce, having addressed the region's business innovation award night in 2014, giving the opening keynote address to Armidale's first TechFest in 2015, and delivering many other presentations to either national or local community groups—wearing his futurist hat. He is also an active investor and especially a nascent macroeconomist.

A Technological Tsunami

A range of authors has recently focused on likely technological developments over the medium term, 10 to 20 years from now, and their implications for the transformation of economy and society (Ford, 2009; Hammersley, 2012; Mills, 2013; Rawlings *et al.*, 2013; Stephenson *et al.*, 2013; Berleant, 2013; Brockman, 2014; Brynjolfsson and McAfee, 2014; Cass, 2014; de Waele, 2014; Pentland, 2014; Wood, 2014). In summary, most of this work sees the extension of Moore's Law into a variety of technological arenas such that the pace of adjustment will ramp sharply to perhaps four times the speed that accompanied the industrial revolution between about 1750 and the turn of the twentieth century. Moore's Law, which dates from 1965, foresaw the doubling of semiconductor power roughly every year or 18 months, has mostly proved correct although the time lapse has now extended to two years (Brock, 2006). The rapid transformation of almost every economic activity will see the collapse of many existing enterprises, rising unemployment—especially among low-skilled workers whose jobs can more readily be mechanized, and greater social inequality, but it will also see the creation of many new jobs. Some places that can position themselves to adapt rapidly to the changes occurring and seize evolving opportunities will win from the tide of events—yielding what Sorensen and Epps (2005) term stable adaptation. Others, with a portfolio of declining businesses and inability to focus on the future, are apt to become losers. Thus, in many respects, Hägerstrand's pioneering work in the 1960s on innovation diffusion is likely to be relevant also in the early years of the twenty-first century, except that information and communications technology (ICT) may revise upward the technological and adaptation prospects of larger rural and regional cities.

Table 10.1 identifies 14 potentially transformative technological arenas, all of which are currently active. But a critical feature of the coming 2MA or TIR, which will accelerate the pace of change, is the increasing blending, fusion, or integration of different technologies to create yet further innovation. This is captured exquisitely by the notion of "the internet of things" whereby a host of devices with separate origins and purposes are integrated through ICT (Greengard, 2015), as on the smart farm or in the smart city or home. Many of the components of Table 10.1 could have explosive impacts on rural regions, not least because collectively they may destroy or radically modify 40 percent or more of all existing jobs over the next 20 years. We can readily hypothesize that rural communities with small and perhaps sparsely settled populations may struggle to create the seedbed conditions essential for the rapid development or adoption of new technologies and their subsequent delivery of scarcely imagined goods or services (Hägerstrand, 1967).

Table 10.1 Fourteen Technological Arenas

1	Enhanced ICT	2	Quantum computing
3	Big data/information storage	4	E-tailing and e-governance
5	Transport (e.g. drones, driverless cars and trucks, Elon Musk's vacuum tubes, and aerospace)	6	Human augmentation (wearable ICT, surgical implants as foreseen by Kurzweil)
7	New materials (lightweight, high strength, anticorrosive, good malleability, etc.—graphene and stanene)	8	New Food (e.g. synthetic meat printed on 3D printers; chemical cuisine (or Note-by-Note cooking); synthetic milk; protein from harvesting insects)
9	Smart everything: agriculture, mining, homes, vehicles, cities	10	FinTech (including crowdfunding; and venture capital specialists)
11	Renewable energy generation and especially storage using new battery technologies	12	Robotics/Artificial General Intelligence
13	Automated construction techniques (e.g. DIRTT in Calgary)	14	Bio-medical (cures for many common diseases; GM advances)

Source: author.

Items in no particular order.

Many other factors are likely to contribute to this outcome, ranging from government policy settings, local business cultures, supply of venture capital, degree of regional integration with global economy, the quality and variety of local physical resources, human and social capital, quality of leadership, and environmental hazards. Given that individual localities tend to vary greatly on all of these dimensions, it is also likely that regional responses to impending and often hugely transforming technologies, and the effectiveness of their outcomes, will also diverge significantly and that effective remedial strategies adopted by place 'A' might not suit place 'B.' So rural communities not only face a tsunami of new technologies, but also a steep learning curve in selecting from a multitude of response options designed to enhance and accelerate local adaptive capacity. Unfortunately, these options are clouded in a miasma of uncertainty.

The Dawn of an Age of Fragility: Technology Collides With Society

As noted by Taleb (2012), uncertainty and fragility are the growing hallmarks of our age. Rural Australia has been, and will continue to be, heavily resource dependent through agriculture, forestry, mining, and, increasingly, tourism and related lifestyle activities. The primary sector in particular has always been buffeted by forces beyond its control (ABARES, 2015; Department of Industry, Innovation and Science, 2015). For example, the prices of crops and minerals are set on the Chicago Mercantile and London Metals Exchanges respectively and reflect global patterns of supply and demand. Prices received by producers are also heavily influenced by the value of the Australian dollar relative to other currencies, especially as nearly all minerals and two-thirds of agricultural output are exported rather than consumed locally. Shipping costs also vary from time to time, along with seasonal conditions. Many parts of rural Australia have unstable climates that lurch between drought and flood, but rarely on any regular timetable. Australia's many bilateral and multilateral free trade agreements sometimes regulate the export of specific commodities, while domestic prices for farm output are often rigged by major supermarket chains.

Moreover, uncertainty frequently arises from conflicts over resources within rural regions. For example, farmers frequently dispute among themselves, with mining companies and surrounding communities such issues as:

- access to irrigation water,
- fracking and removal of overburden for mining, and
- preservation of ecologically important vegetation and wildlife corridors.

Debate over foreign ownership of land is also heating up as Asian countries in particular try to secure food and fiber for their increasingly wealthy and discriminating populations. The impact of uncertainty on Australia's rural society is also likely exacerbated because this nation operates, by global standards, a relatively pure market economy—ranking fourth after Hong Kong and Singapore in the Heritage Foundation's 2015 Index of Global Economic Freedom (Country

Rankings, 2015). In short, both federal and state governments in Australia traditionally run tight fiscal and expenditure settings. They recoil from providing subsidies to help local producers compete in corrupt world commodity markets. They also spend relatively little on regional policy, although observing universal and community service obligations (USOs and CSOs) in providing many essential educational, medical, and infrastructure services (Productivity Commission, 2005; Sorensen, 2000, 2002, 2009a, 2009b; Sorensen *et al.*, 2007).

In addition, primary industries can experience rapid and significant market shifts in commodities demanded by overseas customers, so production traditions often mean little. For example, demand for wool slumped over the decade 2005–2015 while demand for sheepmeat and beef soared. Simultaneously, the number of cattle rose and of sheep declined. Likewise, cotton output expanded relative to coarse grains—reflecting demand conditions and the greater profitability of cotton production. And some new agricultural industries have recently appeared overnight. Soaring Middle Eastern demand for camel milk and meat has been met from the domestication of wild camels in Central Australia (Edwards *et al.*, 2008). Australia, amazingly, has the world's largest herd of wild or feral camels, estimated by some at about one million.

Fortunately, Australian agriculture is for the most part large scale and technology focused (Sorensen, 2009a, 2011a). Aided by many government-funded research organizations, some of which are also industry co-funded, the farm sector's total factor productivity growth has been far faster than any other industry sector since the 1980s through both the rapid uptake of new production techniques and access to the necessary investment capital. This technology focus has undoubtedly helped producers to survive and prosper in a complex and uncertain operating environment, where multiple fast-changing variables intersect and their relationships are rarely linear. Taleb (2007) brilliantly anticipated in precise detail how such complex and opaque environments could lead directly to the 2008 global financial crisis, which was beyond the control of most governments. Imagine, then, the limited capacity of individual farmers to control their operating environments. Thus they, like most private producers of commodities, goods, or services have little option but to be flexible and adaptable, using the kinds of optionality strategy outlined by Taleb (2012).

We must now add consideration of the many fast-changing dimensions of human and social capital which are in some ways unconducive to both adaptation to new technologies and consequent economic renewal. One would expect rural society's aging and typically conservative populations, which often lack fresh leadership and technological knowledge, to lag in the innovation stakes. Moreover, Australians are more mobile in seeking jobs or life experiences than in many other countries, which leads to the rapid out-migration of the young or skilled pursuing better opportunities. Society is also fragmenting. The binary class system, whose conflicts dominated philosophy, culture, and politics from the start of the industrial revolution, has shattered into many different conflicting groups. A recent British study identified seven classes in that nation and much of the developed world would be little different (Savage *et al.* 2013). In one way this is a good thing, bringing many more ideas and preferences to the negotiating table. Simultaneously, it makes it more difficult for rural society to sing with the unified voice that resonated politically in the past. On the other hand, the spread of high-speed broadband is enabling the emergence of numerous theme-oriented networks in virtual space actively pursuing participants' interests. Some seek to defend existing entitlements or viewpoints, while others act as harbingers of the future. Past studies of regional leaderships, who were often crucial to local economic and social development, focused on just one or two highly skilled individuals (Sorensen and Epps, 1996), but it seems likely that fragmenting society will entail many more leadership participants with high-class negotiating and motivational skills (Pentland, 2014).

Figure 10.1 illustrates the complex range of potential participants in shaping rural futures and their preferred knowledge and behavioral attributes for navigating fragile and fast-moving economic and social conditions. Our emergent world often provides us with few clues as to what is going on and where events are heading. As noted earlier, regional problems and prospects are also likely to be diverse, depending on each location's portfolio of resources, geographical accessibility, the quality of human and social capital, and business culture. Different problems will likely entail different solutions.

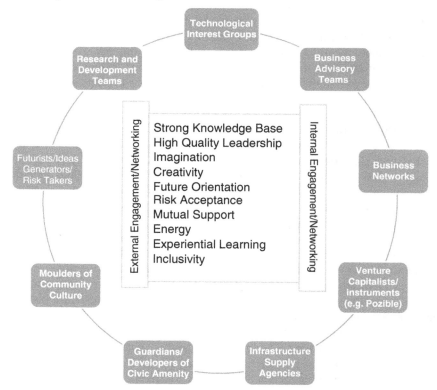

Figure 10.1 Networks of Everything
Source: author.

Complexity and Atrophy of Government

Since the 1960s, rural communities have looked to superior tiers of government, national or provincial, to engineer development via the creation of regional development agencies, infrastructure funding, industrial decentralization, seed-funding of endogenous business development, and provision of good quality services. From an Australian perspective, it is doubtful if any of these strategies have done much to alter development trajectories that would have occurred under a largely market-based economic system (Sorensen, 2002; Daley, 2012). And it is likely that governments' capacity to manage place prosperity will shrink further in an age of fast-moving technology and increasing complexity.

The reasons are simple, but potentially devastating for rural communities. Governments have minimal control over the evolution and spread of technologies, most emanating from the private sector for commercial gain. Connected with this, they also lack understanding of the threats posed by the 2MA or TIR until much too late and are congenitally unable to spark business innovation or identify new business options. Increasingly, too, they have become subservient to the tyranny of the macro where the following domestic or international macroeconomic considerations all loom much larger in public debate than place prosperity:

1 fiscal and expenditure settings and a preference for government budgetary surpluses,
2 lowering Reserve Bank discount (and interest) rates—subject to inflationary constraints,
3 prudential financial regulations,
4 competition policy,
5 balancing international trade,
6 national prosperity relative to our international peers, and
7 promotion of Australia Inc. or its constituent States in global arenas.

Rising aversion and failure of imagination about potential futures and how best to achieve them lead most politicians to prefer *waterfall* over *agile* projects. This distinction, which originated in the fields of project management and ICT, is now used to distinguish between the creation of infrastructure monuments and working toward honing people's adaptive capacities. There may be many more votes in building dams (and opening them) compared with fostering imagination and creativity. And few national or provincial governments have ever successfully managed policy arenas involving changing a broad spectrum of people's and communities' psychologies—their perceptions, attitudes, opinions, imaginations, creativity, ambitions, risk acceptance, and so on (Sorensen, 2010). Finally, governments are constrained by their reliance on courting conservative electorates fearful of change and by a rising difficulty in forming governing majorities in societies whose social and cultural structures are rapidly diversifying. Coalition formation and maintenance is frequently a time-consuming business at the very moment when agile decision-making is required to manage rapid change. Put another way, we face a new and rising form of democratic deficit.

Table 10.2 Some Macroeconomic Considerations Testing Governments

1   Fluid flows of capital and investment
2   The restructuring of corporate landscapes through takeovers, divestments, or collapses
3   Piles of government debt in some countries that have effectively mortgaged future generations or may potentially bankrupt individual nations
4   A messy plethora of bilateral and multilateral trade agreements
5   Rising mobility in international labor markets
6   Increasing imbalances in resource supply and demand

Source: author.

To make matters much worse still, consider this. Economic globalization has the potential to introduce massive instabilities for nations, provinces, and their constituent regions that may be sudden and barely controllable in the short term. It seems likely that the conditions shown in Table 10.2 could trigger global shocks, which few nations could anticipate yet alone manage, whose underlying processes resemble some unholy combination of complexity, information, chaos, socionomic, and tipping point theories (Diamond, 2005; Sorensen, 2011b). Take the last 20 years, since the 1990s. We have witnessed massive commodity booms and busts; the Tech-Wreck of the early 2000s; financial crises in Asia and the United States— both of which had global ramifications; economic meltdowns in the European Union and some of BRIIC[1] nations; the near bankruptcy of Greece and Argentina; and massive economic growth in China capped by a spectacular crash of the Shanghai Stock Exchange. Difficulties in managing or responding to such events often distract governments from focusing on the problems of domestic regions.

Creating Creative Communities (CCC)

How can peripheral regions navigate such turmoil? Given all these fast-moving complexities and uncertainties, it seems unlikely that national or provincial governments will play a large role in promoting regional well-being beyond several traditional roles. These include providing basic infrastructure and social services mandated by USOs and CSOs, funding various kinds of regional development organization, or facilitating research and development. The last named is important for Australia's agriculture and environment. Government subsidies for agriculture amount to *c.*5 percent of gross value of output, among the lowest in the developed world, but much of it is directed to research and development, which has a major impact on the sector's competitiveness (Sorensen, 2011a).

Australian local governments also typically have few resources, accounting for about 5 percent of government outlays, coupled with increasing demands being placed upon them by the state government. From a development perspective, their main role is likely to lie in improving local amenity and lifestyles, providing basic infrastructure such as local roads or water supply, and protecting human and environmental heritage. So the task of adapting local economies to the tsunami of new technologies appears to lie with local businesses and institutions. Existing businesses will have to adapt to changing circumstances as best they can following Taleb's (2012) antifragility precepts—and especially the notion of optionality, while new enterprises will emerge by embracing new niches provided by some combination of (1) technology, (2) local communities' evolving needs or preferences under rising per-capita wealth, and perhaps (3) visitors pursuing intense leisure and recreation goals. Moreover, in the twenty-first century those niches might increasingly involve providing high quality and competitive goods or services to national and international markets.

The task of navigating the turmoil essentially involves the transformation of business cultures to grow a region's or locality's number of business enterprises and improve their commercial success. In the past, governments attempted this role by providing such incentives as cash grants, subsidies, tax holidays or concessions, protective trade barriers—whether regional or even international—and maybe such infrastructure as industrial estates or technology parks. Nearly all these measures have been dismantled in Australia and other advanced nations. In their place, regional and business development strategy has embraced psychology (Sorensen, 2010; Taleb, 2012). Such thinking has been underwritten since the turn of the century by a large raft of economics literature which has dethroned the concept of *Homo Economicus* (see for example Prechter, 2001, 2003; Kahneman, 2011; Rifkin, 2011; Pentland, 2014; Thaler, 2015). They, in turn, build on earlier reservations voiced by some of the discipline's greatest thinkers, including Veblen, Keynes, and Simon. Such geographers and urbanists as Jacobs (1984), Florida (2005), and Glaeser (2011) have also distilled the environmental and behavioral attributes conducive to creation and innovation. The best summary of all this work from a regional development perspective is probably provided by the Startup Genome (Techcrunch, 2015), now the StartupCompass organization.

The Startup Ecosystem Report for 2012 ranked cities globally on six indices: funding, performance, talent, support, mindset, and trendsetter. Excluding the *performance* dimension, which is likely to be slight in most rural regions, we can define the remaining dimensions as follows:

1   Funding: the volume of activity transacted, range of risk capital funding sources, and their breadth of application;
2   Talent: the age and education of those involved in start-ups, length and quality of experience in the industry sector concerned, capacity to handle risk, previous success rates with start-up enterprises;
3   Support: from mutual networks, external mentorship, service providers (inputs), and funding agencies;
4   Mindset: attitudes of business founders—vision, resilience, high risk appetite, strong work ethic, ability to overcome typical start-up challenges; and
5   Trendsetter: ability to embrace new technologies, management processes, business models.

These five dimensions all have a strong psychological component. However, we should probably add three more items to the list. Florida's work demonstrates the importance to innovators of both environmental and social amenity of the kinds discussed by Argent *et al.* (2013) in a rural context. Second, there is Taleb's (2012) insistence on optionality—the constant pursuit and analysis of alternative future business options—as a crucial dimension of business survival which also appears relevant. In other words, we should always be scanning the future under rapidly changing, complex, and uncertain conditions. Finally, the diversity and contest of ideas, which Jacobs notes in her work, could also be crucial. The old idea of developing blueprint plans for regions that governments and businesses should pursue in single-minded fashion appears absurd in the uncertain and fast-moving economic order of 2015. Note, once again, that the application of this broad psychological agenda to particular regions will likely vary according to their local geography, resources, and human capacities.

How, then, do we encourage would-be entrepreneurs to get going or, in effect, translate the innovative culture of places like Silicon Valley into Australia's remoter and sparsely settled rural regions? More precisely, how can we mold communities that think about, explore, and welcome the future; develop and invest in innovative business ideas; start up new enterprises; network comprehensively; develop the sharing economy, and mutually help each other? Adherence to tradition and conservatism are unrealistic options for the survival of businesses or communities. One of this chapter's initial quotations from Jack Welch is spot on on this theme: "If the pace of change on the outside exceeds the pace of change on the inside, the end is near." Alarmingly, it would appear that only a handful of Australia's rural communities or businesses are aware of, or understand, the struggle they face to avoid Welch's dire outcome or the mind-shift necessary to embrace the future creatively. For example, Kotey and Sorensen's (2014) study of small enterprises in country towns servicing cotton production found that business innovation was patchy and often awaited such difficult trading conditions as brought on by drought, far from Taleb's advocacy of optionality. High-quality and future-oriented leadership will become much more important in separating winners from losers than earlier studies in the field (for example, Sorensen and Epps, 1996) revealed. And the locus of leadership will almost certainly shift from mayors and local governments to the business community and social institutions.

Navigating Turmoil in Practice

We now turn to an exploration of how our case study locations, NI and Armidale, have both combined in creative and sometimes complex ways to take innovative local development into their own hands. Figure 2.1 (in the first of the Australia chapters in this collection) locates these jurisdictions. The Regional Development Australia—Northern Inland (RDA—NI) is one of a national network of RDAs sponsored by the Federal Government. Covering 98,606 square kilometers (or 314 km²), its fairly static population of 176,000 yields a low average population density of about 1.8 persons per km². Armidale is Australia's highest city at an altitude of around 1,000 m and its regional population, including its agricultural hinterland, is about 25,000.

A quick glance at Table 10.3 reveals that Armidale and the NI are immensely different across a wide range of indicators, even though the former comprises about 14 percent of the whole region's population. Armidale ranks highly within Australia as a whole on such dimensions as innovation, infrastructure and essential services, human capital, technological readiness, and community skills base. In contrast, NI ranks nationally in the middle of the pack across many indicators, although its clear forte is in agricultural production. What the table does not show is Armidale's high-quality lifestyle amenity. It is home to spectacular waterfalls and gorges in a World Heritage listed landscape, cool climate wineries, boutique shopping, award-winning coffee shops and restaurants, elegant cathedrals, grand pastoral homesteads and other heritage buildings, fascinating museums and galleries, and a constellation of high-culture performances—operatic, theatrical, orchestral, or Broadway musicals. It is also only a magical two-hour drive to the Coast whose climate is somewhat Caribbean. In short, it is a high-amenity location.

Table 10.3 Regional Development Australia (RDA) National Rankings of the Northern Inland and Armidale on Regional Performance Indicators

Theme and Sub-theme	Northern Inland RDA		Armidale-Dumaresq Council	
	Rank/ 55 RDAs	*% Rank lower better*	*Rank/ 560 LGAs*	*% Rank lower better*
Innovation	25	45	9	2
Business Start-ups	55	100	371	34
Research and Development Managers	23	42	36	6
Presence of Research Organizations	14	25	7	1
Institutional Foundations	25	45	136	24
Leadership Capacity	16	29	168	30
Community Skills Base	32	58	79	14
Natural Resources	43	78	495	88
Agriculture	5	9	333	59
Infrastructure and Essential Services	31	56	46	8
Economic Fundamentals	40	73	422	75
Business Turnover	17	31	330	59
Human Capital	29	53	58	10
University Qualification	30	55	76	13
Labor Market Efficiency	38	69	296	53
Technological Readiness	35	64	110	20
Employment in Technology-Related Industries	37	67	122	22
Broadband Coverage	21	38	10	2
Access to Local Finance	33	60	33	6
Demography	47	85	253	45
Population Turnover	16	29	344	61
Dependency Ratios	47	85	200	36

Source: Extracted from the Regional Australia Institute's InSight Database. See http://insight. regionalaustralia.org.au/.

Note
Shading indicates superior ranking on each indicator. 50 percent scores indicate a midpoint in rankings for either RDAs or Local Government Areas (LGAs), both urban and rural combined.

Armidale is rare among most of Australia's inland regional communities because it hosts a university—the University of New England (UNE), which ranks 650 to 700 in the world and makes up roughly 40 percent of the local economy. Over the 80 years since its foundation, a tiny rural town became a sophisticated and cosmopolitan small city whose well-educated and diverse population generates a high standard of living and facilitates change. UNE is, however, highly integrated with the wider NI economy through its strong focus on agricultural production, environmental management, and regional development. For example, the New England region is renowned for its fine wool and beef production, and Armidale is home to at least 14 different cattle breed societies. They, in turn, were attracted to the town because of UNE's focus on animal genetics, numerous agricultural research institutes, and former Beef Cooperative Research Centre. In 2015, Armidale also became the first place within Australia to complete installation of Australia's National Broadband Network (NBN).

The remainder of this chapter examines the tactics and strategies employed in both the NI and Armidale to accelerate the arrival of the future via participant observation. I am a member of RDA—NI's Digital Economy Taskforce (DET) whose primary roles are to maximize regional NBN coverage and then encourage the use of ICT to improve the performance of existing business, social, and government activities; encourage business start-ups; attract existing business activities into the region from elsewhere—and especially capital cities; provide support mechanisms for innovators; and ultimately reorient community culture in favor of experimenting with, adopting, or blending new technologies. The DET has 29 members, although only about ten of those participate actively in regular weekly discussions about opportunities and progress. As a regional organization most constituent Local Government Areas (LGAs) are represented via either one or two delegates, making up 14—or roughly 50 percent—of the taskforce's membership. Regular participants represent such organizations as the RDA—NI secretariat, the NSW Department of Trade and Industry, the NSW Business Council, Ausindustry, NBN Co. (the organization charged with implementing the nation's National Broadband Network), and myself. In short, DET's work is mainly in the hands of government actors charged with business development who form an inner group termed the Digital Economy Implementation Group (DEIG).

The region's DET and DEIG operate both region-wide and locally within Armidale and its hinterland. Initially it focused on the implementation and extension of the NBN system throughout RDA—NI. This infrastructure supply role is still there. After completely connecting Armidale to the system, whereby all landline telephony is now VoIP enabled, its attention turned first to securing high-speed broadband services for the region's major centers including Tamworth, Gunnedah, Narrabri, Moree, and Inverell. Even within these localities, problems often persist in gaining full coverage since the network seems to have blind spots needing remediation—or alternatively some residents and businesses fail to see the need for the upgrade from earlier Internet systems and fail to campaign for NBN access. Smaller centers are now being fully connected and attention then turned to connecting what Australians call rural residential subdivisions—clusters of homes each on several hectares of land and, where possible, farms beyond roughly ten kilometers from town centers. Since it is impractical to connect all farms via fiber-optic cable, Australia is, at the time of writing, about to launch two satellites to deliver higher Internet speeds to remote locations.

The DET also recognized early on that many of the region's small retail and service businesses could be damaged by the rise of extra-regional e-tailing enabled by high-speed broadband. I am part-owner of an Australian-based but internationally focused surf-ware company by grabbing the opportunity to participate in its initial public offering (IPO) early in 2015. Its market is the 15 to 35 age group, which buys a lot of goods online, so the investment looked a sure thing… and so it proved. The DET response, in which I played a part, was to develop a strategy to help local small businesses to establish an online presence by publicizing the opportunity and assisting applicants with help in web design. A second arm of the strategy was recently completed and concerns the development of a regional portal for Internet-based trade called *Come On Shopping* (2015). Many people still wish to obtain goods from within their region, as Pritchard *et al.* (2012) and McManus *et al.* (2012) point out, and this portal will enable people to shop locally, where local is defined as the RDA—NI region. Consumers might like to compare stores in towns A, B, and C and get the best deals in terms of merchandise and price before having their purchases delivered by Australia Post, who are part of the system. Through participation in the DET and DEIG, I was also invited to deliver the address to the region's annual business innovation awards in late 2014, where an earlier version of the ideas in this chapter was voiced publicly to an attentive audience. The taskforce saw this as an opportunity to stress the importance of this region's full participation in our technological future.

Focusing more on Armidale, the DEIG has worked in all sorts of innovative ways to leverage on the city's being the first location in Australia where NBN installation was completed together with both its technology prowess and amenity. It has secured financial support from the NSW government for a data center primarily focused on cloud information storage by regional business and it seems probable that it will be located at UNE. Allied to this, UNE is working with other regional universities to become Australia's Big Data hub for GPS data connected with agriculture and environment. UNE also has many other research centers dealing with such topics as farm management, genetics, smart-farm data management, agriculture-law nexus, and rural futures, each creating a large amount of information, which could broaden the data center away from the likes of precision agriculture.

It also assisted in staging Armidale's and the wider region's first TechFest in 2015 with the aim of it becoming an annual event to familiarize residents on the Northern Tablelands, and especially young people, with forthcoming technologies and their potential uses. Interestingly though, the impetus for TechFest came from eminent local business leaders working in the ICT sector. One such enterprise called WhiteHack is hired by businesses nationwide and even overseas in East Asia to deliberately test their Internet defenses against malicious hackers and remediate lapses before valuable information is lost into cyberspace. On another occasion, the DEIG organized for one of Australia's Internet gurus to come to Armidale in an attempt to persuade local ICT-related businesses to migrate from Internet Protocol (IP) 4 to IP6. This later version is increasingly used in China, India, or other densely populated Asian countries to provide a multiplicity of new domain names unavailable with restricted IP4, and is crucial if local businesses want to trade or enter partnerships with Asian countries.

DEIG members have also piloted Armidale's nomination for the Intelligent Community of the Year award for 2016, an international competition organized by the Intelligent Community Forum based in New York. In late 2015, Armidale made the initial cut from over 400 entries to join the Smart21, alongside many much larger competitors including Montreal, Ottawa, Winnipeg, Hamilton and Oshawa (Ontario), Surrey (British Columbia), San Diego, and New Taipei City and Kaohsiung (both Taiwan). Many of our remaining competitors in the second stage of the competition now under way have populations of more than one million inhabitants—or 40 times Armidale's population, but fortunately the competition is assessed on a per-capita basis. Such participation is another way of informing our community, both business and social, about its potential leadership role in the 2MA and create a culture of hope and expectation, as distinct from more typically fearful responses.

The DEIG also arranged for Armidale and the wider NI region to be showcased in 2015 at CeBIT,[2] a global business-focused technology event organized by Hannover Fairs, a subsidiary of Deutsche Messe, and held in Sydney during May 2015. Armidale and NI were among very few non-metropolitan regions to demonstrate their technological prowess at this meeting and attracted considerable attention. In a globalizing world, with fast Internet connections, regional manufacturing, and service enterprises have an immense opportunity to extend their business horizons far beyond the local. Participation in international trade exhibitions is one path to wider spatial recognition. It is for a similar reason that the DEIG entered into negotiations with a Korean Trade Mission in Canberra in October 2015, leading to their attending an Embassy banquet and a parliamentary breakfast. The aim here was to try to strengthen ties between, on the one hand, leading manufacturers like Samsung and, on the other, local research teams developing sensing technologies like those at UNE's Smart Farm or a local business involved in environmental monitoring. For example, one enterprise has developed products that sense for environmental dangers like forest fires and floods, while the Smart Farm is trialing equipment, some now manufactured locally in Armidale, for measuring in real time such important attributes as soil moisture and nutrients, animal health and weight gain, the height and quality of crops or pasture and so on. Armidale also has an experimental smart home crammed with just about every conceivable electronic gadget and there may be some mileage in negotiating with leading Korean manufacturers about commercializing the systems we have developed.

DEIG members are also working with community groups like the Friends of the Library and the city council to include a Maker Lab, also known as Makerspaces or Innovation Labs, in Armidale's proposed new library facilities. Many North

American cities have incorporated such labs into their libraries, with Chicago[3] and Toronto being prominent at the top end, and perhaps the one at Fayetteville, a suburb of Syracuse in upstate New York, being one of the most renowned. But few exist in Australia. The argument has been made locally and elsewhere that they are useful in helping ordinary members of the public and especially young people to experiment with and get to know new technologies. Such experimentation could become a core component of local psychological reorientation toward a more entrepreneurial and risk-accepting culture able to expand regional businesses horizons nationally and even globally. Furthermore, such labs have, overseas, contributed to new business start-ups which are badly needed in rural Australia. Talking of which, the issue of starting up a regional venture capital fund has also surfaced in DEIG discussions and it is likely to be taken further, especially as I have been invited to host a forum on the subject at Armidale's 2016 TechFest. This has been given added impetus by Malcolm Turnbull's accession to the role of Australia's prime minister, and his strong advocacy of making us an innovation nation, as set out in his 2015 release of a national innovation and science agenda (see Australian Government, 2015).

Discussion

All the actions in which the DEIG has been involved bring together a series of crucial themes for technological development, and its adaptation to or commercialization in particular communities, especially in more remote locations. Such themes are critical to community survival in the 2MA or TIR where we are entering a world not previously experienced and there are few markers to guide us forward. In this landscape our prime task is to create networks of individuals enthusiastic about technology to come together and, through action gain experience about what works and what does not. For me, this makes de Montaigne—the philosopher of experience—the guru of the twenty-first century, even though his ideas were first published over 400 years ago (de Montaigne, 1580). Taleb (2012) incidentally agrees. Actions of the kind documented here concerning DET are the means to gain experience and bring about changes in communities' psychological profiles. In a way, our actions may achieve the same effect as laying a place like Armidale down on the psychologist's couch and trying to diagnose its views of the world and then adapt them to contemporary circumstance—but perhaps much more subtly. If various community groups, DEIG included, embark on discussion of the future; diagnose problems and suggest solutions; demonstrate successes— but learn from rather than abjure failures; improve quality of life and help the technologically challenged; engineer modern infrastructure; develop new and better services; and increase diversity, income, and wealth; then we are likely to transform people's behavior sets for the better. They will be less conservative and more welcoming of change; more risk accepting, creative, and imaginative; more welcoming of diversity and dissent; thirstier for new knowledge and ideas—all preconditions for joining the mainstream of the twenty-first century and the culture of the world's leading techno-poles.

In my view, the actions of the DET and DEIG are all primed to shape this desirable outcome, but there are other social and economic groups in Armidale and the wider region working toward not dissimilar ends which should not be forgotten. If there is a criticism of our work it is that it has far less publicity than it deserves and that we need to work harder on local media management.

Perhaps the most important conclusion of these thoughts lies in economic development theory and the role of clusters popularized by Porter (1990). He sees competitive advantage for firms emerging where groups of businesses in a particular sector can work together competitively in both output and innovation senses, and with suppliers to generate even greater efficiencies. However, that is not the whole story—perhaps not even half of it. Some clusters work if they are able to move with the times, but they can be deadly otherwise. Take Detroit, the headquarters of the US car industry, but now a bankrupt city with almost half the population it had 30 years ago. The world has many other examples of cities whose key industry cluster collapsed with local devastating consequences over the last 250 years since the start of the industrial revolution. Perhaps we should talk no longer about clusters of industries, but rather about clusters of people with the kinds of behavior sets discussed earlier found in successful start-up ecosystems. Moreover, they should be heavily networked as discussed by Pentland (2014) and busily engaged in creative discussion or debate about the future. Not only will this, but the business models they should be adopting will be almost flat rather than the lumbering and hidebound bureaucracies favored by most corporations. Try reading Catmull's (2014) dissection of the successful filmmaker Pixar to see what I mean about the advantages of flat administration. This company has many independent and competing task-oriented groups whose culture is to consult widely—even with people performing such menial jobs as the proverbial tea-lady.

In other words, future success, not failure, is likely to stalk those rural communities trying to emulate Armidale. We are not perfect, but we are trying to get the future discussion going in a broad-based fashion and in line with the recommendations for Australia as whole just published by the joint academies of the Sciences, Social Sciences and Humanities (Williamson *et al.* 2015). Perhaps Armidale has exceptional advantages in this emerging game, but if the community succeeds it will be because it has capitalized on these advantages using cutting-edge behavioral approaches to inventing the future. Locations with fewer resources have little option but to follow in Armidale's cultural-change footsteps—using to best advantage whatever assets their communities possess. However, there is no single approach to this task, which must be tailored to local portfolios of human, social, physical, finance, and built capital. This said, it would also be valuable if various communities' development experiences—the explanation of their successes and failures—could be catalogued for future reference, in line with de Montaigne's philosophy.

Notes

1   Brazil, Russia, India, Indonesia, China.

2 CeBIT = Centrum für Büroautomation, Informationstechnologie und Telekommunikation.
3 See Harold Washington Library Center (2015) for details of Chicago's operations.

References

ABARES. 2015. *Australian farm survey results 2012–13 to 2014–15.* Canberra, Australia: Australian Bureau of Agricultural and Resource Economics and Sciences.

Argent, N., Tonts, M., Jones, R., and Holmes, J. 2013. A creativity-led rural renaissance? Amenity led migration the creative turn and the uneven development of rural Australia, *Applied Geography* 44: 88–98.

Australian Government. 2015. National innovation and science agenda. Available online at: www.innovation.gov.au/. Accessed December 7, 2015.

Berleant, D. 2013. *The human race to the future: What could happen—and what to do.* Minden, NV: Lifeboat Foundation.

Brock, D. (ed.). 2006. *Understanding Moore's Law: Four decades of innovation.* Philadelphia, PA: Chemical Heritage Press.

Brockman, J. 2014. *What should we be worried about? Real scenarios that keep scientists up at night.* New York, NY: Harper Collins.

Brynjolfsson, E. and McAfee, A. 2014. *The second machine age: Work, progress and prosperity in a time of brilliant technologies.* New York, NY: Norton.

Cass, S. (ed.). 2014. *Coming soon enough, six tales of technology's future.* New York, NY: IEEE Spectrum Magazine.

Catmull, E. 2014. *Creativity Inc.* London: Bantam Press.

Come On Shopping. 2015. Available online at: http://comeonshopping.com.au/. Accessed December 17, 2015.

Country Rankings. 2015. Available online at: www.heritage.org/index/ranking. Accessed May 3, 2014.

Daley, J. 2012. *Critiquing government regional development policies.* Melbourne, Australia: The Grattan Institute.

de Montaigne, M. 1580. *Essais.* Bordeaux: Simon Millanges.

de Waele, R. 2014. *Shift 2020: How technology will impact our future.* Kindle version.

Department of Industry, Innovation and Science. 2015. *Resources and Energy Quarterly, September Quarter.* Canberra, Australia: Department of Industry, Innovation and Science. Available online at: www.industry.gov.au/Office-of-the-Chief-Economist/Publications/Documents/req/Resource-and-Energy-Quarterly-September-2015.pdf. Accessed December 17, 2015.

Diamond, J. 2005. *Collapse: How societies choose to fail or succeed.* Camberwell, Victoria: Penguin Group.

Edwards, G., Zeng, B., Saalfeld, W., Vaarzon-Morel, P., and McGregor, M. (eds.). 2008. *Managing the impacts of feral camels in Australia: A new way of doing business.* Alice Springs, Australia: Desert Knowledge Cooperative Research Centre, Report 47.

Florida, R. 2005. *Cities and the creative class.* New York, NY: Routledge.

Ford, M. 2009. *The lights in the tunnel: Automation, accelerating technology and the economy of the future.* USA: Acculant Publishing.

Glaeser, E. 2011. *Triumph of the city: How our greatest invention makes us richer, smarter, greener, healthier, and happier.* London: Macmillan.

Greengard, S. 2015. *The internet of things.* Cambridge, MA: MIT Press.

Hägerstrand, T. 1967. *Innovation diffusion as a spatial process*. Chicago, IL: University of Chicago Press.

Hammersley, B. 2012. *64 things you need to know now for then*. Sydney, Australia: Hodder.

Harold Washington Library Center. 2015. Available online at: www.chipublib.org/makerlab/. Accessed December 18, 2015.

Jacobs, J. 1984. *Cities and the wealth of nations: Principles of economic life*. New York, NY: Vintage.

Kahneman, D. 2011. *Thinking fast and slow*. New York, NY: Farrar, Straus and Giroux.

Kotey, B. and Sorensen, A. 2014. Barriers to small business innovation in rural Australia: A case for local solutions, *Australasian Journal of Regional Studies* 20(3): 405–429.

McManus, P., Walmsley, J., Argent, N., Baum, S., Bourke, L., Martin, J., Pritchard, W., and Sorensen, A. 2012. Rural community and rural resilience: What is important to farmers in keeping their country towns alive? *Journal of Rural Studies* 28(1): 20–29.

Mills, D. 2013. *Our uncertain future: When digital evolution, global warming and automation converge*. San Diego, CA: Pacific Beach Publishing.

Pentland, A. 2014. *Social physics: How good ideas spread*. New York, NY: The Penguin Press.

Porter, M. 1990. *The competitive advantage of nations*. New York: The Free Press.

Prechter, R. 2001. Unconscious herding behavior as the psychological basis of financial market trends and patterns. *Journal of Psychology and Financial Markets* 2(3): 120–125.

Prechter, R. 2003. *Socionomics: The science of history and social prediction*. Gainesville, GA: New Classics Library.

Pritchard, W., Argent, N., Baum, S., Bourke, L., Martin, J., McManus, P., Sorensen, A., and Walmsley, J. 2012. Local—if possible: How the spatial networking of economic relations amongst farm enterprises aids small town survival in rural Australia, *Regional Studies* 46(4): 539–557.

Productivity Commission, 2005. *Trends in Australian agriculture*, Canberra, Australia: Productivity Commission Research Paper.

Rawlings, C., Smith, J., and Bencini, R. 2013. *Pardon the disruption: The future you never saw coming*. Shelbyville, KY: Wasteland Press.

Regional Australia Institute. 2015. InSight Database. Available online at: http://insight.regionalaustralia.org.au/. Accessed December 15, 2015.

Rifkin, J. 2011. *The third industrial revolution: How lateral power is transforming energy, the economy, and the world*. London: Palgrave Macmillan.

Savage, M., Devine, F., Cunningham, N., Taylor, M., Li, Y., Hjellbrekke, J., Le Roux, B., Friedman, S., and Miles, A. 2013. A new model of social class: Findings from the BBC's Great British class survey experiment, *Sociology* 47(2): 219–250.

Sorensen, A. 2000. *Regional development: Some issues for policy makers*. Canberra, Australia: Research Paper No. 26 1999–2000, Department of the Parliamentary Library.

Sorensen, A. 2002. Regional economic governance: States, markets and DIY. In S. Bell (ed.), *Economic governance and institutional dynamics* (pp. 262–285). Oxford: Oxford University Press.

Sorensen, A. 2009a. Creativity in rural development: an Australian response to Florida (or a view from the fringe), *International Journal of Foresight and Innovation Policy* 5(1/2/3): 24–43.

Sorensen, A. 2009b. Local development under uncertainty: Australia's rural perspective. *Rural Studies* (Polish Academy of the Sciences) 20: 7–26.

2

267*

Sorensen, A. 2010. The psychology of regional development, *Australasian Journal of Regional Studies* 16(1): 85–98.

Sorensen, A. 2011a. Australian agricultural R&D and innovation systems, *International Journal of Foresight and Innovation Policy* 7(1/2/3): 192–211.

Sorensen, A. 2011b. Quantum dreaming: The relevance of quantum mechanics to regional Science, *Australasian Journal of Regional Studies* 17(1): 81–99.

Sorensen, A. and Epps, R. 1996. Leadership and local development: Dimensions of leadership in four Central Queensland towns. *Journal of Rural Studies* 12(2): 113–125.

Sorensen, A. and Epps, R. 2005. The idea of stable adaptation and its origins. In A. Mather (ed.), *Land use and rural sustainability* (pp. 1–10). Aberdeen, Scotland: International Geographical Union Commissions on Land Use/Cover Change and the Sustainability of Rural Systems, University of Aberdeen.

Sorensen, A., Marshall, N., and Dollery, B. 2007. Changing governance of Australian regional development: Systems and effectiveness, *Space and Polity* 11(3): 297–315.

Stephenson, N., Brin, D., Egan, G., Powers, R., Robson, J., Watts, P., Aldiss, B., Ridbom, C., McAuley, P., Kress, N., Steele, A., McDonald, I., Fulda, N., and Goonan, K.A. 2013. *Twelve tomorrows*. Cambridge, MA: Technology Review, Inc.

Taleb, N. 2007. *The Black Swan: The impact of the highly improbable*. London: Penguin

Taleb, N. 2012. *Antifragile: Things that gain from disorder*. London: Penguin.

Techcrunch. 2015. Startup Genome Ranks the World's Top Startup Ecosystems: Silicon Valley, Tel Aviv & L.A. Lead the Way. Available online at: http://techcrunch.com/2012/11/20/startup-genome-ranks-the-worlds-top-startup-ecosystems-silicon-valley-tel-aviv-l-a-lead-the-way/. Accessed November 11, 2015.

Thaler, R. 2015. *Misbehaving*. New York, NY: W.W. Norton.

Williamson, R., Nic Raghnaill, M., Douglas, K., and Sanchez, D. 2015. *Technology and Australia's future: New technologies and their role in Australia's security, cultural, democratic, social and economic systems*. Melbourne, Australia: Australian Council of Learned Academies.

Wood, D. (ed.). 2014. *Anticipating 2025: A guide to the radical changes that may lie ahead, whether or not we're ready*. London: Futurists.

11 Building for the Future

Community Responses to Economic Restructuring in Mackenzie, British Columbia

Greg Halseth, Laura Ryser, and Sean Markey

Introduction

In previous chapters, we explored the impacts of accelerating globalization on northern British Columbia's (BC) forest industry (Chapter 3) and the follow-through impacts of these changes on the local labor force (Chapter 7). In this chapter, we complete the review by looking at how small forest-dependent communities have responded to the sweep of changes occurring in their key local economic sector. These changes include the collision of political and economic restructuring that has led to the transformation and reorientation of local government operations from 'managerialism' to 'entrepreneurialism.' In concert with this shift has been the adoption of various aspects of community economic development, as communities seek new local opportunities and alternatives to replace lost or declining economic activities. Through this chapter we will: (1) interrogate rural renewal for the supports and mechanisms important in these processes, and (2) consider the relative roles of a variety of influencing factors, including local capacity, collaboration, leadership, social capital, public policy, geographic variables of location and access, and local innovation.

We used two methods to explore how changes in BC's central interior forest industry have affected the small forest-dependent communities and local governments. First, we conducted ten key informant interviews that asked about important factors in how the community is responding to change. Second, we reviewed local government planning documents. As with the earlier chapters, the work focuses on the community of Mackenzie, BC where we have a long-term research relationship. Our key informants had extensive community and local government experience. As with the other data used in our chapters, the interviews were recorded and transcribed before transcripts were shared back with the participants for review. We then used latent and manifest content analysis to compile themes from the data (Krippendorff and Bock, 2009; Andersen and Svensson, 2012).

Place in the Global Economy

Our interest in how forest-dependent communities are responding to the pressures of economic and workforce restructuring is motivated by several observations.

The first is that many similar communities in BC's central interior are themselves the very definition of forest industry-dependent places. After World War Two, they grew as a result of significant forest industry investment and the resulting boom in forest industry employment. With few other major economic activities aside from the public sector, these communities experience the raw ups and downs of the forest industry (Barnes and Hayter, 1997; Horne, 2004).

Second, and more generally, our interest is also spurred by the growing literature on the importance of place in the global economy (Markey *et al.*, 2006, 2008a; Halseth *et al.*, 2010). As argued by Bradford (2003, 2005), it is 'on the ground' in local places that the impacts of global economic restructuring, shifting international trade, and various national and regional policy initiatives, etc. are all keenly felt. As well, agreements easing the international flow of capital has meant that small differences between places can determine whether or not capital invests or remains in place. In other words, as 'space' has become less important in the global economy, 'place' has become more important.

Third, the growing importance of place means that more attention is needed on such questions as the 'who' and 'how' of local places organizing to respond to both dramatic and gradual transformation. Aarsæther and Bærenholdt (2001; see also Aarsæther and Suopajrvi, 2004) have argued that this requires more focus on local government and governance regimes. As Markey *et al.* (2012) highlight, there are many more players and interests active in local debates and responses than were countenanced 30 to 50 years ago.

Following from these points is recognition that local responses now demand much more from local capacity. This includes not just local actors and institutions, but also the partnerships, collaborations, and relationships needed to bring knowledge together and then mobilize plans into action (Bryant, 1995, 2010; Markey *et al.*, 2008b). As we detail below, these additional demands on local capacity are challenged by the withdrawal of senior governments from some of the roles they have historically played in resource-dependent regions and communities.

Impacts on Places: The Political and Economic Restructuring Literatures

Marchak's (1983) detailed study of BC's forest industry and its forest-dependent communities identified many themes that continue to resonate over time. The starting point for Marchak's work is the inherent instability and vulnerability of staples-dependent resource-based economies. Her description of the increasing influence of capital through large corporate interests, and of the close ties that are forged between labor and capital in the resource extractive project, mirror the updated story portrayed in Chapters 3 and 7, and the wider Canadian forest industry history (Paillé, 2013).

Workers

With attention to the impacts of this transformation on individuals, households, and communities, Marchak (1983) highlights several key points. The first is that the general economic vulnerability within the industry creates a general sense of instability in the workplace. Between 1983 and 2013, the general pattern of employment has been one of continuing production increases with fewer firms and fewer workers. Instability of workplace, within a highly structured unionized setting, has been felt most keenly by younger workers. These younger workers hold less seniority and are most likely to be laid off under economic exigencies. Table 11.1 highlights the growth of two forest-dependent communities in BC's central interior. As the forest industry matured, the communities experienced population stagnation and decline as the industry pursued efficiency gains via the substitution of capital for labor.

Halseth (1999a, 1999b) adds to Marchak's portrait of employment changes in BC's central interior. The influx of young workers with young families coming for the work spurred population growth in many small forestry towns through the 1960s and 1970s. The transitions since that time in local employment show not only an aging workforce, but also the outmigration of young people. Also evident is the failure of many forest-dependent communities to attract new economic sectors or actors that would add significant new employment opportunities so as to attract the 'next generation' of young workers and families.

Forest industry towns also display highly gendered working environments. This is part of a dual economy—a high-wage, unionized, 'male dominated' industrial working environment and a low-wage, non-unionized, 'female dominated' service sector. Service sector employment was also subject to higher levels of part-time work, casual work, and marginal employment. These issues impact earnings levels. However, as Marchak (1983 p. 213) describes,

> though women are not employed in the forest industry in these towns, their presence is an important part of the context for these industrial processes. Women do the maintenance tasks in the homes and the service tasks in the offices, stores, shops, schools, and hospitals. In their absence, the forest company employers could not maintain company towns, and the overall cost of maintaining a male labour force would sharply increase.

Table 11.1 Population Change Over Time

	Mackenzie	*Houston*
1971	n/a	
1981	5,890	3,921
1991	5,796	3,628
2001	5,206	3,577
2011	3,507	3,147

Source: Statistics Canada, Census (1971, 1981, 1991, 2001, 2011).

Reed (2003) updates the portrait of gendered roles, relations, and workplace opportunities in forest-dependent communities. Like Marchak, she argues that "within a framework of social embeddedness, the workplace, family, and community dynamics are important elements in an analysis of paid work in forestry communities" (Reed, 2003 p. 81). Central to her argument is that while significant income and occupational differences between men and women persist, standard measures of these differences often miss the myriad ways women are participating in the forestry sector. This applies especially in the technical and professional jobs now so crucial to forest manufacturing and land-based operations, but which are not often included in standard classifications of 'forestry' or 'resource' employment. She concludes:

> women's relationship to paid work is contradictory... Their employment choices cannot be explained by singular expressions of material desire or maternal practice. Rather, they represent part of a more complex network that embeds their understanding of the paid work of women in local sociopolitical, environmental, and economic practices and meanings. These practices and meanings in forestry communities place women's paid work in a marginal economic position in relation to the paid work of men.
>
> (Reed, 2003 p. 113)

A further consequence of the substitution of capital for labor efficiency trend has been workforce aging. The population pyramids shown in Figure 11.1 and 11.2 illustrate this phenomenon. The community of Quesnel has a significant forest industry base, and it experienced both the intense upswing of industrial investment through the 1970s and the slow loss of employment in that sector since the early 1980s (see Chapter 7 for additional details).

Figure 11.1 shows the demographic structure of Quesnel's population in 1981. This is after the period of significant expansion and before workplace contraction. The population is dominated by young workers and their families who have come to the community for the new opportunities in the growing forest industry. With stable employment, these households are having children and putting down roots in the community.

Figure 11.2 on the other hand, shows the demographic structure of Quesnel in 2011, a point 30 years into employment contraction within the local forest industry. The impact of such contraction in this unionized sector is clear. The workforce has aged in place and is now clustered in the 50–59 years age groups. The lack of significant new job creation in the community is also clear in the gap within the local population in the 20–39 years age groups. Youth are leaving after high school, and young workers (and their families) are not flocking to the community as they once did. The implications of this demographic shift are significant for the capacity of the community to respond to ongoing economic change.

In addition to these overall trends, communities also went through shorter cycles of instability over time. In forestry communities such as Mackenzie, the early years of industrial start-up were characterized by a high degree of transience.

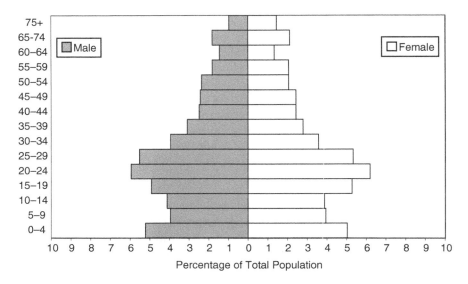

Figure 11.1 Quesnel, 1981.
Source: Statistics Canada, Census (1981).

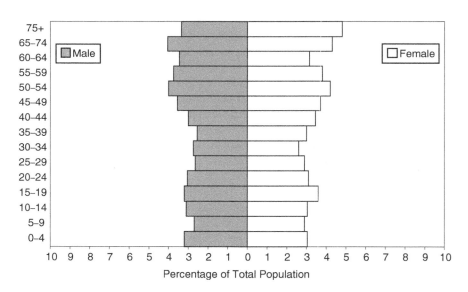

Figure 11.2 Quesnel, 2011.
Source: Statistics Canada, Census (2011).

First, construction workers building the town and its industrial facilities came and went. Second, worker turnover was very high once production got under way in the early start-up years. Marchak (1983) estimates that depending upon the company and type of operation, annual worker turnover might have been between 60 percent and 95 percent.

Communities

Forest-dependent communities in BC have two general formative pathways: instant towns and historical trading towns. The simplest to explain is the 'instant town.' Commensurate with the provincial government's post-World War Two policies to grow and extend industrial resource development across the province was the need for communities within which to house workers and their families in order to establish labor stability. Under legislation, the provincial government created a suite of tools that would allow a new town to be incorporated and built if it supported a significant new industrial resource development opportunity (Halseth and Sullivan, 2002). These towns were typically designed using comprehensive planning principles so as to create attractive, full service communities designed for postwar baby-boom families (Porteous, 1987; Bowles, 1992). Writers such as Lucas (1971) portrayed these towns as part of a unidirectional development cycle that reached from construction through to maturity—both in terms of physical and social infrastructure. The course of their history, however, reflects the instability and vulnerability of staples-dependent economies. As noted by Marchak (1983 p. 304), "these communities exist and are stable to the extent that the resource they produce is in demand on markets over which they have no control and to the extent the companies consider the investment in the particular plant profitable." Mackenzie is an example of a forest-dependent instant town in BC.

Another common group of forest-dependent towns are those that grew from an existing small town base. The town of Quesnel is one such example. Founded as a commercial center during the 1860s Cariboo gold rush, the town was officially incorporated in 1928. Located at the confluence of the Fraser River and the Quesnel River, the early history of the community was as a small supply-center for the fur trade, the gold rush, and then early ranching and small-scale forestry. Onto this foundation came the 1960s' and 1970s' expansion of the industrial forestry model and the construction of a number of new sawmills and pulp mills. While the town retains its role as a service center for the region, it is the forest industry that dominates local employment and the local economy.

Community Transition: From Managerialism to Entrepreneurialism

How are local communities and local governments reacting to the pressures of change that are transforming the forest industry and forest-dependent places? Hayter (2000) writes about the challenges facing these communities, especially since the global economic recession in the early 1980s:

During the boom years of Fordism, many forest towns enjoyed prosperity and relative stability. For these communities, local development was equated with the strategies of the dominant employers typically headquartered elsewhere. Locally, the promotion of industrial development was a nonissue, and local government dealt primarily with managing basic community services. The underlying vulnerability of forest towns, however, was starkly revealed by the sudden, substantial employment downsizing of dominant employers that began in the early 1980s.

(Hayter, 2000 p. 288)

The crisis of capitalism, when linked to longer-term processes such as the rise of neoliberal public policy, meant a transition in the practice of local governance. Hayter (2000 p. 288) draws on the work of David Harvey to describe this transition from 'managerialism' to 'entrepreneurialism,' where "forest towns had to contemplate becoming entrepreneurial and try to create ideas for development from within the community." He uses the notion of an 'unruly' process to describe this new reality for local development because it was so different from the organized and structured ways the community had worked under the earlier Fordist management framework of large corporations and senior levels of government.

The shift to an entrepreneurial approach to local development and governance brought a variety of new challenges. One key challenge has to do with timeframes: economic diversification generally takes a great deal of time while the needs of families displaced by forest industry restructuring are immediate. Another challenge is the lingering nostalgia for the paternalistic firm. Halseth (2005) describes how many local governments will talk diversification, but will focus their attention on attracting replacement large industries. Workers and local government leaders remember somewhat nostalgically earlier times when a single large employer meant relative stability and good paying jobs. Freudenburg (1992) discusses how resource towns become 'addicted' to these sorts of resource-dependent relationships. Hayter (2000 pp. 316–317) describes how the:

forces constraining the diversification of forest towns run deep. Problems of isolation are entrenched by organizational structures, and by development psychology and attitudes that collectively militate against diversification ... Company towns are union towns whose workers are well paid and specialized, hold benefits that increase with seniority, and may have deeply engrained antimanagement attitudes. In general, institutional arrangements and local attitudes in forest towns in BC reinforced one another during Fordism to create a culture inimical to entrepreneurship ... This legacy, combined with geographic marginality, has created massive obstacles to local economic diversification.

Another challenge in the BC context is the 'decoupling' hypothesis (Hayter, 2000). During the 1950s to 1970s Fordist era, the core urban region of metropolitan Vancouver-Victoria was intimately connected with the resource-producing hinterland of the province. Since that time, the economy of the urban core has itself diversified, and while still very dependent on the export wealth generated by non-metropolitan areas, to the urban population and governments (including the provincial government) these critical ties are now more obscured.

The demise of the Fordist development ideal revealed two additional challenges for the future economic diversification of forest-dependent towns: geography and shifting expectations and values associated with both environmental conservation and Aboriginal rights. Geography, or more specifically spatial relations, poses a distinct suite of challenges for economic diversification in forest-dependent towns. For those communities closer to urban centers, or within high amenities regions, there are increased opportunities for diversification or for attracting new residents and new businesses. On Vancouver Island and in southern BC, some former forestry towns have capitalized on their relative urban fringe location and landscape amenity assets to add new economic sectors (such as amenity and retirement migration). More isolated forest-dependent communities do not have such ready options. The result is that there is an increasing diversity of economic transformations being experienced across previously forest-dependent communities. As Hayter (2000 p. 319) notes:

> Forest towns, slowly, are becoming different places. The massive forces of standardization associated with Fordist production—especially commodity production and Taylorist labour relations—are breaking down ... In this context, unruly implies a broad definition of entrepreneurialism, connoting a patchwork of bottom-up, entrepreneurial developments, only loosely coordinated, it at all, by broader planning frameworks.

Stevenson *et al.* (2011 p. 101) reinforce how changing expectations associated with environmental awareness and the exertion of Aboriginal rights have challenged natural resource management and planning: "decision makers are under increasing pressure to incorporate a range of hard-to-define values, including recreational values, spiritual values, and biodiversity values, into the planning process." They add that "Cultural values, especially spiritual values, do not fit within the traditional framework of professional land management" (Stevenson *et al.*, 2011 p. 113).

These forces affect the dynamics and role of the traditional forest sector, yet, economic diversification and the attraction of new residents and businesses can also create challenges. Hayter (2000 p. 298) describes how such success can itself create "a 'cultural clash' with long-time residents, especially with respect to the benefits of large-scale resource development." Wider changes and social expectations are also layered upon the local development transition. As these towns work and plan toward diversification:

> environmental and Aboriginal interests can no longer be ignored as they were under Fordism. For residents of metropolitan Vancouver, environmentalism and aboriginalism may appear as relatively abstract forces, seen only via the new media. It is in resource towns where not only direct confrontation occurs

but where solutions must be forged, through various forms of cooperation that will potentially help shape business practice, work habits, and the nature of communities.

(Hayter, 2000 p. 299)

Opportunities for an Effective Transition

The previous sections described many changes within forest-dependent places and the local government transition from managerialism to entrepreneurialism. The challenge facing resource communities is to effectively navigate these transitions and create a new and robust platform to support future, and ongoing, community development and community economic development. This section examines the literature on local economic development, community economic development, and regional development in BC.

Local Economic Development

A first response to both the transition from managerialism to entrepreneurialism and the deep restructuring of BC's forest industry was that small communities adopted a local economic development approach. This approach, with deep roots in local boosterism traditions, seeks to entice new economic activity into the community. Towns across northern BC set up economic development offices to do this function and have sought to use tools such as property tax relief and other such incentives to lure in new businesses.

Local economic development often focuses upon the 'big win.' That is, trying to bring another very large employer to the community. This is an attractive strategy given that large numbers of direct jobs and local spending will create a multiplier effect across the entire local economy. As Halseth (2005) argues, this is also the familiar pathway for northern BC's resource-dependent communities that had grown so used to a single large local industrial employer. Even where the economic development plans call for economic diversification, the desire to secure a replacement single large industrial employer often overwhelms efforts toward meaningful diversification.

Markey *et al.* (2008b) looked at a large number of economic development plans and strategies across northern BC. They found that a "common refrain within rural and small-town economic development networks is that local development policies are either not working or not having the impact communities and governments might like" (Markey *et al.*, 2012 p. 152). They went on to identify five issues that undercut the effectiveness of local economic development planning:

1   Economic development process lack depth of analysis.
2   Recommendations often fail to account for issues of jurisdiction and meaningful levels of local control.

3 Contracting out responsibility for local development planning limits opportunities to build community buy-in and may limit process accountability.
4 Social and economic planning are not well integrated.
5 Doing things is important, but a coordinated development strategy to facilitate commitment to implementation over the longer term is often lacking.

(Markey *et al.*, 2012 p. 54)

Markey *et al.* (2012) also examined the process of doing local economic development planning and identified critical problems with its execution. Building on a three-stage model they noted that effective local economic development involved a strategy stage where local participation and understanding could be marshaled into a broad process of visioning and goal setting—all linked to local values and assets. A second stage included looking at blue sky options to identify potential opportunities and then assessing the business case for those opportunities against the context of the place (its assets, infrastructure, regional setting, etc.). The third stage of the generic local development model involved active implementation, together with monitoring and the flexibility to respond to changing circumstances and opportunities over time.

The critique of local economic development planning is that it had become 'stuck in the middle' (Markey *et al.*, 2008b). Too often, local or senior governments would fund a blue sky options study of economic possibilities for a region or community undergoing economic distress. When looked at collectively, these plans almost always have the list of options—as if they were downloaded from some master economic development consulting template. There is little or no attention to stage one (local involvement, participation, understanding, vision, and assessment of the context of place), and the funding never includes support for effective implementation or monitoring/adjustment over the 10–20-year periods that research has shown is needed to transform rural and small town economies. In the end, the local economic development approach has seen lots of action, and consumed lots of fiscal resources, but has produced little.

Community Economic Development

Commensurate with the economic restructuring of BC's resource sector after 1980, and the neoliberal public policy shift toward entrepreneurial local governance, many places looked to community economic development (CED) as a solution. CED, as opposed to local economic development, is about endogenous economic growth. It is also generally directed at addressing some form of local social need or issue. It has been defined as: "a process by which communities can initiate and generate their own solutions to their common economic problems and thereby build long-term community capacity and foster the integration of economic, social, and environmental objectives" (Markey *et al.*, 2005 p. 2).

One constraint on CED is access to financing. Limitations may come from the level of experience on the part of the borrower, level of awareness on the part of the lender, the degree of geographic isolation, and perceptions of risk versus rate and timing of return on investment. In general terms, communities must invest in four types of infrastructure to support community development and community economic development strategies. These include the physical, human, community, and economic infrastructure. Yet, such infrastructure investments are costly (or viewed only as costs and not investments). Partners in the public and private sectors are usually needed—further complicating arrangements and extending timeframes.

Another challenge to the CED framework, and to the transition toward entrepreneurial development in general, is the need for supportive public policy. Markey *et al.* (2012 p. 132) describe how the BC provincial government's thinking about community development and its community economic development spending has shifted from an investment approach to an expense mindset: "The withdrawal of government from the reproduction of rural and small-town BC's social and economic infrastructure contrasts sharply with a dynamic period of province-building investments in the period immediately following the Second World War."

The same applies to public policy. The constitutional structure of government in Canada allocated discrete powers to the federal and provincial governments. To the provincial government went matters of local concern. In BC, local governments function only within a mandate defined for them by provincial legislation. The result is that whenever local governments seek to be entrepreneurial, they inevitability need a great deal of policy support from senior government (usually from multiple departments/agencies).

Taken together, CED and local economic development have the potential to assist in strengthening local economies and building some resilience into those economies. However, each has been limited in its application even though considerable time and money has been applied. The critical shortcoming seems to be with senior governments: they have downloaded responsibility for community and economic planning to the local level but have not followed through with an appropriate downloading of autonomy or fiscal capacity, and have been slow with the development of supportive policy frameworks for these approaches.

New Regionalism

A third, emergent, approach to the challenges of neoliberal policy and the entrepreneurial transition in governance involves scaling up to the regional level. Markey *et al.* (2012 p. 64) argue that the:

> origins of new regionalism are linked with the broader economic transformation to post-Fordism and the subsequent attention that this brought to the question of regional disparities that were, to some degree, hidden by a combination of the Fordist industrial structure and government support.

While the literature on 'new regionalism' is broad (Pierce, 1992; Savoie, 1997; Barnes and Gertler, 1999; Polèse, 1999; Porter, 2004), we wish to draw out several salient aspects. The first is that there is an inherent synergy between local and regional actions and activities around social and economic development. This synergy demands awareness at both local and regional levels. It also needs institutions or forums to support dialogue and awareness building. Second, rural and small town places are continuously challenged by capacity issues. By working more cooperatively as a region, communities are able to share workloads and build on collective skills and expertise. At the same time, the region remains a reasonable scale for understanding impacts and working toward solutions. As well, the region is a broader and more appropriate scale at which to evaluate the large infrastructure investments needed to assist both regions and places in constructing a more competitive framework for attracting economic activity and workers.

While arguments in support of local *and* regional approaches have made headway, the region remains a scale challenged by new understandings of governance. Few jurisdictions have managed an appropriate balance of power, authority, and representation that supports both local initiative and regional cooperation.

Place-Based Community Development: A Better Approach

A number of places across northern BC have been successful in navigating the restructuring of the forest sector and the governance transition from managerialism to entrepreneurialism. Lessons from these examples support the notion of place-based community development as a better foundation for addressing long-term rural and small town change. This section explores some examples.

Markey *et al.* (2012) detail two northern BC towns that have been successful in navigating change. The first is Valemount. Located in the Robson Valley, part of the Rocky Mountain Trench, Valemount is located about four hours' drive from the regional centers of Prince George and Kamloops. Since its founding around 1914, the town and surrounding region of about 2,000 people functioned as a small forest-dependent economy. Twenty years ago there were two small sawmills and most of the population was employed in some form of forest management, harvesting, transportation, or manufacturing. Community leaders saw changes coming in the forest economy and they looked at the assets of their community— identifying that they were at a natural transportation crossroads, they were the entrance community to the northern Rocky Mountain national parks, they had a wide variety of recreational and wilderness amenities surrounding the community, and they had a strong foundation of local services.

The town initiated a long-term economic development strategy that sought to mobilize a wide range of economic sectors. They stayed on this course of investing all of their activities toward a new suite of economic futures. Twenty years later the local forest industry is gone, but Valemount survives. Today, they have significant highway commercial services catering to the truck transportation that goes through the region. There are also significant winter and summer tourism activities that have been developed, together with large numbers of new hotels and restaurant facilities. The town has also experienced significant amenity migration and retirement migration taking advantage of the stunning landscape and small town atmosphere. There are also some additional resource extraction industries such as sand and gravel production, and most recently a newly announced community forest.

Markey *et al.* (2012) also described the town of Terrace. Located in northwestern BC, the town began its development around 1912 with the coming of the northern transcontinental railroad line (Grand Trunk Pacific). Since that time, it has been a major forest industry community. Like with Valemount, about 25 years ago community leaders in Terrace noticed the increasing uncertainty in the forest industry. They did not have to change as the economy at the time was exceptionally robust for there were three very large forest-industry facilities and most of the local economy was based around those three large mills.

However, they did embark on a 20-year diversification strategy based upon a simple idea—that Terrace was at the vital crossroads point of northwestern BC. Today, the two largest forestry facilities are gone, the third has had numerous short-term closures, and there is very little forest-harvesting activity in the region. Yet, Terrace survives. Today, it is a service center for northwestern BC. It has significant retail sector activities and considerable new investment in this sector. It has become a hub of government services and activities. It is a regional education center with programs that are unique to the region (such as mining training). And, it has also become the healthcare center with significant new investments in those facilities. All of these sectors are stable and provide well-paying jobs.

Mackenzie, BC

Given the above-noted transitions and transformations, this section of the chapter explores the case of Mackenzie, BC (introduced in Chapter 3). It explores the evolution of the community's approach to restructuring and transition through local economic development, community economic development, regional, and place-based frameworks. As background, we need to realize that Mackenzie is very much a forest-dependent town and local economy. As noted by one of the interviewees:

> Mackenzie really did strike me as being one of the most forestry dependent communities I've experienced. That was always sort of the talk about Mackenzie, is that it was very much a forest-dependent community. In terms of development opportunities, certainly development opportunities in relation to the forest industry, but there was a lack of diversity in town. We noticed that when we first moved here, we kind of had a background concern about it.
> (Participant P6, 2014)

Another noted:

> The people were all in forestry. People didn't worry about anything. They had a job. They had their toys. They could go on vacation. Their kids went to

school. It was a nice community to live in. ... There wasn't a lot of layoffs per se. They didn't start until the mid-2000s as far as I know. Everything that happens within industry, no matter which industry, affects the community. That's part of the problem if you don't diversify.

(Participant P10, 2014)

Economic change and uncertainly is hard in this setting. One interviewee reflected this in a comment about the strikes that were becoming more commonplace after 1980:

Some of the strikes were really hard on the community. Some of them were very ill advised, because the communities were so dependent on the forestry industry. There was no tourism, there was no mining, basically it was forestry or nothing. So, those kinds of strikes were pretty much devastating for the community.

(Participant P9, 2014)

Legacies of Local and Community Economic Development Strategies

A review of local economic development strategies over time in Mackenzie reveals a community struggling in the transition from managerial to entrepreneurial governance. It also shows a community stuck in the old approaches to economic development strategies and planning. Post-2008, however, there appears to be a successful break from this legacy.

In 1991, an economic development strategy for Mackenzie was completed by a consulting firm from Vancouver (Crane Management Consultants). Using a SWOT (Strengths, Weaknesses, Opportunities, and Threats) analysis typical for the time, the principal recommendations called for:

- The establishment of a local economic development office;
- Work on economic development in collaboration with regional authorities; and
- The establishment of an economic development network with representatives from key senior government agencies, departments, and ministries.

The report also recommended undertaking strategic initiatives across four areas. These included:

1 Entrepreneurship
— Stimulating local people to enter the retail sector;
2 Communications and information sharing
— Involving luncheons and newsletters;
3 Diversification of the local economy
— Through 'buy-local' and 'smokestack chasing' initiatives; and
4 Continuing investment in basic infrastructure.

This approach and these recommendations follow directly from the neoliberal transition in governance toward more entrepreneurial local government. This includes having local government take on additional functions, including being the focal point for local and regional economic development coordination. Such an approach also follows the older style of economic development planning as critiqued above by Markey *et al.* (2008b).

This report was followed by some local action. In 1992, for example, a District of Mackenzie Downtown Revitalization Strategy and Concept plan was completed (District of Mackenzie, 1992). In 1994, the Mackenzie Economic Development Committee (created on the recommendation of the 1991 strategic plan) initiated a community economic development program. Their first steps included another SWOT type analysis of the external environment (including globalization, trade, etc.), local and regional development infrastructure reviews, the community's population and economic profile, and sector analyses within forestry, mining, and tourism. These analyses were equivalent to 'blue sky' dialogues asking generally about 'gaps' and 'opportunities.' As reflected by one interviewee:

> I think the mid-90s was the first push to look at mining and tourism as diversification. The 1990s was when we ... started with an economic development officer. I think the mining and the tourism started to show up on council's strategic plans more, those types of things.
>
> (Participant P3, 2014)

Drawing on the 1991 economic strategy, and its focus on traditional economic sectors, in 1997 the District of Mackenzie Forest Advisory Committee hired an outside consulting firm to look at forest-based economic development opportunities for the District of Mackenzie (KPMG Consulting, 1997). With a focus on the "recreation and community development opportunities, rather than business opportunities" (KPMG Consulting, 1997 p. 1), the final report describes a number of projects that could be organized into reasonable proposals to senior government (this time the provincial government's funding arm—Forest Renewal British Columbia) for further feasibility studies. Each proposal included a summary of the opportunity, the availability of local supports, and an evaluation of needed budgets. In addition to sounding like a make-work project for the consulting firm, most proposals were oriented toward 'smokestack chasing.' There was one—the creation of the Mackenzie Community Forest—that would put local resources into local hands for the first time (see below).

In 2007, yet another economic development strategic plan was created (Synergy Management Group Ltd., 2007). As with previous plans, it included a number of short- and long-term opportunities in natural resources and supporting services. It also identified funding opportunities and partners for these various opportunities. However, one especially valuable new addition in that strategic plan was a detailed review of past economic development strategies and reports. The idea was to draw additional value out of those earlier planning investments, to critique those earlier studies, and to collate their findings into a comprehensive action plan.

From its founding in the mid-1970s, through to 2008, Mackenzie had endured increasing cycles of economic downturns in its dominant forest-industry sector. Despite a flurry of activity in and around each of these downturns, little came from efforts or strategic plans to diversify the economy and the community. Each time there was a downturn or a forest sector closure, there would be debate and planning, but each time the forest industry rebounded and workers went back to the mills, both the imperative and the momentum to change or diversify evaporated. Not only were such exercises generally ineffective, but the lack of meaningful and ongoing engagement meant that even active community people did not know about plans, strategies, and priorities. As one engaged interviewee said: "until the mid-2000s, I don't know that there were any economic development strategies in our community. ... Forestry was here so why would we do any economic development?"(Participant P10, 2014).

Mackenzie has experienced remarkable periods of boom and bust since the economic recession of the early 1980s. The volatility of global markets for wood, pulp, and paper products had direct impacts on the community. As one interviewee described her experiences:

> When I moved here ... the town was booming. There wasn't an apartment for rent. There wasn't a hotel room. The campgrounds were full with workers who were here for the summer. At one point there was a little panic because there was no place to live. People who were coming here to work couldn't find a place to live ... When we went into the downturn, five or six years ago, people were giving their houses away, just move in and pay the mortgage. Now we've made the shift again the other way where rent is high, and places are hard to find and rent is expensive because the demand is there ... So I have been through the up and the down swing and then back up again for how the economy has shaped what's going on here in town.
>
> (Participant P1, 2014)

Another interviewee noted that:

> They've been interesting changes. In the 1970s, it was a lot more labor intensive in the forest industry. The work force was totally different than it is now because you've got technology, which has changed things quite a bit. ... sometimes there was a loss of jobs due to technology and restructuring in the forest industry.
>
> (Participant P4, 2014)

Mired in ineffective economic development strategies, Mackenzie had not been preparing for the changes already happening all around them. As one interviewee noted, the town: "was slow to respond during the 1990s and 2000s, the issues that forced changes were obviously the economy and then ... when the town woke up again it was also a whole different demographic" (Participant P3, 2014).

284   *G. Halseth* et al.

But the economic downturn of 2008–2010 was significant. As described in Chapter 3, the entire economic base of forest industry mills was shuttered. As described by one interviewee, the impacts were dramatic: "When everything closed around 2008, we had marriages break up, we had a suicide. People were just going to the bank and saying 'here are the keys.' We were the hardest hit forestry community" (Participant P2, 2014).

Following the economic downturn of 2008, Mackenzie faced a further challenge. The forestry sector in BC had, since the 1980s, been aggressively seeking ways to lower its operating costs. This included the taxes and royalties paid to various levels of government. It had also been busy marshaling its resources into a property tax revolt against local government. Now to be fair, there were some local governments in rural BC that had placed almost the entire local property tax burden onto its forest industry base—something that was unfair—but most local governments had a more balanced sharing of the burden among industrial, commercial, and residential taxpayers. Attention to property tax issues is especially important in Canada because, unlike some other national contexts, our local governments get almost all of their operating revenue from taxes levied on local properties. In Mackenzie, as part of an effort to get the local forest industry back into operation following its 'indefinite closure' in 2009, and against the backdrop of the industry's tax revolt and reduced operating-costs strategies, Mackenzie granted significant tax relief to its three major forest-industry firms.

As shown in Table 11.2, each of Mackenzie Pulp, Canfor, and Conifex were granted two-year municipal tax exemptions. The exemptions were designed to assist with restarting the mills and getting the local operations of the company into a more competitive economic position. The exemptions were dependent upon the companies beginning full-time operation, with stipulations generally including minimum levels of employment, as well as average annual and weekly operating schedules.

But something else also changed after the 2008–2010 period. Mackenzie had weathered the closure of its entire forest industry base through the use of an economic emergency toolkit created by the University of Northern British Columbia's Community Development Institute (Halseth *et al.*, 2008a, 2008b). As part of that toolkit, there were clear framework steps toward creating a long-term economic diversification strategy—diversification strategies that were to be built from wide and ongoing public involvement, and meant to mobilize an understanding of place-based community development. With strong local leadership from the mayor, elected council, and local government staff, Mackenzie has stayed to this course.

Table 11.2 Company Comparisons

Company	Tax Exemption Years	Minimum Employment	Minimum Operating Year	Minimum Operating Week
Canfor	2010, 2011	50 full-time	43 weeks	5 days
Mackenzie Pulp	2011, 2012	220	43 weeks	7 days
Conifex	2011, 2012	no minimum	43 weeks	5 days

Source: District of Mackenzie (2010a) Bylaw 1258; District of Mackenzie (2010b) Bylaw 1257; District of Mackenzie (2009) Bylaw 1245.

They call it 'Mackenzie-in-Motion,' and it is an ongoing and inclusive community-based approach to community development and economic diversification (District of Mackenzie, 2012). The planning process and approach reflect recognition of the typical failures in local economic development planning approaches. Instead, it was built around significant and ongoing community engagement and the collection of relevant information that can be used to support a realistic appraisal of Mackenzie's position in the regional and global economy.

The Mackenzie-in-Motion process includes community surveys, community events, and technical analyses. These feed into regular community vision and goal-setting exercises. In turn, the vision and goal processes feed directly into council priorities and local government workplans to implement and monitor progress on those goals and priorities. This was clearly something new. It was a new process, but it was also a new approach: "we never had a process like Mackenzie-in-Motion that drove our everyday lives. … I think it's the change in the way our council and where our municipal leadership is going" (Participant P3, 2014).

Inclusion was always something Mackenzie was good at. In supporting a new foundation for community development, one interviewee highlighted:

> You either do it yourself or you enable a group to do it. And in helping to enable a group to do it was often us identifying those outside resources that they can go to whether it was bringing in or sponsoring programs, those types of things. So that was one of our roles in that, we'd do that.
>
> (Participant P3, 2014)

Instead of overview plans, Mackenzie began work on detailed strategies, often with regional or provincial partner organizations. These included tourism (Tourism British Columbia, 2008), a community energy plan (BC Hydro, 2012), and the delivery of healthcare and care services (Northern Health, 2013).

Taking the need to partner regionally seriously, Mackenzie has also hosted community-to-community forums involving the District of Mackenzie, the Regional District Fraser-Fort George, and the McLeod Lake Indian Band (District of Mackenzie, McLeod Lake Indian Band, and Regional District Fraser-Fort George, 2013). The wider regional partnership is especially important. As noted by one interviewee:

> I think probably, but it's just part of the bigger picture because I think the two communities have at least in the last ten years or so, if not longer, made a real conscious effort to be … truly be partners. … I think the District of Mackenzie itself, as well as the McLeod Lake Indian Band, have done a lot of work fostering understanding and cooperation. … Just by having and speaking with a common voice, it makes it easier for government and industry and entrepreneurs if they are looking at this area or considering it for one thing or another, they are hearing a common voice.
>
> (Participant P6, 2014)

Many community people agree that these regional relationships are good. As one interviewee noted: "with the McLeod Lake band, we probably have one of the best relationships that there is in the province. It is very good" (Participant P8, 2014).

Within the Mackenzie-in-Motion framework, the community identified 12 goals (Table 11.3). Of these, the top five (*) were adopted as priorities by the local government council for the 2012 through 2015 period.

The Mackenzie-in-Motion framework has also shown the community that when you have a robust action plan, even crisis management can be turned toward supporting long-term community development goals. As described by one interviewee, relief work during the 2008–2010 downturn yielded lasting community benefits:

> They brought in funds, I think it was Council, to have a work program in Mackenzie so that the guys could work in town and not have to go Timbuktu to go to work. So they built roads all around town. They put up picnic tables in different areas of town. They made a cement ramp leading up to the radio station door. That was all done by the work program. So we have got an access road now all the way around town to get out.
>
> (Participant P2, 2014)

Another interviewee commented that:

> The job opportunities funding program provided labor for the community wild fire protection program, as well as the community infrastructure, trails and hiking trails, and the community garden. You know there were a lot of those community improvement projects that got completed.
>
> (Participant P6 2014)

Table 11.3 Mackenzie-in-Motion: Council Priorities for 2012–2015

Community Goals
1　***Good Governance**—Good delivery of services and infrastructure, and a strong, open relationship between staff, Council and the community.
2　***Fiscal Health**—A balanced District budget and healthy cash flow.
3　***Economy**—A diverse, stable economy and job base.
4　***Business Community**—A strong, community-supported local business community.
5　***Attractiveness**—An authentic, attractive community.
6　**Climate and Energy**—Significantly reduced District and community carbon emissions.
7　**Natural Environment**—Clean air, clean water and healthy ecosystems.
8　**Community**—A strong community that supports one another.
9　**Recreation and Entertainment**—Exceptional indoor and outdoor recreational and entertainment opportunities.
10　**Housing**—Housing choice that meets the needs of all residents.
11　**Health Care and Social Services**—Sufficient health care and social services.
12　**Education**—Good educational opportunities for residents.

District of Mackenzie (2012).

As noted, the Mackenzie-in-Motion process was community-driven. A typical critique of local planning efforts focuses on the degree to which people are involved in the process, and how possible development opportunities identify with people's visions or aspirations for their community into the future. Even a place-based community development planning exercise can encounter challenges around this matter of involvement:

> We need to get the public participation in it if we want this town to improve or to grow or whatever; we needed community participation. To me that's Mackenzie-in-Motion, or the best way to describe it. ... Mackenzie-in-Motion is resident participation in council decisions.
>
> (Participant P7, 2014)

And in Mackenzie, they seem to have achieved the needed engagement and participation:

> They are engaged in the community at every step of the way. I don't know how that gets sustained over time, or if it will, but I know that at these various meetings you certainly see a decent turnout when they are having public meetings related to Mackenzie-in-Motion.
>
> (Participant P5, 2014)

As in all community change processes, there are challenges. As one interviewee noted:

> With Mackenzie-in-Motion, I think they've made a lot of progress, but I again you run up against issues of how do you finance all the things we would like to do? ... I guess the one difficulty you face is 'how do you sustain that over time'?
>
> (Participant P5, 2014)

Others spoke about the fit, or sometimes the lack of fit, that comes along during plan or strategy development. As one interviewee described for a recent Mackenzie-in-Motion strategy:

> I think we did a good job of it, but I think there was a bit of visioning there where we missed ... I mean they had, you know, community meetings, and they unveiled their plan for downtown Mackenzie, and it would be wonderful if they could put into place all of the things ... little avenue with apartments above the stores, ... but Mackenzie wasn't ready for that. And so I think they lost some support as far as the plan goes because people looked at that and said this is not Mackenzie ... I think we were a bit enthusiastic, optimistic.
>
> (Participant P1, 2014)

Another challenge is impatience. The focus on the long-term process of transition and change will require staying the course over the long term as well. As one interviewee noted: "I know when we talk about economic development and we have an economic development officer, everyone expects everything to be happening now in leaps and bounds. It is a process and it takes time as well" (Participant P4, 2014).

One answer to impatience is action—and the Mackenzie-in-Motion strategy has included considerable action. In addition to the items described above, another significant action was the establishment of the McLeod Lake Mackenzie Community Forest (MLMCF). While mentioned in local economic development reports as early as 1977, solid action did not really start until 2008. It is a joint partnership between the McLeod Lake Indian Band and the District of Mackenzie—a partnership that was possible only because of all the regional relationship building work that the communities had invested in. The MLMCF has access to an annual timber harvest of 30,000 m³. As with most community forests in BC, this small harvest makes it difficult to earn a profit, but the partners work on other benefits such as employment and work for local businesses. The MLMCF is governed by a seven-person board made up of three members appointed by the McLeod Lake Indian Band, three appointed by the District of Mackenzie, and one appointed by a rest of the board. In its mission statement, the MLMCF seeks to:

> fulfill its environmental, economic and social objectives. The community forest will be managed under the principles of ecological sustainability, economic viability, local employment, localized value-added or manufacturing opportunities, forestry education and training, identification and recognition of culturally significant areas, and outdoor recreation opportunities.
>
> (British Columbia Community Forest Association, 2014)

In 2013, a report card on the progress of the Mackenzie-in-Motion work was shared with the community. It builds upon a specific community vision:

> From its roots as a new town for forestry workers, Mackenzie has grown into a strong and supportive community that residents are proud to call home. Supported by a healthy environment, Mackenzie's economic base is now diverse and robust, providing consistent employment for residents. Recreation is key to our high quality of life and healthy lifestyle, with exceptional natural features drawing residents outdoors. Great community services and facilities complement the outdoors with opportunities to meet and engage with neighbours, and the town takes pride in how attractive it is for both residents and visitors.
>
> (District of Mackenzie, 2013 p. 6)

The report card goes on to clarify for everyone the good progress being made on the five key council priorities, as well as the larger set of 12 community goals.

Clearly, this community-driven process appears more likely to be successful than any previous economic development initiative over the previous 40 years. As another interviewee noted:

> I think that is driving the District through that program… as well as the community in general. It's sort of recognizing the need to diversify … Those kind of economic diversity things are more front and center in people's minds. And so I think it's a good climate for fostering those kinds of diversification opportunities.
>
> (Participant P6, 2014)

Discussion

As detailed in earlier chapters (Chapter 3 and Chapter 7), the pressures of long-term and ongoing restructuring in the natural resource sector is having tremendous local impacts on small, remote towns and communities that are dependent upon these industries for their economic base. That large industries create significant local impacts in the small places where they operate is not a new revelation of course. Our purpose in this chapter, however, has been to examine how small places have responded to the accelerating pace of restructuring and change in these natural resource sectors. Using the forest industry as our example, and the forest-dependent town of Mackenzie as our case study, we have looked at the impacts of two themes. The first is the transformation of local government from its historic 'managerial' role to what is now a much more 'entrepreneurial' role. The second is the struggle within this entrepreneurial turn to adopt and use different economic and community development planning strategies.

As shown in the Mackenzie case, the shift from a managerial to an entrepreneurial role has been difficult for both the local government as well as the local community. While the social, demographic, employment, and economic landscape changed, the people in leadership remained very dependent upon, and comfortable within, the paternalistic role that large industry had played in the community since its early years. They remained dependent even though the industry had clearly moved away from any interest in maintaining its stewardship roles. The community's dependence is reflected in the failure to take seriously the need to diversify the local economic base as well as the inability to get traction on any of the many economic and community development planning strategies that had been developed over the years.

From the 1970s until 2008, Mackenzie's approach to economic and community development planning was a combination of local economic development and CED concepts. These imported with them some critical elements that reinforced the likelihood that resulting plans and strategies would be ineffective. To start, such plans were typically developed with limited public involvement or input. They were also developed over short periods of time that failed to allow for sufficient local debate or reflection. Without these first elements properly dealt with, the resulting plans were not supported by effective local or regional collaborative partnerships. They also lacked the local champions in both the civic and civil society leadership structures who would advance the agenda. They did not demand much of local capacity and local leadership as they were developed by outside consulting firms. As a result, however, there were also limited opportunities to appreciably grow local economic development planning capacity through the processes themselves.

A further point about local economic development centered approaches is that they play a deliberate role in furthering the neoliberal policy turn by highlighting and reminding the community that now they were in charge of their own economic futures. The result was that Mackenzie, like so many rural and small town places, hired an economic development officer and added economic development as a local government function, even though no serious framework for effective local economic diversification ever developed. The best these plans achieved was to support 'smokestack chasing'—trying to recruit new and large industrial players to relocate into the community. With Mackenzie's timber supply already fully allocated, attention turned to the other large industrial sector of BC's central interior—mining.

Reflecting on the CED approach that came into vogue in the 1980s, its value and success was muted by its (mis)placed application. To start, CED is a complex approach, but at its core is an internal focus on addressing some key social needs or issues, as well as adopting a 'bootstrap' approach to encouraging local entrepreneurship. In Mackenzie, none of the economic plans or strategies identified key social needs or issues to be addressed beyond concerns for jobs when the forest sector was in a downturn. This is quite remarkable given that even when the forest industry bounced back, the now well-entrenched processes of substituting capital for labor meant layoffs, a steady decline in local jobs, and the attendant social impacts and issues.

In terms of encouraging local entrepreneurship, while this was mentioned in numbers of plans and strategies, these were not grounded in an understanding of how the changing local economy and its employment losses were eroding the local service and retail base. Without recognition of its place in the region, there was also no recognition of the increasing retail leakage to the regional center of Prince George as highway improvements were made over the years. Encouraging local entrepreneurship in a community with a declining population and increasing retail sector linkage makes little sense—and even less sense without a comprehensive strategy to support local entrepreneurial initiative in those sectors where it might lead to success (such as hunting/guiding, logistics, and mine equipment supply for example).

The more recent embarkation on the Mackenzie-in-Motion process seems to signal a maturation away from older approaches. Within the 'entrepreneurial turn' of the neoliberal policy shift, the local government and civic leadership in Mackenzie seems to better understand and be more committed to its recast roles and responsibilities. There are a fewer appeals to local industry for salvation and assistance—in fact, the opposite has occurred as the community offered short-term assistance to each of the three large forest-industry firms in the town. As well, community development and economic development actions are no longer isolated within an economic development office or officer. It now seems to be inculcated across all facets of local government.

The process itself also seems to have adopted approaches that are more likely to garner success. Public involvement is increasing, the process is expressly community-driven, and it is widely recognized as an ongoing process that will evolve and adapt along with the community to changing circumstances. Collaboration between the public, private, and non-profit sectors is also a key element of the process. Collaboration is not only about engaging, but also about harnessing the capacities and skill sets of these partner sectors. Community and economic development planning today puts great pressure on local capacity and it is only by working cooperatively that some of this challenge and burden can be shared. Finally, the process is embedded in ready mechanisms for implementation both within the local government office, and within partners across the community.

A key third step in the transition from older approaches is that Mackenzie now works collaboratively with its regional partners. As with local collaboration, this is not an easy path as it demands both time and money, and must be constantly tended. However, the benefits are already clear. The partnership with the McLeod Lake Indian Band, for example, is the foundation for the new community forest. It also supports new local entrepreneurship in the forest and construction sectors more generally. While each community has its own development destiny, there is a shared recognition now of the value of having the region 'speak with one voice.'

The Mackenzie-in-Motion process highlights several things. The first is the importance of social capital and social cohesion in contemporary economic development and community development planning. The role of relationships and networks, of trust and participation, are part of a more successful package to support change and the dialogue for planning on how to successfully engage with that change.

The process also highlights the importance of leadership. While leadership exists across sectors, and can be shared, the past inability to stay focused toward economic diversification reinforces the need for educated and committed community leadership. This leadership, as well, must be committed to partnerships and regional collaboration.

The process also suggests that aspects of a more place-sensitive or place-based approach to community development may be taking hold. Strategies with the Mackenzie-in-Motion process seem to recognize not just local assets, but also the very real limitations on the community of realizing some economic development options. A more realistic appraisal of opportunities against the constraints of accessibility and infrastructure is important, as is the recognition of the jurisdictional limits to local government action in both economic and community development—a point that further highlights the need for partnered and collaborative approaches.

As is clear from the Mackenzie-in-Motion vision statement, the potential development of community and economic development assets has also been given a defined set of community aspirations against which to evaluate and choose options. The emphasis on creating a "supportive community residents are proud to call home" which is set within a "healthy environment" where residents are able to combine a "high quality of life" together with a "healthy lifestyle" and get out on a routine basis to enjoy the outdoors means that Mackenzie is not seeking just any economic development opportunities, it is seeking opportunities that enhance their natural and community environments without sacrificing either.

Conclusion

Social, political, and economic restructuring are transforming rural and small town places. While all such places are challenged to respond, those whose economies are dependent upon natural resource production are especially challenged given the dramatic transformations occurring within those sectors. As evidenced in this chapter, industry transformed its approach long before communities did so. Drawing upon the example of British Columbia's central interior, with case evidence more specifically from the forest-dependent community of Mackenzie, we have highlighted that after decades of fruitless community and economic development strategic planning processes, some inroads are perhaps now being made toward a new approach. Having gone through processes of local economic development and CED, there seems now to be more attention to an increasingly place-sensitive approach to community development in support of long-term economic transformation and diversification.

References

Aarsæther, N. and Bærenholdt, J. 2001. Understanding local dynamics and governance in northern regions. In J. Bærenholdt and N. Aarsæther (eds.). *Transforming the local: Coping strategies and regional policies* (pp. 15–42). Copenhagen, Denmark: Nordic Council of Ministers.

Aarsæther, N. and Suopajrvi, L. 2004. Innovations and institutions in the North. In N. Aarsæther (ed.). *Innovations in the Nordic periphery* (pp. 9–35). Stockholm, Sweden: Nordregio: Nordic Centre for Spatial Development.

Andersen, J. and Svensson, T. 2012. Struggles for recognition: A content analysis of messages posted on the Internet, *Journal of Multidisciplinary Healthcare* 5: 153–162.

Barnes, T.J. and Gertler, M.S. (eds.). 1999. *The new Industrial Geography: Regions, regulation and institutions*. New York: Routledge.

Barnes, T.J. and Hayter, R. (eds.). 1997. *Troubles in the rainforest: British Columbia's forest economy in transition*. Victoria, BC: Western Geographical Press, Department of Geography, University of Victoria, Canadian Western Geographical Series, vol. 33.

BC Hydro. 2012. *District of Mackenzie community energy & emissions plan.* Approved by Council Resolution on August 27, 2012. District of Mackenzie. CEEP: QuickStart.

Bowles, R.T. 1992. Single-industry resource communities in Canada's north. In D.A. Hay and G.S. Basran (eds.), *Rural sociology in Canada* (pp. 63–83). Don Mills, ON: Oxford University Press.

Bradford, N. 2003. Public–private partnership? Shifting paradigms of economic governance in Ontario, *Canadian Journal of Political Science* 36(5): 1005–1033.

Bradford, N. 2005. *Place-based public policy: Towards a new urban and community agenda for Canada*. Ottawa: Canadian Policy Research Networks.

British Columbia Community Forest Association. 2014. Available on-line at: www.bccfa.ca/index.php/becomeamember/members/item/60-mcleod-lake-mackenzie-community-forest. Accessed September 10, 2014.

Bryant, C. 1995. The role of local actors in transforming the urban fringe, *Journal of Rural Studies* 11(3): 255–267.

Bryant, C. 2010. Co-constructing rural communities in the 21st century: Challenges for central governments and the research community in working effectively with local and regional actors. In G. Halseth, S. Markey, and D. Bruce (eds.), *The next rural economies: Constructing rural place in a global economy* (pp. 142–54). Oxfordshire: CABI.

Crane Management Consultants. 1991. *District of Mackenzie economic development strategy*. Prepared for Prince Regional Development Corporation. January 1991. Vancouver, BC.

District of Mackenzie. 1992. *District of Mackenzie downtown revitalization strategy and concept*. Mackenzie, BC: District of Mackenzie.

District of Mackenzie. 2009. *Canfor revitalization tax exemption bylaw No. 1245, 2009*. A bylaw of the District of Mackenzie to grant a revitalization tax exemption. Mackenzie, BC: District of Mackenzie.

District of Mackenzie. 2010a. *Conifex revitalization tax exemption bylaw No. 1258, 2010*. A bylaw of the District of Mackenzie to grant a revitalization tax exemption. Mackenzie, BC: District of Mackenzie.

District of Mackenzie. 2010b. *Mackenzie Pulp mill development corporation revitalization tax exemption bylaw No. 1257, 2010*. A bylaw of the District of Mackenzie to grant a revitalization tax exemption. Mackenzie, BC: District of Mackenzie.

District of Mackenzie. 2012. *Mackenzie-in-Motion: Strategic priorities 2012–2015*. Mackenzie, BC: District of Mackenzie.

District of Mackenzie. 2013. *Mackenzie-in-Motion: Annual report*. Mackenzie, BC: District of Mackenzie.

District of Mackenzie, McLeod Lake Indian Band, and Regional District of Fraser-Fort George. 2013. *Regional community to community forum: Summary report—Meeting #2 (Larger Forum)*. February 27, 2013. McLeod Lake Auditorium, McLeod Lake, BC. Mackenzie, BC: District of Mackenzie and McLeod Lake Indian Band.

Freudenburg, W.R. 1992. Addictive economies: Extractive industries and vulnerable localities in a changing world economy, *Rural Sociology* 57(3): 305–332.

Halseth, G. 1999a. Resource town employment: Perceptions in small town British Columbia, *Tijdschift voor Economische en Sociale Geografie* 90(2): 196–210.

Halseth, G. 1999b. 'We came for work': Situating employment migration in B.C.'s small, resource-based, communities, *Canadian Geographer* 43(4): 363–381.

Halseth, G. 2005. Resource town transition: Debates after closure. In S.J. Essex, A.W. Gilg, R.B. Yarwood, J. Smithers, and R. Wilson (eds.), *Rural change and sustainability: Agriculture, the environment and communities* (pp. 326–342). Oxfordshire: CABI Publishing.

Halseth, G. and Sullivan, L. 2002. *Building community in an instant town: A social geography of Mackenzie and Tumbler Ridge, British Columbia*. Prince George, BC: University of Northern British Columbia Press.

Halseth, G., Killam, S., and Manson, D. 2008a. Working framework for economic emergencies for smaller municipalities—Part I, *Municipal World* 118(3): 35–39.

Halseth, G., Killam, S., and Manson, D. 2008b. Working framework for economic emergencies for smaller municipalities—Part II, *Municipal World* 118(4): 35–38.

Halseth, G., Markey, S., and Bruce, D. (eds.). 2010. *The next rural economies: Constructing rural place in a global economy.* Oxfordshire: CABI Publishing.

Hayter, R. 2000. Flexible crossroads: The restructuring of British Columbia's forest economy. Vancouver, BC: University of British Columbia Press.

Horne, G. 2004. *British Columbia's heartland at the dawn of the 21st century: 2001 economic dependencies and impact ratios for 63 local areas.* Victoria, BC: Ministry of Management Services.

KPMG Consulting. 1997. *Forest-based economic development—Opportunity for the District of Mackenzie.* Project Report. Prepared for District of Mackenzie Forest Advisory Committee. Edmonton, AB: KPMG Consulting.

Krippendorff, K. and Bock, M. (eds.). 2009. *The content analysis reader.* Thousand Oaks, CA: Sage Publications.

Lucas, R.A. 1971. *Minetown, milltown, railtown: Life in Canadian communities of single industry.* Toronto, ON: University of Toronto Press.

Mackenzie Economic Development Committee. 1994. *Mackenzie Economic Development Planning Discussion Paper.* Mackenzie, BC: Mackenzie Economic Development Committee.

Marchak, M.P. 1983. *Green gold: The forest industry in British Columbia.* Vancouver, BC: UBC Press.

Markey, S., Halseth, G., and Manson, D. 2006. The struggle to compete: From comparative to competitive advantage in northern British Columbia, *International Planning Studies* 11(1): 19–39.

Markey, S., Halseth, G., and Manson, D. 2008a. Challenging the inevitability of rural decline: Advancing the policy of place in northern British Columbia, *Journal of Rural Studies* 24(4): 409–421.

Markey, S., Halseth, G., and Manson, D. 2008b. Closing the implementation gap: A framework for incorporating the context of place in economic development planning, *Local Environment* 13(4): 337–351.

Markey, S., Halseth, G., and Manson, D. 2012. *Investing in place: Economic renewal in northern British Columbia.* Vancouver, BC: University of British Columbia Press.

Markey, S., Pierce, J.T., Vodden, K., and Roseland, M. 2005. *Second growth: Community economic development in rural BC.* Vancouver, BC: University of British Columbia Press.

Northern Health. 2013. *Healthy northern communities 2013: Mackenzie.* Prince George, BC: Northern Health Authority.

Paillé, G. 2013. *A history of forestry in Canada.* Québec, QC: Les Publications du Québec. Natural Resources Canada, FPInnovations, Cégep de Sainte-Foy.

Pierce, J.T. 1992. Progress and the biosphere: The dialectics of sustainable development, *The Canadian Geographer* 36(4): 306–320.

Polèse, M. 1999. From regional development to local development: On the life, death, and rebirth (?) of regional science as a policy relevant science, *Canadian Journal of Regional Science* 22(3): 299–314.

Porteous, J.D. 1987. Single enterprise communities. In C.N. Forward (ed.), *British Columbia: Its resources and people* (pp. 383–399). Victoria, BC: Department of Geography, University of Victoria, Western Geographical Series, volume 22.

Porter, M. 2004. *Competitiveness in rural US regions: Learning and research agenda.* Boston, MA: Institute for Strategy and Competitiveness, Harvard Business School.

Reed, M.G. 2003. *Taking stands: Gender and the sustainability of rural communities.* Vancouver, BC: University of British Columbia Press.

Savoie, D. 1997. *Rethinking Canada's regional development policy: An Atlantic perspective.* Ottawa, ON: Canadian Institute for Research on Regional Development.

Statistics Canada. 1971. *Census of Canada.* Ottawa: Statistics Canada.

Statistics Canada. 1981. *Census of Canada.* Ottawa: Statistics Canada.

Statistics Canada. 1991. *Census of Canada.* Ottawa: Statistics Canada.

Statistics Canada. 2001. *Census of Canada.* Ottawa: Statistics Canada.

Statistics Canada. 2011. *Census of Canada.* Ottawa: Statistics Canada.

Stevenson, S.K., Armleder, H.M., Arsenault, A., Coxson, D., DeLong, S.C., and Jull, M. 2011. *British Columbia's inland rainforest: Ecology, conservation, and management.* Vancouver, BC: University of British Columbia Press. With B. Drinkwater, A. Fredeen, B. Heise, P. Laing, Z. Lindo, P. Sanborn, and J. Shultis.

Synergy Management Group Ltd. 2007. *Business welcome. Fun included. Mackenzie.* Mackenzie, BC: District of Mackenzie Economic Development Strategic Planning Committee.

Tourism British Columbia. 2008. *Mackenzie tourism plan: Final.* Victoria, BC: Community Tourism Foundations Program.

12 Resource Town Transitions in Finland

Local Impacts and Policy Responses in Lieksa

Juha Kotilainen, Maija Halonen, Eero Vatanen, and Markku Tykkyläinen

Introduction

As a general trend in Finland, there has been a constant migration from remote rural areas to urban centers and their surroundings since the 1960s. The case study resource town, Lieksa, has been no exception. The municipal and other local actors have sought to find suitable strategies to address this issue. However, it is not only the local actors that have been involved in designing responses to the problems of economic restructuring and population loss. Typically for Finland, the state has had a very active role in promoting regions and localities in their attempts to overcome the impacts of structural economic and demographic transformations. Over the decades, these strategies have had some success in the short term. In the long term, the success of these strategies has, however, been meager. In this chapter, we explore the changing demography of the case resource town and examine the various strategies that have been implemented to deal with the adverse impacts of restructuring of the economy and population change.

Resilience, Adaptive Capacity, and Reactions to Pressures to Change

Resource cycles (Hayter and Patchell, 2011), and more broadly, industry life-cycles can be understood by drawing from discussions on economic, social, and environmental resilience of natural-resource-dependent communities (Wilson, 2012). The life cycle of an industry is a result of evolution of the economy when new technologies and shifts in consumption patterns create series of emergence and disappearance of industrial activities, leading to processes of adaptation in production systems (Brezis and Krugman, 1997; see also the companion Chapter 4 on Finland). These evolutionary processes consist of the stages of growth, decline or shake-out, and adaptation to a changed situation. The possibilities for a local or regional economy to manage a phase of decline are dependent on its adaptive capacity, which is related to resilience.

Resilience is a concept that originates in research seeking to understand human–environment interactions (Adger, 2000; Folke, 2006), but it has also been utilized in analyses of the evolution of regional economies (Christopherson *et al.*, 2010; Martin, 2012; Boschma, 2014). Resilience is a notion that refers to the ability of a system or region to cope with change. The distractions that a social-ecological system or a region faces have often been seen as abrupt, but there are also slower processes that can be seen to cause a threat to a system's persistence. Within this foundational understanding, the concept of resilience has been given various connotations, from the interpretation that resilience is about a system's ability to resist change, through a system's capacity to adapt in order to be able to cope with a new situation, to its learning capabilities (Folke, 2006).

In research pertaining to social-ecological systems, resilience has largely been a normative concept, with the idea that the more resilient the social-ecological system is the better, and resilience should be promoted by social action (Folke *et al.*, 2010). However, resilience should not be seen only as a positive ideal. It could easily be thought of as systems connecting the political, the economic, and the ecological through, for example, the maintenance of extraction and utilization of fossil resources for producing energy instead of developing renewable energy, the resilience of which may not be seen as a goal by many. Nevertheless, if the problems of regions that are facing economic shocks are considered, it is easy to see the resilience of a region or a locality as something worth striving for. Resilience, in such a case, could be seen as social and economic capacity ensuring the opportunities of a region or community to maintain development and well-being (Martin, 2012; Wilson, 2012).

One of the central arguments within resilience research has been that systems at various scales are interlinked, and a disruption in a system at one scale is likely to cause disruptions in related systems on larger or smaller scales (Folke, 2006). Often the resilience of systems at different scales may be in contradiction, and the resilience of a system at one scale (e.g. global) may even prevent resilience in another system at another scale (e.g. local) (MacKinnon and Derickson, 2013). Regarding the transformations in the case of Finland and the case study resource town, it is noteworthy that in the Nordic countries, governmental regulation with regional policy and the Nordic welfare regime (see Chapter 8 on labor issues in Finland) have played a central role in local adaptation. Thus, local adaptive capacity and governmental regional and welfare policies have been intertwined.

In exploring regional resilience, Martin (2012) has identified several options for a region to react to economic pressures. Engineering resilience would result in the rebound of a region back to its previous state. The concept of ecological resilience resonates with the idea of regional economic hysteresis, where the regional economy finds its previous growth trend but from a different starting point. Adaptive resilience, in turn, would lead to realignment of the constituents of the regional economy. More concretely, there could be in principle four different ways for a region to react to a state of economic shock. Resistance could be measured by the degree of sensitivity or depth of reaction of a regional economy to a recessionary shock. The speed and degree of recovery of a regional economy would signal its return to the state that existed prior to the phase of decline. Reorientation would mean the extent of adaptation of a regional economy in response to a recessionary shock. Finally, renewal would be measured by the extent to which a regional economy renews its pre-recession growth path or shifts to a new growth trend.

Within this framework, adaptive capacity can be taken to mean the ability of a system consisting of local and governmental actors to prepare for stresses and changes in advance or to adjust and respond to the effects caused by exogenous or endogenous processes. Increasing adaptive capacity improves the opportunities of a region or community to manage the varying ranges and magnitudes of adverse impacts, while allowing for flexibility to rework approaches if deemed at a later date to be on an undesirable trajectory (Engle, 2011). Adaptability can be conceived of in the sense that the actors and institutions from the local level to the senior governmental level try to prognosticate the stresses and pressures for transformations, thereby seeking to create procedures of planned adaptation.

As has been illustrated in the previous chapters on Finland's resource regions (Chapters 4 and 8), the resource periphery in Finland and the case study resource town of Lieksa have been struggling to maintain their employment figures. Intimately related to dwindling employment, the actors in the resource town have also been struggling with a declining population. In what follows, we examine the reactions in the resource town to the continuous pressures to reorganize local assets so that the inhabitants would have opportunities for employment. However, as a specific condition in Finland, the local communities have not been struggling alone. Regional development policies have been present since the mid-1900s, and they have included strong state interventions in the economic development of regions and remote municipalities facing rural and industrial decline. We therefore present a brief analysis of regional development policies in Finland in order to make the local responses to crises more comprehensible. First, however, we examine demographic change.

Demographic Change in Lieksa

The rates of urbanization and industrialization were record-breaking in Finland in European terms in the 1960s and the 1970s (Tervo, 2005). The proximity of the growing European timber market had expanded the utilization of timber resources and increased the demand for local labor since the beginning of the twentieth century (Aarnio, 1999). Through the increased use of natural resources, industrial activities expanded to marginal areas, which accelerated rural population growth. In addition, rural population growth escalated in the post-World War Two years as a consequence of the Land Acquisition Act, which redistributed 9.1 percent of the land area in Finland to veterans and refugees. This policy increased the amounts of agricultural and non-agricultural one-family rural housing (Tykkyläinen, 1995). In Lieksa, the size of the rural labor force and rural population peaked in the early 1960s.

At first, the growing industries in small towns and rural areas offered new jobs for the growing populations. However, less than two decades later, the rural periphery faced a structural change and depopulation. The postwar baby-boom generation entered the labor market simultaneously with the rationalization of primary production. The consequence was rural overpopulation and large-scale migration from rural areas to cities mostly in Finland and Sweden (Rannikko, 1999). Lieksa lost about 7,000 inhabitants due to migration in ten years alone (Figure 12.1) during the 1960s and 1970s. The socioeconomic restructuring processes were mitigated by the establishment of spatially equal welfare services and decentralization of public tasks in the late 1960s and the 1970s, and regional policy funding was allocated to disadvantaged regions from 1966 (Moisio and Leppänen, 2007; Sippola, 2011). However, these policies were insufficient to stop the vicious circle of diminishing employment and population, and the growing proportions of aging population in places such as Lieksa (Figures 12.1, 12.2, 12.3, and 12.4).

While the lack of employment opportunities largely explains migration from Lieksa, there are other reasons as well. During the 1960s, the general urbanization process with new lifestyles and opportunities for higher education attracted people to the regional centers and cities in Finland and Sweden. Apart from clear individual economic push–pull factors, the social chain migration (see MacDonald and MacDonald, 1964) impacted on the migration of networks of relatives, friends, and villagers, including those who actually had a workplace or probably could have had the chance to work or have vocational training in Lieksa. On the other hand, the out-migration opened opportunities for local and regional migration, especially to the town center, which was expanding, and the residential

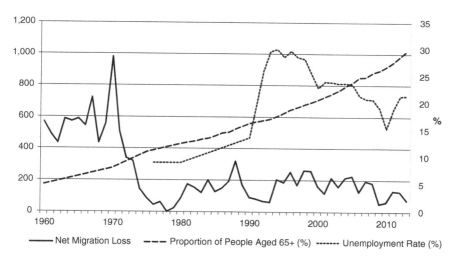

Figure 12.1 Annual Net Migration:[1] Loss: the Proportion of People Aged 65 and Over[2] to the Total Population, and Unemployment Rate[3] (%) in Lieksa (Present-Day Area).

Sources: Lieksa (1980); Official Statistics Finland (1960–1986, 1982, 1990, 2014a, 2014b, 2015c).

Notes
1 Intermunicipal net migration is the difference between intermunicipal in-migration and intermunicipal out-migration (Official Statistics Finland, 2015a).
2 According to demographic dependency ratio people aged 65 and over are calculated as elderly persons (Official Statistics Finland, 2009).
3 Unemployment rate is the proportion of the unemployed people to the active population (labor force) (Official Statistics Finland, 2015b).

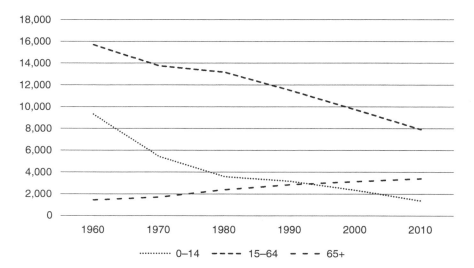

Figure 12.2 Changes in the Age Structure of Population, Lieksa (Present-Day Area), 1960–2010.
Sources: Lieksa (1980); Official Statistics Finland (2015c).

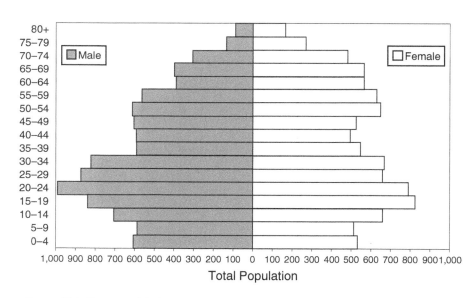

Figure 12.3 Demographic Structure of the Population in Lieksa, 1980.
Source: Official Statistics Finland (2015c).

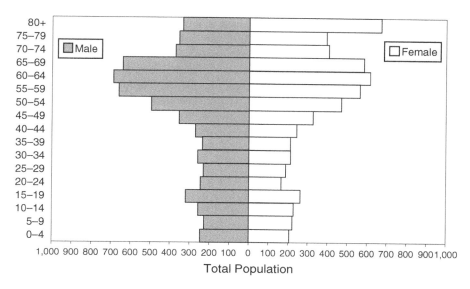

Figure 12.4 Demographic Structure of the Population in Lieksa, 2014.
Source: Official Statistics Finland (2015c).

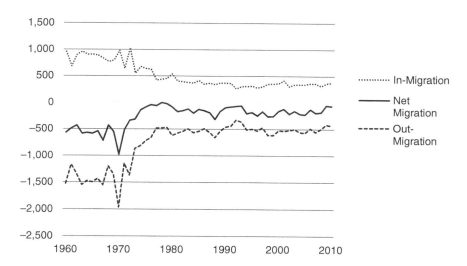

Figure 12.5 In-Migration, Out-Migration and Net Migration: Lieksa 1960–2010.
Sources: Official Statistics Finland (1960–1986, 2011).

area next to the Pankakoski Board Mill, where new residential areas were planned (Lieksan kauppala, 1961, 1969; Pielisjärvi, 1969). These trends are revealed in the statistics as countermigration which certainly has been less massive than out-migration, but has restrained the decrease in population numbers (Figure 12.5). While changes in municipal status and boundaries before 1973 limit the interpretation of statistics, the main point from the 1960s and the early 1970s is that while structural urbanization led to the remote town of Lieksa losing inhabitants through out-migration, the inhabitants in the area began to migrate also from the most sparsely populated areas to the more urban areas locally.

While the migration during the late 1970s can still be explained by structural causes, there was an increased impact from the policies and actions targeted at the migration from such remote areas. However, the principles of migration kept changing through the 1980s, and though the stabilized curve of in- and out-migration has its partial basis on the balanced structure of the local society and the decreased size of the population, the emphasis of the migration lies more and more on individual life courses and lifestyle choices. Therefore, the opportunities for structural control and creation of a certain type of development in the long term have diminished. In this regard, migration since around 1980 can be seen as a reflection of individualization, with a connection to the waning of normative and standardized political steering of people's behavior (see Beck, 1992).

This demography, as well as the economic challenges and the transformations in industries presented in the previous chapters, form the framework in which the local community has struggled to maintain its ability to provide an economically feasible environment for its population. In what follows, we explore these attempts one by one. We also draw from the perspectives on regional and local resilience that seek to understand how communities could cope with transforming conditions which affect their economic basis, social structures, and thus even their existence. First, however, we provide a view on regional policies in Finland, as the strategies at the local scale cannot be understood without reference to these national-scale policies.

Regional Policy Impact

Regional Policies in Finland

It is important to emphasize that in Finland the policies to help local communities and regions to deal with adverse economic conditions have been a combination of national and local efforts. Thus the responsibilities related to mitigating the impacts have not been left to the local communities alone, but this does not of course remove the problem that the communities nevertheless must compete with one another for entrepreneurs, business, and production and it is hardly possible to reach a situation in which all communities are on a winning side (MacKinnon and Derickson, 2013). Beyond this general principle of national- and local-scale interaction, national development policies on regions and localities, during their existence for about half a century, have been transforming from being industrialization-oriented rural policies toward policies emphasizing the competitiveness of regions and cities (Moisio, 2012).

Although surveys carried out on the rate of regional development since the nineteenth century as well as early industrialization policies and activities by the state and national government can be seen as predecessors of regional policies, true regional policies in Finland emerged in the 1960s (Jauhiainen and Niemenmaa, 2006). The targets of regional policies were institutionalized in the national legislation, with six successive laws on regional policies preceding Finland's membership of the European Union in 1995. These policies were a reaction to decreasing employment in many eastern and northern parts of the country, especially in rural areas. The regional development policies were guided by an ideology that the opportunities for employment, education, and well-being (including healthcare and social services) should be equally distributed across the country, with the double aim of also utilizing the labor input by the inhabitants throughout the regions, for economic growth and an increase in wealth nationally.

It has been suggested in retrospect that regional development policies in Finland until the late 1990s could be divided into three main phases (Vartiainen, 1998). In the first phase, which lasted until the mid-1970s, policies concentrated on industrializing less-developed parts of the country. As the country was still very rural in the 1960s and lagging behind in comparison to the level of urbanization in Europe, the target of industrializing the rural areas was defined as central for the regional policies. The second phase, from the mid-1970s until the late 1980s, was characterized by the rise of spatial and strategic planning in the regions. Industrialization was no longer the most important goal, but regional development was understood as taking more varied forms. The national regional policy measures were at their height in the 1970s (Sippola, 2011). Starting in the late 1980s, the third phase consisted of development actions based on specific development programs. While in the early phases it was the national government, ministries, and state-run development organizations that were responsible for advancing regional development, in the latter phases this responsibility was transferred to the regions themselves, with the regional councils becoming the chief organizations planning for regional development. The increase in the weight of regional organizations in regional development was also due to the membership of Finland of the European Union (EU) in 1995, which brought with it the pivotal role of regions in the allocation of EU structural funds. With Finland's membership of the EU, additional instruments were introduced into the regional policy repertoire. These included the EU structural funds and LEADER (from the French *Liaison Entre Actions de Développement de l'Économie Rurale*) policy measures, which is a local development method seeking to mobilize local rural actors on the European scale (European Commission, 2015). Therefore, over the decades, there has been a shift from supporting large-scale manufacturing industries to an emphasis on the competitiveness of regions in the global economy. The most recent developments in the political discourse seem to favor the spatial movement of labor force instead of the formerly strong principle of moving positions of work.

The notion of a decentralized welfare state has been used to describe the larger political framework of regional development policies of the late twentieth century (Moisio, 2012). In the background, there were politics of identities and a foundational idea about achieving national coherence, so that rural and urban populations and various social groups and classes would be amalgamated. The means included the expansion and intensification of activities governed by the nation-state throughout the state territory and regional development measures were a concrete tool in this endeavor. On the one hand, there was an underlying tenet that capitalism as a rule produces differences in regional wealth which must be evened out by state intervention. On the other hand, the existence of the nation-state was seen to be crucially based on the overall availability of and access to natural and human resources. This led to the aim of industrializing the national territory throughout, and regional development projects were a crucial part of this aim. This sort of welfare capitalism was based on extensive regulation by the state, expansion of the public sector, a significant role for planning in contrast to free markets, as well as creating economic growth by increasing public spending. State-owned companies were major players, including Enso-Gutzeit described in the earlier Finnish chapters. Gradually the regional policies were expanded from being driven by industrialization policies to an expansion of public welfare services to the regions. This practical aim was accompanied by the political principle of treating all the regions, places, and citizens equally.

Transformations in Regional Policies Affecting Lieksa

Nationally led regional development policies did have a significant impact on Lieksa, since as part of the industrialization policies the local economy was diversified in terms of the variety of products manufactured there. The strong development policies of the 1970s, therefore, created an increase in jobs in manufacturing in Lieksa at a time when forestry work was on the decrease. This pattern was empirically described in Chapter 4. Similarly, the shifts in the emphasis of the development policies are reflected there. It was seen in Chapter 8 as well how employment in the services sector expanded in Lieksa due to the increase in welfare services. Also the later transformations in the focus of regional policies and abandonment of the industrialization paradigm are visible in the curves on the sectoral effects of employment in Lieksa. The regional policies of the twenty-first century have been focused on competitiveness of regional urban centers, which have been configured to distribute wealth and well-being to the surrounding communities and rural areas (Moisio, 2012). In such policies, places such as Lieksa do not have the role they used to have in previous development policies with the goal of territorially even development.

In terms of employment, Lieksa came to a turning point in 1990, as there has been no growth of employment in the main industries since then. Instead of an abrupt collapse, there was a steady trend of reduction in employment. Several simultaneous larger-scale disturbances deepened the loss of jobs. One of the most unfavorable processes was the nationwide recession in the early 1990s, caused by the chain effects of several factors which were mainly started by excessive foreign indebtedness combined with simultaneous devaluation; it eventually led to a plunge in demand in the domestic market and the cutting of public spending (Kiander,

2001). At the same time exports to the Soviet Union market came to an end. In Lieksa, the unemployment rate surged to 30 percent (Figure 12.1).

In this turmoil, governmental support for the services of the welfare state and regional policy measures was reappraised. The reduction of public spending was partially an outcome of the economic recession, but the time was also favorable for a policy change from nationally regulated social equity-oriented goals toward an internationally oriented capitalist society regime (Julkunen, 1992, 2001). The political aspirations of that time as well as the accession of Finland to the EU in 1995 stressed the strengths of specialized and competitive regions in regional policy instead of aiming at abolishing the disadvantages of developing areas (Kortelainen, 2010). The new EU policies and funding mechanisms such as regional structural funds and LEADER-funding for rural areas reformed and partly replaced the former regional policies (Eskelinen, 2001; Danson and de Souza, 2012). The ideology of regional development shifted from the nationally governed top-down format into a combination of integrated programs regulated by the EU and regionally based bottom-up development projects (Malinen, 1998). However, the post-1995 development in Lieksa shows that the newest development policy instruments have had only meager impacts on development. Although Finland's membership of the EU brought about new regional and local policy instruments, they have not significantly created new jobs in Lieksa since the mid-1990s.

Looking more closely at the local scale, there have been a variety of detailed development strategies that have sought to bring change into the local trajectories. Elsewhere, strategies to deal with decline in Lieksa have been identified (Kotilainen *et al.*, 2012, 2015). These include the further industrialization of the local economy as well as its diversification through an industrial park; developing the service sector; and new forms of utilization of local natural resources. Each of these strategies incorporates varying more detailed substrategies. We next describe these strategies and seek to put them in a larger-scale context.

Local Strategies to Provide New Opportunities

Diversifying the Economy as a Means to Provide Employment: The Industrial Estate

The most visible strategy to support the resource town in its struggle to overcome the crisis in employment caused by restructuring of the forest industry has been the establishment of an industrial estate in the early 1970s (Vuorenmaa, 2003). In terms of the different versions of regional resilience (Martin, 2012), this strategy, as far as it has been successful, would be about a realignment of the assets of the local economy, with a further aim of its reorientation. The explicit aim of the industrial estate was to diversify the local economy, but this aim was built on the foundations of industrial traditions prevailing in the resource town.

It is noteworthy that the strategy to diversify the local economy, with its materialization in the industrial estate, was a combination of local- and national-scale efforts. It thereby also illustrates the way the efforts for supporting community and regional resilience can be a blend of input from various scales. As described above, there was a wider ideology behind the emergence of this multiscalar effort, as the policies and strategies in Finland for dealing with regions, towns, and rural areas with problems related to their economies started to be executed on national and local scales from the 1970s. In Lieksa, the establishment of the industrial estate was the greatest achievement of a regional policy that operated by providing various subsidies to firms that decided to relocate their production to peripheral municipalities undergoing restructuring. Lieksa was one of the first municipalities to benefit from the new industrial estate instrument.

There were also other larger-scale political-economic processes that helped the industrial estate project in its early success. Foreign trade across the borders of Finland was deregulated during the same decades, as Finland became an associate member in the European Free Trade Association (EFTA) in 1961, made a free trade agreement with the European Economic Community (EEC) in 1973, and a special agreement with Council for Mutual Economic Assistance (SEV/Comecon) led by the Soviet Union, in the 1970s. Moreover, the Finnish mark was strongly devaluated in 1967, which, together with the opening of the European markets, generated favorable conditions for the diversification of the industrial structures.

The prerequisites for the investments in the industrial estate in the 1970s included, first, availability of labor force, a result of a large generation entering the labor market and a sharp decline in employment in the primary sector. Second, local industrial culture in the community gave competitive advantage in relation to other, more rural, Finnish municipalities. Third, regional policy instruments enabled the attainment of financial support from the government for investments, research and development, the training of labor, and wages for a few years after the enterprise was founded. Moreover, loans were available from the state-owned regional development fund KERA / Finvera *(Kehitysaluerahasto)* (Tykkyläinen, 1992; Yli-Jokipii and Koski, 1995).

From the start, measured by employment figures, the strategy to diversify the local economy was clearly partially successful, as many rubber and plastic products manufacturers and clothing industries decided to relocate in Lieksa, and the number of workers employed in factories almost doubled from 1970 to 1980. However, the solution was only moderate, as a relatively abundant number of inhabitants, slightly less than 10 percent, were still struggling with unemployment (Figure 12.1). In terms of the variations of resilience, the shift from the previous path of forest industry dependency was made clear by turning away from local natural resources. The new industries were calculated to grow on imported raw materials. For instance, clothing factories and metal products workshops were established, and the rubber industry started its production.

As a result, Lieksa's economy became consciously diversified in the 1970s. It could be assumed that this diversification should have led to a situation in which the local economy was less vulnerable to disturbances, as it was no longer dependent on a single resource or a single line of production. Interestingly, this was not the case in the long run. After ten years of relative success brought by incoming investments by companies and the national government, a sharp decline in manufacturing jobs, that continues today, began in the 1980s. The roots of these long-term failures lay in the very means designed for fighting the decline. As the diversification of the local industry was based on imported raw materials, it was easy to relocate this manufacturing as its competitiveness in this location declined. A larger process of deindustrialization prevailed in Finland in the 1980s, and these new industries in the marginal areas became vulnerable with the waning of regional policy support. The prices of many products manufactured by the industries in Lieksa were high for the domestic market and could not compete with imported products. The industries in Lieksa had to improve their cost-efficiency, which led to redundancies and even shrinking turnovers. An increasing part of the blue-collar manufacturing activities in high-cost peripheries found themselves on the losing side of the spatial margin of profitability (Hayter and Patchell, 2011; Smith, 1981).

Therefore, there was a downside to the industrial park strategy. The newly created manufacturing units that refined imported raw materials (textiles, rubber, steel, and plastic) were based on capital loans and subsidies. The benefits turned out to be temporary, as changes in the global market, production technologies, and the strategies of firms have caused manufacturing units to decrease their production figures, relocate again to other regions and countries, or close down for good.

Re-exploitation of Local Natural Resources

There are other strategies that could be characterized as aiming at either recovery or reorientation of the local economy (Martin, 2012). As the revitalization strategy that drew from imported resources has been in decline in the long run, a more recent industrial strategy has been built, again, on the exploitation of local natural resources. There are different strands within this local natural resource strategy, but they all draw on the use of timber. It seems that the causes for this return in local strategies to one that is focused on the local resource can be found in the figures that illustrate that despite large-scale technological transformations in the forest industry that led to the decrease in the number of jobs in recent decades, the utilization of forest resources for industrial purposes still dominates the local economy. It has been estimated that the utilization of local natural resources today provides for about 25 percent of all local jobs, which is high compared to the Finnish average, of about 10 percent, and the forest industry makes up about half of all manufacturing jobs in Lieksa (Vatanen, 2010). The traditional forms of forest resource utilization, that is, by the forest industry, keep playing a major role as an employer (see Chapter 8). This production includes cardboard, sawn timber, and glue-laminated timber. However, reliance on this kind of industrial production is not really a strategy for the local actors; rather the forest industry continues functioning in the town despite any strategies.

However, the potential of industries drawing from the forest is seen in local strategies to be more diversified today than they used to be. There are local development strategies that focus on utilizing timber for energy production. In these plans, the scale of production may vary from small-scale firewood entrepreneurs to larger-scale industrial production. An example of new plans is a bio-oil refinery. Lieksa Development Agency (2014) is in charge of a plan for establishing a bioenergy production plant in the vicinity of the Kevätniemi sawmill. The general goal of the project is to strengthen the forest cluster locally. This plan is thus far waiting for the licenses and financing needed for the construction to start. The product would be bio-oil produced from timber with annual planned production figures between 90,000 and 180,000 tonnes. The aim is that the wood-based bio-oil would have commercial potential by replacing fossil fuels in industries and heating systems, and later also as fuel for vehicles.

The employment impacts of such new industries are speculative and various scenarios can be created (Lehtonen and Okkonen, 2016). Unfortunately for local employment opportunities, nevertheless, the applications of these new automated technologies usually require fewer workers than the forest industries that dominated production in the twentieth century. Employment figures for a bioeconomy that exploits local natural resources at large in Lieksa have been calculated by Vatanen (2010) and Vatanen *et al.* (2012). According to these calculations, the forest industry provides employment for about 550–600 persons, tourism (which in Lieksa is related to forest environments, spectacular landscapes, and natural sceneries) employs about 200 persons, while collecting wood for energy production and production of wood chips would employ about 30 to 40 persons. Agriculture employs about 250 persons.

Service Sector

There have also been developments that imply the form of resilience as renewal, but on a closer look point toward reorientation (Halonen *et al.*, 2015). The industry life-cycles have not rested on manufacturing industries only. Employment grew continuously in the service sector from the 1920s until around 1990. Until the mid-1960s, this was a consequence of colonization, and the expansion of the primary sector and forest industries increased the demand for services as the size of the population grew. After that, much of the increase in employment in services can be explained by the construction of the Nordic welfare state, where public healthcare and social services were to be provided evenly across the country.

The intensive construction of the welfare state began in the early 1970s, and the idea was to create local services that were administrated, produced, and financed by the municipalities, with additional financial government support (Kortelainen, 2010). In Lieksa, this reform produced a considerable need for educated employees, especially in the healthcare sector, and the reforms were possible only with a simultaneously created system of state subsidies (Lieksa, 1975, 1976). Compared with the decline of employment by more than 5,000 persons over about two decades, the increase in jobs in the service sector was about 1,000 jobs. Hence, adaptive capacity, although supported by regional policy and the expansion of the welfare state, was not sufficient as the overlapping growth cycles in the service sector and manufacturing could not create enough resilience to prevent continuing population loss.

There are two current strategies related to the service sector that cover areas other than the nationally regulated welfare services. Services for tourism are seen as a way forward from the local problems, and there is actually a strong heritage in the tourism industry within the municipal boundaries. The hilly and forested Koli National Park, located across the lake from the municipal center, is one of the best-known natural sceneries in the country. Legacies of former development include a hotel and the oldest ski lift in Finland (in operation since 1939). There is also another park within the municipal boundaries, part of the marshy Patvinsuo National Park, administered by the Finnish Forest and Park Service Metsähallitus. As another attraction, the forested Ruunaa area with its river and rapids is also an important site for recreation. Nevertheless, the employment opportunities in tourism services are unlikely to reach the level provided by processing industries in the past.

As another form of services, but only on a minor scale, call-center firms have been locating their operations in Lieksa in recent years, providing services through the Internet and telephone. The reason for this choice of location has been the relative abundance of a local workforce.

Migration to the Rural: Can It Bring New Growth?

Finally, we can identify a strategy that is closest to potential renewal of the local economy, as it builds not on the existing or former industries at all, but aims at attracting incomers on the basis of alluring housing conditions. It is hoped that spacious living conditions will attract incomers who would prefer the relative benefits of the area in comparison to more densely populated areas. Wealthy and healthy senior citizens are generally the most desired returnees, but there are also foreign immigrants from the neighboring Russian Federation and EU countries as well as refugees from outside Europe.

If the narrative of individualization is combined with the metanarrative of urbanization and lost jobs, understandably the questions of 'who' and 'why' one would migrate to Lieksa are difficult to answer. As the question of migration was asked of a group of municipal representatives, the conversations turned immediately to the out-migration and the structural changes in the past. The only clear group of new incomers that were mentioned were the refugees from Somalia who mainly began to migrate to Lieksa in 2010 after a number of flats became available for rent. For the time being, the long-term economic outcome of this migration can only be speculative and is dependent on how the migrants adapt and find a livelihood. Nevertheless, during the integration period the municipal administration receives financial compensation from the state, which comes in addition to the benefits for the local economy from the rents of apartments, wages of the employees managing the integration process, and income tax, as well as the input to the local economy through purchases of services (Vatanen and Halonen, 2013).

In the same interviews, returnees were mentioned by the municipal representatives as another group of in-migrants, in a sense that there are every now and then some returnees coming but not en masse. The returnees can be divided into two groups: young adults and pensioners. The most recognizable young adults were those who have gained experience via education or training somewhere else and return to a farm or house they have inherited. In some cases, pensioners return to their previous homes but according to the interview material it is more common that they settle closer to the center and the services than their original place of domicile. On the other hand, the line between an actual return classified as in-migration and long-term residency for instance in an old home which has been changed into leisure property can be very thin. There is some housing potential as there are cottages. Moreover, there are old houses which are now classified as second homes (Table 12.1), which are a common feature in Finland (Pitkänen, 2011).

From the point of view of the town representatives the migration of young adults would certainly be favored. Though the young childbearing and working-age adults were mentioned as especially beneficial in-migrants for the town, the overall view was that any migrants—pensioners, early-stage refugees, and those who are outside of the employment activity—are better than no migrants at all. Indeed, the out-migration and population loss in any form has been seen more problematic than the skewed age distribution resulting in the negative dependency ratio (Figure 12.4).

From the point of view of migration, rural areas of the municipality can be divided into two sections: the western side close to Lake Pielinen and the eastern side in the forested wilderness. Practically, the lakeside area has been noticed as a potential attraction for new incomers and worthwhile for planning and development. On the other hand, the municipality has no special interest in the village areas with the legacy of small-scale farming and forestry. There are random incomers who have found a home in the old forestry villages since the turn of the millennium. According to interviews with a selection of in-migrants (totaling 11), individual choices characterize this group of newcomers. Above all they represent a form of counterurbanization, as they feel they find better quality of life in the peripheral areas than in the population centers (Jones *et al.*, 1986). The interviewed migrants were coming from more populated centers either from southern Finland or other parts of Europe. Compared with the returnees, these migrants had no emotional or cultural bonds with Lieksa. The location and the town were actually quite irrelevant to them. The most important reasons behind their decisions to move were the atmosphere in the wilderness, a nice house and plot of land, availability of outdoor activities and, a little surprisingly, relatively good infrastructure as well as services in the town center. In addition, those who were planning to be entrepreneurs, mainly in the field of small-scale tourism, saw suitable facilities for their business as the most critical point for a choice of location.

Table 12.1 Cottages and Second Homes in Lieksa, 1970–2014

Year	1970	1980	1990	2000	2010	2014
Number of second homes in Lieksa	717	1,195	1,720	2,341	2,638	2,806

Source: Official Statistics Finland (2015d).

At the moment, incomers in the remote area are very microscale examples, but a small potential of chain-like in-migration can be noticed. As some of the interviewees described, their migration has drawn positive attention among people in their place of departure, which may lead or has already led to additional in-migration. This was the case for instance with a few entrepreneurs and employees in the tourism business who had previously been seasonal workers but after a while settled down. From the point of view of development, tourism was seen to provide the main potential for the area. Entrepreneurs from abroad were especially wondering why the town administration has not shown more interest in tourism development as they saw more possibilities for new entrepreneurs in the field, without the place turning into a mass tourism center, which these entrepreneurs definitely wished to avoid.

Conclusions

Struggling with gradually declining industries and loss of inhabitants, the actors associated with the local and national scales have sought to find ways to overcome crises in the local economy. The results of these attempts can be seen in the industry cycles presented and analyzed in the previous chapters on Finland. The transformations from one industry cycle to another can be seen as an expression of resilience. The case study aptly illustrates how resilience of a local community is not only generated at the local scale by local-scale actors; on the contrary, national-scale policies have had an essential impact on the capacities to cope with adverse conditions in the case study resource town, and the transformations internationally within the forest industry and even geopolitics have had an impact on the development options of the locality.

With the decline of one industry cycle, the locals and stakeholders have attempted to search for new sources of livelihood. Resilience can be observed in the phases where the shifts of the emphasis from one sector to another and toward newer, more productive technologies have compensated for the loss of mature businesses. There has been reorientation and renewal (Martin, 2012) of the local economy as a response to declining industries. The role of the state has been significant in providing institutional and economic conditions for local resilience and the new development cycles that have emerged as a result. Resilience as capacity for reorientation and renewal has been enabled through institutional regulation, investments in infrastructure, and government subsidies. The increase of the service sector was financed mainly by taxes from the governmental budget. The larger conditions of the growth of the forestry and manufacturing industries originated very much from the global market. All the policy reactions from the above have been based on the capacity of the state and limited to a particular period of time. Hence, policy measures are not automated, but dependent on governmental resources, public-spending priorities and decision-making. Markey *et al.* (2008) give an example of how the state can alter and attenuate government and industry commitments to peripheral areas. That reorientation of regional policy is comparable to what has happened in Finland (Suorsa, 2007).

As different sectors and industries react differently to changing conditions and have different life cycles, successful resilience periods generate industry life-cycles originating from the success of enterprises. The first cycle of lake iron ore production has disappeared in full, and a great part of agriculture (as measured in the number of jobs) has disappeared. Similarly, the forestry sector, from logging to final production, has been strongly rationalized and restructured several times. There are many devolutionary processes, and intercyclical transformation is full of the risk of failure. If a region remains unattractive to new, potential industries, resilience in the form of reorientation or renewal may be hindered. For instance, the short wave of footloose industrialization is over in Lieksa and there are no signs of a significant recovery. The new industry life-cycles of bioenergy and tourism are often mentioned in regional and local plans and newspapers as a panacea, but their realization is risky and dependent on various factors of development.

Cold, remote peripheral areas are not generally target areas of young generations (Tuhkunen, 2007) or amenity migration (Partridge, 2010). The increasing number of elderly newcomers will create the risk of making the demographic structure ever-more biased toward older generations. The employment rate in Lieksa is already very low in a Nordic context (Roto *et al.*, 2014). From a purely economic perspective, it can be estimated that in the short run, all migrants are beneficial to the local economy by bringing with them income from external sources. Their consumption, therefore, has a positive economic effect on the revenues of the local economy. It can be prognosticated, however, that in the long run a large number of elderly incomers may cause budgetary problems for the local administration through their need for public services that are, according to the national legislation, the right of every citizen (Kotilainen *et al.*, 2012).

According to Lehtonen and Tykkyläinen (2012), through investments in innovations, technologies, and labor quality and skills, developing industries benefiting from rural economies and the promotion of lifestyle changes could slow down rural job decline. A more passive form of adaptation would consist of an increase in the flexibility of factor prices outside urban centers, which would lead to better price competiveness and a higher demand for labor. However, it may remain less beneficial for a renewal of local economies and for a creation of new industry life-cycles. This is nothing new in the context of current economic literature, but as the state and the EU off-load a great deal of development responsibilities onto regional and local actors, no large nation-state level governmental initiatives can be expected in the current economic climate. Thus, in terms of policies and strategies for dealing with change, adaptation is supposed to emerge endogenously in the declining peripheries. Yet, thus far the impacts of EU policy instruments have not succeeded in changing rural decline. The rural renewal, such as rapid modernization and growth of small businesses, has been insufficient from the viewpoint of job growth.

In the resource town that has been scrutinized in these chapters, the balance between competitive factors in different spatial scales has shifted over time. The attractiveness of local natural and human resources and governmental interventions in addition to market demand were crucial in generating booms and resilience in the sense of reorientation in the early long cycles. In the case of the industrial estate, local attractiveness rested on subsidized human resources trained for factory work and on investment grants and R&D grants, while local natural resources had only a minor role. Similarly, in the case of increasing services, local natural resources as inputs played a minor role as only a fraction of growth came from tourism, although the introduction of nature-tourism services has increased the importance of the landscape as a local resource.

The question remains, therefore, about the future of the resource periphery. When decline seems inevitable, gradual adaptation to decline (Sousa and Pinho, 2015) could be a reasonable alternative for resource towns such as the one scrutinized here. If there is new growth, on the basis of this research it seems that it is most likely that the resilience of the local economy will prove to occur in the form of reorientation, where the local assets are organized and aligned in new ways. Nevertheless, the conditions for local resilience in resource towns such as the one investigated here, are immensely complex, and chance, surprises, and contingencies play such major roles in their trajectories, that predicting the future of a resource periphery is, after all, a complicated task.

References

Aarnio, J. 1999. Kaskiviljelystä metsätöihin: Tutkimus Pielisjärven kruununmetsistä ja kruununmetsätorppareista vuoteen 1910. Joensuu, Finland: PhD dissertation, Department of Geography, publications, University of Joensuu.

Adger, N.W. 2000. Social and ecological resilience: Are they related? *Progress in Human Geography* 24(3): 347–364.

Beck, U. 1992. *Risk society: Towards a new modernity.* London: Sage.

Boschma, R. 2014. Towards an evolutionary perspective on regional resilience, *Regional Studies* 49(5): 733–751.

Brezis, E. and Krugman, P. 1997. Technology and the life cycle of cities, *Journal of Economic Growth* 2(4): 369–83.

Christopherson, S., Michie, J., and Tyler, P. 2010. Regional resilience: Theoretical and empirical perspectives, *Cambridge Journal of Regions, Economy and Society* 3(1): 3–10.

Danson, M. and de Souza, P. 2012. Nations and regions in Northern Europe. In M. Danson and P. de Souza (eds.), *Regional development in Northern Europe: Peripherality, marginality and border issues* (pp. 98–117). Abingdon: Routledge Regional Studies Association Series on Regions and Cities.

Engle, N.L. 2011. Adaptive capacity and its assessment, *Global Environmental Change* 21(2): 647–656.

Eskelinen, H. 2001. *Aluepolitiikka rautahäkissä.* Kunnallisalan kehittämissäätiön Polemia-sarjan julkaisu 41. Available online at: www.kaks.fi/sites/default/files/Polemia%2041. pdf. Accessed March 18, 2014.

European Commission. 2015. *The European Network for Rural Development (ENRD). LEADER Gateway.* Available online at: https://enrd.ec.europa.eu/en/leader. Accessed November 13, 2015.

Folke, C. 2006. Resilience: The emergence of a perspective for social-ecological systems analyses, *Global Environmental Change* 16(3): 253–267.

314   *J. Kotilainen* et al.

Folke, C., Carpenter, S.R., Walker, B., Scheffer, M., Chapin, T., and Rockström, J. 2010. Resilience thinking: Integrating resilience, adaptability and transformability, *Ecology and Society* 15(4): 20.

Halonen, M., Kotilainen, J., Tykkyläinen, M., and Vatanen, E. 2015. Industry life cycles of a resource town in Finland: The case of Lieksa, *European Countryside* 7(1): 16–41.

Hayter, R. and Patchell, J. 2011. *Economic geography: An institutional approach.* Don Mills, ON: Oxford University Press.

Jauhiainen, J. and Niemenmaa, V. 2006. *Alueellinen suunnittelu.* Jyväskylä, Finland: Vastapaino.

Jones, H., Caird, J., Berry, W., and Dewhurst, J. 1986. Peripheral counter-urbanization: Findings from an integration of census and survey data in northern Scotland, *Regional Studies* 20(1): 15–26.

Julkunen, R. 1992. *Hyvinvointivaltio käännekohdassa.* Tampere, Finland: Vastapaino.

Julkunen, R. 2001. *Suunnanmuutos: 1990-luvun sosiaalipoliittinen reformi Suomessa.* Tampere, Finland: Vastapaino.

Kiander, J. 2001. *Laman opetukset: Suomen 1990-luvun kriisin syyt ja seuraukset.* Helsinki, Finland: Government Institute for Economic Research, Publications 27(5).

Kortelainen, J. 2010. Aluepolitiikka. In P. Niemelä (ed.), *Hyvinvointipolitiikka* (pp. 346–366). Helsinki, Finland: WSOYpro Oy.

Kotilainen, J., Eisto, I., and Vatanen, E. 2012. Search for sustainable means for managing shrinkage in a peripheral city in Finland. In C. Martinez-Fernandez, N. Kubo, A. Noya, and T. Weyman (eds.), *Demographic change and local development: Shrinkage, regeneration and social dynamics* (pp. 65–70). Paris, France: OECD LEED.

Kotilainen, J., Eisto, I., and Vatanen, E. 2015. Uncovering mechanisms for resilience: Strategies to counter shrinkage in a peripheral city in Finland, *European Planning Studies* 23(1): 53–68.

Lehtonen, O. and Okkonen, L. 2016. Socio-economic impacts of a local bioenergy-based development strategy: The case of Pielinen Karelia, Finland, *Renewable Energy* 85: 610–619.

Lehtonen, O. and Tykkyläinen, M. 2012. Työpaikkakehityksen alueelliset kehitysprosessit Itä-Suomessa 1994–2003 /[THIN]Spatial processes of job growth in Eastern Finland, 1994–2003, *Terra* 124(2): 85–105.

Lieksa Development Agency. 2014. Kevätniemen biojalostamo ja bioterminaalihanke. Ympäristövaikutusten arviointiselostus. Lieksa, Finland: Report on the Environmental Impacts of the Kevätniemi Biorefinery and Bioterminal. Available online at: www.lieksada.fi/sivut/userfiles/file/YVAselostus_Kevatniemi_24092014_FINAL-www.pdf. Accessed November 13, 2015.

Lieksa. 1975. *Municipal report of Lieksa 1974 I.* Lieksa, Finland: Lieksan kirjapaino.

Lieksa. 1976. *Municipal report of Lieksa 1974 II.* Lieksa, Finland: Lieksan kirjapaino.

Lieksa. 1980. *Municipal report of Lieksa 1979.* Lieksa, Finland: Lieksan kirjapaino

Lieksan kauppala. 1961. *Municipal report 1960.* Lieksa, Finland: Lieksan kirjapaino

Lieksan kauppala. 1969. *Municipal report 1968.* Lieksa, Finland: Lieksan kirjapaino

MacDonald, J.S. and MacDonald, L.D. 1964. Chain migration ethnic neighborhood formation and social networks, *The Milbank Memorial Fund Quarterly* 42(1): 82–97.

MacKinnon, D. and Derickson, K.D. 2013. From resilience to resourcefulness: A critique of resilience policy and activism, *Progress in Human Geography* 37(2): 253–270.

Malinen, P. 1998. Yhdentävä maaseutupolitiikka ja paikallinen omaehtoisuus. *Maaseudun uusi aika* 2: 22–27.

Markey, S., Halseth, G., and Manson, D. 2008. Challenging the inevitability of rural decline: Advancing the policy of place in northern British Columbia, *Journal of Rural Studies* 24(4): 409–421.

Martin, R. 2012. Regional economic resilience, hysteresis and recessionary shocks, *Journal of Economic Geography* 12(1): 1–32.

Moisio, S. 2012. *Valtio, alue, politiikka: Suomen tilasuhteiden sääntely toisesta maailmansodasta nykypäivään.* Tampere, Finland: Vastapaino.

Moisio, S. and Leppänen, L. 2007. Towards a Nordic competition state? Politico-economic transformation of statehood in Finland, 1965–2005, *Fennia-International Journal of Geography* 185(2): 63–87.

Official Statistics Finland. 1960–1986. *Population: Intermunicipal migration.* Volume 6 A. Annual publication. Helsinki, Finland: Official Statistics Finland.

Official Statistics Finland. 1982. *201—Population over 15 years by sex and belonging to labour force 1980.* Unpublished data system printout. Helsinki, Finland: Official Statistics Finland.

Official Statistics Finland. 1990. *Census of Population.* Volume 7 C. Helsinki, Finland: Official Statistics Finland.

Official Statistics Finland. 2009. *Population projection 2009–2060.* Available online at: http://tilastokeskus.fi/til/vaenn/2009/vaenn_2009_2009-09-30_en.pdf.   Accessed February 12, 2015.

Official Statistics Finland. 2011. *Population: Intermunicipal migration 1987–2010.* Available online at: http://pxweb2.stat.fi/. Accessed April 20, 2011.

Official Statistics Finland. 2014a. *010—Population by area, main type of activity, sex, age and year 1987–2013.* Available online at: http://pxweb2.stat.fi/. Accessed February 10, 2015.

Official Statistics Finland. 2014b. *Immigration and emigration by age, sex and area 1987–2013.* Available online at: http://pxweb2.stat.fi/. Accessed February 10, 2015.

Official Statistics Finland. 2015a. *Concept and definitions: Intermunicipal net migration.* Available online at: http://tilastokeskus.fi/til/muutl/kas_en.html. Accessed February 11, 2015.

Official Statistics Finland. 2015b. *Concept and definitions: Unemployment rate.* Available online at: http://tilastokeskus.fi/meta/kas/tyottomyysaste_en.html. Accessed February 11, 2015.

Official Statistics Finland. 2015c. *Population according to age (1-year) and sex by area 1980—2013.* Available online at: http://pxweb2.stat.fi/. Accessed March 18, 2015.

Official Statistics Finland. 2015d. *Number of free-time residences by region 1970–2014.* Available online at: http://pxnet2.stat.fi/PXWeb/pxweb/en/StatFin/StatFin__asu__rakke/030_rakke_tau_103.px/?rxid=7e654011-1a7a-4ca7-b11d-28ed5973e142. Accessed May 28, 2015.

Partridge, M. 2010. The duelling models: NEG vs amenity migration in explaining US engines of growth, *Papers in Regional Science* 89(3): 513–536.

Pielisjärvi. 1969. *Municipal report 1968.* Pielisjärvi, Finland: Pielisjärvi.

Pitkänen, K. 2011. Contested cottage landscapes: Host perspective to the increase of foreign second home ownership in Finland 1990–2008, *Fennia* 181(1): 43–59.

Rannikko, P. 1999. Savottojen ja väestökadon Suomi. In M. Löytönen and L. Kolbe (eds.), *Suomi: Maa, kansa ja kulttuuri* (pp. 211–221). Jyväskylä, Finland: Suomen Kirjallisuuden Seuran Toimituksia.

Roto, J., Grunfelder, J., and Rispling, L. (eds.). 2014. *State of the Nordic Region 2013.* Nordregio Report 2014:1. Stockholm, Sweden: Nordregio.

Sippola, M. 2011. Kehitysalueista aluekehitykseen. Suomen virallisen aluepolitiikan 30 ensimmäistä vuotta 1966–1995. Työ- ja elinkeinoministeriön julkaisuja 31/2011.

Smith, D. 1981. *Industrial Location*, 2nd edition. New York: John Wiley & Sons Inc.

Sousa, S. and Pinho, P. 2015. Planning for shrinkage: Paradox or paradigm, *European Planning Studies* 23(1): 12–32.

Suorsa, K. 2007. Regionality, innovation policy and peripheral regions in Finland, Sweden and Norway, *Fennia* 185(1): 15–29.

Tervo, H. 2005. Regional policy lessons from Finland. In D. Felsenstein and B.A. Portnov (eds.), *Regional disparities in small countries* (pp. 267–282). Berlin: Springer.

Tuhkunen, A. 2007. *Between location and a sense of place-observations regarding young people's migration alacrity in Northern Europe*. Tampere, Finland: Tampere University Press.

Tykkyläinen, M. 1992. Solutions to mine closure in Outokumpu. In C. Neil, M. Tykkyläinen, and J. Bradbury (eds.), *Coping with closure: An international comparison of mine town experiences* (pp. 225–246). London/New York: Routledge,

Tykkyläinen, M. 1995. Asutustoiminnan taloudelliset vaikutukset. In E. Laitinen (ed.), *Rintamalta raiviolle: Sodanjälkeinen asutustoiminta 50 vuotta* (pp. 139–158). Jyväskylä, Finland: Atena.

Vartiainen, P. 1998. *Suomalaisen aluepolitiikan kehitysvaiheita*. Helsinki, Finland: Sisäaisainministeriö, Aluekehitysosaston julkaisu 6/1998.

Vatanen, E. 2010. Lieksa—luonnonvaroista riippuvainen kaupunki. In J. Kotilainen and I. Eisto (eds.), *Luonnonvarayhdyskunnat ja muuttuva ympäristö—resilienssitutkimuksen näkökulmia Itä-Suomeen* (pp. 41–54). Joensuu, Finland: Publications of the University of Eastern Finland, Reports and Studies in Social Sciences and Business Studies 2.

Vatanen, E. and Halonen, M. 2013. Maahanmuuttajat maaseutua uudistamassa: Esimerkkinä Lieksan matkailuelinkeino, *Maaseudun Uusi Aika* 2(3): 78–85.

Vatanen, E., Eisto, I., and Rannikko, P. 2012. Luontopalvelut ja matkailu syrjäisen maaseudun elinkeinojen uudistajana: Tapaus Lieksa. *Kunnallistieteellinen aikakauskirja* 2/2012: 89–113.

Vuorenmaa, R. 2003. *30 vuotta: Lieksan Teollisuuskylä Oy*, Lieksa, Finland: Lieksa Development Agency.

Wilson, G.A. 2012. *Community resilience and environmental transitions*. Abingdon: Routledge.

Yli-Jokipii, P. and Koski, A. 1995. The changing pattern of Finnish regional policies, *Fennia-International Journal of Geography* 173(2): 53–67.

13 Community Responses to Restructuring

Sean Connelly and Etienne Nel

Introduction

As discussed in Chapters 5 and 9, regional and rural New Zealand has experienced a profound process of institutional, economic, and social transformation since the 1980s which has fundamentally impacted on local governance, community well-being, and employment (Peet, 2012). The state's wholesale adoption of neoliberalism, the trimming of welfare state benefits and support to rural and deprived areas, the privatization of state economic entities with severe impacts on rural employment levels, the cessation of forestry operations in areas with indigenous forests, and the restructuring of employment relationships and the role unions once played were all hallmarks of this era. The preceding has directly impacted on the viability and well-being of large numbers of small towns and rural communities, particularly those in the resource-frontier regions of the country (Roper, 2005; Lattimore and Eaqub, 2011; Maunder, 2012). Added to these upheavals was the decision by the state in the late 1980s to amalgamate several hundred borough councils and local authorities to form the current 76 territorial authorities which form the basis of the country's local government system, leading to the loss of local small town autonomy and the silencing of the voice of the smaller communities (Nel, 2015).

Having detailed these broad processes of change in previous chapters, this chapter examines what the local response in two rural regions in southern New Zealand, particularly at the regional level and, second, at the community-level, has been. This chapter considers the situation in these economically challenged areas and the degree to which local/regional and community initiatives have variously been able to respond to externally imposed economic changes, the weakening of state support, the loss of local autonomy, the role of leadership, the different methods used to address regional development, and finally the effect of business responses in an economy directly exposed to external market forces.

This chapter focuses on how the regions of West Coast and Southland have experienced these changes and the degree to which local communities have been able to respond to the employment gaps which have occurred as a result of the neoliberalization of the economy and the associated impacts on local employment and economic and social well-being. Initial state support for areas experiencing restructuring is outlined before overviewing, over time, a range of local initiatives, at both the regional and community/local authority levels in the context of significantly reduced state support and regional economies increasingly subjected to externally driven processes of change. Significant in this overview are the different approaches adopted to achieve regional development in the two case study regions. Finally, as will be discussed below, while local initiatives are occurring in both regions driven by local individuals, organizations, and by community groups, which may strengthen the communities' sense of cohesion, the impact on economic development is minimal. There is also some very small indication of economic development being self-driven by a tiny scattering of new niche, externally focused, businesses choosing to locate in small towns.

The Impacts of Change on Local Communities

As discussed in Chapter 5, the rationalization of state economic activities, the loss of subsidies, and the reduction in state employment devastated many small town communities in West Coast and Southland of New Zealand, particularly those which had depended on resource exploitation. As detailed in Chapter 9, mining towns such as Ohai, Nightcaps, and Blackball and timber-milling towns such as Tuatapere have experienced extended demographic and economic decline and the effective loss of the initial reason for their existence. While there has been dairy-related recovery in the farming economy, the initial impacts of the loss of farming subsidies on farming communities and rural service centers was devastating with towns such as Gore experiencing a significant loss in their business and employment base (Wilson, 1995). Parallel changes in global trade regimes and the loss of state support have exacerbated long-term decline in the small manufacturing economy in the two regions, which has negatively impacted on towns such as Westport, Greymouth, and Mataura where factory closures in the clothing, paper, and meat processing industries has weakened local employment. Added to this, the state's decision to halt the exploitation of indigenous forests and the designation of extensive tracts of reserve land in both regions in 1986 (amounting to 85 percent of the surface area of the West Coast) (Britton *et al.*, 1992) was seen by the local residents as an affront to the autonomy of their regions and a victory of the conservation movement which local people feel does not understand the needs of their population.

Within this broad context, the once-powerful unions, which had their genesis in these regions and which had been advocates of worker rights and community well-being in the face of exploitation since the late 1800s, lost their voice as the state, in support of business, introduced more flexible employment conditions, which over time has seen the casualization of labor, contract-based employment, and the fly-in-fly-out system on the remaining mines. This weakened the once-powerful bond of solidarity between unionized workers and small town communities, further depriving local communities of a voice and local organizational skills, and weakening their ability to respond effectively to economic change (Maunder, 2012).

A study of the town of Reefton undertaken in the 1990s (in Le Heron and Pawson, 1996) illustrates the impact of state restructuring. In 1987, out of the town's population of 1,100, 125 worked in various state agencies including the railroads, state coal, the Ministry of Works, and the post office. By 1994, this number had fallen to 21, while 37 of the former state employees were now self-employed or employed in the private sector in the town, 15 were retired or unemployed and 45 had left the town. Within the West Coast region more broadly, state forestry employment was reduced by 90 percent in the early 1980s and state coal mine employment was halved in the same period and some mines were closed. By 1987, coal mining (both state and private) had fallen from 24 percent to 4 percent of male regional employment, while it was estimated that some 900 state jobs had been lost by that year in a region which, at that stage, only had a population of 35,000 (Britton *et al.*, 1992).

Key employment and demographic trends in the two regions have included near static population growth levels in both regions and their major centers and significant demographic decline in almost all small towns, with the exception of small towns that are lucky enough to benefit from tourism growth. In employment terms, there has been a hollowing out of traditional employment mainstays in mining, state employment, and forestry. That said, the service sector has grown significantly, particularly in the larger centers, which to some degree has compensated for losses experienced at the regional level but not at the local level. Both regions have suffered from the out-migration of skilled workers, particularly after each round of restructuring, and at present there is a clear erosion of the post-20 years of age demographic bracket, as revealed in Figures 13.1 and 13.2, which weakens both local employment and family bases.

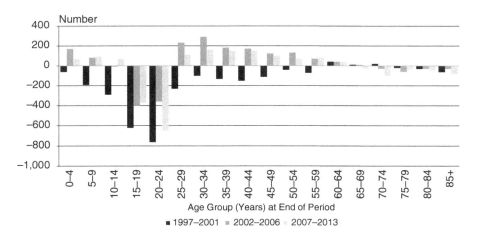

Figure 13.1 Net Migration Rates, West Coast.
Source: Statistics New Zealand (2015) and licensed by Statistics NZ for re-use under the Creative Commons Attribution 4.0 International license.

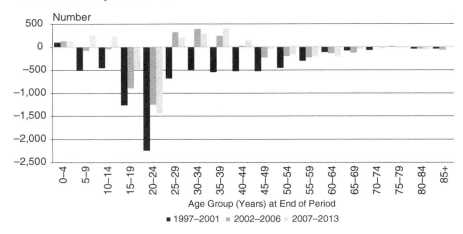

Figure 13.2 Net Migration Rates, Southland.
Source: Statistics New Zealand (2015) and licensed by Statistics NZ for re-use under the Creative
Commons Attribution 4.0 International license.

Initial Responses to Change

Following the regional-level shocks which were experienced, there were some
initial efforts in the West Coast and Southland regions to seek economic and
employment diversification. For a brief period, the state supported 15 Social
Support Coordinating Committees around the country to assist retrenched workers
and communities to adjust. These initiatives appeared to have had limited impact
given government's decision in 1987 that "regional assistance schemes belonged
to the past" (in Britton *et al.*, 1992 p. 247). In the early 1990s, the state's
Community Employment Group (CEG) scheme supported local initiatives to
promote self-employment and assist through the provision of self-employment
subsidies. Parallel efforts were undertaken to support community businesses.
Despite some initial successes, employment levels were not sustained and none of
these interventions appears to have generated any significant impacts on the local
employment and economy base, although in Southland there is some evidence
that community businesses which received state funds to improve state housing
and environmental protection in the 1990s did enjoy a limited measure of success
(Scott and Pawson, 1999).

Local efforts included a lackluster attempt to establish a small fertilizer
company in Westport by the Buller Community Development Corporation, which
was inspired by the experience of community development in Scotland and which
did receive some degree of state support. The enterprise was designed to reintegrate
retrenched workers back into the labor force; however, it failed to grow or
diversify into new enterprises as was initially proposed (Britton *et al.*, 1992). In
both Westport and Greymouth, workers retrenched from closed clothing factories
set up clothing cooperatives in the early 1990s with support from the Department

of Internal Affair's Co-operative Loans scheme. Difficulties with operating at scale and competition from cheap foreign imports negatively affected the prospects of these undertakings (Le Heron and Pawson, 1996).

The state has since removed support such as the Community Employment Group (CEG) and other supports such as the Community Organisations Grants (COGS) have been reduced with some funds being transferred to the Department of Internal Affairs (DIA) to support three-year duration community development positions or activities in a few localities nominated as requiring assistance (Department of Internal Affairs, 2015). A very small amount of assistance was, until very recently, given via the Ministry of Social Development (MSD) to a few selected isolated and deprived rural areas to partially fund a community support worker to assist communities to access government social welfare services; however, these have recently been closed due to a fatal shooting incident in one center, resulting in the cessation of the work of eight support workers in Southland (Ministry of Social Development, 2014). Minor funding is also given to REAPs (Rural Education and Activity Programmes) in rural centers to help rural communities' access parenting and community education support (Rural Education and Activity Programme, 2015).

In New Zealand, government-led economic development is currently undertaken by the Ministry of Business Innovation and Employment (MBIE). They have a focus on fostering a competitive and productive economy and improving the public service. Invariably this will privilege growing economic sectors and regions and not declining areas or struggling businesses, though special mention is given to supporting Māori business initiatives in some of the more economically marginal parts of the country (Ministry of Business Innovation and Employment, 2015). Hence current state support for economically struggling rural communities in New Zealand is virtually nonexistent, with the state focusing instead on growing regions and high growth potential business sectors, reflecting New Zealand's now long-term acceptance of its neoliberal policy.

Regional Responses to Change

In comparison with international responses to economic crises, regionally based responses in the New Zealand case study regions of West Coast and Southland were rather late in coming. This is surprising given the magnitude of the change experienced.

In the New Zealand context, it is difficult to differentiate between rural regional development and export-led economic development. The developmental history of New Zealand is such that it has always been dependent on exports of agricultural products, timber, and mining resources, first for the UK and more recently focused on Asia (Le Heron and Pawson, 1996). However, in contrast to the focus on national economic development policy that primarily seeks to facilitate the extraction of globally competitive commodities, attempts at regional economic development have been made that seek to generate local economic activity by virtue of their place-linked activities. Similar to what Markey *et al.* (2007) describe in the Canadian context, we see in New Zealand limited regional development strategies more focused on proactive attempts to improve regional competitive advantage based on local capacity and resources.

However, the transition from sectoral to territorial policy development or a 'new regionalist' approach described in the literature (Tomaney and Ward, 2000; Marsden and Sonnino, 2005; Markey *et al.*, 2007) is problematic in the New Zealand context. Regional economic development of any type is limited. Regional development initiatives that do occur are often framed as a means of assisting the resource-based economy, as there is much local-level political and cultural capital tied up in resource-based economies. The mentality that boom–bust commodity cycles are a part of rural life persists, and this mentality serves to limit the extent to which proactive community development focused on the quality of life and diversification in the regions can gain traction (see below). Exploring the uneven development within and between regions in New Zealand offers a unique vantage point from which to understand the complexity of multifunctional rural places. As Markey *et al.* (2000) state, the transition from productivist to post-productivist promotion of place is complex and needs to accommodate a diverse range of issues, stakeholders, and contextual diversity that may be both productivist and post-productivist.

For example, while economic development on the West Coast is closely tied to global market demand for commodities, there is increased reliance on local actors to lure investment, and attract people and other resources to maintain the viability of rural and marginal places (Conradson and Pawson, 2009). Similarly, in Southland, changes to the labor structure of farms, the conversion from sheep and beef to dairy, and the uneven impact of restructuring on individual farms has resulted in the loss of jobs, decline of small towns, and school closures (Smith and Montgomery, 2004). It is increasingly up to individuals and communities to compensate for the population-based rationalization of government services through investments of social, cultural, and human capital to maintain rural quality of life. As Stern and Hall (2015) state, with neoliberalism and the competitive nature of chasing scarce resource, some communities have the capacity and resources to provide for the amenities and services that contribute to the quality of life in certain places, while others lose out. Those communities with proactive citizens are those that 'win' grants that allow for improved amenities for their communities, reinforcing already existing disparities between rural places.

It is thus challenging to engage in rural community-driven development within the constraints of global development where endogenous development is marginalized in the pursuit of attracting foreign investment and improving access to global markets. The restructuring of the New Zealand economy that occurred throughout the late twentieth century was anticipated to release the innovation of people and places from the constraints of government and allow them to prosper through their own initiative, but in reality that has only exacerbated uneven development (Conradson and Pawson, 2009). Additionally, community development in New Zealand is shaped by a social service rather than developmental legacy. The first community development offices created in local councils were initiated to support greater coordination of service delivery between voluntary and statutory agencies, to build community capacity to cope with change, and to administer social service funding for employment or housing challenges (Chile, 2006). As a result, they tend to be reactive in nature, responding to crises after they appear, rather than acting proactively. Service provision for state contracts takes precedence over community mobilization and social transformation (Chile, 2006).

In the section below, we discuss the approach to regional development in Southland and the West Coast. The approaches adopted in the two case study regions differed significantly and this reflects on local/regional perceptions on the need for change, how best to respond, and whether collective action was deemed necessary or effective. Equally important have been questions around access to compensatory funds from the state and how best to utilize them at the regional level. The two regional responses were also funded differently, one from a collaboration of the three councils and funded from their rates (local tax) base, the other via a trust set up to manage a compensation fund given by the state to address the negative effects of new legislation prohibiting the logging of indigenous timber. Other New Zealand regions have not had access to compensation funds of a similar scale, or have had mixed results in working collectively as a region.

Southland Region

In Southland, following local government amalgamation and the devolution of greater powers to local authorities, the three territorial authorities, recognizing the value of joint action, established a regional economic development agency in July 2001 called Venture Southland (Venture Southland, 2015). As an economic development agency, the purpose of Venture Southland is to promote the region, to act as a facilitator for economic and community development opportunities, and to work with groups and organizations to identify opportunities and facilitate the development of projects and initiatives that will benefit Southland communities (Venture Southland, 2015). It is funded by annual grants from the three councils.

Venture Southland has three key functions. First, it is engaged in business development to identify, support, and promote opportunities for economic diversification and employment and business growth in the region. In this area, it has enjoyed some degree of success over the years. For example, the 2012–2013 Venture Southland Annual Report indicates approximately $2.4NZ million was spent on business development in that year including investigating options for: Stewart Island energy, silica mining for photo voltaic use, support for the aluminum smelter and waste product reuse, supporting European Space Agency programs and developing new oat-based products. In addition, support was given for: agriculture (including the development of new crop types) and improved on-farm efficiency, Information, Communication and Technology (ICT) (including a program to reduce farm costs), support for manufacturing, and business mentoring. Second, it is focused on destination promotion for tourists, new migrants, investors, and students. Activities in this area include investments in cycle trails, promotion of free tertiary education in the southern city of

Invercargill, tourism support, event management, and business attraction (promotion accounts for approximately half of the economic development budget).

Finally, Venture Southland supports groups and organizations to achieve community development by advocating for communities and offering advice to community groups on how to access services. Community development was allocated approximately $1.5NZ million (about one third of the total budget) and this includes support for the undertaking of community planning strategies, if requested, in many of the local communities, supporting trusts in their activities such as: events, local museum support, history, arts, rural health, hiking trails, etc. (Venture Southland, 2013, 2015). In addition, there was partial funding of a community development worker position in Gore and Mataura (Venture Southland, 2013). Support has also been given for a search and rescue system in one of the more remote communities and for the development of rural broadband links (Key Informant 1, personal communication, 2012, 2015; Key Informant 2, personal communication, 2013, 2015). These small community projects are often tourism related and aimed at diversifying the local economy and potentially building community cohesion. Out of the $3.9NZ million annual budget, the majority of funds spent in 2013 were for operating expenditure, predominantly wages for staff and $350,000NZ for project costs. This indicates a modest budget, mostly utilized to cover the cost of staff rather than direct project implementation costs.

One of the successes of the Venture Southland model is that the investment in capacity building, relationship formation, and knowledge expansion in the region which allows Venture Southland staff to play the roles of effective development facilitators and coordinators. Venture Southland provides the capacity for the Southland districts to address issues around strategic regional development rather than relying on external consultants that take a 'cookie-cutter' approach that would not account for the diversity within the region (Key Informant 2, personal communication, 2015). Efforts to address youth unemployment in the region are a good example. Nearly 20 percent of the region's youth are out of work or out of training and Venture Southland was able to make the case that this has considerable long-term implications to the economic development of the region. Evidence suggested that the first job was critical, so a program was developed to identify the education and training programs that were available with actual employment opportunities (Key Informant 1, personal communication, 2015). The Invest in Youth program draws on linkages with industry, businesses and employers, and education and training institutes to develop youth-friendly employment practices (rosters and working hours) and opportunities through internships, training, mentoring, and holiday work opportunities (Venture Southland, 2015). Venture Southland has been able to engage partners in seeking to address the root causes of youth unemployment and facilitate a proactive regional response.

While local community initiative tends to be rather muted in the Southland there are a few exceptions, in the largest population centers in the region as well as some in the towns with smaller populations. Table 13.1 provides a list of examples of community-based initiatives from Southland.

Table 13.1 Community-Based Initiatives From Southland

Invercargill	Partly through the leadership of the center's charismatic mayor, an ongoing program promotes the town to new residents, and supports the development of recreational and cultural assets. A significant local initiative is the support for a 'zero-fees' enrolment system as the local tertiary training technical institute designed to boost the number of young people in the town and to encourage them to stay on after completing their studies (Key Informant 2, personal communication, 2012).
Gore	In Gore, the promotion of lifestyle i.e. 'city living in a rural setting,' heritage promotion, local museums, and a country music festival are key local icons and perceived strategies to attract tourists and investors (Key Informant 9, personal communication, 2013).
Lumsden and Athol	In the small town of Lumsden, and nearby in Athol, there are niche entrepreneurs selling landscape art and fishing flies predominately via the Internet. These businesses are voluntarily and independently proactive in local/regional economic development and have helped diversify their local economies to a limited extent (Key Informant 10, personal communication, 2012).
Mataura	The residents of the small town of Matura have shown their strong ability to debate different forms of economic development, which include lignite conversion to oil and reusing aluminum waste from a nearby smelter. These discussions were encouraged and facilitated by the Gore Council, a Venture Southland funded community development position, and a local politician but has yet to bear fruit (Key Informant 9, personal communication, 2015).
Nightcaps and Ohai	In contrast, economic development was lacking in the declining mining towns of Nightcaps and Ohai. The focus of community engagement in these centers was predominately on social needs via a MSD funded community worker. Though external funds and advice were potentially available, the community was not in a strong enough position to apply for them, with political representation being distant (Key Informant 11, personal communication, 2013).

West Coast Region

"Well, it's people in Auckland that want to save their conscience by protecting the West Coast because they've destroyed their environment in the city" (Key Informant 6, personal communication, 2013).

The sense of outsiders controlling the destiny of the West Coast is strong and has been reinforced in particular by debates about the management of indigenous forests that resulted in the creation and demise of the West Coast Forest Accord (WCFA) (1986–2002). The WCFA had sought to balance the competing interests of conservation with the preservation of timber forestry on the West Coast by allocating large tracts of the West Coast to the newly formed Department of Conservation (DoC). DoC would be responsible for stewardship and managed forestry at existing yields until such time as forestry could shift from indigenous species to plantation forests (Memon and Wilson, 2007). The accord unraveled in the face of competing agendas, with West Coast councils uniting with the timber industry to form the West Coast Resource Interests and taking the government to court over the right to harvest trees, while the government was pressured from the other side by environmental groups, based largely in the urban centers, that wanted all harvesting of indigenous timber stopped (Memon and Wilson, 2007). The end of the WCFA led to the end of native logging on Crown land, significant loss of forestry jobs, and placing 85 percent of the surface area of the West Coast into a conservation estate to be managed by the DoC. Government provided a $120NZ million package to the West Coast to assist communities to adjust to the loss of the logging industry, $28NZ million of which was a direct payment to Buller, Grey, and Westland District councils and to the West Coast Regional Council. The remaining $92NZ million was put into a trust called 'Development West Coast' (DWC) which was set up to manage the fund to promote sustainable employment opportunities and to generate sustainable economic benefits for the West Coast, both now and into the future (Development West Coast, 2015).

The 2004, DWC Annual Report indicated initial investigations into potential projects in forestry, mining, sphagnum moss, film, tourism, and aquaculture, and investments in these activities (Development West Coast, 2004; Conradson and Pawson, 2009). The Trust initially pursued a traditional, but questionable, approach of 'smokestack' chasing, funding several specific small industrial enterprises (Key Informant 4, personal communication, 2014; Key Informant 5, personal communication, 2015; Key Informant 6, personal communication, 2015). The subsequent failure of a number of these investments (for example: in manufacturing i.e. ice cream and investment in the development of a cranberry farm) led to a strategic rethink on the part of the organization which now, controversially in the region, adopts a more conservative approach to development, tending rather to conserve and build their cash base, which unfortunately has recently been eroded by share market fluctuations, and distribute the interest annually, this being $4.6NZ million in 2012. There are competing views of what kind of role DWC should play. Some think it should act more like an economic development agency and play a more proactive role by investing in and attracting industry and business development. Others point to its status as a charitable trust and the commitment to manage the $92NZ million endowment from government for future generations indicating the more conservative approach which the trust is currently following. As one key informant commented:

> of course the money that Development West Coast was given from the Government was all about forestry, every time some other industry falls over or the coal mining stops or the Holcim (cement factory) perhaps pulls out of Westport and things or a big wind comes along and blows something over um, Development West Coast is looked to as the rescue agency and that's been quite an interesting thing in the last wee while, perhaps some people do see that when bad things happen, we've got this huge pot of money, it's only

human nature ... but we're still not at the point where Development West Coast is going to open up a factory of some sort.

(Key Informant 3, personal communication, 2014)

The 2012 DWC Annual Report showed how the funds were reinvested, and that the interest was used to support DWC operations and an annual grant made to each of the three district councils of $400,000NZ to be used to upgrade a wide range of sports or community facilities such as halls and information centers (this included Society for the Prevention of Cruelty to Animals kennels, a kindergarten, and a cycle trail) (Development West Coast, 2012, 2015). In addition a one-off grant of $2NZ million was also given to each council for facility upgrades. There has, over the years, been some direct investment in a very limited number of local businesses. For example, the 2012 DWC Annual Report shows that the largest local investment was $5NZ million for a 43 percent stake of a dairy farm, and that the DWC continued to own a Karamea tourism business which is now leased to a trust. In addition, the DWC helped to establish a cranberry cooperative with the DWC-owned cranberry farm now being sold; a loan was provided to a laundry; and assistance was also given to a restaurant. In terms of economic development, general business mentoring is also undertaken, business awards are supported and there is representation in regional and national horticultural and mineral forums. There were also one-off payments to two cycleways of $1.5NZ million in total, and $1NZ million was paid toward a multipurpose training facility in Rapahoe in memory of lives lost at a mining accident at Pike River. Community assistance is limited to an annual grant of $90,000NZ for a community trust to distribute separately and $10,000NZ annually is paid to support amateur sport.

An overview of the Development West Coast annual reports shows the existence of a relatively substantial fund generated from interest earnings. This is unlike the case of Venture Southland which was funded from local government taxes. The report suggests a preference toward funding facility upgrades rather than economic development. The exceptions are for general business mentoring, and a few direct investments into West Coast business ventures in agriculture and tourism, via commercial finance through loans and equity investments in West Coast businesses to help them develop or expand their operations (Development West Coast, 2015).

In contrast to Venture Southland, Development West Coast has tended to follow an approach of being anchored to the region's traditional strengths as epitomized in the region's current economic development strategy (West Coast Regional Council, 2015). Another point of difference was releasing funds to contribute toward the maintenance of the facilities in their region, while having the advantage of considerable investments separate from rates taxes and access to the returns on these investments.

In the West Coast region, high degrees of local autonomy in the different territorial authorities appear to have reduced the capacity for collaborative action and it is only in 2013 that work on a Regional Development Plan 2014–2030 (West Coast Regional Council, 2015) was finally initiated. This strategy, in its current form, revolves around historic economic strengths in the region and, with the exception of a new tourism focus (Key Informant 4 2015), the strategy does not seem to suggest at a break from the region's traditional economic path-dependence. While it suggests diversifying the economy is a key strategy, it recognizes that the foundation of the economy is unlikely to change. The Regional Economic Development Plan sets aspirational targets for 2030 based on 25 percent growth in job numbers to 19,450 full-time equivalents, population growth of 15 percent to 36,970, GDP growth by 35 percent to $1.98NZ billion, and exports as a proportion of GDP that exceeds 40 percent (currently at 36 percent) (West Coast Regional Council, 2015). These outcomes are all dependent on the traditional strengths of the West Coast economy, as one key informant noted: "we've got an economy that's based on three elements really, it's the mining, it's the tourism and it's dairy farming or agriculture generally but it's mostly dairy farming" (Key Informant 5, personal communication, 2014). Action items over the short term are focused on building collaboration among the three district councils and the regional council so that there is consistency in planning and policy development in support of the economic strategy targets, developing a mineral development strategy in partnership with Minerals West Coast, working with the national government to reduce regulatory process delays, enhancing tourism marketing, and working with Westland Milk Products Ltd. to ensure continued employment growth in the region.

Anecdotally, this view of the natural resource bounty of the West Coast being the foundation for past, present, and future wealth is prevalent in the region and comes through the economic development strategy. The focus of the economic development strategy is almost entirely on taking back control of an economy that exists to provide resources for others:

> There is a view that 'We don't need the rest of New Zealand. We've got all the timber, all the coal, all the gold, all the water for power schemes. All we need is someone to cut the red tape and we've got to look after ourselves.' But, but we get controlled by Auckland. That's where all the majority of the people are.
>
> (Key Informant 6, personal communication, 2013)

The regional economic development strategy (and the associated mineral development strategy) is focused on removing regulatory barriers for investment to promote externally dependent extractive industries and tourism. In contrast, alternative development pathways focused on the quality of life and the internal economy of communities are also being discussed. However, these initiatives are constrained by the long history of boom–bust cycles of resource extraction that limit possibilities of talking about alternative economic development pathways. As one key informant put it:

> there's been quite a culture of dependency that's grown around the West Coast, but certainly in the past decade or slightly longer, there's been more of a, sensitivity to changing global prices, especially with coal … and so the area

has been subject to the, the boom and bust cycle of fossil fuels, but, there's a certain acceptance of that here, that that's the way it is and, we just need to, see it through to the next coal mine opening or next big industry investment that comes to the area, looking for resources.

(Key Informant 7, personal communication, 2013)

However, it is the downturns in the economic cycle that open up opportunities to discuss alternatives. Community development initiatives throughout the region were able to use the economic downturn in the coal industry strategically to engage residents in discussions about the kind of community that they want:

Even before the closure of the Spring Creek mine which was 200 plus jobs lost, we had begun work on place making, 'cause I think that's, one of the um, top issues for us … it certainly ran counter to prior policy. It was 'let's make our area an attractive place for residents and they'll bring their jobs with them' … which essentially seems like a more 21st century approach, rather than we will create jobs and they will come.

(Key Informant 8, personal communication, 2013)

On one level, economic development in the region is dominated by the key players in industry that are focused on creating optimal conditions for investment in extractive industries and tourism once global economic conditions rebound (fueling rises in prices for coal, dairy, or international tourism). However, at another level, there is widespread community support for initiatives that contribute to the quality of life of current residents and a belief that investing in communities as good places to live will result in migrants who will bring their mobile jobs with them. Unfortunately, these initiatives focused on the external and internal economy respectively; they do not appear to be working in collaboration with each other.

In the West Coast a number of community organizations have emerged, perhaps in the absence of a regional actor equivalent to Venture Southland. The strongest in this regard was in Hokitika, however, other smaller towns, in particular Blackball, showed a degree of self-generated community and entrepreneurial driven economic development. Table 13.2 provides noteworthy examples of community-based initiatives from the West Coast.

Table 13.2 Community-Based Initiatives From the West Coast

Hokitika	The larger town of Hokitika, following the earlier loss of population and the closure of a regional mental health facility, has experienced something of a revival as a result of both its attraction as a tourism center and the decision of the regional dairy industry to significantly expand its production facility in the town. A local group, Enterprise Hokitika, and the local tourism agency promotes the town and business activity and has supported a well-established annual 'Wild-foods festival' which has raised the town's profile nationally and internationally as a recognized tourism destination (Key Informant 12, personal communication, 2015).
	The well-established greenstone-carving industry based in Hokitika has begun to train staff in basic Mandarin to liaise better with customers and to think about new innovative jewelry products that suit both the general market and the Asian market (Key Informant 13, personal communication, 2013). The West Coast as a whole is building on of the accolades of the Lonely Planet listing the region as one of the country's top ten tourist destinations in 2013, in addition to Hokitika taking advantage of being the setting for the Booker Prize winning book *The Luminaries* (Key Informant 14, personal communication, 2014).
Blackball	In the small former coal-mining town of Blackball, where the labor movement in the country was founded, a small local initiatives have been undertaken to celebrate the town's socialist history (Key Informant 14, personal communication, 2015). As in Lumsden, the promotion projects are independently driven by local niche entrepreneurs who have attracted outside custom via niche salami exports or niche tourism through the socialist-themed Hilton hotel.
Greymouth and Westport	The two largest towns of Greymouth and Westport have had the challenge of trying to diversify their economies away from mining and toward tourism, including the promotion of industrial and mining heritage. The Westport local council are active in promoting the town as a place to invest in and retire to, in an attempt to reutilize its housing. Development West Coast has supported the establishment of the West Coast Construction Alliance among the various construction, engineering, and mining contractors so that they could pool their skills and resources and develop joint bids for large-scale construction projects, particularly associated with the Christchurch post-earthquake rebuild. Most of these industries and companies were formerly engaged in mining but have diversified to sustain employment numbers. Alliance members are committed to keeping work and jobs local through the use of local subcontractors and promote the diverse skill based in the region (Key Informant 16, personal communication, 2015; Key Informant 17, personal communication, 2015).
Reefton	The small gold-mining town of Reefton is currently experiencing the downscaling and planned closure of its last remaining mine. Community-driven initiatives there have sought to diversify the town's economy through a focus on tourism alternatives. These include signage, an information bureau, tours, a historical trail, and successful links with international tour operators who have included the town on a tour itinerary (Key Informant 15, personal communication, 2011).
Ross and Kumara	The two very small towns of Ross and Kumara have active environmental and resident groups and community projects possibly due in part to a former charismatic mayor residing in Kumara and enthusing project leaders and local businesses, and also due to the allocation of a DIA worker to assist both towns. Both towns are making efforts to promote tourism, in particular targeting the Chinese and to promote the cycle trail (with national government support). Ross is focused also on town beautification and celebrating the town's 150th anniversary and activities are led by the Westland Environmental Network. In Kumara, a trust (the Kumara Residents Trust) has been promoting the town via a series of historic panels and efforts to beautify the town and remove derelict buildings (Key Informant 12, personal communication, 2015).

Differences in Regional Support

While regional development in Southland tends to be associated with the endeavors of the council-funded regional agency Venture Southland, which investigates alternative economic options and liaises with various business and community actors while providing some support for complementary community development initiatives, a significant difference exists with the West Coast. In the latter region a different model has been established based on independent funding, and initiatives tend to be far more locally than regionally focused and predominately relate to supplementing the development of local facilities with limited direct investment into a few selected businesses.

Regional Initiatives Provided by the State

In addition to external community support provided by the rates funded Venture Southland, or the one-off government grant funded West Coast Development Board, as noted above, the government's DIA provides salary support for community workers for up to three years in selected areas, though this is more targeted to a specific area than being regionally focused. Workers are tasked to help facilitate community development initiatives and funding applications. One current shared position has been allocated to the small towns of Kumara and Ross on the West Coast, and there were previously allocated positions in the small towns of Karamea on the West Coast and Kaitangata, Gore, and Mataura in Southland. Staff are engaged to help build community capacity rather than manage economic development or direct project interventions (Department of Internal Affairs, 2015).

The MSD, until recently, provided ongoing partial funding of support staff in some specific small towns where mines and industries had closed, such as Nightcaps and Lumsden in Southland. Workers were tasked to provide ease of access to state support and advice to beneficiaries. Unfortunately, as noted above, these have recently been closed until further notice (Ministry of Social Development, 2014).

Various government departments also supported the establishment of REAPs in rural communities including the West Coast and Southland. Activities undertaken include adult and community education, literacy, addressing parenting supports, truancy, early education issues, etc. (Rural Education and Activity Programme, 2015). More recently, because of an influx of new migrant workers (often from the Philippines) which has occurred in Southland to meet the dairy industry's requirements, there has been the establishment of various migrant support groups in small towns, such as in the service town of Winton which has a particularly strong new migrant center. These migrant workers have reinvigorated the church community in many of these small towns, with the Catholic churches in the area offering special services for the Filipino community and Catholic school rolls have increased (Harding, 2011). Similar support groups for newcomers have also established on the West Coast with support from REAP, Development West Coast, and others.

Community Initiatives

In addition to ongoing regionally based support, there are some smaller, more localized initiatives. At the community level in Southland, there is a traditional focus on the retention of social infrastructure, such as trying to ensure that local community swimming pools remain open, as in Mataura (Key Informant 9, 2015). At the community level, there appears to be less of a focus on economic development projects, other than work readiness training, to address the needs of those with limited work experience attracted to the low-cost housing available in some declining rural areas.

One of the reasons for the lower emphasis paid to economic activities in Southland has been the current high levels of rural and small town employment because of the strength the region's dairy industry has enjoyed in recent years, absorbing people who lost their jobs in other resource-based industries in the region. Within this scenario, population loss following earlier rounds of restructuring also needs to be considered as impacting on the numbers of those remaining and in search of work. In terms of other community initiatives, Māori indigenous people operate Marae (community facilities for tribal members) in rural areas, often focus on the development of their community buildings and community activities. Likewise churches predominately focus on their constituents and buildings, rather than on economic development initiatives.

Niche business and tourism have also had a small impact. A few small Southland and West Coast towns have seen the arrival of a scattering of businesses which are notable in that they gain a large proportion of their trade from outside the region, either through Internet sales, the export of niche products like salami from Blackball, or from attracting tourists from outside of the region (as opposed to passing travelers). These niche businesses, though small in number, have improved local income flows and have created some economic diversity in the towns they locate in. They tend to support town promotion via their presence on the Internet and can potentially attract other businesses to colocate nearby. Their facilitation of economic development is largely through informal and voluntary coordination with like-minded entrepreneurial neighbors. The impact of these businesses, which draw in external income, on economic development could be as significant as the impact of formal regional development initiatives.

Discussion and Conclusion

From the above discussion it is apparent that economic and institutional restructuring since the early 1980s has had a profound impact on regional and rural New Zealand. As shown with respect to the two case study regions, it would be difficult to argue that they have returned to former levels of employment and economic activity as a result of either recent economic change or localized responses. Rather, while both regions have been able to benefit from a period of prosperity in the dairy industry and recent growth of tourism and the service sector, deeper structural changes related to deindustrialization and the effective collapse of the mining and timber industries have not been replaced by economic activities of a similar scale, to the detriment of the economic well-being of communities and towns throughout both regions. Local and community responses to change seem to have been slow in coming in comparison to international responses to economic crisis, and there seems to have been an initial expectation that the state would respond, which did not match with New Zealand's emerging neoliberal economic policy from the 1980s. Where initiatives have been undertaken they often tend to have a social, or sports and community facility focus, though sometimes with a tourism component.

The difference between the two regions is significant, with Southland adopting an approach of investigating regional economic alternatives including community initiatives whereas in the West Coast recent activities tend to be more focused on subsidizing localized facility upgrades or direct investment into a few individual traditional businesses such as mining, dairy, and tourism. Clearly significant challenges remain and while the larger centers such as Invercargill and Greymouth may well have reached a new equilibrium where they are experiencing modest economic growth and demographic stability but not real growth, the same cannot be said for many of the smaller communities and towns (with the exception of tourism towns and some of the rural service centers meeting farming needs). Most small towns appear to still be locked in long-term structural decline and population loss which current, socially focused community initiatives are unlikely to alter. It should, however, be noted that a scattering of individual businesses offering niche products and pulling the majority of their trade from outside of the wider region have managed to create a small degree of economic diversity and are creating economic development from their own initiative. Such small niche businesses, however, are unable on their own to turn the tide of economic decline.

The following, unfortunately, seems to remain true for many communities in the West Coast and Southland study areas: "local initiatives in marginalized places around New Zealand have only a small effect on the social and geographical inequalities generated by the processes of globalization and national restructuring" (Scott and Pawson, 1999 p. 193). It seems that the impact of community initiatives on the economics of a small town, whether undertaken by a financially well-resourced or an investigative style of development board, a council or a community worker, are only marginal, especially if the predominate focus is on social projects or facility upgrades. There is, however, some hope where an organization undertakes investigations into economic alternatives as has been done by Venture Southland and Development West Coast; however, these need then to spread into real projects adopted by local actors. An alternative route is where there is a focused initiative led by a passionate local mayor or community leader as has occurred in Hokitika and Invercargill. New Zealand's neoliberal focus on growth industries and growth centers leaves little resources to support declining rural communities. There is, however, a glimmer of hope in the small businesses who lure their income from outside of the region, who decided to locate in these declining towns: while they are unlikely to restore the economic prosperity these towns formally have enjoyed, they do give these towns a sense of new economic life and the hope and character that comes with this.

References

Britton, S., Le Heron, R., and Pawson, E. 1992. *Changing places in New Zealand: A geography of restructuring*. Christchurch, New Zealand: New Zealand Geographical Society.

Chile, L. 2006. The historical context of community development in Aotearoa New Zealand, *Community Development Journal* 41(4): 407–25.

Conradson, D. and Pawson, E. 2009. New cultural economies of marginality: Revisiting the West Coast, South Island, New Zealand, *Journal of Rural Studies* 25: 77–86.

Department of Internal Affairs. 2015. *Community development scheme*. Auckland, New Zealand: Department of Internal Affairs. Available online at: www.communitymatters. govt.nz/Funding-and-grants---Crown-Funds---Community-Development-Scheme. Accessed August 18, 2015.

Development West Coast. 2004. *West Coast Development Trust, 2004 annual report.* Available online at: www.dwc.org.nz/images/02.ABOUT_DWC/04.KEY_ DOCUMENTS/Annual_Reports/2004_Annual_Report.pdf. Accessed August 23, 2015.

Development West Coast. 2012. *Development West Coast annual report 2012*. Available online at: www.dwc.org.nz/images/02.ABOUT_DWC/04.KEY_DOCUMENTS/ Annual_Reports/2012_Annual_Report.pdf. Accessed August 23, 2015.

Development West Coast. 2015. *About DWC*. Available online at: www.dwc.org.nz/about-dwc/about-dwc. Accessed August 18, 2015.

Harding, E. 2011. Dairy boom boosted by Filipinos. *Southland Times.* Available online at: www.stuff.co.nz/southland-times/news/5569199/Dairy-boom-boosted-by-Filipinos. Accessed August 26, 2015.

Lattimore, R and Eaqub, S. 2011. *The New Zealand economy*. Auckland, New Zealand: Auckland University Press.

Le Heron, R. and Pawson, E. 1996. *Changing places: New Zealand in the nineties*. Auckland, New Zealand: Addison-Wesley Longman.

Markey, S., Pierce, J.T., and Vodden, K. 2000. Resources, people and the environment: A regional analysis of the evolution of resource policy in Canada, *Canadian Journal of Regional Science* 23(3): 427–454

Markey, S., Manson, D., and Halseth, G. 2007. The (dis?)connected North: Persistent regionalism in Northern British Columbia, *Canadian Journal of Regional Science* 30(1): 57–78.

Marsden, T. and Sonnino, R. 2005. Rural development and agri-food governance in Europe. In V. Higgins and G. Lawrence (eds.), *Agricultural governance: Globalization and the new politics of regulation* (pp. 50–68). New York: Routledge.

Maunder, P. 2012. *Coal and the coast.* Christchurch, New Zealand: Canterbury University Press.

Memon, P.A. and Wilson, G.A. 2007. Contesting governance of indigenous forests in New Zealand: The case of the West Coast Forest Accord, *Journal of Environmental Planning and Management* 50(6): 745–764.

Ministry of Business, Innovation and Employment. 2015. *Our purpose*. Auckland, New Zealand: Ministry of Business, Innovation and Employment Available online at: www. mbie.govt.nz/about/who-we-are/our-purpose. Accessed August 18, 2015.

Ministry of Social Development. 2014. *Satellite sites to remain closed until further notice.* Auckland, New Zealand: Ministry of Social Development. Available online at: https://www.msd.govt.nz/about-msd-and-our-work/newsroom/media-releases/2014/satellite-sites-to-remain-closed-until-further-notice.html. Accessed August 18, 2015.

Nel, E.L. 2015. Evolving regional and local economic development in New Zealand, *Local Economy* 30(1): 67–77.

Peet, R. 2012. Comparative policy analysis: Neoliberalising New Zealand, *New Zealand Geographer* 68(3): 151–167.

Rural Education and Activity Programme. 2015. REAP work. Available online at: www.reapanz.org.nz/reap-work. Accessed August 18, 2015.

Roper, B.S. 2005. *Prosperity for all: Economic, social and political change in New Zealand since 1935.* Auckland, New Zealand: Thomson.

Scott, G. and Pawson, E. 1999. Local development initiatives and unemployment in New Zealand, *Tijdschrift voor Economische en Sociale Geografie* 90(2): 184–195.

Smith, W. and Montgomery, H. 2004. Revolution or evolution? New Zealand agriculture since 1984, *GeoJournal* 59(2): 107–118.

Statistics New Zealand. 2015. *Local population trends.* Auckland, New Zealand: Statistics New Zealand. Available online at: www.stats.govt.nz. Accessed May 23, 2015.

Stern, P. and Hall, P. 2015. *The proposal economy: Neoliberal citizenship in 'Ontario's most historic town.'* Vancouver, Canada: UBC Press.

Tomaney, J. and Ward, N. 2000. England and the 'new regionalism,' *Regional Studies* 34(5): 471–478.

Venture Southland. 2013. *Year in review 2012–2013.* Available online at: www.venturesouthland.co.nz/Portals/0/Documents/R_14_1_633.pdf. Accessed August 23, 2015.

Venture Southland. 2015. *Venture Southland.* Available online at: www.venturesouthland.co.nz. Accessed August 1, 2015.

West Coast Regional Council. 2015. *Regional economic development plan.* Available online at: www.wcrc.govt.nz/our-region/Pages/Economic%20Development.aspx. Accessed May 23, 2015.

Wilson, O.J. 1995. Rural restructuring and agriculture-rural economy linkages, *Journal of Rural Studies* 11(4): 417–431.

14 Rural Restructuring
Conclusion

Sean Markey and Greg Halseth

Rural Restructuring: Documenting Experience

The introduction and the contributions from Roger Hayter provide a summary of the core purpose of this volume, being to describe the processes of transition in rural resource-dependent communities and regions, driven by industrial restructuring, government policy retrenchment, and the actions of communities themselves. The rich, theoretically informed, and highly contextually nuanced contributions from the international teams lead to a single overwhelming conclusion: that despite the speed and intensity of global forces, and the predominance of a market-oriented ideology that has governed the developed world for the past 30 years, history and geography still matter in the twenty-first century. While this will be great news to geography and history departments around the globe (and others employing political economy perspectives), the fact remains that rural communities themselves, and the governments charged with defending the broader public interest, are less aware of this impactful reality to the condition and viability of rural places.

As Halseth states in the introduction,

> while corporate interests have quite deliberately recognized the changing competitive environment of the global economy, and have made decisive moves to reposition themselves to be more competitive in that environment, public policy and local community efforts have not been as transformative.

Put another way, as corporations have sought to embrace the potential of being, in essence, placeless (and therefore unaccountable to the rigidities of local labor conditions, communities, environmental responsibilities, and other regulatory burdens), labor and communities remain rooted in place. Trends in labor mobility are challenging what is emerging as a preferential norm, but the rootedness of home and community remain. Overall, governments and communities are trying to catch up, experimenting with different policy and programmatic interventions (with varying levels of sincerity and effectiveness). What remains is a patchwork quilt of case stories that has yet to coalesce into a coherent theoretical and programmatic response. This is what is leading to the 'uneven development of neoliberalism' that is outlined in the chapters from New Zealand and Australia, while being acknowledged in the other countries.

Rural and resource sector researchers, including all of those within this volume, have done a remarkable job of documenting the processes of change that have affected rural regions since World War Two. As outline particularly in the BC and Australian chapters, we can divide the postwar period leading up to the present in a series of 30-year phases. The first 30 years following the war (1950–1980) are defined by what is generically described as the long-boom. The demand for resources driven by postwar reconstruction, combined with progress in social policy and labor standards, created a period of tremendous growth in rural regions throughout the developed world. The trilateral partnership that united governments, industry, and labor (combined with policies of protectionism) created a period of relative stability, and rural and small town expansion.

The following 30-year period, from the early 1980s through the first decade of the twenty-first century, is documented within the literature as a time of intense restructuring, driven by interwoven patterns of market liberalization, industrial restructuring (responding to low-cost global competition—and ultimately seeking to substitute capital for labor), and varying forms of neoliberal government transformation (which aligns with industrial restructuring by supporting market-oriented policy, deregulation, and overall decreased levels of government interventionism).

The chapters within this volume recount the literature that well documents this 60-year period. By employing a series of theoretical devices, we can unravel the structural forces of change and understand how they touch ground within rural and small town communities and regions. Theoretical devices such as staples theory, long wave theory, and evolutionary economic geography provide rural researchers with powerful conceptual tools with which to document and illustrate just how history and geography have mattered.

But what next? What does this history teach us about what to expect from the next 30 years? How will history and geography matter to rural communities and regions as they seek to react to the changes they have been impacted by in order to maintain—or pursue—a viable future? This question is particularly important given that the patterns of change will likely continue to accelerate, where the cycles of crisis and recovery will likely continue, and where new challenges such as climate change will express themselves with ever-increasing force. The chapters in this volume use the already mentioned theories, and a selection of other emergent ideas within the literature, to offer some robust and exciting insights.

In the following sections, we begin with a review of the broad themes that outline the restructuring experience of rural and small town places. We offer these themes with recognition that the generalities of restructuring and transition are always shaped by the context of place in terms of any specific locale in question (Massey, 2005). The second part of the chapter seeks to build on this foundation of material and knowledge to discern the discourses and patterns that are emergent in shaping our understanding of rural restructuring and change in the forthcoming 30-year period, to complete our 30-30-30 year analysis.

Rural Restructuring in Theory and Context

The three dominant theories used within the book to explore rural restructuring are staples theory, long wave theory, and evolutionary economic geography. First, as Argent states in Chapter 2, "Innis' staples theory is best regarded as a broad approach to understanding the causes of uneven development over space and time (Hayter and Barnes, 1990)." More specifically, the focus of staples theory is on the effects of transporting raw resource materials over long distances (causing weaknesses in other lines of development); dependence on external industrialized areas for value-added processing, markets, and supplies of manufactured goods; and dependence on external sources of capital to cover the high costs of resource development (Hayter and Barnes, 1990). This theoretical framework offers a particularly robust and contextually grounded approach to understanding the impacts and patterns of development. It is also important in terms of its embrace of history and geography for countering modular understandings of development processes forwarded by more neoclassical oriented theories.

Second, Tykkyläinen *et al.* employ long wave theory in their analysis in Finland. In Chapter 4, they conceptualize:

> local development processes as industry life cycles (Peltoniemi, 2011; Potter and Watts, 2011; Edenhoffer and Hayter, 2013), which we associate with an evolutionary framework of development. In this context, techno-economic paradigms are seen to generate global-local conditions and modes of production for industry cycles (Perez, 2010).

They identify five industry waves in their case community of Lieksa since the nineteenth century: (1) lake iron ore; (2) colonization; (3) forest mills; (4) manufacturing; and (5) services. The recognition of historical importance is clear within their use of this theoretical approach. Again, however, their research uses this life-cycle analysis to provide a contextually rich picture of development within Finland and their specific case study.

Finally, Argent in Chapter 2 describes evolutionary economic geography as being, "concerned with explaining the transformation of economic landscapes over various temporal and spatial scales and, in particular, explicitly recognizing and accounting for the causal roles of time and space in economic change and continuity (see Boschma and Martin, 2010)." As Martin (2012 p. 180) has argued, "any convincing theory of regional development needs to give explicit recognition to, and account for, the roles of history and path dependent dynamics and outcomes." But rather than viewing path dependence as inevitably supporting "locked-in" regional economies, he further argues that there must be room to admit other "more incremental and developmental patterns of evolution" (Martin, 2012 p. 183). This point is critical to our understanding of rural community and regional restructuring as it leaves space for agency, particularly important as we ponder the more structural global-local dynamics which shape patterns of development.

Drawing from the analysis derived from these theories allows the collective voices within this volume to emphatically state that history and geography matter. History matters because of the extent to which development is an evolutionary process. The decisions, impacts, investments of the past create a legacy and trajectory that shapes and influences future pathways and possibilities. Geography matters because of the resource endowments of particular places, the collection of policies that frame development processes, connectivity to markets, and local cultures and histories. Wider changes (such as the emergence of new techno-economic paradigms) that radically shift geographic positionalities and relationships are a vital evolutionary element in how such past legacies and trajectories are disrupted.

Before proceeding to our culmination of generalized findings, it is also worth noting that 'rural' also matters. Despite the incredible diversity of rural communities (which has lead Ray Bollman, an outstanding Canadian rural researcher, to note, "if you've seen one rural community ... you've seen one rural community") and differences that are remarkable within a 30-minute drive, to say nothing of different international and cultural settings, rural places do share certain characteristics. Most importantly, concerning the dynamics of restructuring and change, the structural realities of *distance* and *capacity* are critical dimensions of the rural experience. Distance makes both investments and market access more expensive, thereby embedding a competitive disadvantage before you have even begun to assess local attributes and opportunities. Relatedly, rural capacity is notoriously less plentiful than in metropolitan places given both limited overall population scale (which makes infrastructure investments more expensive per capita) and human capital to engage with development processes (both in terms of sheer numbers of people to engage in or support development activities, and also as a generality, rural places contain a less educated and trained population).

These structural conditions are important to keep in mind as we assess the impact and outcomes of various development initiatives, be they transformations in the industrial make-up of a region or local/regional initiatives designed to diversify or promote the local economy. These realities are reflected in connection to Ocean Falls, a small isolated coastal community in British Columbia, Canada. As highlighted by Hayter in the introduction to Part III of this volume, the corporate executive who stated, "Whatever you can do at Ocean Falls you can do better somewhere else," is confronting (in part) the realities of isolation and capacity. Our own research in Ocean Falls reveals another dimension of the story, in that their town slogan (painted on a sign at the entrance to the village) is "home of the rain people." While communicating an embrace of the heartiness of the rural lifestyle (and rural sense of humor!), viewed from a lens of restructuring, it is an entirely inward worldview that speaks to a false sense of stability attributed to a single resource economy.

At a larger scale, the extent to which rural matters may also be evident in the assessment provided by Kotilainen *et al.* regarding the impact of European Union funds to support rural regions, stating in Chapter 12, "[y]et, thus far the impacts of EU policy instruments have not succeeded in changing rural decline. The rural renewal, such as rapid modernization and growth of small businesses, has been insufficient from the viewpoint of job growth." This is a sobering assessment, particularly as the EU regional and declining rural regions policies and programs have long been the envy of North American rural researchers and practitioners. In the dichotomous world of sticky and slippery places, in terms of their ability to retain capital and people within a globalized world, rural regions face barriers associated with their inability to adequately match up to checklists of economic success factors, lists which tend to favor urban characteristics and fail to adequately conceptualize the rural context and a rural perspective.

With these theoretical and contextual definitions and foundations now in place, we turn our attention to a summary of some of the core 'knowns' concerning rural community and regional restructuring. Following the structure of the volume, we begin by discussing broader patterns of restructuring, before turning our attention to labor and community dynamics within rural regions.

Restructuring forces since the early 1980s, driven by increasing global competition and the reduction of global trade barriers, have impacted rural resource regions in three fundamental ways. First, competition from lower-cost producers has resulted in a drive to enhance productivity and, relatedly, reduce costs of production. Technology has replaced labor and entire production processes have been relocated to lower-cost regions. These structural conditions are responsible for the statistical certainty that if your economy is based on the extraction and processing of natural resources, your employment levels in those industries will decrease over time. As Bollman (2007) argues, there are three drivers for rural Canada: technology, prices, and demography. In terms of technology, the ongoing substitution of capital for labor means primary sector industries will employ fewer people. If rural development means the growth of jobs and/or local population, then resource production will not be the future driver of rural development. As a result, successful communities will necessarily have to find new goods or services to 'export.'

Related specifically to industrial restructuring, as Hayter alludes, the drive for flexibility in the production process, which has supplanted traditional notions of Fordist labor organization (and the large numbers of jobs it supported), has been fully embraced and complemented by the "flexibility mantra of neoliberalism" (introduction to Part I of this volume). Neoliberalism has dominated public policy since the 1980s and has resulted in a process of government deregulation, the withdrawal of program supports, and the dismantling of central planning policies of government intervention (Peck and Tickell, 2002). Jessop (2002) describes how neoliberal policy shapes economic, political, and social relations by endorsing the market economy, minimizing government intervention, and maximizing the freedom of individuals. One consequence has been the removal of regional equalization policies that provided communities with some protection from fluctuating global markets and the mobility of foreign resource-based companies (Polèse, 1999).

The retrenchment orientation of neoliberalism has also meant that rural and small town places have been pushed by senior levels of government to compete in the global market to attract private investment to support economic development and fund local infrastructure and services. The ideology, and corresponding approach to government, is redefining the roles and responsibilities of government and industry in resource-based rural regions. As senior levels of government promote resource development, they—along with industries—are reducing their direct financial support for local communities (Markey *et al.*, 2008a; Polèse, 1999). The social contract that once bound resource industries, senior governments, and rural regions together is broken and policy-makers, researchers, and practitioners have not yet forged a coherent response to the post-1970s/1980s restructuring of the political economy of resource-dependent communities and regions.

Second, all of the chapters in this volume reference the decline of unions. The combination of increasing demands for labor flexibility and neoliberal labor policy eroded the Keynesian compromise that delivered employment growth and (relative) stability in the 30 years immediately following World War Two. These changes appear most severe in New Zealand. As Connelly and Nel report in Chapter 9, union membership fell from 603,118 in 1991 to 384,777 members by 2008. The impact of changes to labor regulations, including removal of collective bargaining and other labor rights, has resulted "in some of the weakest employment protection systems in the OECD." These patterns are reflective of changes in Australia and Canada.

The story from Finland shows it to be a relative outlier in terms of resisting some of the pressures of neoliberalism. As Halonen *et al.* state in Chapter 8,

> the key principle of the labor market system in Finland, as in other Nordic countries, has been based on the ideology of corporatism with having an economic tripartite negotiation system between the state and both employers' and labor organizations, herewith affecting not only the position of the employees but also the employer's possibilities to respond to the development of industries.

The social contract remains a more significant force in Finland, providing an interesting contrast to the dominance and stated 'common sense' associated with the application of neoliberal policies in other OECD nations.

Third, community and regional transformations associated with restructuring have been dictated by the physical reality that while capital (and to a lesser extent labor) may be mobile, communities are not. Changes in the economic production system and public policy have combined to result in the depopulation of many rural regions (while acknowledging growth that may occur in certain boom sectors and places) and resource frontier aging (Skinner and Hanlon, 2016). Rural communities have become smaller and older over the past 30 years.

Some of the depopulation change may be attributed to previous unsustainable harvesting rates, in which case it can be argued that certain communities should never have reached their peak labor force. However, it is clear from the chapters in this volume that the key contributors to relative rural decline are intentional: related to corporate decision-making driven by competitive pressures and the reluctance of senior governments to invest in rural regions. From a governance perspective, Markey *et al.* (2008a), refer to this phenomenon as the 'resource bank,' the idea being that corporations and senior governments view rural resource regions as a bank from which they can withdraw funds to support public expenditures. The shift since the 1980s, however, has witnessed a failure of both corporations and governments to reinvest in rural resource-bank regions. The social contract that once tied resource development with social development has been abandoned, while the extraction of funds (i.e. resource wealth) continues.

Other 'knowns' associated with community and regional transition include the local government shift from managerialism to entrepreneurialism of the local economy. As senior governments have downloaded responsibility to local governments, industries have abandoned their economic stewardship for the resource communities in which they are based. As Halseth states in Chapter 1,

> local government has, at times, struggled with the transformation from managerialism to entrepreneurialism. For some, there is a desire to return to the halcyon days of the 1970s when big industry brought large numbers of jobs and significant local tax revenue such that local government really had little to do beyond managing basic infrastructure maintenance. Today the circumstances are more dynamic and complex.

Aside from the reduced budgetary capacity of local governments, the transition to more local stewardship of the local economy has also been hindered by early economic development efforts. Initial forays into local economic development really simply channeled the principles of neoliberalism to the local scale (and it can be argued served to justify the broader neoliberal position). An early focus on market-oriented approaches (that ignored the contextual dynamics of place) resulted in little other than glorified smokestack chasing and a complete underappreciation of the time and resources required to support comprehensive economic transition and the human capital and governance components necessary to make it all work. This fundamental confusion of 'growth' for 'development' delayed the necessary work to fully reorient and restructure community and regional economies. At its worst, it served to depress support for future localist initiatives, as communities felt that they have 'been down that road before' when new economic development planning initiatives are suggested, with only the sting of failure (and no real learning) to frame their memories.

Anthony Sorensen contributes an interesting complement to the strategic challenges of local development, being a failure of imagination and creativity to define what might be possible for rural development. This mirrors and extends the arguments in Markey *et al.* (2012) that rural communities need to adopt a more place-based orientation to the reimagining and then creative rebundling of local assets so that emergent development opportunities and pathways fit better with local aspirations. In the absence of imagination, governments and communities rely on conservative tactics, which emulate the failed but familiar patterns of the past. Communities and governments at all levels have failed to adequately understand the risks associated with rural reinvestment in new pathways, and the risks associated with doing nothing. Markey *et al.* (2008b) have framed this failure as an inability to adequately incorporate the context of place in planning and decision-making. Without adequately understanding local conditions and capacity, the proverbial laundry list of economic development opportunities that usually accompany studies into local economic diversification are ultimately destined for failure because of the mismatch between place and project.

Sorensen also discusses the success story of Armidale, Australia, in exemplifying what is possible when the rural imagination is fully engaged. While containing 'exceptional advantages' (high amenity natural and built environment, a thriving arts sector, a university, and proximity to the coast), the story speaks to the importance of networking and creativity in exploring economic diversification rooted in the local assets of place. As Hayter alludes, it is never clear how we may transfer the success of one place to another, but the process and openness to possibility speak beyond contextual specificity.

Case transferability raises an interesting challenge to rural researchers and practitioners who are seeking new rural development pathways. As alluded to above, community and regional development suffer from a dearth of more intense scrutiny and theorizing. This is magnified in the rural setting, where there are simply fewer researchers engaged in the work. If rural development suffers from 'case studyitis,' then it is through collaborations such as this volume where we have an opportunity to delve more deeply into case conditions, compared across a series of international jurisdictions, and offer what are (hopefully) more robust theoretically informed, and theory-forming insights. This is the purpose of our final section.

Rural Restructuring: Future Directions

The authors in this collection employ a variety of concepts to chart existing and emergent characteristics of rural development that may inform our understanding over the next 30 years. Embedded within these ideas are lessons from the two previous 30-year periods, while also incorporating new ideas—or creativity—in how we may reimagine, approach, research rural development. The concepts of regional development, resilience, and place-based development find their way into most of the national case studies.

Regional development refers to programs that prioritize a territorial approach to investment and intervention in society and economy. As the chapters illustrate, various regions have gone through various phases of regional intervention. Historically, there were top-down programs designed to stimulate or diversify economic activity through the placement of major industrial infrastructure. Following some of the now well-documented failures of this approach (that it was poorly coordinated, based upon weak theories, assumed that rural regions were homogeneous, needs-based, and fostered dependency, see Markey *et al.*, 2005), regional development, or what is now often referred to as *new regionalism*, maintains a territorial focus, but adopts a much more participatory and integrated or holistic approach.

New regionalism has emerged as both a reactive and proactive response to recent forces of political and economic restructuring. Reactively, rural regions are pursuing collaborative approaches to help mitigate the loss of senior government and industrial interventionist roles in the development process. They are working together to pool capacity in the absence of support. Proactively, integrated development, at a regional scale, offers opportunities to address the complexities of territorial planning and to mobilize the strategic competitive advantages of place-based assets within a globalized economy (OECD, 2006; Shearmur, 2010).

Resilience is a concept that has been gaining currency within both the regional and rural development literatures. Kotilainen *et al.* (Chapter 12), provide a straightforward definition of resilience as, "a notion that refers to the ability of a system or region to cope with change." In Chapter 2, Argent extends from this notion to link to evolutionary economic geography and differentiates the concept from how it is applied in an ecological setting, stating that:

> it seeks to encompass the frequently complex and complicated process of adaptation and adjustment that occurs in empirically real rural settings when social, demographic, cultural, and economic systems are challenged or threatened. The concept enables the exploration of the multiple trajectories that 'the community' may embark upon, or be forced into, taking into consideration the influential role of past experiences and multiscalar forces.

Finally, Halonen *et al.* in Chapter 8 highlight the core focus of place-based development, as development that considers the "variability of local assets and local capabilities." It is a collaborative and co-constructed approach (meaning it requires the active participation of all levels of government and communities within a territory) that seeks to understand and unlock the inherent competitive advantages of communities and regions for development purposes. It provides an opportunity to harness collective strength, address some of the traditional rural challenges around capacity, grow the critical partnerships needed to realize effective and positive change, and stimulate greater creativity.

Each of these concepts are constructed from—and applied to—the case communities and regions as a collection of policies, programs, and actions that define the rural development enterprise. Borrowing from the approach of grounded theory, these concepts may be defined as abstract ideas, but they must interact with the ground somewhere. How do generalized approaches or policy directions work themselves out in real places? It is through a synthesis of the case studies within this volume where we may identify some common elements that both inform theory-building, and offer guidance to rural communities themselves. In the remaining section we highlight five factors: (1) understanding and mobilizing local assets; (2) reimagining rural community and economy; (3) leveraging human and social capital; (4) collaboration and scale; and (5) benefits and reinvestment.

First, rural development must begin with an understanding of the local assets of place. Previous approaches that treated rural regions as if they are all the same, or as passive recipients of blunt top-down policies, will either immediately fail or embed deficiencies that will hamper adaptive capacity over time. As Halseth *et al.* highlight in the town of Mackenzie, following some early stumbles in their economic development efforts, once the town sought to engage and understand the local community (place the community and not an external consultant at the center of the planning process), their work is proving much more successful and seemingly durable. Similarly, as highlighted above, the development success from Armidale, Australia is attributed entirely to the make-up of their local assets. It is a story that other communities can seek to learn from. While the examples may not be entirely transferable, the more general lessons may be informative.

Second, rural development must proceed from a position of being informed by the past, but not bound by either nostalgia or the comfort of repetition. Sorensen in this volume (at Chapter 10) speaks about the need to reimagine rural futures. This creative impulse may be reframed from a strategic perspective in terms of having a vision for rural development at different scales. Done well, visions are important for communicating and establishing a shared perspective about future directions. They may also enable institutional stability at all levels over the long periods required for redevelopment and reorientation, helping to mediate internal tensions and facilitate continuity and capacity building, further reinforcing the vision itself. We see in virtually all chapters, with Finland as somewhat of an outlier, the challenge posed to rural communities and regions as senior government abandoned any commitment to a rural development vision in favor of market fundamentalism, and local communities were unprepared (lacking entirely in past experience) to forge direction on their own.

Third, perhaps the principal ingredients in our appreciation and utilization of local assets are to understand and facilitate human and social capital development. This includes engaging and encouraging the emergence and initiative of local leadership; fostering skills to take advantage of new opportunities; convening and supporting the development of multidirectional networks (meaning intra- and intercommunity networks, in addition to networks that bond together different governance scales); and—perhaps most importantly—actually listening to the aspirations of different peoples and places. These factors are evident in the examples in this volume from Canada (Mackenzie-in-Motion) and New Zealand (Venture Southland and Development West Coast). Pushing further, the Australian example of 'creating creative communities' not only involves the story of an innovative Digital Economy Taskforce undertaking groundbreaking planning work, but also the dedication and commitment of moving plans into action through a Digital Economy Implementation Group. Within all of these stories and examples, the appreciation of local assets and local social capital development is critical; and, the Finnish case reminds us all about how chance, surprise, and contingency can play unexpected roles and our places must be resilient to these as well.

Fourth, rural communities must see themselves as part of a region. In the absence of equity-oriented senior government policy (which defined the immediate postwar period), communities must leverage the scale of collaboration for both advocacy and investment. Regional advocacy is required to offer any kind of substantive resistance to the negatively perceived actions of resource industries (be it related to labor or environmental impacts) and the senior governments that facilitate their operation. A regional investment mentality is required to overcome the definitional characteristics of rural identified above, being that the replacement and/or construction of development infrastructure is hindered by the realities of distance and scale. We see these cuts most dramatically in the cases provided by Canada, New Zealand, and Australia in this volume. Finland offers some insights in terms of their willingness to preserve some of the conditions of the Keynesian compromise that defined the postwar period into the post-1980s restructuring era. Their emphasis on employment, education, and well-being fundamentally rewires the metrics of success for rural development. Even if the findings from the research show that the programs are not having the desired impact on employment in the case community of Lieksa, perhaps the real question linked to well-being is whether that alone is being valued by residents.

The emphasis on well-being is echoed in the research from New Zealand that comments specifically on the negative impacts of neoliberal restructuring on the well-being of rural communities in that country. In another source of alignment, the emphasis on well-being offers an interesting connection with why people choose to live in rural places. Research done in British Columbia, for example, reveals that the value rural residents place upon preserving their rural lifestyle is a key driver of how they wish to approach development opportunities (Halseth et al., 2006).

Fifth, all of the cases within this volume speak to the challenges of maintaining or reconsidering rural investment in a political environment that prioritizes the narrow outcomes associated with the vagaries of the market. If the first 30-year period of our analysis here prioritized and linked social investment as a way to secure and ground economic investment, the 30-year period following the early 1980s abandoned that investment mentality. Unfortunately, as we have learned, this resource-bank approach continued on the roads, rail, pipes, and runways of a previous generation. Now in the early years of our next 30-year period, the twentieth-century infrastructure that many rural communities continue to rely upon is near or completely at the end of its life cycle, with no systematic plan or vision for replacement.

The connection between resilience and reinvestment is particularly cogent for rural regions. As with the other items in this synthesis list, reinvestment requires action from all sectors. Communities must not see themselves as passive recipients of government programs or corporate giving. As part of the reimagination process, communities must become stewards of the resources that surround them and view their involvement in the exploitation/use of those resources from a perspective of ownership and sense of place. Governments must be willing to explore new revenue-sharing agreements. Benefits must flow to rural communities beyond the metrics of jobs and income, particularly as they live with the externalities that may be associated with resource development. Finally, companies themselves must move beyond stakeholder management to positions where they embrace a shared wealth perspective that repositions the corporate enterprise within an integrated development landscape in rural regions.

Closing

It is clear from each of the research teams involved in this international edited volume that resource-dependent rural and small town places within developed economies are struggling to find their footing after 30 years of economic restructuring and policy change. To allow for comparison of cases, each team committed to an historically informed political economy approach that would explore the global-local linkages that first structured and then stressed their respective local and regional economies. They then explore the implications of change within the community and region via employment and labor force transformation. Finally, each explore the responses that places and regions are using to build more sustainable and resilient communities and economies.

The four national cases make clear that external forces heavily influence the restructuring of resource-dependent regions, and yet the contemporary challenges of securing an alternative rural development future have been pushed off to the communities and regions themselves. Over the past 30 years, both the state and global capital have fundamentally changed the way in which they support rural development. Unfortunately, neither has been able to identify a robust new policy or program approach that would align their 'top-down' contributions to the 'bottom-up' community development and economic development planning efforts of resource-dependent rural and small town regions.

The initial policy and program supports for regional or local development offices trying to replace one large industry with another single large industry have not proven very successful. Instead, flexible and inclusive place-based approaches that recognize local assets and operations, that have a commitment to implementation over the long term, and that recognize the realities of both place and the opportunities of those places within the contemporary global economy, are needed. Lessons and examples within this volume point to some promising potential.

The theoretically informed cases in this volume suggest important directions for advancing our discussions and debates about rural renewal. To start, the different theoretical approaches used both complement and extend one another. In the complexity that is 'rural,' such theoretical inclusiveness is needed. That said, there is also strong evidence to support ongoing attention to the 'unique' within the general problem of rural development. As we have noted, both geography and history matter! Further engagement with theoretical questions is needed to push the insights from case study research, and further research is needed to test the applicability and value of theoretical explanations 'on the ground.'

Comparative research is, of course, by definition very difficult. The complexities and differences between cases can overwhelm and obscure the topics or issues being compared. In this volume, each of the national research teams has narrowed their investigations to allow for a greater level of comparability. Yet, while we see general trends quite clearly, we also see nuances, uniqueness, and difference. Clearly, comparative research on the political economy of restructuring in resource-dependent rural and small town places needs to continue and needs to both push and test the findings, suggestions, and directions highlighted in this book. For rural researchers and rural communities, both time and the economy move along relentlessly. We need to recognize that, in such a context, doing things to better understand rural restructuring and rural community development will matter and not doing things will have consequences.

Finally, the rural and small town regions and places described in this book have made, and continue to make, vital contributions within their respective countries. They have shown a willingness to meet difficult challenges head on and the persistence to find successful pathways to creating more sustainable economies and resilient communities. The chapters in this edited volume seek to add to both theoretical and policy debates about rural and small town economic and community change, but they are also most certainly dedicated to the people who everyday are working to define and realize their 'next rural economies.'

References

Bollman, R.D. 2007. *Factors driving Canada's rural economy, 1914–2006*. Ottawa, ON: Statistics Canada.

Boschma, R. and Martin, R. (eds.). 2010. *The handbook of evolutionary economic geography*. Cheltenham: Edward Elgar.

Edenhoffer, K. and Hayter, R. 2013. Restructuring on a vertiginous plateau: The evolutionary trajectories of British Columbia's forest industries 1980–2010, *Geoforum* 44: 139–151.

Halseth, G., Manson, D., Markey, S., Lax, L., and Buttar, O. 2006. The connected north: Findings from the Northern BC Economic Vision and Strategy Project, *Journal of Rural and Community Development* 2(1): 1–27.

Hayter, R. and Barnes, T. 1990. Innis' staple theory, exports and recession: British Columbia, 1981–86, *Economic Geography* 66: 156–173.

Jessop, B. 2002. Liberalism, neoliberalism and urban governance. In N. Brenner and N. Theodore (eds.), *Spaces of neoliberalism: Urban restructuring in North America and western Europe* (pp. 105–123). Malden, MA: Wiley-Blackwell.

Markey, S., Halseth, G., and Manson, D. 2008a. Challenging the inevitability of rural decline: Advancing the policy of place in northern British Columbia, *Journal of Rural Studies* 24: 409–421.

Markey, S., Halseth, G., and Manson, D. 2008b. Closing the implementation gap: A framework for incorporating the context of place in economic development planning, *Local Environment* 13(4): 337–351.

Markey, S., Halseth, G., and Manson, D. 2012. *Investing in place: Economic renewal in northern British Columbia*. Vancouver, BC: University of British Columbia Press.

Markey, S., Pierce, J.T., Vodden, K., and Roseland, M. 2005. *Second growth: Community economic development in rural British Columbia*. Vancouver, BC: University of British Columbia Press.

Martin, R. 2012. Re(placing) path dependence: A response to the debate, *International Journal of Urban and Regional Research* 36(1): 179–192.

Massey, D. 2005. *For space*. London: Sage.

OECD. 2006. *The new rural paradigm: Policies and governance*. Paris: OECD.

Peck, J. and Tickell, A. 2002. Neoliberalizing space, *Antipode* 34(3): 380–404.

Peltoniemi, M. 2011. Reviewing industry life-cycle theory: Avenues for future research, *International Journal of Management Reviews* 13(4): 349–375.

Perez, C. 2010. Technological revolutions and techno-economic paradigms, *Cambridge Journal of Economics* 34: 185–202.

Polèse, M. 1999. From regional development to local development: On the life, death and rebirth (?) of regional science as a policy relevant science, *Canadian Journal of Regional Science* 22(3): 299–314.

Potter, A. and Watts, H.D. 2011. Evolutionary agglomeration theory: Increasing returns, diminishing returns, and the industry life cycle, *Journal of Economic Geography* 11(3): 417–455.

Shearmur, R. 2010. Space, place and innovation: A distance-based approach, *The Canadian Geographer* 54(1): 46–67.

Skinner, M. and Hanlon, N. (eds.). 2016. *Ageing resource communities: New frontiers of rural population change, community development and voluntarism*. Oxford and New York: Routledge.

Index